WITHDRAWN

WESTERN 'CONTAINMENT' POLICIES IN THE COLD WAR

The Yugoslav Case, 1948-53

WESTERN 'CONTAINMENT' POLICIES IN THE COLD WAR

The Yugoslav Case, 1948-53

Beatrice Heuser

ROUTLEDGE
London and New York

First published in 1989 by
Routledge
11 New Fetter Lane, London EC4P 4EE
29 West 35th Street, New York, NY 10001

© 1989 Beatrice Heuser

Typeset by LaserScript Limited, Mitcham, Surrey

Printed in Great Britain by TJ Press (Padstow) Ltd.,
Padstow, Cornwall

British Library Cataloguing in Publication Data

Heuser, Beatrice
Western containment policies in the Cold War: the Yugoslav case,
1948-53.
1. Western bloc countries. Foreign relations with Yugoslavia,
1948-1953. 2. Yugoslavia. Foreign relations with Western bloc
countries, 1948-1953
I. Title
327'.0917'3

Library of Congress Cataloging-in-Publication Data

Heuser, Beatrice, 1961-
Western containment policies in the cold war.
Bibliography: p.
Includes index.
1. Yugoslavia–Foreign relations–1945-
2. Geopolitics–Yugoslavia. 3. Yugoslavia–Strategic aspects. 4. World
politics–1945-1955. 5. United States–Foreign relations–Yugoslavia.
6. Yugoslavia–Foreign relations–United States. 7. United
States–Foreign relations–1945-1953. I. Title. II. Title: Containment
policies in the cold war.
DR1303.H48 1989 327.497 88-23914

ISBN 0-415-01303-8

Contents

Contents

Contents

Preface

It is customary to start with a note of thanks, and I am very glad that this will give me an opportunity at least to mention all those to whom my work and I myself owe so much, although I feel that I shall never be able to thank them fully. Starting with institutions, I wish to acknowledge with gratitude the grants, scholarships and research fellowships I received from the following: the Economic and Social Research Council, the Harry S. Truman Library Foundation, the North Atlantic Council, and St. John's College, Oxford.

I should like to mention my surprise and delight at all the help I received from total strangers, who allowed me to interview them: I must admit that at times my work seemed almost like an excuse for meeting the most fascinating people, whose kindness and hospitality were baffling. Here I should like to mention M. Jean Gueury, Sir Fitzroy Maclean, Mr. Ernest Davies, Sir Denis Wright, Admiral Irvin, Dr. Louis Dollot, Général Renault, M. Jean Laloy, M. Burin de Roziers, Dr. Le Breton, Lady Peake, Dr. John Campbell, Admiral Carney, and George Allen Jr. I should like to thank Mr. Hilary King in particular, who has offered copious advice on a whole range of problems and has done so much to enable me to imagine what times were like in Yugoslavia during the period I am discussing. His letters and our conversation have been a wonderful source of inspiration to me.

I also received a great deal of advice from many other academics, including Prof. Adam Roberts, Dr. Robert Blum, Dr. Henry Bill Brands, Prof. Raymond Poidevin, Dr. Branko Pribicevic, Prof. Maurice Vaïsse, Dr. James Tang, Dr. Anne Deighton and Sheila Kerr, to mention but a few. Dr. Anne Deighton, Rachel Ashley and Vasso Spanos have helped tremendously, not only forcing me to clarify my ideas, but also helping me turn my gobbledegook into intelligible English, so that I owe the correct spelling of just about every other word to them! Even then, Dr. Avi Shlaim and Prof. Geoffrey Warner were able to point out many errors to me, and I am very grateful to them for this and for their very constructive suggestions about final improvements of the text, and for their encouragement.

Preface

I met with enormous amounts of patience and tolerance from my supervisor, Dr. Richard Kindersley, who has been a very kind and caring *Doktorvater*, being very constructive in his copious criticism; I am very much aware how much I owe him. It is only right that he should head the list of those whom I wish to thank most. Next, I want to express my gratitude and rather belated appreciation to Francis Wyman, from whom I have received more advice on recent publications than I could cope with at times, who has helped me more than anybody else to take the plunge into the Cold War, even if he never approved of my methods and approach. Further, I want to thank Prof. Adolf Birke, who gave me much encouragement and friendly support when I needed it most.

And now a word about Muses. Muses are not simply ornamental characters, who sit around decoratively, inspiring you in some irrational way (although there may be a tiny element of irrationality). A Muse is a sort of deity who feeds you the ideas and dreams and thoughts (preferably entirely unrelated to your field of academic research), whom you admire profoundly and who (in this case at least) is far, far above you, in intellect and maturity and in many other ways. I have such a Muse, and I can only say how lucky I am in having one, who has saved me from mental starvation by dishing up banquets of ideas, knowledge and imaginary worlds. To my Muse I thus owe my mental survival; need I explain my gratitude further?

Finally, I owe everything else to my parents, my best friends. There are no words to thank them adequately, as my debt is boundless. They have been very understanding and supportive, but then they both know what it's like to do research. I want to dedicate this book to them, but also to the memory of one who was not only a great academic adviser, but also a great friend, and a person who has become an ideal that I should like to try to live up to: Elisabeth Barker. Journalist, scholar, linguist, she was the most open-minded, sharing, generous, kind, welcoming, inspiring and interesting person I had met. Her death in March 1986 made the writing-up of this thesis a very melancholy process, and I shall continue to miss her advice and her friendship, and to treasure the memory of the precious times I had with her.

D.B.G. Heuser, Oxford

ix

Introduction

In this work the wide field of Western Cold War perceptions and policies is examined with a searchlight concentrating on the impact of the Tito-Stalin split on Western perceptions, and on the policies adopted (mainly towards Yugoslavia, but also towards other Communist régimes) as a result of this. The reason for the choice of this particular searchlight is that more than most other problems of Western foreign policy-making of that time (with the exception of Germany), Western views of and policies towards Yugoslavia reflect the great issues, perceptions and policies of the Cold War. Yugoslavia's Communist government, expelled from the family of Socialist states, was at the focal point of the tensions between two conflicting ideologies in the form of two opposing power blocs. On the day of its expulsion it faced the profoundly anti-Communist Western powers, who were terrified by the threat which they perceived as emanating from the Soviet Union and all its satellites (including Yugoslavia). They had hitherto only perceived Communism as a monolithic, expansionist movement, but their perception was changed profoundly, so that they now saw Communism as a movement that might break up into rival factions, if existing tendencies were encouraged skilfully. Western policies towards Yugoslavia were also conditioned by perceptions of other major events of the Cold War, such as the civil war in Greece, and the invasion of South Korea, and by the policies the West adopted and implemented to deal with them.

The policies of the governments of the United States, Britain and France towards Yugoslavia, starting with the expulsion of Yugoslavia from the Cominform on 28 June 1948, and ending with the death of Stalin on 5 March 1953, have so far only been studied in part. There have been examinations of American policy towards Yugoslavia[1], of individual episodes in Anglo-Yugoslav relations[2], and even of the relations between "Tito, Stalin and the West"[3]. Few of these, however, make use of the governmental working documents, which have recently been made available in the archives[4], and those that do, particularly the very valuable and detailed study by Joze Pirjevec, only cover the period up to 1948/1949[5]. None studies the interrelation of American, British and French policy throughout this period, in the context of both Soviet and Western Cold War aims and actions. The co-ordination of these policies makes it imperative to study all three governments' attitudes towards Tito and the influence they had on each other; unless all three sides are examined, there remain serious gaps in the explanation of policy formulation and execution.

The years we are dealing with fall roughly into two periods: first, June 1948 until June 1950 (the beginning of the Korean War) in which Yugoslavia was seen and treated more as an ideological wedge or spearhead in the side of the supposedly crumbling Communist monolith; secondly, June 1950 until March 1953, when her function as a defensive shield for NATO territories was her primary importance for the Western powers. Our period cannot be understood without some explanation of previous developments; nor are all the developments originating in this period concluded by the death of Stalin. Therefore the discussion of the "setting" in which the expulsion of Yugoslavia from the Cominform occurred (Chapter 1) will contain a brief examination of Soviet and Western policies before June 1948. The last chapters will include brief sketches of subsequent developments.

In trying to understand Western policies — "Western" will be taken to mean "American, British and French" — the attempt will be made for both three-year periods to reconstruct the situation as it was, as far as this is possible with all the information now available, trying to get a picture of what Stalin's overall foreign policy might have been. This is probably the closest we can get to the "reality" of the situation. We still lack access to the archives of the Soviet government which would give us certainty, and it is clear that even now it is far from certain what Stalin's motives and policies really were; accordingly, there is a strong element of hubris in calling our reconstruction "reality". Nevertheless, since the period we are dealing with, students of Soviet foreign policy have painstakingly gone over all available evidence and have put together a picture of Stalin's overall policies which at times differs decisively from the assumptions and interpretations of contemporary Western decision-makers[6]. Additionally, the accessibility of Western archives gives the foreign policy analyst extensive knowledge of the top secret information available to (in this case, three) governments at the time. Some of this information on events in the Soviet orbit, which was not always shared by the three governments concerned, retrospectively corroborates the picture sketched by the Soviet foreign policy specialists[7]. It is assumed here that this picture is the closest approximation to "reality" that we can find for the time being, and it will have to serve as such, while mental reservations will always be made. Chapters 1 and 5 will contain this reconstruction of "reality".

The next step (also in Chapters 1 and 5) will be to contrast this "reality" with its perception by the Western decision-makers. This can be done with as great an accuracy as that with which any historian could ever reconstruct the thoughts, ideas, perceptions and motivation of any group of people, since for this period, in spite of some retention of sensitive material by the three governments, a super-abundance of documentation is available in the form of internal government documents, public statements and speeches, memoirs, and even oral histories and interviews. With knowledge of the perceptions, it is easy to understand the policies adopted subsequently. These were designed to turn the perceived situations to the advantage of these governments, and their understanding of the situation determined the choice of options and the imagined possible developments which might be brought about[8]. The contrast between perceptions and reality will later help us to account for the lack of success of certain policies adopted by the Western powers.

Chapters 2, 3, 4, 6 and 7 will explain how the Tito-Stalin split's perceptions by the Western powers were built into and modified their overall policies; what individual policies were adopted towards Yugoslavia and for what reasons. In each case, the result of these policies or actions will be examined: if possible, it will be asked whether they were successful; if they were clearly not successful, it will be asked how far they failed because of the misperceptions on which they were based.

The difficulty of this section is to assign outcomes to any single cause: if the aim of a policy was or was not realized, this may be due to other factors and circumstances outside the decision-makers' control, and in some cases there is no way of telling whether a policy had any impact on the outcome of the event. For example, we very rarely have even the slightest indication regarding the factors which influenced Stalin's reasoning in taking individual decisions; or, for the Yugoslav side, in spite of the publication of memoirs, the hard documentary evidence for the motivation of decision-making in individual cases is still hidden away in mostly inaccessible archives[9]. There are also differences in scale: while it may be possible to reconstruct general tendencies of Stalin's or Tito's policies from official communications, public statements, measures that could be monitored from the outside, memoirs and interviews of participants or defectors, the minutiae of decision-making can very rarely be reconstructed in this way. This is the lesson drawn from a comparison of the information contained in the Western archives with the information about Western decision-making and policies reconstructed from interviews, memoirs and public statements. It is reasonable to assume that the same or even more pronounced differences exist between our present knowledge of Stalin's policies and the knowledge we might have had if we had access to Soviet archives.

Interviews seem most unrewarding from a factual point of view, as the time-lag between the events examined here and the present is nearly forty years. While they are invaluable for character-sketches and an impression of the atmosphere of the time, both interviews and memoirs bring with them the danger of distorting the past. Perceptions of the situation, own motivation, or facts are recalled not only with a failing memory but also with the interpretation of hindsight. Often the memory of a major event blots out in the minds of contemporaries other simultaneous developments, which may not have reached the climactic dimensions of the former event. Thus for example few contemporaries now recall the threat of an invasion of or civil war in Yugoslavia (1949-51) which was constantly regarded as a major danger by Western intelligence services during these years, and which evidently gave the Western powers cause for concern, as we know from the now available documents (see Chapters 4, 5 and 6). On the other hand the invasion of Korea is remembered very vividly, while its occurrence was neither regarded as likely (in the specific isolated form in which it took place) or important (if it should happen) by Western military and civilian intelligence before June 1950[10]. In the spring of 1950, Korea therefore hardly featured at all in the minds of decision-makers, while Yugoslavia featured fairly prominently. This would come as a surprise if one relied solely on interviews and memoirs for a reconstruction of this period.

Nothing is therefore better evidence than a dated and signed document laying out a decision-maker's view at the time of the decision. Nevertheless, one has to be aware of contemporary distortions of explanations or interpretations. Thus a presidential appeal to Congress for the release of funds for arms aid for Yugoslavia is likely to paint an exaggerated picture of the particular threat facing that country, in order to convince Congress. In reality, the granting of arms aid might be more of a preventive measure, designed generally to strengthen a recipient country which would be an asset to the West in case of a general war, even if this is not thought imminent.

In this study of Western policy-making, most emphasis will be on internal governmental documents, such as memoranda drawn up within the foreign ministries, letters from ambassadors, ministerial briefs, cabinet papers, most of which were classified, i.e. regarded as "confidential", "secret" or even "top secret". These are found mainly in the public archives of the US, Britain and France, but also in some private collections. These documents are used mainly to illustrate the perceptions of a situation, but as letters or telegrams sent by ambassadors contain both factual reports and interpretations (usually sent separately), these archives also serve as a major source of factual information which is used for the reconstruction of "reality".

In spite of what has been said about the abundance of material (e.g. British files on economic aid negotiations) there are important gaps in other sectors of the archives (e.g. French files on tripartite economic aid negotiations, American NSC documents after 1950, later American intelligence reports after 1950, all British intelligence reports, several aspects of military negotiations, and minutes of the meetings of certain crucial committees, such as the British Permanent Under-Secretary's Committee, the incompletely accessible minutes of the meetings of the Conseil des Ministres in France, and the absence of records of private conversations between decision-makers, etc.). On the whole, however, these gaps can be filled by partial reconstruction, and one is rarely left with the impression that the decision-making process or the final decisions cannot be traced closely enough to answer questions raised by this study. The area where there are most gaps, not surprisingly, is that of strategic planning and military policy.

The quantitative limits of this study make it impossible to deal with Western policies towards Yugoslavia, the decision-making process and the implementation in detail, which is a pity, as this would contribute to the understanding of why the implementation of the adopted policies often differed so much from the original designs of the policy-makers. As these processes have more to do with governmental machineries, with the technical side of administration and the problems of the Yugoslav economy, this omission does not, however, make the study of the discrepancies of "reality", perceptions, decisions and aims impossible. The decision-making processes are known and can be reconstructed. Where possible, references will be given to published sources or secondary literature dealing with these developments in detail.

Finally, a short explanation of who the decision-makers were, and what machineries they operated with, is called for. What is meant by Western "governments" is those who take decisions, and those within the government who advise and influence them. Adapting Richard Snyder's definition of the state, one could say that "government action is the action taken by those acting in the name of the government. Hence, the government is the decision-makers."[11] By this definition, the US Congress must be regarded as part of the US government, while in this case-study the British Parliament and the French Assemblée Nationale could almost be left out as they only rarely had the power to make decisions regarding policy towards Yugoslavia, and on those occasions made no attempt to change the policies they were asked to endorse. Only once did the British House of Commons push the "government" to take action, and that was in a direction it had intended to pursue anyway (see Chapter 5). Both Parliament[12] and the Assemblée Nationale[13] were not, generally, interested in minor questions of foreign policy (among which we must count Yugoslavia), while they could develop great interest in some major issues (e.g. in the UK later the debate about Suez, in France the German question or the related issue of the European Defence Community). The foreign policy consensus in Britain[14] and the continuous obstruction on the part of the Communists on most foreign policy issues in France, which rarely elicited serious responses by the other parties in this period[15], contributed to this picture of unconcern regarding minor issues. The American Congress, however, was more frequently asked to endorse action by the executive, had more opportunities to make decisions, and showed greater reserve, although it did not, on any occasion concerning Yugoslavia, seriously alter decisions already taken by the other decision-makers, or obstruct their implementation[16].

In the US, the decisions are made by the President (in our period, Truman, then Eisenhower), who acts with the advice of his Secretaries, the government departments, the military, etc., but who has no obligation to follow their advice. In this study, all basic policy decisions were made on the recommendation of the State Department's Policy Planning Staff, which sent a draft decision to the National Security Council (NSC). This consisted of the President, the Secretaries of State, Defense, Army, Navy and Air Force, and the Chairman of the National Security Resources Board. The NSC was not unlike the Cabinet Defence Committee in Britain, except that no NSC decision counted without the President's approval. Once he had given it, however, it had the quality of law. The State Department, the military establishment, and the Treasury would then act as executors of the presidential orders, deciding minor points on the basis of this overall policy decision. Changed circumstances therefore required a new basic NSC/presidential decision. In the US, the "government" therefore is taken to consist of the main decision-makers (the President, Congress) and those who advise them (mostly represented on the NSC), thus having influence on the formation of policy[17].

In Britain, the system of Cabinet responsibility means that no single individual is held responsible for decisions. As Cabinet decisions do not, however, require the consent of all members of the Cabinet, and can be made by a very small inner Cabinet or Cabinet Committee, or even by the Foreign Secretary in consultation with the Prime Minister only, it is chiefly these two individuals who must be regarded as responsible for the decisions made. The Cabinet (or the Cabinet Committee, or the Prime Minister) were advised on matters of foreign affairs by the Foreign Secretary, the Chancellor of the Exchequer (Treasury), and the Minister of Defence with the Chiefs of Staff, who each drew on their respective ministries for advice and information. Within the Foreign Office, at the time, two Committees were of crucial importance for Cold War policy-making: the Russia Committee, established in 1946, and the Permanent Under-Secretary's Committee established in 1947 as a conscious effort to copy the American Policy Planning Staff[18]. These committees would study reports prepared by Departments within the Foreign Office, or individual ambassadors, and propose policies which would be enacted with the authorization of the Foreign Secretary, who would consult the Prime Minister or even the Cabinet as a whole or one of its Committees, if the importance of the issue warranted it. Ultimately, in the British system, who makes foreign policy depends on the relationship between Foreign Secretary and Prime Minister. In our period the Foreign Secretaries Bevin and Eden had much power, and in most matters concerning us here, enjoyed the full confidence of their respective Prime Ministers (Attlee and Churchill). Bevin and Eden were thus the crucial decision-makers, usually on the basis of general policies adopted by the Cabinet as a whole or in one of its major Committees[19]. Herbert Morrison, however, was in a much weaker position.

In France, joint ministerial decision-making in the IVth Republic was much less formalized, but as in Britain the main policy decisions were taken by the ministers collectively (in the Conseil des Ministres, the records of which are only partly accessible, however[20]). All other decisions were either taken by the Foreign Minister (in our period, successively, Georges Bidault, Robert Schuman, and once again Bidault) or delegated by them to the Secrétaire Général of the Quai d'Orsay, who provided for greater continuity than the very swiftly changing governments. The French Foreign Minister appears to have had more responsibility and authority than the Secretary of State in the USA, and even than the Foreign Secretary in Britain, in all but the most popular questions of foreign policy-making (such as the German question or Western alliances and pacts). Decision-making in France was often a secretive process, with ministers trying to keep information even from their colleagues, or else playing an elaborate game of leaking it to the press, and blackmailing each other with it, with top civil servants also involved extensively[21].

One must not underestimate the importance of the respective bureaucracies and ministries in day-to-day decision-making. It was usually the desk officers in the respective foreign ministries who drafted new policies; the diplomats stationed in the country concerned, and the military also made recommendations. However much the rôle of the diplomat in another country may seem to have become that of an errand-boy in the modern world of improved communications, where an increasing number of decisions can be referred back to the ministry at home, these decisions are still made with the advice given by the diplomats in mind, who thus have a very important advisory function in the decision-making processes at the highest level. Within the ministries, the senior minister (in Britain, the Foreign Secretary, or in the US, the Secretary of State) usually only gives his attention to particularly critical and exceptionally important questions. When lesser decisions are called for, they are usually taken by a junior minister (in the case of Britain, the Minister of State or the Parliamentary Under-Secretary of State; in the case of France during Bidault's second term of office, the Secrétaire d'Etat, a post created by him), or a high-ranking civil servant (the Permanent Under-Secretary in the British system, or the semi-political Secrétaire Général in the French system; the head of a department or section, depending on the nomenclature of the ministry). Therefore these people in practice play crucial rôles in the decision-making process; if they do not take decisions themselves, it is they who decide that an issue is important enough to warrant putting it to the minister himself. As this is done with prepared drafts of decisions and policy recommendations, their views are certain to reach the ultimate decision-maker(s).

As has been mentioned above, the military also has an important input into the decision-making process. The high priority accorded to anything concerning "national security" in the United States gave the advice of the military establishment particular importance in our period. This was paralleled to some extent in the government of Britain and, less so, in France, but the severe constraints on the rôle these two countries could play in military (and economic) aid relations with Yugoslavia correspondingly gave their military (and the treasuries) an almost purely advisory function. The French and British treasuries acted mainly as brakes on government spending in foreign policy[22].

We turn now to the context in which the Tito-Stalin split occurred, to explain how the expulsion of Yugoslavia from the Cominform fitted into Stalin's foreign policy, and Western perceptions of it.

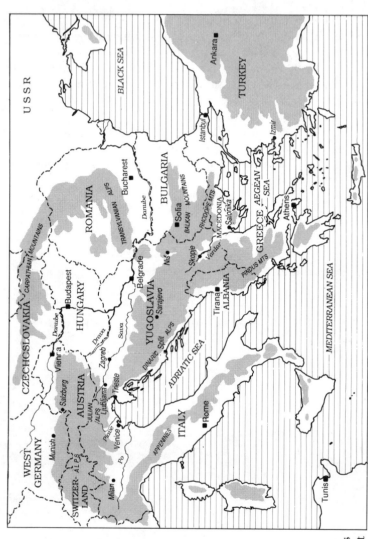

Yugoslavia in its
geo-strategic context

1

The Setting

To understand the state of mind of the foreign policy-makers of Britain, France and the United States at the time of Yugoslavia's expulsion from the Cominform, it is necessary to sketch their perception of the situation before this event and their policies in response to it. This study is neither concerned with the causes or the origins of the Cold War itself, nor will it deal with the question of responsibility for its outbreak and escalation from disagreements between negotiators at international conferences to war-scares. Instead, the focus of this chapter will be on the Western decision-makers' perceptions of the Soviet threat and of the origins of the Tito-Stalin split. The latter will be contrasted with Stalin's general policies and his particular policies towards Yugoslavia, as far as these can be reconstructed with historical hindsight.

Western Perceptions of a Soviet Threat

Military establishments, in war or peace, have to make contingency plans for any threat that is likely to arise to their country, taking into account any potential enemy's capabilities, given the worst possible circumstances. Thus in Britain and the US military planners even during the Second World War regarded their strong ally, the USSR, with some suspicion, seeing a potential threat from those quarters earlier than the great majority of diplomats and politicians. These suspicions did not arise merely from the different ideologies adhered to by the Eastern and Western Allies. They were also rooted in the unsatisfactory experiences in wartime of the excessively secretive and suspicious behaviour of the Soviet armed forces, as it seemed to Westerners[1].

In addition to the military planners, the British Prime Minister, Winston Churchill, and some other key politicians also began to fear and distrust the Soviet leaders. Their attitudes towards the rulers of the Soviet Union were shaped not only by the amicable toasts drunk at conferences planning the joint counter-offensive against their Fascist enemies. Ernest Bevin, for example, the Foreign Secretary (1945-1951) of Clement Attlee's Labour government, had many years of conflict with the Moscow-led Communists in Britain to look back on, having himself served as secretary general in trade unions. Bevin was thus passionately anti-Stalinist[2]. Truman, US President from April 1945 until January 1953, after the invasion of the USSR by the Germans had expressed his hope that they would finish each other off, with the implication that he thought them equally distasteful[3].

There was, however, tremendous appreciation among the general public in the West, of the Soviet contribution towards the victory over Fascism[4]. Suspicions regarding Stalin's intentions, harboured by Western foreign policy-makers, would not have stifled the wartime alliance permanently, if it had not been for quarrels concerning postwar arrangements. Western relations with the USSR focused on these matters, however, and there was ample scope for profound clashes. For the deluge of the war had not only destroyed possessions and lives, but it had also carried away kings and governments and had broken down frontiers. Old power-structures had gone, and new ones had to be set up. The power vacuum left by the defeat of the German and Italian empires created a vortex like a low-pressure zone on a weather chart, and it was in precisely this area that the greatest amount of friction occurred.

Disagreements over Soviet occupation policies in those Eastern European countries that had been liberated by the Red Army served to catalyse the recognition of the differences between the British and the Americans (and, to a lesser extent, of the French) on the one hand, and the Soviet Union on the other[5]. At the peace conferences and the meetings of the Council of Foreign Ministers in 1945, 1946 and 1947, Western participants increasingly felt that their Soviet interlocutors were unreasonable and stubborn. The question of how occupied Germany should be treated led to particularly many clashes during attempts to co-ordinate the joint occupiers' policies[6].

Even now it needed more than this to turn such disagreements between allies into enmity. Further Soviet moves after the Second World War led Westerners to perceive a threat. Soviet occupation forces in Iran stayed on for months after they should have left in early 1946. In 1945-1946 the Russians once again tried to realize the old Tsarist dream of gaining a say in the control of the Bosphorus and the Dardanelles, urging a revision of the Treaty of Montreux. They further asked Turkey to cede her eastern provinces of Kars and Ardahan to the Soviet Republic of Armenia. On both occasions the Soviet Union was frustrated, but the realization in Western minds that these Soviet moves were of an expansionist nature created a charged atmosphere[7].

This was increased by the Communist radio- and press-campaigns waged by Communists throughout the world, denouncing the 'imperialism' of Britain and France, and, increasingly, of the US. This old axe had been ground with the British by Communists since Marx and Engels, but having just emerged from a war in which Communists, Socialists and Conservatives alike had fought jointly, this was a bitter pill for Westerners. In his famous speech given in Fulton in the American state of Missouri in March 1946, Churchill, the leader of the British Conservative Party (then in opposition) pointed to this threat, referring not only to his disapproval of Soviet policy behind what he called the Iron Curtain, but also to Stalin's probing in Germany, Turkey and Iran[8]. In his equally famous "Long Telegram" of 22 February 1946, George Kennan, an American diplomat and expert on Soviet politics, similarly pointed to the threat which Soviet policy posed to the West. He explained that Stalin denied the possibility of peaceful co-existence of both a "socialist center" and a "capitalist center", the two of which would have to battle "for command of world economy". He explained:

Whenever it is considered timely and promising, efforts will be made to advance official limits of Soviet power. For the moment, these efforts are restricted to certain neighbouring points conceived of [in Moscow] as being of immediate strategic necessity.... However, other points may at any time come into question, if and as concealed Soviet political power is extended to new areas.

Communist parties in other countries were in his view unofficial agents of this Soviet policy whose leaders were believed by Kennan to be "working closely together as an underground operating directorate of world communism, a concealed Comintern tightly coordinated and directed by Moscow". In the same way he identified as "agencies utilized for promulgation" of Soviet policies those

> Governments or governing groups willing to lend themselves to Soviet purposes in one degree or another, such as present Bulgarian and Yugoslav Governments, . . . Chinese Communists, etc. . . . Not only propaganda machines but actual policies of these regimes can be placed extensively at disposal of USSR.

The Soviet belief underlying this policy was, in Kennan's view, "that with US there can be no permanent *modus vivendi*": the Soviets saw a clash as ultimately inevitable[9]. It is warranted to quote Kennan's perceptions at such length, as he gave the State Department "new intellectual moorings" by offering "a new and realistic conception" to which the State Department, having been "floundering about", could "attach itself ", which it did: the telegram was widely circulated by Kennan's superiors who shared the views he had been the first to put into words[10]. Kennan's views were taken so seriously and regarded as so wise that he was appointed Director of the newly formed Policy Planning Staff in the State Department in early 1947, from where he strongly influenced American thinking until late 1949[11].

Frank Roberts, a senior diplomat in the British embassy in Moscow, equally saw a threat to British interest arising from Soviet policy. This he saw partly in the form of the economic isolation of Eastern Europe which would be lost to British trade. Beyond that, Soviet-led Communism, with its old hatred for Socialists who had forsworn the doctrine of the inevitability of revolution, was a challenge to the Labour government, as Soviet propaganda in Britain's colonies troubled the autumn of her imperial rule. In dealing with the Soviet Union, Roberts found that

> She has interests everywhere . . . her policies are entirely
> flexible and can be pressed, adapted or temporarily
> shelved to suit the needs of the moment. . . . In the long
> run she thinks she is bound to win out and can afford to
> be patient, provided always that she can defend herself
> against what she regards as a potentially hostile world.

Roberts agreed with a British intelligence report and with his
American colleague, Kennan,[12] that the USSR would seek to
avoid a major war at least until their current five-year plan
would have ended (i.e. 1950). Nevertheless, he regarded the
Soviet régime as expansionist, with long-term ambitions
dangerous to vital British interests[13]. Like Kennan's "Long
Telegram" in the US State Department, Roberts's dispatches
were well received in the British Foreign Office, and
Christopher Warner, the head of the Northern Department,
indicated that he regarded them as a guideline which the
British could use in dealings with the USSR[14]. In response to
them, Warner wrote a paper on 2 April 1946 on "The Soviet
Campaign against this Country", in which he claimed that with
its recent behaviour,

> the Soviet Union has announced to the world that it
> proposes to play an aggressive political role, while
> making an intensive drive to increase its own military and
> industrial strength. We should be very unwise not to take
> the Russians at their word, just as we should have been
> wise to take *Mein Kampf* at its face value. All Russia's
> activities in the past few months confirm this picture. In
> Eastern Europe, in the Balkans, in Persia, in Manchuria,
> in Korea, in her zone of Germany, and in the Security
> Council [of the UN]; in her support of Communist
> parties in foreign countries and Communist efforts to
> infiltrate Socialist parties and to combine left wing
> parties under Communist leadership; in the Soviet
> Union's foreign economic policy (her refusal to
> co-operate in international efforts at reconstruction and
> rehabilitation, while despoiling foreign countries in her
> sphere, harnessing them to the Soviet system, and at the
> same time posing as their only benefactor); in every word
> on foreign affairs that appears in the Soviet press and

broadcasts ... the Soviet Union's acts bear out the declaration of policy referred to above.

Warner's memorandum was highly influential and shaped the ideas of the British government[15].

While American and British views of the Soviet threat were converging and overlapping by 1946, the French were still much more concerned with the danger emanating in their view from a potential revival of Germany. The wartime alliance with Communism had been even closer for France than for the other Western Allies because of the crucial rôle played by the Parti Communiste Français (PCF) in the Résistance. As a result of this, there was much greater sympathy for Communism among workers and intellectuals alike. Consequently, the postwar PCF had nearly a quarter of the votes in general elections and until 1947 was represented with ministers in the successive French governments. Due in part to this domestic political climate, in the words of a French historian, "French awareness of the Russian threat was belated and reluctant."[16] In the immediate postwar years a Gaullist streak in French foreign policy, aiming at independence from both East and West, provided for a neutralist France as mediator between the Russians and the "Anglo-Saxons"[17]. This only gradually evaporated with the dissipation of wartime agreement, marked by the failure of the subsequent meetings of the Council of Foreign Ministers. This led to a gradual line-up of France with the United Kingdom and the US, which had crystallized by the second half of April 1947 when the Moscow meeting failed. Strikes organized by the PCF between June 1947 and December 1948 created a feeling of fear of Communism in the minds of those Frenchmen who were not sympathetic, and they served to polarize French politics[18], leaving the PCF isolated. Its leader Maurice Thorez lost support outside his own party when he proclaimed that France would not wage war against the Soviet Union even in self-defence[19].

If the years 1945 to mid-1947 saw the gradual development in the British and American foreign ministries of a perception of a threat emanating from the USSR, the moves made by the Soviets within the Eastern bloc from the summer of 1947 onwards until the expulsion of the Yugoslavs from the Communist community in mid-1948, put the West in a state of outright alarm. In the autumn of 1947 Zhdanov proclaimed at the founding conference of the Communist Information Bureau (the Cominform) that there were now two camps in the world, a Socialist one and an imperialist one. Christopher Warner noted on 20 October 1947 that in his view this meant the end of another "Popular Front" phase, and the beginning of a new phase, in which there was the opposition of "Communism versus the rest".[20] It was thus assumed in the West that this recognition of East-West antagonisms was a step undertaken by Stalin to increase the tension, as it was assumed that Zhdanov spoke with Stalin's authorization[21]. The London Conference of Foreign Ministers of November/December 1947 was an utter failure because of the stubbornness, in the eyes of the West, of Molotov, the Soviet Foreign Minister[22]. When in February 1948 the Communist coup in Czechoslovakia turned that country into another Soviet satellite, Western indignation increased decisively. Westerners saw parallels between this event and the fall of Czechoslovakia on the eve of World War II, and they were determined not to engage in "appeasement" of Stalin. A CIA report at the time pointed out that "the psychological reaction to the Czech coup appears to have been out of proportion to its actual significance."[23] Although the American National Security Council (NSC) had studied this CIA report, they in turn produced one on 30 March 1948 which read; "The USSR has engaged the United States in a struggle for power, or 'cold war', in which our national security is at stake and from which we cannot withdraw short of eventual national suicide." The report asserted that "the ultimate objective of Soviet-directed world communism is the domination of the world."[24]

Western Measures to Counter the Soviet Threat

The events in Czechoslovakia could not have been reversed by the West by anything short of military intervention. Although the Western powers were not prepared to go that far, their determination was strengthened to resist any further Soviet move which looked expansionist. Thus the Brussels Treaty, signed in March 1948 by Britain[25], France[26] and the Benelux countries, contained a commitment to mutual defence, and likewise the Vandenberg Resolution of the summer of 1948 which allowed the US to commit itself to the defence of Western Europe. This was the first commitment of the sort made in the history of the United States in peacetime, and it was the necessary prerequisite for the conclusion of the North Atlantic Treaty in the following year. These two decisions were encouraged by the escalation of fear of the Soviet Union in the West, resulting from what proved to be a grave miscalculation on the part of Stalin: the Berlin blockade, which started in mid-June 1948. Like the Korean War two years later, the Soviet Union's forcible attempt to oust the Western powers from an area that was of little value to them strategically, resulted in their stubborn insistence on the freedom of that area, in this case, of West Berlin. They were even prepared to go to war over this strategically untenable part of the city[27]. In the words of a senior British Foreign Office official, Sir Gladwyn Jebb, "What the French call a 'grande peur' seized the Western world."[28] This feeling was not changed in any way by the relatively cool and level-headed CIA reports[29] or by Kennan's estimates that the USSR was not likely to risk a world war within the next decade or so[30].

But besides the fear of an attack, there was a fear that, having "established themselves solidly in Eastern Europe", the Soviets would "from these secure entrenchments . . . [seek] to infiltrate into Western and Southern Europe. Tactically they have been concerned to probe along the Western line in the hope of finding a weak spot and so of effecting a penetration which would cause the whole line to collapse." As Geoffrey Wallinger and his Southern Department in the Foreign Office noted, "there is no indication that [Western counter-measures] have deflected the Soviet Government from their purpose." This view was shared by Bevin and Attlee, who approved the Southern Department's crucial statement of British perceptions and policies, known as the "Bastion Paper", communicated to the State Department in early August 1948. Soviet aims were thus at this stage seen by the British as well as the Americans as "the political domination of Europe and eventually of the whole world"[31].

The perception of the threat emanating from the Soviet Union required a policy to counter it. After the end of the Second World War, the US armed forces had been largely demobilized: the number of soldiers had been reduced from 12 million on VE Day to 1.6 million in 1947, and the defence expenditure for the fiscal year 1945 of 81.6 thousand million dollars had been cut down to 13.1 thousand million in the fiscal year 1947[32]. Similarly, the British armed forces worldwide were cut from 5.1 million men and women at the end of the war to about 1.2 million at the end of 1946 [33]. Britain and the US in close succession established specialized committees to formulate policies to deal with the Soviet threat. In the spring of 1946 the British set up the "Russia Committee" in the Foreign Office[34]. In early 1947 the State Department's Policy Planning Staff (PPS) was created, and the National Security Council of the United States (NSC)[35]. Nothing comparable to the American PPS or NSC was set up in France, however, nor was an overall policy developed, such as the American doctrine of "containment"[36]. The initiative lay with the Americans and the British in the early postwar years.

The next step was the formulation of policies to deal with the threat. The Americans developed the policy of "containment". This is a concept difficult to sum up accurately and often misunderstood, even by top American decision-makers at the time[37]. Its partial ambiguity resulted largely from the style in which its spiritual father, George Kennan, expressed himself: he had a great weakness for mixing metaphors and for insinuating, but never clearly setting out what his views were. It was probably because of the vagueness of his writing that so many American diplomats, strategists and politicians found expressed in it, or thought they found, what they had been sensing about American-Soviet relations. As Director of the Policy Planning Staff, his was the most important influence on American foreign policy-making until his resignation in late 1949 [38]. Yet his policies had come to stay, having had such a profound influence on the initial moulding of American policy-makers' attitudes towards the Soviet Union and on their vision of possible measures to counter the Soviet threat.

Kennan's proposed strategy[39] was shaped by his personal perception of the threat. As we have seen, he did not expect Stalin to risk a world war in the foreseeable future to gain his desired aims, namely the victory of his system over the rival West; Kennan thought the USSR would take its time pursuing this goal. He therefore did not advocate any hasty measures of self-defence, and he never seems to have contemplated a pre-emptive strike against the USSR, or, indeed, all-out rearmament. The hallmark of Kennan's strategy was, instead, the economic and psychological strengthening of the democratic forces of the West, which in turn would frustrate Soviet attempts politically to subvert the masses of the West European countries that had a potential for social discontent and unrest, on account of the economic exhaustion of the ruined postwar Europe. Kennan saw only five areas in the world as crucially important, namely the five (real or potential) centres of industrial-military strength: the US, the United Kingdom, Germany (or the industrial area along the Rhine), the USSR and Japan. Of these, only the USSR was hostile towards the US at the time, so it was vital for the United States to prevent the other three from also falling under the Soviet sway. These areas in Kennan's view were strongpoints which had to be defended. Any other area on the periphery of the Soviet empire was not worth a defence commitment on the part of the US[40].

On a non-military level, however, Kennan envisaged extensive American activity: apart from helping the economic revival of Western Europe, the United Kingdom and Japan, which would create self-confidence and would diminish vulnerability to Communist subversion, he hoped that the US could in the long term influence the Soviet Union to modify its concepts of international relations. This would be done, as Kennan put it in his famous article in *Foreign Affairs* in 1947, by showing the Soviet Union that it would be met "with unalterable counter-force at every point where they show signs of encroaching upon the interests of a peaceful and stable world". This should be done morally rather than militarily: the US should oppose the Soviet Union by assuming "the responsibilities of moral and political leadership", and by projecting itself as "a country which knows what it wants, which is coping successfully with the problems of its internal life and with the responsibilities of a World Power, and which has a spiritual vitality capable of holding its own among the major ideological currents of the time".[41]

But beyond these purely defensive measures, he thought the US could also "influence by its actions internal developments, both within Russia and throughout the international Communist movement, by which Russian policy is largely determined". One of the means he mentioned explicitly was that of "informational activity". Yet it is known that he also favoured subversive operations against the governments of the Soviet-dominated areas of Europe, which, as we shall see presently, was a very militant, aggressive side of containment. This, combined with the portrayal of the US as the radiant incarnation of the better alternative to Socialism and Communism, could "increase enormously the strains under which Soviet policy must operate, . . . and . . . promote tendencies which must eventually find their outlet in either the break-up or the gradual mellowing of Soviet power".[42] Kennan's plans for the "containment" of Soviet Communism were therefore by no means purely passive or defensive, as was alleged later by John Foster Dulles (see below, Chapter 7).

The policies proposed by Kennan were largely implemented by the American administration. The economic (and psychological) revival of Western Europe and the United Kingdom were achieved mainly through the administration of Marshall Aid. This American grant aid, which had Kennan's full support[43], aimed at restoring the European economies to health: their recovery from the devastations of the war had been proceeding all too slowly, giving the Communists greater leverage. American military planning focused mainly on the defence of certain key areas[44], which were indeed, as Kennan had postulated, Britain, Western Europe and Japan, plus the Mediterranean as an important supply-route and the Middle East as a strategic air base[45], although the Middle East by agreement with the UK was mainly regarded as a British defence responsibility[46]. The American-subsidized economic revival of the United Kingdom and France would, it was hoped, enable the Americans to share with these countries the burden of defending the "Free World": they would take on the defence of areas which the Americans did not see as crucial, together with their own home-territories. This in turn would effectively allow the Americans to concentrate their forces on the defence of areas vital to them (e.g. Japan and the Pacific) while once more acting as an arsenal for Europe in case of an emergency.

All in all, this policy proved considerably cheaper than the one which seemed contained in the words of the Truman Doctrine of March 1947. Committing the US to the defence or support of all "free peoples who are resisting attempted subjugation by armed minorities or outside pressures" this crudely exaggerated America's commitment to the defence of the "Free World"[47]. The Truman Doctrine, which was formulated over the issue of giving aid to Greece, was given this universal applicability, paradoxically, to gain the support of Congress. Yet it must not be forgotten that the promise of "cheap" measures to achieve "national security", as are found in Kennan's policy of defending strongpoints only, which would keep the defence budget within reasonable limits, was also popular with Congress[48].

Kennan opposed the Truman Doctrine because in his view it over-extended American commitments. Yet his own strategy of strongpoint defence proved contradictory to his strategy of strengthening the morale of the populations in the key areas, in order to help achieve the former: if a country of minor importance but of clearly non-Communist character, such as Greece or Korea, were attacked by Communist forces, and the US would not come to its aid, this would in turn demoralize the nations in the strongpoint areas, who would then become more vulnerable to Communist subversion. They might well fear that the Americans would leave them to fight a Soviet attack on their own if they were attacked, as the Americans would be suspected of attempting to keep out of any military conflict. This would undermine the determination of the populations in the key areas to fight back if attacked. Because it was important to keep up the morale in these areas, the Americans were effectively unable to tolerate the loss of a country even of minor importance, as would become evident with the attack on South Korea in 1950. But already the need to come to the aid of Greece, a country not included in Kennan's list of strongpoints, showed his strategy of strongpoint defence to be unworkable, as we can say with hindsight, and its replacement by a US commitment to the defence of the "Free World" as a whole, with a rocketing defence budget, already existed in embryonic form in the Truman Doctrine, to be born in 1950 in the form of NSC 68 (see Chapter 5)[49].

Yet the Truman Administration's policy of "containment" cannot be translated purely as the defensive attempt to stop the Soviets from extending their influence beyond the Iron Curtain into the "Free World". Like Kennan's plans, the implemented form of "containment" was two-pronged, containing a militant, aggressive policy aimed at actively undermining Soviet control of Eastern Europe, besides the defensive policy aiming at boosting Western economies and Western morale. On 17 March 1948, George Marshall informed some of the US Ambassadors that

> Ultimate United States objectives toward Sov [*sic*] Balkan satellites — Yugoslavia, Albania, Bulgaria, Rumania and Hungary — may be summarized as establishment [of] those states as democratic independent members [of the] family of nations, under conditions guaranteeing people's effective enjoyment [of] human rights and non-discrimination against US interests and interests of other peace-loving states.

This amounted to the American hope for a liberation of Eastern Europe from the "totalitarian Soviet Balkan hegemony" which had "thwarted the democratic majority of the people"[50]. The US was to encourage this process actively: publicity for the cause of freedom and democracy, of the American way of life and the superiority of American ideas, was increased through an expansion of the radio broadcasts of the Voice of America. With its transmissions to Eastern Europe it was supposed to put strain on the relations between the Communist rulers and the people, and between Moscow and the populations of the satellites, by revealing the truth about how badly the Moscow-led Communists were treating their subjects.

But this "informational activity" on the part of the US did not constitute the limit of the active, offensive side of the Truman Administration's "containment" policy, as Bennett Kovrig would have us believe[51]. Already the policy paper NSC 7 of 30 March 1948, entitled "The Position of the United States with Respect to Soviet-Directed World Communism" had the conclusions:

> The defeat of the forces of Soviet-directed world-communism is vital to the security of the United States. . . . This objective cannot be achieved by a defensive policy. . . . The United States should therefore take the lead in organizing a world-wide counter-offensive aimed at mobilizing and strengthening our own and anti-communist forces in the non-Soviet

world, and at undermining the strength of the communist forces in the Soviet world.

To achieve these aims, the US should "Develop a vigorous and effective ideological campaign. Develop and at the appropriate time carry out, a co-ordinated program to support underground resistance movements in countries behind the iron curtain, including the USSR. . . . Establish a substantial emergency fund to be used in combatting Soviet-directed world communism."[52]

If this is seen in conjunction with NSC 10/2 of 18 June 1948, the "NSC Directive on [the] Office of Special Projects" (within the CIA), it becomes clear that the US Administration was authorizing "activities . . . against hostile foreign states or groups or in support of friendly foreign states or groups but which are so planned and conducted that any US Government responsibility for them is not evident . . . and that if uncovered the US Government can plausibly disclaim any responsibility for them." These activities were to include "propaganda, economic warfare, preventive direct action, including sabotage, anti-sabotage, demolition, and evacuation measures; subversion against hostile states, including assistance to underground resistance movements, guerillas and refugee liberation groups, and support of indigenous anti-communist elements in threatened countries of the free world." Because other sections of the CIA or the military establishment were to deal with "armed conflict by recognized military forces, espionage, counter-espionage, and cover and deception for military operations", these tasks were not on the agenda of the Office of Special Projects[53].

As we shall see, this policy was enacted. Even if it did not meet with great success within the period under consideration, the historian John Yurechko is right in arguing that the Truman Administration did not distinguish itself fundamentally from the Eisenhower Administration in its policy towards the satellites of the Soviet Union, even if it was the Eisenhower Administration that, particularly through the mouth of the Secretary of State, John Foster Dulles, so loudly proclaimed its commitment to the concept of a liberation of Eastern Europe from Communist dictatorship, claiming that the previous Administration's "containment" policy had been passive and defensive only[54].

It is of importance to note that prior to the Tito-Stalin split all these offensive activities aimed at encouraging popular uprisings that would overthrow the Communist governments within the satellites and the Soviet Union, which seemed the only way in which the burden of Stalinist oppression could be shaken off. Also it was still thought that *any* Communist government in power would necessarily be inimical to the US. Yet the occurrence of schisms between Communist governments within the Soviet dominated part of the world was already thought possible by Kennan. In a lecture at the University of Virginia in Febrary 1947, he talked in particularly woolly terms about the possibility of a Communist régime which had "come to power in a country not contiguous to the borders of the direct military power of Russia" (what he probably meant was a country far away from Moscow, not easy to subjugate by the Red Army because of the sheer geographic distance) turning on its masters in Moscow, successfully defying the Kremlin's attempts to control it. He gave the example of a Communist China, which would have the potential ability to break away[55]. While Yugoslavia would equally have fitted the description, there is no evidence that Kennan thought of her in those terms.

Kennan would have regarded such a schismatic Communist régime as of advantage for the West, because in splitting away it would weaken the power-base of the Soviet Union. Did he, then, envisage any active Western support for the development of a schism? Gaddis infers that Marshall Aid was designed as a tool to break up the Soviet orbit by straining the relationship between the Kremlin and the Communist rulers of the People's Democracies. Gaddis points out that Kennan expected Stalin to forbid the satellite governments to accept Marshall Aid, which in turn must have seemed to them like a missed opportunity to restore the economic health of their countries[56]. This disappointment on the part of the satellite régimes would have been the side-effect, however, and definitely not the main aim, of Marshall Aid. There is thus no evidence for the existence of a concept of active encouragement of schisms within the Communist world prior to the Tito-Stalin split.

British policy to counter the Soviet threat differed from that of the US, in that the British did not have the economic means

15

to adopt a strategy of propping up the economies of countries more directly menaced by the Soviet Union, to the extent that the US did. Nevertheless, they agreed that the economic and psychological strengthening of governments in threatened areas would result in greater resistance to the threat. They therefore eventually participated in many economic aid schemes in conjunction with the US and with France, as far as their limited resources allowed (see particularly Chapters 3, 6 and 7).

The British equally believed that self-help in Europe was necessary for the building up of the morale and strength of Europe. The crucial difference in perspective here was that British planning to meet the Soviet challenge in Europe hinged on an American guarantee. It was not yet clear even to well-educated Britons that this effectively meant the end of Britain's great power status: Britain was still the leading force in the Commonwealth and dominated large parts of the Middle East and Asia. In 1948 even Bevin was dreaming of a leading rôle for Britain within a union or loose federation of Western European states, "independent both of the United states and of the Soviet Union"[57]. Yet Bevin knew that for the time being a consolidated Europe alone, even with the backing of the Commonwealth, was not enough to meet the strategic and ideological threats emanating from the USSR: Europe was economically weak, and on the military side lacked the nuclear power which could have made up for its manpower deficiencies in comparison with the Soviet Union[58].

In the summer of 1948, the British Foreign Office at Bevin's request produced a memorandum referred to within Whitehall as the "Bastion Paper". Approved by Bevin and Attlee, it was communicated to the State Department as representing "the general views of H.M.G.", and can be regarded as the most important summary of the British defensive policy *vis-à-vis* the Soviet Union before the outbreak of the Korean War. While the "Bastion Paper" was drawn up originally to review the problem of the Greek Civil War, Bevin decided that this problem must not be looked at in isolation but "in the framework of the general European [and Middle Eastern] situation". After analysing the Soviet threat to "the Western Powers in Europe and the European flank in Turkey and Persia", it described the policy of consolidating "the West in the face of this [Soviet] menace". The measures taken so far were listed as Marshall Aid, the Brussels Treaty, the Truman Doctrine, and the actions of the US and Britain to prevent a Communist victory in the Italian elections. The paper concluded, however, that the measures taken so far were not enough.

> If the Soviet advance is now to be halted, the Western nations must continue to develop the policy on which they have embarked. This will necessitate perseverance over a long period, since the Soviet Government will not abandon their fundamental aims at the first sight of opposition. It will also require constant vigilance and a firm resolve to parry each threat as it develops. Only a sustained effort of this character will prevent a breach in our defences which might bring down the whole line.[59]

The paper stated that the struggle between East and West was "now concentrated with a varying degree of intensity on the principal bastions of the Western line of Europe: Germany, Austria, Trieste, Greece and Turkey". This did not, however, mean that the British government advocated the defence of certain strongpoints only, as Kennan did. In spite of what its title seems to imply, the paper called for the defence of the entire periphery of the Soviet orbit. Any breach in this line would enable the Soviets to penetrate Western Europe and "cause the whole line to collapse". Penetration of this sort was not just seen in military terms, but even more in the realm of politics and ideology.

In either case it definitely meant that in the British government's view, any Soviet step across "the line", politically or militarily, had to be fought. It could be argued that this clashed with British defence strategy, which did not at the time provide for the use of any British troops on the continent, other than the occupation forces in Germany[60]. These military plans, however, only concerned the initial stages of a defensive war in which, before the foundation of NATO, the British could not count on American participation.

British support for the concept of peripheral defence (military, political and economic alike) fell in with the more costly and less limited side of Kennan's proposed policy of "containment", and helped shift the balance of Anglo-American policy-making towards a commitment to the defence of all (free) nations against a threat emanating from armed minorities within or from powers without, which had been formulated in the Truman Doctrine. This was happening much to the horror of Kennan and high-ranking men in the State Department, who regarded it as an over-extension of US commitments. It is important to keep this in mind in view of the situation in which Yugoslavia was soon to find herself.

The French Foreign Ministry had no such global policy, but was torn between the fear of a resurgent Germany and the fear of a Communist victory within, while the military was fighting unrest and insurrection in French colonies in Africa and South East Asia. Policy decision-making in the Conseil des Ministres was paralysed until 1947 by the presence of Communist ministers, and the Gaullist trend was still felt, delaying the formulation of a strategy that would be in line with those of Britain and the United States. When France finally came down on the Anglo-American side in 1947/48, it was more in response to British moves rather than to French initiative[61]. Nevertheless, this resulted in France's joining the Western Union and NATO. It was not until 1950 that the French began to take the initiative with various specific schemes designed to consolidate areas of particular concern to them against the Soviet threat. They did not, however, adopt a global strategy[62].

Western Relations with Yugoslavia until 1948

Of the Western powers, the British had had most contact with Yugoslavia since 1941, having supplied Tito's Partisans with arms during the Second World War[63]. But while Churchill and Stalin had agreed in October 1944 in their famous "percentages agreement" that both should have an approximately equal share of influence in Yugoslavia after the war[64], within a year the British had lost most of it[65]. Charles Stefan, who was a diplomat at the US embassy in Belgrade at the time, recalled that "no other regime in Eastern Europe had moved as rapidly down the road to Soviet-style communism and one-party government as had Tito's Yugoslavia."[66] Although the British made efforts to stay on good terms with Tito[67], his foreign policy clashed with British interests in the cases of his claims on parts of southern Austria (Carinthia), Trieste, and his support for the Greek Communists in the Greek Civil War.

The Americans clashed with the Yugoslavs on the same issues as the British. Worse still, in August 1946 the Yugoslavs shot down two American transport planes, killing two crew, as the two aircraft had violated Yugoslav airspace. This embittered relations considerably[68]. Franco-Yugoslav relations were fairly insignificant in this period. In 1948, during the great strikes in France, the Communist Party of Yugoslavia (CPY) and the Yugoslav trade unions angered the French government by giving financial support to the striking workers and miners in France[69]. French relations with Yugoslavia remained very distant until 1950.

On the whole, Western relations with Yugoslavia were a small-scale version of their relations with the Soviet Union. Stefan remembers that "In the area of foreign relations, the Yugoslavs appeared to be the staunchest and most militant of all the Soviet satellite states."[70] In January 1948 the Foreign Office described Yugoslavia as "the undoubted prize pupil of all the Eastern European states within the Soviet orbit — the most monolithic, to use the Marxist terminology"[71]. As late as 22 June 1948 the French Ambassador in Belgrade, Payart, thought Yugoslavia was aspiring to be "la fille aînée de l'église communiste"[72]. The Western powers thus thought of the Yugoslavs as the most orthodox proponents of the Communist line in foreign policy, which in their view emanated from a thoroughly centralized government in Moscow under its all-powerful supremo, Stalin. Occasions were observed by Western politicians and diplomats, on which the Yugoslavs took orders from the USSR to change their policy on certain international issues when these were discussed at conferences[73]. Yugoslav propaganda-battles seemed to be directed at the same issues as those of the Soviet press and radio broadcasts[74]. Their foreign policy seemed to Western observers part of the expansionist strategy of the Soviet Union. Hence came the assumption in the British "Bastion Paper" that pressure (from Yugoslavia) on Trieste was part of the Soviet overall strategy, and likewise the inference that the Yugoslavs were acting on behalf of the USSR in the matters of Carinthia and Greece[75], at the time when the USSR was concentrating its attention on the Berlin blockade. In the same way, in

Kennan's words, even the best-informed American officials saw Communism as

> a monolithic structure, reaching through a network of highly disciplined Communist parties into practically every country of the world. In these circumstances, any success of a local Communist party, anywhere, had to be regarded as an extension in reality of the political orbit, or at least the dominant influence, of the Kremlin. Precisely because Stalin maintained so jealous, so humiliating a control over foreign Communists, all of the latter had, at that time, to be regarded as the vehicle of his will, not their own. He was the only center of authority in the Communist World; and it was a vigilant, exacting and imperious headquarters, prepared to brook no opposition.[76]

In reality, however, this was one of the Western misperceptions of the Communist world, as we shall see presently, based on the mistaken assumption that Stalin was always completely in control, as sole commander of a thoroughly monolithic, centralized and homogeneous world Communist movement. The following analysis of the origins of the Tito-Stalin split will attempt to reconstruct what the real state of the Communist movement was in 1947-48, what shape Stalin's policies eventually took, and in what way Tito's policies clashed with them.

The Origins of the Tito-Stalin Split

There had been conflicts of some importance between Tito and Stalin ever since the CPY took up arms in resistance to the Fascist occupiers in 1941, but these had been a well-kept secret[77]. They mainly revolved around the insufficiency of support which the Yugoslav Communists received from Stalin, who even during the war seemed anxious not to offend his Western allies by withdrawing recognition from the royal Yugoslav government-in-exile.

But the wartime disagreements gave way to a period of honeymoon from 1945 until 1947, in which Tito was seen by

East and West alike as Stalin's most loyal and favourite disciple, and Stalin singled him out for preferential treatment on several occasions[78]. The Yugoslavs seemed to model their government on that of the Soviet Union, with a dictatorial administration backed by a secret police force; the Yugoslav constitution of 1946 was very similar to that of the Soviet Union, and like the USSR, Yugoslavia adopted a Five Year Plan for the industrialization of her economy.

This, however, was to become a point of contention between Tito and Stalin, who sought to make the satellites serviceable to the Soviet Union's planned economy. He thought the Yugoslav Five Year Plan over-ambitious and unrealistic while Tito was not enforcing collectivization at the same rate as the Soviet Union had done[79]. This was a concession the Yugoslav leaders made to the peasants, knowing how much they had relied on them in the war. They were regarded as "the strongest pillar of our State order", which, according to Stalin, was "in complete contradiction to Marxism-Leninism" which considered "that in Europe and in the countries of people's democracy, the working class and not the peasantry is the most progressive, the most revolutionary class". Stalin also accused the CPY of having let itself become submerged in the People's Front[80], which was the continuation into peacetime of the wartime coalition between the CPY and any other political group willing to unite with them to fight the occupying forces.

Further, the Cominform criticized the fact that the majority of the members of the Central Committee of the Party had been co-opted, not elected by the members of the CPY. This criticism was justified: the Central Committee was indeed a club of old friends who were soon to show their solidarity, with the exception of Žujović and Hebrang. These two men had sided with Stalin on the issue of the Five Year Plan, as a result of which they were expelled from the Central Committee of the CPY and later imprisoned[81]. This had angered Stalin, who on other occasions had unsuccessfully tried to establish closer ties with other members of the CPY[82] and with Žujović and Hebrang lost his leverage inside the CPY's leadership. The criticism concerning the composition of the Central Committee reflected the hope that new members could be brought into it through elections, people who might be more open to pressure from Stalin.

21

A further issue was the Yugoslav request for a withdrawal by the Soviet Union of 60% of their military and civilian advisers in Yugoslavia. They had begun to irritate their hosts, receiving higher pay than their Yugoslav colleagues, and attempting to establish an espionage network in Yugoslavia. The Soviets reacted angrily by withdrawing the remaining advisers in March 1948, and accused the Yugoslavs of having treated them like agents of a hostile power[83]. The Yugoslavs were also reluctant to accept Soviet advice on military matters, as they had been successful during the Second World War with the strategies they had used, and thought them more appropriate to the Yugoslav situation than Soviet military doctrine[84]. Tito and his friends also refused to allow the Soviet military a greater control of the Yugoslav army which the Red Army Command requested in the context of the military centralization and re-organization that was initiated in early 1948[85].

The Yugoslavs were then accused of being unwilling to accept the criticism of the Communist Party of the Soviet Union (CPSU) and to mend their ways. They themselves, however, had been happy to mete out criticism to others at the founding conference of the Cominform, where they had attacked the French and Italian Communist Parties for allying themselves with bourgeois parties. The Yugoslavs also declined to come to the Cominform meeting of June 1948, when these points of criticism were to be discussed with them[86]. This provided the justification for their expulsion from the Cominform.

There was one further accusation which constituted only a fragment of the first sentence of the Cominform communiqué of expulsion, which read: "The information Bureau notes that recently the leadership of the CPY has pursued an incorrect line on the main questions of home *and foreign* policy, a line which represents a departure from Marxism-Leninism."[87] This is virtually the only mention of foreign policy in the entire correspondence, and no further explanation of this allegation can be found anywhere. But in one of the letters from Stalin there is a revealing paragraph mentioning Trotsky. While all other criticism was aimed at Yugoslav domestic policies, the reference to Trotsky came in isolation and not in connection with internal affairs. It was alleged several times that the

Yugoslavs talked about the CPSU as degenerate[88], and Stalin's and Molotov's letter of 27 March 1948 read:

> ...one might mention that, when he decided to declare war on the CPSU, Trotsky also started with accusations of the CPSU as degenerate, as suffering from the limitations inherent in the narrow nationalism of great powers. Naturally he camouflaged all this with *left slogans about world revolution.*[89]

This point opens up new dimensions of the Tito-Stalin controversy. To understand it fully it is necessary to consider Stalin's overall policy towards the satellites, other Communist parties, and towards the West, in the increasingly tense atmosphere of the Cold War.

Between 1945 and early 1947, Stalin encouraged flexibility and diversity among the various Communist parties who were told to follow whatever way seemed most promising for them to establish themselves in their respective countries. In other words, they were allowed to follow "separate roads to Socialism", concentrating on domestic issues and on dealing with internal opponents, with considerable freedom to choose the most appropriate means[90]. It may be recalled that this was the period in which Communist régimes took roots in the Eastern European countries, when Communists got into the French government, when the Italian Communists in alliance with the Nenni-Socialists were close to gaining an overall majority in the general election, and when the Greek Civil War was revived. Tailoring policies to fit local needs was of great importance particularly in Eastern Europe: the consolidation of the Communists' hold on those countries had to come in stages, as they were in a minuscule minority of the population (with the exception of Czechoslovakia) immediately after the war. In all states except Yugoslavia and Albania they were almost foreigners in their own native countries, as they had spent the war years in Russia or in concentration camps, rather than organizing resistance movements within their own countries[91]. At the same time Stalin was probing on a diplomatic level and at peace conferences to see what he could get out of the postwar settlement for himself, as we have seen. It was a period of "catch as catch can".

During this period he also tried to effect instability in Western Europe; his attempts were reflected in his negotiations with the Western powers regarding Germany. He wanted to keep Central and Western Europe weak and divided, while giving the Soviet Union and the satellites time to recover. Security for the USSR meant the weakness of Western Europe. As we have seen above, this led to the perception of a threat in Britain and the United States and they took measures to meet it, adopting the strategy of "containment". Here was the extreme opposite of what Stalin had hoped to achieve: with the Truman Doctrine and particularly with the Marshall Plan Western Europe was being strengthened[92]. Therefore Stalin seems to have changed his strategy, trying thenceforth to give less offence to the Western powers in order to slow down or even to stop their drawing together in reaction to his earlier policies[93].

Already in April 1946 Stalin began to withdraw some of his more exaggerated claims, for example to Cyrenaica. After the proclamation of the Truman Doctrine, Stalin gave an interview to a Western journalist, denying the inevitability of an East-West conflict[94]. The initiation of a less offensive foreign policy also required the reining in of all Communist parties world-wide, so that Stalin could be in control of their activities, domestic and foreign. This meant that a period of centralization and *Gleichschaltung* was necessary. The phase of diversity was thus ended by the foundation of the Cominform, which was designed to achieve these new aims[95].

Following this interpretation by the historian Brzezinski, McCagg and Ra'anan have shown that in 1947-48 there was a factional conflict at the highest level within the Soviet leadership[96]. Of the two factions, one was headed by Zhdanov and included Molotov, who was so uncompromising at the London Council of Foreign Ministers in late 1947. This Zhdanovite faction was in favour of following a radical, revolutionary line, encouraging Communist parties outside the Soviet orbit to take a belligerent stance, to stage strikes and to rise in arms to overthrow colonial powers[97]. This faction had the sympathetic support of Tito and Mao, but together they assumed also that they had the full backing of Stalin, who in their view could not but agree with their revolutionary ambitions, especially as nothing in his rhetoric led them to believe otherwise[98].

The rival faction was that of Malenkov, Suslov (Zhdanov's personal rival) and the economist Varga, who favoured a line which was really closer to Stalin's nature, namely that of consolidation and centralization, which McCagg calls "Stalin's 'Statism'"[99]. On the whole, Stalin had a deep dislike for coups and revolutions, and personally preferred gradualism, as Louis Fischer has demonstrated[100].

Stalin, away from Moscow more frequently in this period, suffering from illnesses which cut him off from some of the developments in Moscow, must have been lacking complete awareness of the issues involved and the extent to which this rivalry went until late 1947 to early 1948; but perhaps he allowed his subordinates to be at each other's throats, as long as he could be sure that he could interfere at any time and still come out on top. For our purposes it is important to show that Zhdanov's extremely radical faction had the support of Tito, and that the CPY agreed with the Zhdanovites that revolutions should be encouraged world-wide[101].

The CPY was the only European Communist party to send representatives to the Second Congress of the Communist Party of India in Calcutta in February-March 1948, and to the Southeast Asian Conference of the World Federation of Democratic Youth at the same time. The Yugoslavs on these occasions advocated insurrection as opposed to compromises with the existing Indian government; soon afterwards the Communist Party of India replaced its general secretary Joshi by Ranadive, who was the major proponent of insurrectionism. The Youth Conference was also attended by representatives from the Communist parties of Burma, Malaya and Indonesia, all of which experienced Communist insurrections during 1948. This is not to say that the Yugoslav delegates in the name of the Cominform gave them the order to go ahead: the explosive situations in Malaya and Indonesia existed already, and since 1946 peasants in Hyderabad had been involved in an armed uprising. The Yugoslavs did, however, on the occasion of these conferences express that "in the face of the whole system of violence and suppression, the people [of Southeast Asia] had no way but to reply in kind: by force, by revolution." Dedijer, a member of the Yugoslav delegation, recalled that "we did not try to conceal our opinions. We had just emerged from the revolution, we were young and full of enthusiasm. We wanted to help all the world's oppressed to liberate themselves as soon as possible. But all we did was to agree with the assessment that Asian communists themselves had made."[102]

The Southeast Asian insurrections all proved abortive, and were given little or no support by the USSR, as the Yugoslavs alleged, because Stalin was afraid of antagonizing the Western powers in an area which was not of vital concern to him[103]. There was one uprising in the Far East, however, that was on its way to victory, in spite of the absence of support from the Soviet Union, as Stalin himself admitted to Milovan Djilas, one of the closest associates of Tito[104]: that of the Chinese Communists. Here again we find an aspect of the disagreement which began to crystallize between the radical and the Statist factions: the Yugoslavs were very supportive of the Chinese Communists and thus of the radical side[105].

Questions of foreign policy were thus at the heart of the differences between Tito and Stalin. Of these, the Greek Civil War seems to have loomed largest in Stalin's mind. Yugoslav involvement dated back to 1943[106]. Yugoslavia supplied the Greek rebels with arms and ammunition during the second and third rounds of the Civil War (1946-49), and allowed them to use Yugoslav territory as a base for operations. All the other satellites except Poland helped as well, albeit on a much more modest scale. Tito's friend Dedijer speculated that this could not have happened without Stalin's approval[107].

Stalin's attitude towards the Greek Civil War was not clear-cut. In the percentages agreement with Churchill of October 1944, their interest in Greece and other Balkan states had also been discussed, and it had been agreed that Britain should have 90% influence in Greece, and the USSR only 10%. It seems that Stalin took this commitment seriously[108]. In January 1946, Dimitrios Partsaliades, one of the leaders of the KKE (the Greek Communist Party) visited Moscow and was advised against resuming the armed conflict, although he was told that it was up to the KKE to decide[109]. This fell into the time of "diversity" as discussed above, where the various Communist parties were left to decide many issues for themselves. According to Dedijer the Yugoslavs received a telegram from Stalin in March 1947 saying that "what we were doing [namely giving aid to the Greek guerrilla forces] was good", after which aid from Yugoslavia increased significantly. Dedijer also claims that the Soviets sent about 30 anti-aircraft guns, which were earmarked for Greece, but for some unexplained reason remained in Yugoslavia[110]. Nevertheless, Vukmanović-Tempo claims that on the whole "the leadership of the Soviet Union has no interest whatsoever in a victory of the people's revolutionary movement in Greece". In Tempo's view this was demonstrated by the percentages agreement; also, the Greek Communist Party was not invited to the first Cominform meeting, nor did the Greek Communist leader Zachariades have his articles published in the Cominform journal *For a Lasting Peace, For a People's Democracy*[111].

According to McCagg, the first Cominform meeting in September 1947 was designed by Stalin not only to centralize Soviet control over the European Communist parties in general, but also more specifically to bring the Poles and the Yugoslavs into line: the Poles, because under Gomułka they were actually coming much nearer to a nationalistic line than any of the other satellite parties, including the CPY, and the Yugoslavs because of their radical foreign policy particularly regarding Greece. Instead, contrary to Stalin's intentions, Zhdanov and the Yugoslavs turned the meeting into an occasion on which they sharpened the division between East and West, and, as had been said earlier, attacked the French and Italian Communist parties for their policies of compromise[112]. Perhaps Stalin noticed then that things were not going the way he wanted them to: Zhdanov's decline set in at the very time the conference took place, when Suslov suddenly rose to great prominence in Zhdanov's CPSU Secretariat for dealings with foreign Communist parties. In October 1947 in an interview with a Western journalist, Stalin tried to play down the importance of the Cominform. He further suppressed the records of the Yugoslavs' attacks on the French and Italian representatives on account of the coalition policy of their Communist parties[113].

If it is true that in 1947 Stalin had to some extent lost his control of the factions within the Kremlin, due to illness and periods of absence from Moscow, in 1948 he once again assumed control, coming down on the side of the faction of Malenkov which favoured Statism and consolidation. He crushed the radical Zhdanovite faction and attempted to bring down Tito with it[114]. While in March/April the Yugoslav controversy with the Soviet Communist Party gathered momentum, Zhdanov's fortunes were declining. In April 1948 his journal *Partiynaya Zhizn* ceased publication[115], and he was forced to put his signature to the Cominform's condemnation of his former protégés in June. His own death on 31 August 1948 was followed by the execution or removal in some other way of his supporters. But even before his death there were clear signs that Zhdanov had lost Stalin's favour: for example the Communist *Arbeiter Zeitung* in Switzerland in an article of 2 August 1948 claimed that the Stalin line was now winning over the Zhdanov-Cominform line which had suffered a defeat in the Tito affair[116].

Other aspects of Stalin's foreign policy also need to be seen in this context. When in February 1948 Stalin allowed the Communists to seize power in Czechoslovakia, he yielded to the temptation of an easy victory through action which was not in line with the Statist policy, but aimed at greater consolidation of this part of his empire[117]. This was a miscalculation on his part regarding Western reactions to what must have seemed to him a relatively minor move. Then, with the Berlin blockade, he tried to consolidate his orbit and to delay the integration of Western Germany into the increasingly united Western bloc, which was his ultimate nightmare[118]. Finally, with the attempt to bring the Yugoslavs to heel, he tried to enforce discipline and to eliminate their radical concepts of foreign policy which had resulted in clashes with the Western powers that had been beyond Stalin's control, increasing tension in the relations between the Communist orbit and the Western world, when these were most in need of subtle handling, as the Western reaction to the Prague coup showed.

The issue of the Greek Civil War had remained unsettled after the Cominform founding conference, and had clearly continued to trouble the Western powers. It came to a head when on 24 December 1947 Markos Vaphiades, the highest-ranking rebel leader at the time, proclaimed the establishment of a rival Greek government. At the end of December 1947 the American Under-Secretary of State, Robert Lovett, made a statement condemning Markos's move[119]. On 22 January 1948, after consultation with the US, Bevin made a statement in the House of Commons, confirming British interest in Greece and admonishing the Balkan neighbours of Greece "and their Soviet mentors" to leave Greece alone. "In all solemnity, I would advise great care: Provocations like these lead sometimes to serious developments which we, and I hope they, are anxious to avoid." He therefore entreated the USSR and the satellites to respect the UN Assembly's decision which demanded a cessation of all foreign interference in the Greek Civil War[120].

Stalin was obviously aware of the strong feelings in the West concerning Greece. In February 1948 Yugoslav emissaries, among them Tito, Djilas, and the Bulgarian Premier, Dimitrov, were summoned to Moscow. Tito refused to go, and Kardelj went instead. Stalin told the Yugoslav and Bulgarian representatives that "the uprising in Greece has to fold up". He stated his conviction that the Greek rebels

> have no prospect of success at all. What do you think, that Great Britain and the United States — the United States, the most powerful state in the world — will permit you to break their line of communication in the Mediterranean Sea! Nonsense. And we have no navy. The uprising in Greece must be stopped, and as quickly as possible.[121]

The Yugoslavs seem to have backed down on this question temporarily and never gave official recognition to Markos's government. Further, Dorange, the French Military Attaché in Athens, had information according to which it was decided at a meeting in Belgrade on 17 May 1948 not to give the Greek rebels any further arms aid. Instead, the Vice-Minister of Foreign Affairs, Bebler, is said to have told a member of the British embassy that the Yugoslav government would be willing to re-establish diplomatic relations with the Greek Royalist government, on condition that a coalition government were formed, including the Communists; this of course was precisely the course of collaboration with the bourgeois parties which the Yugoslavs had denounced so vigorously at the Founding Conference of the Cominform[122]. Indeed, Dorange knew that the Greek Chargé d'Affaires in Belgrade had informed Athens "que Gouvernement Yougoslavie manifeste désir entamer conversations pour établir relations normales [sic]". He also reported that day (18 May 1948) that the supply of arms and matériel "a cessé depuis quelques jours"[123].

> Au reçu de cette décision, Marcos aurait manifesté sa colère et son intention de ne pas l'executer estimant

qu'elle était une véritable trahison vis-à-vis du Parti
Communiste Grec et de l'Armée Démocratique.
Zachariades, Secretaire Général du Parti, est intervenu
et, ne pouvant le convaincre, aurait fait appel à Moscou.
Il est vraisemblable que des ordres sont venus
directement de la Capitale Soviétique, puisque les
membres du Gouvernement Marcos ont commenté
favorablement, au cours de leurs entretiens, la position
prise par Molotov[124]. Le dernier en soulignant
l'obligation formelle d'executer la 'décision de *Belgrade*',
aurait insisté sur le fait que les sacrifices consentis ne
l'auraient pas été en pure perte et que le sang versé
trouverait plus tard une large compensation. Mais, pour
le moment, la situation générale imposait un
changement de tactique.[125]

At the beginning of June the Greek rebel radio declared the
readiness of the Communists to negotiate an armistice, which
was said particularly in a radio-speech on 6 June 1948 by
Zachariades. At that time, however, the Greek government
refused to negotiate (a course in which it was supported by the
US and British governments), as the mere readiness to
negotiate would have conferred a certain legitimacy upon the
rebels[126].

We know that the Yugoslavs resumed their aid for the
Greeks at some stage, and according to findings of the UN
Special Commission for the Balkans (UNSCOB) were
supplying them with arms until the spring of 1949[127]. There is
some rather ambiguous evidence that the issue of aid for the
Greek rebels might have been discussed at the Warsaw
meeting of the Cominform, which decided on the
excommunication of Yugoslavia[128]. It is tempting to speculate
that the Yugoslavs might by that time have resumed aid to the
Greeks: in that case the Cominform condemnation of the CPY
might have been issued in lieu of further orders to cease
aiding the fight in Greece, which the Yugoslavs might or might
not heed, due to their differing appreciation of the world
situation. Confirmation of this seems to be what Dr. Korbel, a
former Czech ambassador to Yugoslavia, told two members of
the State Department towards the end of that year. Having
resigned from government service he felt that he could now

speak frankly, and he said that in a recent conversation in Paris, Aleš Bebler had told him

> that the difficulties between the Yugoslavs and the Soviet Union had originated over their conflicting views of the international situation and the control of the Yugoslav Army. The Soviet Politburo, according to Bebler, believed that the possibility of an international conflict was pressing, while the Yugoslav regime thought there was no danger of a war in the near future.

Bebler had said that it was this fear that prompted Stalin to assert his power and influence over the institutions of Yugoslavia (and other satellites) such as the Army, as we have noted above[129].

As we have seen, Stalin's reason for opposing further aid for the Greek Civil War does indeed seem to have been his fear of a direct clash with the British and the Americans over this issue. In supporting the Greek rebels the Yugoslavs were, from Stalin's point of view, putting a dangerous strain on East-West relations. The Yugoslavs, however, chose to regard a different aspect of Stalin's reasoning as predominant. Vukmanović-Tempo claimed that

> the Soviet Government is not at all interested in any revolutionary movement which it cannot control and subordinate . . . to its own hegemonistic plans, but even considers it an obstacle. . . .To realise its hegemonistic policy, the leadership of the Soviet Union has shown itself completely hostile to the revolutionary . . . struggle in any country in which its control was not assured (whether through geographical distance, the 'unreliability' of the leadership, or any other cause), or which may have been fated to be the subject of bargaining with the imperialists (on the principle of spheres of influence).

Tempo thought these were the reasons why Stalin had urged Mao not to oppose Chiang Kai-shek, but to come to terms with him, and why Stalin did not give the Chinese Communists much support, and let down the Communist insurgents in Indonesia, and, of course, Greece[130].

Tempo differentiates between two reasons that Stalin had for not supporting Communists: either that a country was considered to be in the sphere of influence of a Western power (the Yugoslavs knew about the agreement between Churchill and Stalin), or else because Stalin disliked movements which he could not control, as he wanted to subject everything to his "hegemonistic policy". But the latter point is related to the former: in a period of tension between the Soviet Union and the Western powers, was it not important to Stalin that misunderstandings should not occur in the West over what Soviet intentions were? Such a misunderstanding could have arisen from an insurrection as in fact it did over Greece, where the Western powers assumed that the rebels had Stalin's full support, although he had virtually promised to Churchill that he would leave Greece alone. Was it not vital for Stalin to be able to hold back radical Communists in remote areas, when not only Communists world-wide[131], but also the West considered Communism as monolithic? It was therefore perhaps not just pure thirst for power, and intolerance of any other gods before him that led Stalin to enforce the subordination of all Communists and Communist-led projects to Moscow's orders. Although Stalin's drive for domination certainly played a part, the rational (and perhaps rather defensive) element was also there: in the battles of the Cold War the Generalissimo had to be in control of all his forces and all their moves. It was this aspect that was not fully grasped by the Yugoslavs or by Western observers.

For the same reason, other aspects of Yugoslav foreign policy displeased Stalin at this stage, as they were equally connected with his desire not to let Yugoslav moves upset his plans and increase East-West tension. Thus the Yugoslav claims on Trieste and Carinthia antagonized the Western powers, and the Soviet government ceased supporting the Yugoslavs on them[132]. Earlier Yugoslav moves, such as the shooting down of the US aircraft, had already resulted in rebukes from Stalin[133].

A further issue was the Yugoslav domination of Albania, although it differed little from Soviet treatment of Yugoslavia. In both cases the stronger power controlled joint stock companies in the weaker country, and tried to shape its economy and military establishment by sending over advisers[134]. In December 1947 Stalin summoned a Yugoslav representative, Djilas, to Moscow "in order to bring into harmony the policies of the two Governments vis-à-vis Albania". According to Djilas, Moscow was trying to replace Belgrade's influence in Albania[135]. Stalin on this occasion played a very obscure game, even urging his guest to go ahead and "swallow Albania"[136], which seemed so astonishing to Djilas that he decided to act with caution, suspecting a trap. It is not clear what Stalin was getting at when he urged the Yugoslavs to do what he otherwise seemed to want least of all. That he was being contradictory became quite clear when he returned to his earlier accusations regarding Yugoslavia's excessive interference in Albania, in the meeting with Djilas, Kardelj and Dimitrov in February 1948[137]. The Yugoslav plan of integrating Albania, however, was then already being realized, but not in the open form advocated by Stalin in late 1947; it only ground to a halt in the middle of 1948[138].

This instance in turn reflects Yugoslav ambitions in matters of foreign policy. They wanted to dominate the Balkans through a federation which they, together with their Bulgarian neighbours had been planning to set up since the end of the Second World War. Stalin had at times encouraged the plan, but when British opposition had been voiced early on, he had ordered it to be shelved[139]. It can be taken as evidence that Stalin was not informed about all that was going on, when he showed that he had not been aware in 1947 of the revival of the plans for a Balkan Federation by the Yugoslavs, and by the Bulgarians under Dimitrov. Their intention may have been to make use of such a federation, which would have united the Yugoslav and Bulgarian parts of Macedonia, to justify an irredentist claim on the part situated in Greece, thus putting an even greater strain on that country which was already divided by civil war[140]. As a first step, Tito and Dimitrov in August 1947 signed an agreement at Bled forming a customs union and providing for closer integration of their states at a later point. The draft was approved by some high-ranking person in Moscow (possibly Molotov, but not Stalin!); it was amended and turned into the Yugoslav-Bulgarian Treaty of Friendship, Co-operation and Assistance[141].

In January 1948 Dimitrov gave a press interview printed in *Pravda*, in which he expressed his belief in the "inevitability" of a confederation of Balkan states in the future, mentioning not only Yugoslavia and Bulgaria, but also Romania, Albania,

Czechoslovakia, Poland, Hungary and, significantly, Greece. On 28 January 1948 *Pravda* published a criticism of Dimitrov, totally disavowing his project[142]. In the meeting with the Yugoslavs and the Bulgarians on 10 February, Stalin rebuked Dimitrov humiliatingly on account of this plan in the presence of the other representatives from Belgrade and Sofia. Then he changed his approach totally, as he had done on the Albanian issue, and actually ordered his guests to undertake a merger of their two states. Perhaps he hoped that it would shake up the tight-knit Yugoslav leadership and would introduce the "Trojan horse" of the Bulgarians into the Central Committee of the CPY, as the Yugoslav chief emissary on this occasion, Edvard Kardelj, suggested[143]: he thought Stalin intended in this way to secure a firmer grip on Belgrade through some of those Bulgarian leaders who were more subservient to Moscow. The Yugoslavs decided to move slowly and to delay whatever development Stalin wanted to bring about[144]. For the Yugoslavs the February meeting ended, however, with Kardelj being forced to sign an agreement whereby his government was committed to consult the Soviet Union on any future move in foreign politics[145], which once again illustrates the predominance of Stalin's concern about Yugoslav foreign policy in his later decision to chastise them.

It is important to note that this entire meeting was dedicated to the discussion of these questions of foreign policy. On this last occasion on which Yugoslavs talked with Stalin personally, the matters discussed were thus in no way related to the ostensible reason why the Communist parties of the USSR and of Yugoslavia, and later the CPY and the Cominform, clashed.

There is also evidence that the February talks were followed up by concrete measures: already from late January-February 1948 onwards economic pressure was brought to bear by the Soviet Union on Yugoslavia through considerable cuts in trade[146]. Negotiations for the supply of arms and ammunition to Yugoslavia, and for Soviet help with the development of the Yugoslav armaments industry were suspended[147]; Stalin probably intended to force the Yugoslavs in this way to limit their aid to the Greek rebels. Our view that the main cause for the Tito-Stalin split lay in Yugoslavia's foreign policy is confirmed by a statement of Martinov, the Counsellor of the Soviet embassy in Rome, who was regarded by the British embassy "to be the real works there"; this statement reached the British via the Czechoslovak embassy:

> Martinov said that the real quarrel with Tito was on account of the latter's insistence on running too independent a foreign policy. Main points on which Moscow had been urging greater moderation in Belgrade were:
> (a) Yugoslav claim to Carinthia which was preventing the Soviet Government from reaching an agreement on Austrian Peace Treaty.
> (b) that Belgrade was giving more help to Markos [and the Greek rebels] than Moscow considered prudent.[148]

Western Perceptions of the Breach

It is important to contrast what we can reconstruct as the real reasons for the split with Western perceptions, as these were to be the basis of Western decision-making. Western onlookers had a first indication that something unusual was going on in the Balkans when the issue of the Balkan federation came to the fore in January 1948. The French Ambassador in Belgrade, Jean Payart, wrote to the Quai d'Orsay that such a federation would increase the power of the Balkan countries and their independence from Moscow: "je ne vois pas Stalin renoncer de gaîté de coeur au bénéfice que tire sa politique de la pluralité de chefs d'Etat qu'il peut toujours opposer les uns aux autres."[149] Sir Maurice Peterson, the British Ambassador in Moscow, and his British colleague in Sofia, Sterndale-Bennet, used the same reasoning to explain the *Pravda* rebuke of Dimitrov for his statement in January 1948[150].

The dispute between the Yugoslavs and Stalin was a well-kept secret from then until early June. Certain small episodes were recorded, such as the removal of Tito's portrait from Rumanian public buildings, Yugoslav protests against air-space violations, or the absence of a message from Stalin in the Yugoslav press on Tito's birthday (25 May), an important "dog that didn't bark", to use the Sherlock Holmesian concept. These were not enough to alert the West to what was really happening[151]. Other signs were misinterpreted completely, such as the dismissal of Žujović and Hebrang, the two pro-Soviet ministers in the Yugoslav government, in mid-May: it was actually thought that they were punished for being *anti*-Soviet[152].

Thus total bewilderment characterized Western interpretations[153], until on 12 June the USSR sent the Western powers a note proposing that a scheduled conference to settle issues regarding the use of the Danube should not be held in Belgrade, as planned, but elsewhere. The American Chargé d'Affaires, Robert Borden Reams, and presumably also the British Ambassador, Sir Charles Peake, began to see the light when they found out that the Yugoslavs were trying to reverse the Soviet decision, and they even admitted to Peake that they regarded it as a snub. In the absence of Cavendish Cannon, the US Ambassador, it fell to Reams to inform the State Department of this, in the first available telegram to the West that reflected the explosive nature of the situation:

> embassy feels Yugoslav response [to the] Soviet Danube conference note [is the] first direct and irrevocable challenge [by] any satellite to supreme authority [of the] Communist overlords in Kremlin. Tito's apparent decision to challenge Stalin instead of recanting past errors may well be most significant event here . . . and even presages possibility [of] split in Soviet bloc if breach [is] allowed to widen. For first time in history Soviet Union is faced with consolidated Communist régime in power outside own borders willing to risk independent or even contrary course.

The telegram dismissed the issue of the Danubian Conference as of little importance, and similarly the rôle of ideological differences was not thought to be the "basic cause [of the] developing conflict". Instead, "Tito's personal ambitions to lead own sphere in southeast Europe must have cumulatively irritated and perhaps alarmed the Kremlin."[154]

Although this assessment was the first to show where the problem lay, the emphasis of Reams's analysis is wrongly focused. Undoubtedly Tito's personal ambitions did irritate Stalin, but the basic cause of the split lay not so much in Tito's aspirations in the Balkans as the attitude towards Greece in particular and the encouragement of revolutionary movements in general, just those ideological reasons which

Reams dismissed. Also, the Yugoslav insistence on Belgrade as the place for the Danube Conference was more an unloved child pleading for the attention of its parent who was turning away from it, than an act of rebellion. Reams's interpretation was to be the mould for further analyses of the nature and origins of the split by the American and British observers, who were in close contact with each other[155], even though this bold telegram did not evoke any immediate response either from Washington or from the US embassy in Moscow.

On 16 June 1948 Aleš Bebler, the Vice-Minister of Foreign Affairs, in a conversation with Peake vented his anger at the Soviet government for having suggested a change of venue for the Danube Conference, which made it clear to Peake that there were tensions between the two Communist governments[156]. On 18 June he cabled to the Foreign Office his impression "that Yugoslav-Soviet relations are now strained over the whole field of foreign and internal policy". Peake listed the points at the heart of the dispute in his telegram, but without recognizing their crucial importance:

> Fortunes of Markos in Greece seem to be definitely on the wane and there are indications that relations between KKE and Yugoslav Communist Party are strained. The same is undoubtedly true of relations between the Bulgarians and Yugoslav Macedonians. It seems not improbable that Tito, as the self-styled leader of the satellites, shares blame for all this.[157]

Peake knew from Yugoslav press reports that Tito's "portrait was to be found next to Stalin's at congress of the Indian and Burmese Communist Parties", but again, the only conclusion he drew from this was that Tito "has tended to get too big for his boots".

Nevertheless, Peake had at least recognized that there was a "rift in Yugoslav-Soviet relations"[158]. The French government had "similar indications of tension in Yugoslav-Soviet relations" as Sir Oliver Harvey reported from Paris[159]. Yet much confusion was created in the minds of Western diplomats in Belgrade by Yugoslav efforts to comply with Soviet wishes during the second half of May, and the first half of June 1948. For example, the demotion of the Anglophile General Velebit (who, as we now know, had been denounced by Stalin as an "English spy"[160]) from his position as Assistant Minister of Foreign Affairs, was taken in May 1948 as evidence that an anti-Western campaign had begun, particularly when seen in the context of harassments of foreigners[161]. The government's measures taken to refute the charges levelled against them in the correspondence with the Communist Party of the Soviet Union (CPSU), such as the stepping up of agricultural collectivization and the announcement of the Congress of the CPY for that summer, were (rightly) interpreted as meek submission on the part of the Yugoslavs to orders from Moscow[162].

The rift between Stalin and Tito came out into the open on 28 June 1948 when the Cominform expelled the CPY with the aforementioned communiqué. Both immediately before and for about a year after its publication, the Yugoslavs made a great display of loyalty towards the USSR. At the Danubian Conference which did, in the end, take place in Belgrade, they voted with the Soviet representatives and against Western interests on every issue[163]. In the press and in public speeches, the Yugoslavs went out of their way not to say anything blatantly offensive about the USSR, the CPSU or Stalin, other than accusing them of having made a mistake when condemning Yugoslavia. Moreover, at the 5th Congress of the CPY which met in Belgrade on 21 July 1948, Tito concluded his eight-hour speech with the words "Long live the Soviet Union, long live Stalin!"[164]

The only way in which Payart could make sense of Yugoslav behaviour before 28 June was by thinking in terms of pure conflicts of power and interests:

> La tendance de certains chefs balkaniques à se mettre trop en avant et à jouer internationalement dans les milieux communistes un rôle dont les dirigeants soviétiques prennent ombrage, la propension naturelle des Partis à devenir autocéphales et à relâcher les liens qui les rattachent à Moscou, l'importance numérique enfin de la classe paysanne dans ces régions, peuvent provoquer entre la 'patrie du socialisme' et les 'démocraties populaires' des frictions sérieuses.[165]

Yet in spite of Western diplomats' awareness of strains in Soviet-Yugoslav relations, they received the Cominform communiqué with considerable surprise. The US Ambassador in Moscow, Walter Bedell Smith, admitted that nobody had expected "one so important and well trained as Tito" to lead "a revolt", and that the Cominform communiqué astonished his embassy staff[166]. The British and the American Ambassadors were not in Belgrade at the time of the publication of the communiqué, as they had not expected such an event.

The first reaction of the American and British Chargés very closely paralleled the analysis Reams had offered in his earlier telegram, dismissing the official reasons for the expulsion of Yugoslavia and focusing on the clash between Yugoslav and Russian national interests, and rivalry between Tito and Stalin[167]. This interpretation was accepted by the State Department[168], and was shared with insignificant variations by Payart[169], Georges Heuman, the French Consul in Ljubljana[170], Yves Chataigneau, the French Ambassador in Moscow[171], and by Jacques Camille Paris, the head of the Direction d'Europe in the Quai d'Orsay[172].

On the whole, Western diplomats overlooked the disagreements about foreign policy, and if they noted them, they still failed to see their overall significance. The French Ambassador in Prague, Dejean, thought, like Reams and King in Belgrade, that "les raisons d'ordre idéologique (invoquées) ne sont qu'une façade. Le différend est en réalité d'ordre politique." He noted the diverging policies over Trieste and the Balkan federation[173]. In some other dispatches, Trieste, Austria and Macedonia were mentioned; once or twice the differences in attitude towards Greece were also recognized, although not in their full implications, and rarely with the right understanding of what policy Tito had sought to implement there[174]. Only Dejean regarded the foreign policy factor as the crucial point of difference, and his interpretation left no impact.

Western diplomats did recognize immediately that the dispute which was taking place was in fact one between Stalin and the Yugoslavs, and that the Cominform was being used to disguise this[175]. The American Policy Planning Staff paper prepared under Kennan's auspices on 30 June 1948 which became the National Security Council's policy statement on Yugoslavia as NSC 18, epitomized the analysis given in all the American and British telegrams quoted above (with slightly less emphasis on Yugoslav nationalism than found in the French telegrams). Here we read that the CPY's leaders defied "the Kremlin", instead of finding a recognition that it was Stalin who ordered the expulsion of the CPY from the Cominform. Thus the whole incident is made to sound more like an *active decision by the Yugoslavs* to stand up to Stalin than a threatening measure of Stalin's to which the Yugoslavs reacted defensively. Again, "the Kremlin" or "Moscow" was seen as an undivided body, which denies the possibility of factions within it. By casting Yugoslavia in the active part of those who decided to break with "Moscow", the Policy Planning Staff gives them credit for a greater striving for independence than was actually to be found; meanwhile the importance of ideology was underrated significantly.

Why did the Western diplomats' interpretation distort the causes of the split? They did not totally misunderstand the situation. Tito and his supporters did indeed have much greater pride in their own achievements and in their own Communist tradition than any of the other satellite Communist parties, as we have seen, and even their adoption of a defensive stance vis-à-vis the Cominform and the USSR was unprecedented. The members of the Cominform missed no opportunity to claim that the Yugoslav people were victims of the pride and megalomania of their leaders[176]. It is also not surprising that Westerners were to some degree misled by the Cominform communiqué to believe that one of the most important issues was the USSR's interference in Yugoslavia's internal matters, and that it was mainly a question of the Kremlin's imposition of uniformity, which conflicted with Yugoslav "nationalism" and with the wish of Yugoslav leaders to decide their internal affairs without any interference from the outside[177]. It was not wrong to note the Yugoslavs' boldness in defending themselves against the accusations from Stalin and the Cominform.

Yet Westerners made two mistakes in dismissing the ideological foreign-policy disagreements between the Yugoslav leaders and Stalin. First, they failed totally to see the overall context of Stalin's foreign policy, and the reasons why Stalin tried to silence the faction advocating revolutionary adventurism. This is not surprising, as it was nearly totally unknown to the rank and file of the Eastern Communist parties, let alone Western observers, that there was such a factional split high up in the Kremlin and in other Communist governments in Eastern Europe. As we have shown, Westerners regarded the Kremlin as monolithic.

The second mistake was to think that individual Communist leaders or parties outside Russia might *want* to break away from Stalin's tutelage. Westerners mistakenly assumed that disagreements could only arise from right-wing deviationism on the part of non-Russian Communists, and they failed to recognize signs of Tito's ultraleftist, revolutionary foreign policy, which we have identified as the main cause of the dispute. Western observers did not interpret correctly the lengths to which the Yugoslavs went to make amends for their mistakes which Stalin had pointed out to them, short of incurring self-destruction. Otherwise they would have noticed that it was Stalin who had taken punitive action against the Yugoslavs, and it was not Tito who had decided to offend Stalin.

Instead, Westerners assumed that Tito had yearned to break away from the Soviet Union. Prior to the Tito-Stalin dispute, George Kennan had foreseen the possibility that an individual Communist government in a country geographically out of reach for the leaders of the Kremlin could become independent from the USSR, driven by a nationalist quest for self-government without interference from Moscow. Although he had thought of China, his prediction now seemed to be fulfilled by Yugoslavia. A similar, but not as yet outspoken expectation was recorded by Bedell Smith. He claims to have noted in his "journal" in April 1948 that "the undivided allegiance which the Soviet Government expects from foreign Communist Parties can hardly be maintained, now that these governments have come into power."[178]

Bedell Smith was talking about the Communist parties in Eastern Europe, but all of these were in quite a different position from that of the Chinese Communist Party in the late 1950s and 1960s. For more than a dozen years after the end of the Second World War, Communist parties in Eastern Europe and Asia were so supicious of the West that they felt the need for Soviet support against the hostility which the "imperialist powers" seemed to show. Interference from Moscow was decidedly the lesser evil compared with interference from the Western powers, whose aim, as we have seen, was the replacement of the Communist totalitarian governments by freely elected democratic ones[179]. One must also remember the importance of factors such as the Communist parties' dedication to the Communist cause, and their fear of their own populations, who had not brought them into government by majority voting, and their total dependence on the might of the Soviet Union, to whose troops they owed their power.

Instead of seeing the strength of these forces of cohesion between the Communist governments, and their loyalty to Moscow, reinforced by the hostility of the Western world, Westerners like Bedell Smith indulged in the wishful thinking that the personal pride of Communist leaders or parties in Eastern Europe, the national interest of their countries, or their dislike of being ordered about by men in the Kremlin might be reasons for them *to want to break away from Moscow.* Not only regarding the Communist leaders, but also regarding the populations they ruled, Bedell Smith thought of the Iron Curtain which "the Soviets have erected around their part of the world . . . as a dike holding in check the churning torrents of the pent-up emotions of Eastern Europe"[180].

Western policy-makers and diplomats overestimated the assumed readiness of the populations of Eastern Europe to rise up in arms, which was the basis on which the Americans built their original liberation policy. Westerners also overestimated the drive for independence of the Communist régimes themselves, an example of which they erroneously perceived in the Tito-Stalin split. On this misperception they built a new aspect of their liberation policy, as we shall see presently, namely that of encouraging other Communist governments to "follow Tito".

2

The Impact of the Tito-Stalin Split on Western Cold War Policies 1948-1949

A Communist Conspiracy? Tito Remains a Communist

None of the Western diplomats in Belgrade doubted the reality of the split[1]. The State Department's Policy Planning Staff and after it the National Security Council (NSC) immediately took it to be real (see below)[2]. Yet the French Ambassador in London reported that in the British Foreign Office, "On n'exclut même pas la possibilité qu'il s'agisse en occurrence d'une manoeuvre."[3] Geoffrey Wallinger, the head of the Southern Department in the Foreign Office (i.e. the department dealing with Yugoslavia), was temporarily led to believe by Romanian propaganda that Tito might have been put up by the "orbit" to get Marshall Aid; this was in spite of the fact that the British Chargé in Belgrade had stated emphatically as early as 30 June 1948 that the "Yugoslav leaders have surely burnt their boats", and that the rift was genuine[4]. Bevin remained suspicious for several months; as late as February 1949 he called Tito's moves "in the nature . . . of a put up job designed to pave the way for Yugoslavia's return to the Stalinist fold". His initial reactions reflected considerable reserve.

Wallinger, who by this time had been converted to believe in the reality of the split, while expressing his agreement with Bevin's pessimistic emphasis on Tito's obvious wish for a reconciliation with Stalin, nevertheless said that "all our information seems to run counter to the idea of a put-up job."[5] Bevin was gradually coming around to this view, so that by early 1949 consensus was established in Western foreign policy-making circles that the split was not a hoax[6].

Even if the split was real, however, the Yugoslavs were still Communists, and would remain so. This was already acknowledged by the Americans in NSC 18 of 6 July 1948, which read: "Tito's defiance of the Cominform does not mean that Yugoslavia has 'come over' to the West. Yugoslavia remains a communist state and its negative attitude toward the western democracies is as yet unchanged."[7] The French Ambassador to Yugoslavia, Jean Payart, also warned his government on the day after the Cominform Declaration was published, not to expect an imminent change of Yugoslav foreign policy. He added:

> Toute interprétation prémature de cette nature, de la part de la presse, aurait pour résultat d'augmenter la pression que Moscou exerce sur la Yougoslavie, et d'incliner cette dernière chez qui le sentiment de la solidarité slavo-communiste serait ravivé, à se rejeter vers l'URSS qui, en dépit de tout, lui demeure plus proche.[8]

Georges Heuman, the French Consul in Ljubljana, warned the Quai d'Orsay that

> Un différend [entre la Yougoslavie et l'URSS] sur les *moyens* ne saurait donc rompre durablement une communauté de *but* et, . . . il est peut-être raisonnable de supposer que . . . l'Etat rebelle ne saurait, à l'intérieur, être autre chose que l'image et, à l'extérieur, que l'allié du grand Etat socialiste de l'Est.[9]

Dejean in Prague and Contre-Amiral Laurin from the French Ministry of Defence equally pointed out that Tito had not become pro-Western overnight[10].

Policy Option 1:
Overthrow Tito? The CIA's "Liberation" Efforts

In what way, then, could the Western powers take action which could turn this situation to their advantage? There were essentially three possibilities: the first was to perceive Tito's government as isolated and weakened, in which case one could try, according to the policy of working for a liberation of Communist-governed countries from their totalitarian régimes (see Chapter 1), to stage an anti-Communist uprising to overthrow Tito and to replace him by a Western-style government. This policy failed to take into account likely Soviet reactions, which would have provided the ideal excuse for an invasion by Red Army forces; at the very least it would have led to Communist, anti-Titoist, anti-Western participation in a civil war thus created by the West in Yugoslavia.

This highly dangerous policy was indeed adopted by the American Central Intelligence Agency (CIA) towards the end of 1948, and one shocking aspect of this is that it was done almost six months after the US President and the National Security Council had decided against such an option; the CIA thus acted against the explicit presidential orders contained in NSC 18, which defined US policy towards Yugoslavia as one of cautious support. The British Foreign Office had already dismissed the encouragement of such an alternative group as undesirable, recognizing that Tito's followers were in control of the Secret Police and the Army, so that any uprising or civil war in Yugoslavia would either be crushed by the Yugoslav Communists or taken advantage of by the USSR[11]. The CIA, however, obviously decided to ignore this danger. With its new "licence to kill", NSC 10/2 on Special Projects (see Chapter 1), the CIA now leapt into action, glad to have found a target for what may have been the first project of the sort. It began to infiltrate into Yugoslavia right-wing exiles, mainly Serb Chetniks, who had been in a bitter feud with Tito's Partisans during the war, with the aim of overthrowing the Communist government[12]. These men were conspicuously clothed in American Air Force uniforms, and it seems that they were picked up straight away by Ranković's Security Police and led off to some prison or camp, a journey which took them via Belgrade main railway station, where they were seen and recognized as former Chetniks.

The French embassy heard about this and passed on the news to the US embassy[13]. Cavendish Cannon, the Ambassador, was obviously horrified. At the end of January 1949 he sent a telegram to the Department, urging it once and for all to bury the

> view that Tito's downfall would establish conditions for more representative and Western-minded Yugoslavs.

This highly wishful approach to Eastern European political realities ignores . . . [the fact] that Cominform is ready to exploit by force any weakening of Tito's security apparatus. . . . In Yugoslavia there are not three choices but two: Tito or a Moscow tool.[14]

Cannon may well have feared that his views were not being listened to in Washington, as the CIA operation was in total contradiction to his past advice; he therefore passed a copy of this telegram on to the Foreign Office via the British embassy, presumably because he hoped that the British would exert pressure on his own government to follow his recommendations. In the Foreign Office, Charles Bateman, the Super-Intending Under-Secretary of State for the Southern Department, minuted that he regarded the American action as "inconceivably stupid", as it would "only serve to rouse all Tito's worst suspicions about America's real aims". Neither the Permanent Under-Secretary of State, Sir Orme Sargent, nor Bevin himself disagreed with Bateman's condemnation of "this idiotic American behaviour". Bevin therefore informed the State Department: "I entirely agree with Mr. Cannon that any backing of anti-Tito elements, for instance by attempts to use ex-Ustaši or Chetnik elements in the country for any purpose whatsoever, would be playing straight into the Soviet hand."[15] Cannon found that the State Department was sympathetic to his views and that its Policy Planning Staff persuaded the National Security Council to note explicitly that "there is no possibility under the present circumstances that a non-communist 'third force' could take over power should Tito lose his grip on the country. It is either Tito or a Moscow stooge regime in present-day Yugoslavia."[16] Thus an end was put to this foolish and abortive CIA operation. Its lack of success did not, however, stop the CIA from launching other, equally abortive operations elsewhere[17].

Policy Option 2:
Britain and France: "Masterly Inactivity"

If it was unwise to try to overthrow Tito's government, a second option was to keep out of the affair altogether, not taking any action. This stance was taken initially by the British and the French. Neither of them had as yet conceived of the notion of a Western policy designed to encourage actively the "liberation" of Eastern Europe, as the Americans had, and neither had formulated a policy to encourage a process of self-liberation (and indeed, the French never did). In November 1947, the British Cabinet had wisely agreed with its Foreign Secretary's advice that one should not "lead the anti-Communists [in Eastern countries] to hope for support which we cannot give"[18]. Therefore in the summer and autumn of 1948, the British Ambassador in Belgrade, Sir Charles Peake, could not imagine any way in which the West could take advantage of the situation in Yugoslavia. He recommended a policy of "masterly inactivity"[19].

Peake's French colleague in Belgrade agreed with him, and the Quai d'Orsay decided not to interfere in any way. Among the three Western powers, the French were the most reserved in their attitude towards Yugoslavia, and continued to be so until the end of 1950. They also urged the other two Western governments to remain inactive, disapproving of subsequent Anglo-American actions[20].

Bevin, with his suspicions and his strong dislike of Communists, like Peake first thought it advisable "not to do anything ourselves with regard to Yugoslavia — let the Communists quarrel among themselves"[21]. When on 29 June 1948 the US embassy in Belgrade urged their government in Washington to make a public commitment to the preservation of the territorial integrity of small nations, with special reference to Yugoslavia[22], Bevin, who was informed of this proposal, quickly raised the matter with the US Ambassador in London, Lewis Douglas[23]. The Foreign Secretary "suggested that we refrain from issuing any such statement until there has been an appreciation of the Cominform action and [we] have a clearer view of its considerations and significance"[24]. The State Department in turn assured Bevin that they had already taken the same decision[25], in accordance with NSC 18. Later that year Bateman warned the State Department not to depart from a policy of "masterly inactivity" until Tito had made a friendly gesture. Even at the end of 1948 Bevin proposed to have a telegram sent to the US Secretary of State, warning him of Tito[26]. The French and British perception of the possibilities offered by the situation, and consequently the stand-offish policy they adopted, stood in contrast to that of the US State Department.

The American Perception

"The State Department regarded the Cominform's denunciation of Tito as the most significant event which had taken place behind the iron curtain since the war. This episode even over-shadowed the present critical situation in Berlin." Thus the British Ambassador in Washington, Sir Oliver Franks, informed his government on 30 June 1948 [27]. Indeed, Frank Wisner, a senior official in the State Department[28], claimed that "the State Department's Russian and Cominform experts, including particularly Messrs. Bohlen, Kennan and Llewellyn Thompson" had immediately identified the Tito-Stalin split as "probably the most important single development since the conclusion of hostilities as far as international Soviet and Communist internal affairs are concerned, on a plane with the Trotsky fall from grace"[29].

The reason for this excitement in the State Department was to a very large extent the fact that what was seen as Yugoslavia's decision to break away from the Cominform (see Chapter 1) seemed to be fulfilling Kennan's prediction of the possibility of a rift between the USSR and its Communist vassals. Henri Bonnet, the French Ambassador in Washington, informed the Quai d'Orsay of the "satisfaction" that was felt in the State Department, and of the increase of the influence of Kennan and Bohlen, whose theories the rift seemed to confirm[30]. Indeed, the Policy Planning Staff under Kennan on the very day after the publication of the Cominform Declaration stated that "the disunity within the communist world . . . has been demonstrated. . . . The possibility of defection from Moscow, which has heretofore been unthinkable for foreign communist leaders, will from now on be present in one form or another in the minds of every one of them."[31] This view, which was the basis of their policy decision NSC 18 (see below), interpreting the Yugoslav rupture with the Cominform as a potential precedent for further developments of the same nature elsewhere, was immediately publicized by the State Department in its press briefings[32]. Bonnet reported that it was presented to the American public "comme revêtant une importance exceptionelle tant pour les rapports entre l'URSS et ses satellites, que pour l'évolution du Communisme international et même pour le développement de la situation intérieure de l'URSS"[33].

This view was also shared by the British Chargé in Belgrade, Cecil King, although not yet, as we have seen, by the Ambassador Peake. On 30 June 1948 King, who was in close contact with Reams of the US embassy, reported excitedly

> the Yugoslav Party . . . are attempting to set up their own brand of Communism in opposition to the Kremlin Party line. [This is] one of the most important developments in the whole history of Communism. For the first time there is a chance of establishment of a heresy upon a firm territorial basis. [It] raises at once the parallel of the opposition of Constantinople to Rome. The contradiction of Russian imperialism and international Communism becomes even more acute and when, as will now surely happen, every Balkan Communist Party is subjected to even closer Russian control, both the sentimental and practical attractions of the Yugoslav heresy will be strong indeed. This is quite apart from its effects upon the fortunes of Western Communist parties now open to the taunt that they accept Moscow's orders subserviently while the Communist party of a small Balkan country is capable of independent action.[34]

These great hopes were to be disappointed; nevertheless, this was the basis on which the British, too, gradually became convinced that the Yugoslav case might have an impact on world Communism that was in the interest of the Western powers.

Effect of Titoism on Communist Parties in Western Europe

Several Western diplomats and foreign policy-makers were hoping that the minimum effect of the Tito-Cominform split would be to teach the Communist parties in the West a lesson. In May 1947 Kennan had predicted splits between Communists in Western Europe and in the Mediterranean countries, on the one hand, and the Kremlin on the other[35]. Cecil King, as we have just seen, thought that the Cominform communiqué would alienate Western Communist parties[36]. A Foreign Office minute of 6 October 1948 stated the belief that Yugoslav independence in political matters was crushed by Moscow "since it was tempting to other communist leaders, particularly in countries at a distance from Moscow such as China and France"[37].

The two most important Communist parties in Western Europe, those of France and Italy, were not, however, shaken as much by the treatment of Yugoslavia as the Western governments had hoped. Togliatti of the Italian Communist Party (PCI) and Thorez, Cachin and Duclos of the French had of course been deeply resentful of the criticism meted out to them by the Yugoslavs at the first Cominform meeting in 1947[38]. They immediately and unanimously came out against the Yugoslavs when the Cominform delivered its first blast against Tito[39]. As the PCI used the Trieste issue and past animosities to equate Tito with anti-Italian policies, Italian Communist support for Tito was open to charges of the betrayal of Italian interests.

The only gesture of sympathy for Tito occurred later, in January 1951, when a group was formed in Emilia-Romagna under two well-known Communists, Valdo Magnani and Aldo Cucchi, upon their resignation from the PCI itself. The defection of these two men from the PCI seems to have occurred over the issue of Moscow's control. Magnani had served under Tito in an Italian Partisan formation in the Second World War, and their propagation of the concept of "active neutrality" in the East-West conflict, very shortly after Tito began to use it (e.g. in his speech of 16 February 1951), shows up the links which existed with Yugoslav Communism, now that the Yugoslavs had begun to develop their criticism of the Soviet Union. Magnani and Cucchi did not, however, attract much popular support, despite the publicity they received[40]. This is not surprising, because in Italy as in France, the Communist workers were on the whole uninterested in the fate of the CPY.

Of the French intellectuals, the great majority of those who were members of the Parti Communiste Français (PCF) came out against Tito and his followers: the fierce attacks on them by Dominique Desanti, André Wurmser[41], and many others ran strictly along Cominform lines[42]. It was chiefly fellow-travellers who sympathized with the Yugoslav cause, such as Louis Dalmas[43], Marcel-Edmond Naegelen[44], Jean Paul Sartre[45]; the art historians Agnès Humbert[46] and Jean Cassou[47]; the journalist Vercors (*nom de plume* of Jean Bruller)[48]; Claude Aveline, Madeleine Weil, Claude Kahn, David Weill and others[49]. Added to the impact of the subsequent show-trials in Eastern Europe (particularly the Rajk trial), the effect of the Tito-Cominform split was to cement the split between the Stalinist PCF and these left-wing "idealists", as David Caute calls them, who had been fellow-travellers for so long; a very small number even left the PCF on account of their experiences when travelling to Yugoslavia[50]. The show-trials soon spread westwards to France, and two Spanish Civil War veterans, André Marty and Charles Tillon, were accused of various crimes associated with "Titoism", such as ultraleftism, and expelled from the PCF; there is no indication, however, that there was any real link between them and the Yugoslavs[51].

A small and relatively insignificant movement called Mouvement Communiste Français Indépendant was formed under Roger Le Corre soon after the expulsion of Tito; it seems that it was sympathetic to the Yugoslavs. In 1951 it also adopted Tito's motto of neutrality in the East-West struggle. But the MCFI's membership and importance was decidedly limited[52].

On the whole, the Yugoslav expulsion from the Cominform may even have delayed the development of more independent tendencies in Western Communist parties, as for example in Italy[53]; it certainly had little positive effect on the majority of the members of the west European Communist parties[54], as the British and American foreign ministries had to admit when in 1949-50 and 1951 respectively they made studies of "Anti-Stalinist Communism"[55] and "Communist Defections and Dissensions in the Postwar Period"[56].

"Watchful Waiting": Further Satellite "Defections"?

However sceptical the British and French might have been at first concerning possible beneficial consequences of the rift, their diplomats, like their American colleagues, carefully scanned news from the Soviet bloc for indications that the chasm between the Yugoslav Communist Party and the Cominform might be found also within other Communist governments, or between them and Moscow. On 1 July 1948 Cecil King thought that Albania would follow Yugoslavia[57], and even later rumours recurred that the Albanian leader Hoxha was about to throw in his lot with Tito[58]. But the Albanian and also the Rumanian Communist Parties disappointed any Western hopes early on by coming out in full support of the Cominform statement against Yugoslavia[59]. In Hungary, the opposition to the Communist régime was given new hope, according to French observers, while the Communists rallied to Stalin's orders[60]. After a few days of total bewilderment, the Czechoslovak Communist Party also came out against the CPY[61].

The two countries in which the Communist leadership did not automatically put all its weight behind the Cominform were, significantly, Bulgaria and Poland. Dimitrov, the Premier of Bulgaria, was guilty by association with Tito, and like Tito had not received birthday greetings from Stalin that year, a sure sign of his displeasure[62]. It does indeed seem as though Dimitrov had been considerably more sympathetic to the Yugoslavs than most other Communists, attempting not to break off relations with them altogether even after the Cominform denunciation[63]. American and French observers thought they could discern factional strife within the Bulgarian Communist Party at this time[64]. But the Bulgarians were also brought into line in due course.

The Poles under Gomulka had striven for greater national independence from Moscow, and he came the closest to being the right-wing, nationalist deviationist whom Westerners mistakenly thought they saw in Tito[65]. It should be noted here that the Yugoslavs only developed the doctrine of the equality among Socialist states from mid-1949 *in reaction to their expulsion from the Cominform*, which is the reverse of the causality the Westerners imagined to find[66]. Stalin's wilful distortion of the disagreements between him and Tito, reflected in the Cominform Communiqué, had made the Yugoslavs sound like "petty-bourgeois nationalists"[67]: this had the benefit of firing a warning shot at the Poles. Although the Polish Party openly supported the Cominform against Yugoslavia, the British Ambassador in Warsaw, Sir David

Gainer, reported on 2 July 1948 that some Polish Communist leaders were acutely embarrassed, as there had been "a marked tendency" among them "to proclaim that the Communist state which they are constructing will have special Polish characteristics". Gainer did not think, however, that the Poles would dare oppose the Soviet Union, in view of their geographic position[68]. He explained that their tendency to emphasize Polish nationalism or national individualism sprang from their imposition on Poland by means of rigged elections. In his view, they felt so insecure that they disliked nothing "more than to have their Polish background called into question and [there is] nothing that the greater part of the Polish people enjoy more than doing precisely this"[69].

Their emphasis on nationalism had been tolerated by Stalin as a useful means of establishing Communism in Poland in the period of diversity, and it lingered on. On 19 July 1948 Beausse of the French embassy in Warsaw reported that Gomułka had voiced objections to the Cominform's decision. Again, the link with domestic popularity is emphasized when Beausse added, "Songez, me disait . . . un . . . haut fonctionnaire des Affaires étrangères, à l'immense prestige qu'acquérerait tout à coup notre Président, si Moscou lui reprochait publiquement d'avoir mené une politique anti-soviétique."[70] These reports seemed to Western observers to be borne out by Gomułka's subsequent demotion and expulsion[71], which was seen in terms of a "corrosive action" of the CPY on Poland by R.A. Sykes in the Southern Department of the Foreign Office[72]. On 5 October 1948 the Yugoslav Assistant Minister of Foreign Affairs, Dr. Bebler, told Hector McNeil, the British Minister of State, that the Poles had indeed "shown themselves to be sympathetic" to Yugoslavia[73]. Nevertheless, as the French Ambassador in Warsaw, Jean Baelen, noted, all this only meant that the Polish government was the least hostile towards Tito among the People's Democracies[74]. Even that was ephemeral, as by January 1949 the Polish Communist Party was staging vicious propaganda attacks against Tito[75].

Nevertheless, these signs of wavering fanned Western hopes that the seeds of dissent would yet take root and grow in other satellite countries. Apart from Kennan's optimistic expression of this hope in NSC 18, this was said by the US Chargé in Belgrade, Reams, who telegraphed that the "contagiousness of Yugoslav experiment in independence seems to be growing, witness Gomułka episode in Poland", quarrels between the Bulgarian Macedonians and the Bulgarian Communist Party, "reported Czech protests to the Kremlin . . . and signs of schisms in principal Western CP's"[76]. Wallinger in the Foreign Office saw a reverse causality: he thought that already existing rebellious tendencies towards self-emancipation in the other Communist parties had obliged Moscow to make an example of the CPY, "pour discourager les autres" [*sic*][77]. His assistant, Lord Talbot de Malahide, thought there might well be tendencies "present and future" in the other satellite countries to break with Moscow[78].

The Yugoslavs also clung to the belief that at least the populations of the other satellites were sympathetic, even if their leaders did not have the courage or the power to side with Belgrade[79]. When talking to Westerners, they claimed that the satellites were "rapidly veering round in favour of Tito"[80]. The Yugoslavs continued to make these claims in the following two years at least[81].

The Purges of "Titoists" "Prove" the Existence of "Titoism"

When no such further "defections" occurred in the period immediately following the Tito-Stalin rift, this was not seen by Westerners as reason enough to abandon their hope. Paradoxically, they felt confirmed in their belief in the existence of "Titoist" tendencies in other Eastern European countries: they explained the non-occurrence of "defections" with preventive purges which were staged in the Communist parties. For many of the accused individuals were denounced by Moscow as "Titoists", and were to some extent seen by Western diplomats as people who could have led their Communist parties away from Moscow. Indeed, this seems to have been what Stalin feared: the liquidations were therefore described by a victim of the purges as a preventive measure taken at Stalin's orders, affecting those who were in any way "likely to resist Stalin's directives", even if there was no evidence for the existence of conspiracies aimed at securing greater independence from Moscow. Stalin is said to have feared the existence of people likely to resist his orders. The typical victims were Communists who had not been trained in

Moscow, that is, people on whom Stalin had not been able to keep tabs at least at some stage of their lives, thus monitoring their loyalty[82].

Eliminating on average one in every four party members in each of the East European Communist parties between 1948 and Stalin's death in 1953[83], the purges brought down Gomuka on 31 August 1948; he was lucky to survive. Koci Xoxe, the Albanian Minister of the Interior, was arrested on charges of Titoism in December 1948 and executed in June 1949; his colleague Nakos Spirou, Minister for Economic Affairs, had supposedly committed suicide earlier. In February 1949 Markos Vaphiades, the pro-Titoist leader of the Greek guerrilla forces, was called to Moscow and replaced by the anti-Zhdanovite Zachariades. Dimitrov of Bulgaria, who had escaped the fate of a Tito or of a Xoxe by totally submitting to Stalin's demands, died a natural death in 1949; Kostov, however, who had been an enemy of Tito but a defender of Bulgarian interests, was stripped of his powers in March 1949, indicted and executed at the end of that year. The Hungarian Rajk who had been known as a Leftist as well as a Magyar nationalist, was also tried and executed; his show-trial shook some left-wing public opinion more than the expulsion of the CPY from the Cominform[84]. Slansky in Czechoslovakia was executed in 1951, while Zapotocki, Gottwald and Clementis were stripped of their power. Later Ana Pauker, the Romanian Foreign Minister and bitter enemy of Titoist Yugoslavia, became a further victim of Stalin's purges[85].

All these instances led Westerners to believe that "Titoist deviationism" had existed[86], but that it had been nipped in the bud. Nevertheless, it was hoped that the tree that had budded once might bud again: the show-trials were taken as ample evidence that Communism was alive and capable of sprouting new shoots, not a petrified monolith under the Kremlin's strict control. The CIA informed the National Security Council in mid-November 1948 that doubts had been raised regarding the effectiveness of Soviet control of the Eastern European satellites.

These doubts have expressed themselves in the Communist purges in Poland and Czechoslovakia, and it is significant that these doubts are apparently being stifled by a stricter use of the techniques of party discipline and police methods rather than by basic modification of policy.[87]

Stalin paradoxically contributed to this impression. He himself feared and over-interpreted any demonstration of concern for domestic political feelings, on the part of satellite leaders, as nationalism, seeing the potentiality of "Titoism" even where there was none. By stepping up Cominform propaganda to battle with this paper-tiger, and by attempting to bring down Tito almost by all means, he convinced Westerners that there was a potential of nationalism in the satellite governments. Thus the CIA reported to the National Security Council in mid-October 1949:

> The Soviet war of nerves against Tito, which has now led to the abrogation of [the Soviet and satellite] friendship treaties with Yugoslavia, increasingly reveals the disintegrating effect of Tito's defection on the structure of international Communism. . . . Tito's successful defence of his position, by emphasizing a fundamental and resolved strain in Communist doctrine and organization, may develop into a means of pulling together an anti-Stalin opposition.[88]

As we have seen, the British took longer than the Americans to become convinced that what had happened between Yugoslavia and the USSR could occur again. On 25 November 1948 there were still voices in the British Russia Committee stating emphatically "that it was important to realise that the satellites were lost to us for the time being and that we should preserve our attack for places the battle [of the Cold War with the USSR] was actually joined, in Berlin, Greece, China and South East Asia"[89]. On 2 February 1949, however, the Northern Department put forward its view that the impact of Titoism had changed this picture. After describing Soviet measures to consolidate the orbit, the paper read:

> 1948 has seen the emergence of Tito as an anti-Soviet deviationist and opponent of the Soviet Union's hegemony over the Orbit. This development may in the long run, prove more important than the degree of consolidation so far achieved. As long as he is successful

in retaining control, Tito is a reminder to the Soviet Government of the continuing dangers of defection within the camp and a source of encouragement to anti-Soviet elements within the Eastern European countries.[90]

This analysis contains all the mistakes found in Reams's first telegram to the State Department, which had influenced thinking there, supported by Kennan's view. Reams's views, shared and possibly developed in conjunction with Cecil King in Belgrade, had reached the Foreign Office in King's dispatches, influencing diplomats there to talk of the Yugoslavs as "anti-Soviet" and as "defectors". This in turn encouraged the Northern Department to expect the feelings and tendencies supposedly found in Yugoslavia to emerge elsewhere, and thus these British officials gradually warmed to the concept of "Titoism" as a disruptive force.

In this way the uniquely Yugoslav phenomenon of "Titoism" became to Western policy-makers a concept that held out to them the hope of the multiplication of the Yugoslav incident. "Titoism" in late April 1949 was defined by Cannon as a "Communist movement which seeks to establish sovereignty with regard to its internal concerns and equality with other Communist Parties in international relations"[91]. Interestingly enough, Cannon anticipated developments in this case: the Communist Party of Yugoslavia itself had not as yet created this doctrine[92]. Gradually realizing, after months of hoping for a reconciliation with Stalin, that it would not materialize, the Yugoslav leaders had to develop such new doctrines, out of the necessity of convincing the lower echelons of the CPY that they were in the right and Stalin was in the wrong. This body of doctrine was therefore developed a considerable time *after* the split, and because of it; there was no Yugoslav attempt to question the primacy of Stalin before the split, and the later Yugoslav doctrines associated with "Titoism" were thus not a cause of the split. Tito himself denied any ambitions of setting up a new Communist international, and Yugoslavia certainly did not become the New Rome of Communism as Cecil King had thought[93].

Yet the label of "Titoism" was widely used in the press and elsewhere to denote a form of Communism seeking independence from Soviet domination. But the inaccuracy of its connotations, namely, that the Communists thus described were subscribers to a body of thought worked out by and represented by Tito, was soon demonstrated to anybody who cared to study the state of Communism world-wide more seriously than those journalists and politicians fond of catching labels. In August 1948 the Russia Committee in the Foreign Office issued a questionnaire to all missions abroad in order to make a survey of the "Effects of Titoism on Communist Parties in other countries". The answers proved, however, that many Communist parties were not in the least interested in Yugoslavia or in "Titoism"[94], as the "Survey of Communism in countries outside the Soviet orbit", also produced by the Russia Committee, reflected[95]. The final report was therefore headed "Anti-Stalinist Communism", which seemed a more suitable expression than "Titoism". It distinguished two main currents: the first was one associated with Trotsky, Zinoviev, Bukharin, etc., and it was said that this form was virtually extinct both within and outside the USSR, or else of insignificant importance.

> The second type of 'deviation' from Stalinism may be called national communism, involving denial of the basic claim of the Communist Party of the Soviet Union that, by virtue of its greater experience, it is the only infallible interpreter of Marx-Lenin-Stalinism. The obvious present example of this type is Tito's régime in Yugoslavia, but we may sooner or later have another specimen in Communist China. From the beginning there has been implicit in Tito's attitude the idea that no one socialist state or Communist Party is subordinate to another; and it was Tito's refusal to allow his security, military and economic apparatus to be penetrated by agents of the Kremlin, or to agree to absolute Kremlin control of his policy through party channels, which was the real basis of the Soviet grievance against him.

Allegations of ideological heresy that had been made by the Cominform, were dismissed in this report[96]. The incorrectness of the dating of the Yugoslav development of the doctrine of equality among Socialist states misled the Foreign Office in their retrospective interpretation. Yet this interpretation underlay the adoption of policies in the West, having spread from the State Department to the Foreign Office.

Perceptions of Inimical and Neutral Communism

The question still remained as to whether a repetition of the Yugoslav case, or even the formation of an alternative Communist creed, loosely thought of as "Titoism", was in the interest of the West. Peake's advocacy of detachment was based on the argument that

> even should Tito be able to establish a neo-Communism in Eastern Europe . . . I can at present see no reason why such a process need necessarily be to our advantage. Indeed, the existence of a brand of Communism which took more account of individual national feelings might be better calculated to increase the sway of Communism than the reverse.[97]

Peake's view is reflected by sceptical statements made in a Russia Committee paper as late as mid-1949: "Tito is anti-Kremlin but he remains a Communist and his example may do considerable harm to the West."[98]

French reserve was based on the argument that there was no guarantee that he would not turn back to the Kremlin one day, having received aid from the West which would then be a lost investment. The French remained sceptical of Anglo-American hopes regarding the effect that the Yugoslav case might have on the satellites[99].

The American State Department, however, and gradually also the British, saw any potential schism in the Communist movement as something that would, in weakening the forces at the disposal of the Soviet Union, strengthen the position of the West in the Cold War. This, then, implied the understanding that it was not Communism as such that was the worst enemy of the "Free World" (although Communism certainly continued to be seen as an evil), but Communism as a tool of Russian imperialism. But this was a difficult conviction to hold.

Thus the Western powers never in this period abandoned the aim of changing the government of Yugoslavia into a

Western-style democracy. If the Communist régime in Yugoslavia was not to be overthrown by Western secret service operations resulting in civil war, there was still the option of a policy of combined pressure and persuasion, that would result in the adoption of more democratic characteristics by the existing régime. Indeed, this was the State Department's explicit long-term policy towards Yugoslavia in a policy statement of 1 September 1949[100]. It might be termed the peaceful variant of the CIA's violent policy aimed at overthrowing Tito: the nonviolent alternative, consisting of the attempt to press for changes in the way of liberalization (if not liberation) was to survive throughout the entire period. Indeed, as will be demonstrated in Chapter 7, it became more of a short-term policy for the British under the Eden ministry.

Throughout, there were expressions of the moral dilemma facing the Western powers in their sworn anti-Communism and anti-totalitarianism. Any question of aiding the Yugoslavs was always connected with the

> very important consideration of the rectitude of our position and the attendant necessity for avoiding the appearance of a headlong rush to the support of a government which we have consistently condemned for its policies and practices in respect of political persecution and the general denial of individual liberties, etc.

as Frank Wisner of the State Department wrote in July 1948[101]. Even at the end of 1949 a major US foreign policy statement, NSC 58/2, put great emphasis on the fact that Communist deviationism should be regarded as a temporary aim, but not as the ideal or ultimate solution of the problem of Eastern Europe. It was added that

> Communism is inherently opposed to the fundamental principles underlying our form of government and any communist regime is therefore inimical to the United States. Accordingly, the United States should be alert to any opportunity to further the emergence of non-communist regimes in the satellite states, providing such non-communist regimes would have a reasonable prospect of survival.

Further, it was stated that anti-Communist sentiments should be kept alive by US efforts, including once again not only propaganda, but covert operations[102]. It seems that this addition to the text of NSC 58 was made at the request of either the Department of Defense or the National Security Resources Board[103]. It is characteristic for the attitude of greater reserve which the national military establishment in the United States harboured towards Yugoslavia until the end of 1950.

The question of moral rectitude, however, ultimately ranked after the *realpolitisch* consideration that "Titoism should continue to exist as an erosive and disintegrating force within the Russian sphere", as Kennan's policy planners noted[104]. Without ever giving up the long-term hope for Yugoslavia's "genuine re-emergence as a political personality in its own right"[105], the continuation of Yugoslav Communism in the short term was not regarded as particularly objectionable. As early as 30 June 1948 the National Security Council in their policy decision NSC 18

recognize[d] that if Yugoslavia is not to be subservient to an outside power its internal regime is basically its own business. The character of that regime would not, in these circumstances, stand in the way of a normal development of economic relations between Yugoslavia and this country.[106]

This simply phrased policy decision had the supremely important implication, that in the context of the Cold War and increasing paranoid hatred of all things Communist, the US government was prepared to do business with a Communist government, desisting from crude attempts to interfere in its internal affairs, if the Communist government was not a tool of Soviet expansionism.

The British Foreign Office draft minute of 22 December 1948, like NSC 18, made it clear that Tito's ceasing to be a Communist was neither likely nor necessary, and not a matter of top priority for the West[107]. This was also acknowledged a year later in a conclusion of the Russia and Permanent Under-Secretary's Committees in the Foreign Office:

privately and tentatively [Yugoslavia] seems to be moving

towards relations with the Western Powers freed from the assumption of inevitable hostility. If this process continues, it may establish a precedent for a *modus vivendi* between the Western world on the one hand and, on the other, states which without abandoning their Communist beliefs, are not actively working against Western aims and are not part of an exclusively Russian bloc.[108]

This has become the premise underlying Western readiness for peaceful co-existence with non-aggressive Communist governments (such as relations with Communist China two decades later). With the acceptance of the Communist government of Yugoslavia as one that was not inimical, the foundation was laid for the discrimination between a Moscow-led (and thus expansionist, inimical) Communism, and Communist governments who could be regarded as inoffensive in international politics.

"Titoism" as Asset for the West: A New Facet of the Policy of Liberation

But the continued existence of Yugoslav Communism, independent from Moscow, was not merely seen as inoffensive: indeed, the crucial fact was that Western hopes for a disintegrating effect of Yugoslavia's "defection" on the Communist movement turned Tito's political survival into a perceived asset to the West. As Wallinger said on 17 February 1949, the Western powers stood to gain in the short term, "by letting Tito's independent communism continue"[109]. In August 1948, Reams advocated that his government's strategy should be to

> seek maximum exploitation [of the] increasing opportunities to widen the gulf between Yugoslavia and USSR and extend Tito's influence among Soviet satellites. Ultimately Tito's brand of communism may well be more alluring . . . than Stalin's. . . . It represents today the outstanding political possibility in the Soviet sphere.[110]

This view hinged on the continued belief in the possibility of further rifts within the Communist movement. When other Communist parties did not "break away" this did temporarily spread defeatist feelings within the Foreign Office. On 8 October 1948 an Assistant Under-Secretary of State, Sir Ivone Kirkpatrick, expressed his view to Bevin that "it would be wrong to deduce from [the Tito-Stalin split] that the Soviet system in Eastern Europe is crumbling"[111]. Yet by the end of the year, the opinion in the Foreign Office was once more that Tito's

> existence represents the first successful split in the international communist front which it is in our interest to see perpetuated and extended, for as long as the split exists it is bound to hamper and embarrass the Kremlin's policy in the other satellite countries and beyond.[112]

The American Ambassador in Belgrade was even more optimistic, having gradually warmed to the position taken by Reams; on 31 January 1949 he advised his government that the "Tito rebellion represents outstanding political possibility for the United States policy inside Soviet sphere"[113]. He called Yugoslavia the "sole apparent agency for undermining Soviet influence in East Europe"[114]. His view was accepted by the National Security Council and the President as NSC 18/2 of 17 February 1949, the revised version of NSC 18 which we shall discuss presently. Sketching the possible effects of "Titoism" on the satellites (including China), the National Security Council decided that

> Much as we dislike him, Tito is presently performing brilliantly in our interests in leading successfully and effectively the attack from within the communist family on Soviet imperialism. Tito in being is perhaps our most precious asset in the struggle to contain and weaken Russian expansion. He must be allowed to prove on his own communist terms that an Eastern European country can secede from Moscow control and still succeed. . . . Tito for the present must be the example of the prosperous and successful domestically-produced communist who has been able to preserve the national independence of his country.

This, it was hoped, would arouse the admiration of most Communists except those who were "Moscow's stooges and quislings"[115]. George Kennan and his Policy Planning Staff took the same line. At a meeting on 1 April 1949, Kennan

> pointed out that the bond binding the communist leaders in the satellite countries with the Kremlin was a very tenuous one. Everything possible should be done to increase the suspicion between the Kremlin and its agents abroad. Titoism as a disintegrating force in the monolith should be stimulated and encouraged by all devices of propaganda. . . . We should encourage a healthy nationalism within the satellite countries as an antidote to the iron controls exercised by Moscow.[116]

The American Chiefs of Mission to the satellite states, meeting in London in October 1949, equally drew attention to the benefits which were likely to accrue to the West from the "schism" created in the "communist world", setting "back the Soviet Union's initiative against the West"[117].

To the Americans at least, the Yugoslav case and its hoped-for effects on the Communist movement thus fitted in nicely with the American policy of liberation: the encouragement of schisms became a new facet of it. The first time that the policy of "encouraging a retraction of Soviet power and influence from [a] satellite area" was described as including the policy of putting strains on relations between Communist governments and the Kremlin was in the policy paper NSC 20/1 of 18 August 1948. It noted that

> It should . . . be our aim to continue to do all in our power to increase these stresses [between the USSR and the satellite governments] and at the same time to make it possible for the satellite governments gradually to extricate themselves from Russian control and to find, if they so wish, acceptable forms of collaboration with the governments of the West.

The paper went on to say that Tito had demonstrated the ineffectiveness of the Soviet methods of controlling satellite leaders.

Conditions are therefore favorable to a concentrated effort on our part designed to take advantage of Soviet mistakes and of the rifts that have appeared, and to promote the steady deterioration of the structure of moral influence by which the authority of the Kremlin has been carried to peoples far beyond the reach of Soviet police power.[118]

In September 1949 this policy was again emphasized with the adoption of NSC 58 by the American government. Under the heading "U.S. Policy toward the Soviet satellite States in Eastern Europe", its aim was "to find means of improving and intensifying our efforts to reduce and eventually to cause the elimination of dominant Soviet influence in the satellite states of Albania, Bulgaria, Czechoslovakia, Hungary, Poland and Rumania". The paper analysed "The Lesson of Tito" and gave a realistic appreciation of the reasons why Tito and his government were able to withstand the pressure from the USSR. Along the lines of Cannon's telegram of 25 April 1949[119], NSC 58 thus acknowledged that the developments in Yugoslavia had taken this specific course due to the special characteristics of Tito's rule, and it concluded that "conditions do not now exist in the satellite states which would permit them promptly to follow the pattern of Yugoslavia."

The paper then discussed other "Courses open to us". Rejecting the course of war with the Soviet Union, it re-stated, however, that "Our ultimate aim must . . . be the appearance in Eastern Europe of non-totalitarian administrations willing to accommodate themselves to . . . the free world community." As only Czechoslovakia had known democracy, the National Security Council recognized that there were hardly any indigenous democratic forces to draw on. Therefore this was rejected as an immediate goal. "If, however, we are willing that, as a first step, schismatic Communist regimes supplant the present Stalinist governments, we stand a much better chance of success", the paper concluded. It was admitted that "it would be a difficult task to attempt to bring about a severance of satellite ties with the Kremlin". But this would still be nothing in comparison with what it would require to uproot the Communist ideology as such in these countries.

The more feasible immediate course, then, is to foster a

heretical drifting-away process on part of the satellite states. However weak they may now appear, grounds do exist for heretical schisms. We can contribute to the widening of these rifts without assuming responsibility.

The US would thus avoid a direct clash with the USSR. "Such a development could conceivably grow to the point where there would be two opposing blocs in the communist world — a Stalinist group and a non-Cominformist faction, either loosely allied or federated under Tito's leadership." It would then be left to the US to balance the two Communist blocs against each other.

NSC 58 also proposed a series of measures that were to be taken by the US to realize this policy. First, it was to try to get the USSR to withdraw its armed forces from satellite territory. Second, the Stalinist elements in the governments should be isolated, if possible, and put under pressure from popular opinion (presumably also with covert operations to incite the populations in the satellite countries to unrest). Attacks on Stalinism as something opposed to the national interest of the satellites should further be used to encourage nationalist groups. Fourth, attempts should be made to jolt the Comecon and thereby to reduce the effectiveness of Eastern European trade[120].

As noted in Chapter 1, the British had not developed a liberation policy by the time of Yugoslavia's expulsion from the Cominform. Then in response to the events in Yugoslavia, they, too, conceived such a policy as we shall see. The Foreign Office's Russia Committee agreed during 1949 that it should be a British objective "to weaken the hold of Moscow over the countries which it at present dominates; [and] to resist, and if possible to curtail, the influence of Communism with its proclaimed hostility to Western ideals and interests". It was regarded as important to do so in the European satellite states

> before their peoples become so imbued with Soviet propaganda as to follow the lead of the Soviet government without demur. . . . This objective should not be pursued by means likely to increase the risk of war. . . . While constructing a political, economic and social system which could appeal to the satellites and in which a place for them could be found, the Western powers

should at the same time take any positive steps open to them to undermine Soviet control of the orbit. These steps include propaganda, economic inducements and covert activities as may be appropriate.[121]

While it was thus said on the one hand that "the influence of Communism" with its hostility to the West should be curtailed, it was conceded on the other hand that appeal should be made to "the satellites" (by which not only the populations but also the existing Communist governments of the satellites are meant!), to shake off Soviet control.

Policy Option 3:
The Exploitation of the Tito-Stalin Split

This Russia Committee statement of mid-1949 encapsulates the three facets of the third policy option seen by the British and the Americans to exploit the Tito-Stalin split. Yugoslavia was now seen as a spearhead or wedge which could break up the Communist monolith. This wedge could be used in several ways, as we shall see presently. Propaganda was of crucial importance in this context: British ambassadors in the satellite capitals suggested that it should be used to show up the bad treatment the Yugoslavs had received at the hands of the Soviet Union[122]. Further, the bait of trade and economic aid could be held out to Communist governments (Yugoslavia should be made the example of this, as we shall see in the following chapter). This presupposed, however, that these Communist régimes could be reassured that they would not be forced to betray their political creed in order to benefit from trade with the West. Again, if Yugoslavia was to be the exemplary case, the Western powers logically had to adopt a policy of tolerance towards Tito's Communism, i.e. let him "sit on the fence", as the British called it, without forcing him into the "Western Camp".

Accordingly, the Western powers had to avoid excessive pressure on Tito to comply with their political demands. Peake asked this "most strongly" when in February 1949 thought was given in Britain to trading with Yugoslavia[123]. This line of reasoning continued to run through Foreign Office and diplomatic circles until the end of the Labour government in 1951[124].

Equally, on 30 June 1948, Kennan's Policy Planning Staff informed the National Security Council that

> If the Soviet satellite area disintegrates even further, either now or in the more distant future . . . the attitude we take now [towards Yugoslavia] may constitute an important precedent. Furthermore, our attitude at this time may have an important influence on *whether* the rift between Tito and Moscow spreads to Russia's relations with other members of the satellite area or serves to weld those other members still more tightly to the Kremlin.[125]

The Policy Planning Staff therefore recommended that the "western world" by its attitude towards Yugoslavia should take care not to undermine Tito's standing with his followers, nor lay him open to excessive criticism from the Cominform, by being too friendly towards him. Nevertheless, they should not be "too cold toward Tito" if (but only if) the Yugoslavs should make "advances . . . toward closer association with the West", as that would "be used by Moscow Communists as a proof that foreign Communists have no alternative but to stay with Moscow"[126]. Approved by the National Security Council and the US President, this became the foundation of the first phase of American policy towards Yugoslavia as NSC 18. As the Sous-Direction d'Europe Orientale in the French Foreign Ministry summed it up on 9 November 1949, "Pour les Anglo-Saxons, le titisme a été . . . une occasion de créer une fissure dans le bloc des satellites parce que sa doctrine représentait de schismatique. Il fallait donc essayer d'aider Tito sans trop le compromettre au point de vue politique."[127]

Yugoslavia's Special Situation among the Satellites

The reason why other Communist leaders were unlikely to resist the world-wide enforcement of the Party line on the issue of Yugoslavia was at the same time the reason why Tito managed to survive. Tito and his CPY had an exceptional position within the country, paralleled only by the situations in Albania and in China, as already noted in Chapter 1. It was different from that of any other Eastern European Communist party as those relied on the USSR's backing in every respect, and did not have the support of an army and a police or the personal allegiance of the vast majority of the Party members. This point was conceded occasionally by observant Western diplomats. Even Reams commented prior to the Cominform Declaration,

> In evaluating Tito's ability to maintain separatist policy it should be noted that he occupies exceptional position. Other certain Communist leaders were in Russia during the war and returned [to] their countries accompanied by Kremlin picked teams. Tito led resistance and organised own team from ground up [*sic*].[128]

Cannon recognized as early as 5 July 1948 that Tito was in his opinion the only Communist chief capable of holding out against pressure from Moscow: as an experienced fighter leading an army of loyal and excellent soldiers he had the greatest personal "sex appeal" among the European Communist leaders[129]. Ten months later, Cannon drew up an analysis of the characteristics of the CPY, in which he showed that this Party had a very special position as it was so firmly in control of the country. Seventy per cent of its members had been in the Party for less than three years (and thus had no connection with Moscow other than through Tito), while the remaining 30% were "bound by the great emotional impact of war service under Tito"; only a negligible number had an acquaintance with Communism pre-dating the reconstruction of the CPY by Tito in 1939. Cannon did not think that there could be any

> confidence that such conditions as in Yugoslavia and the Communist Party of Yugoslavia produced Titoism . . . would inevitably effect a similar result elsewhere. . . . What can be suggested, however, is that wherever a set of circumstances involving a Communist Party which has largely by its own efforts achieved victory and consolidated its power, a leadership more or less continuous and isolated in some degree from direct Soviet experience, a mass membership new, uneducated, and bound to the leadership by ties of emotion and

nationalism, and an attempt by Moscow to alter policies which are fundamentally organizational — wherever such a set of circumstances, or some combination of them, is to be found, there at least a presumption of the possibility of Titoism may exist. [130]

Although this analysis can retrospectively be credited with a considerable amount of realism, it still presupposed wrongly that Tito's CPY and possibly some other Communist parties had the urge to establish their sovereignty internally and their equality externally. Even so, Cannon's criteria cut the number of possible "defectors" among the Communist parties down to two: those of China and of Albania. In other parties, the Communist leaders did not have a strong enough standing.

Both China and Albania did indeed have a special place in Anglo-American policy-making. The French were left out completely in the case of Albania, as they were not trusted to keep covert operations secret. In the Far East, they were once again excluded to a certain extent, as they had less direct commercial interest in China (as opposed to Indochina) than the two "Anglo-Saxon" powers. It is therefore mainly Anglo-American policy that is of concern to us.

Western Policy Towards China: Drive Mao to Titoism?

As early as 1947 George Kennan had conceived of the possibility of a Communist China distancing itself from the USSR (see Chapter 1). He thought that if the Chinese Communists ever gained control,

> the men in the Kremlin would surely discover that this fluid subtle oriental movement which they thought they held in the palm of their hand had quietly oozed away between their fingers and that there was nothing left there but a ceremonious Chinese bow and a polite and inscrutable Chinese giggle.

Kennan thought that a country out of reach for the Red Army had a greater potential for producing an indigenous Communist movement that could survive without the blessing of the CPSU's leaders, than Russia's satellite neighbours in

Europe. For this is what he must have meant when he suggested awkwardly that China was "a country not contiguous to the borders of the direct military power of Russia"[131].

A year later Yugoslavia, rather than China, seemed to fulfil Kennan's bizarrely worded and premature prophecy. Indeed, Tito and Mao, and their respective Communist parties, had much in common. Both had their own liberation to be proud of, neither of them had received much help from the Soviet Union in coming to power[132] and neither was very close to Moscow geographically; both had Communist-led armies wholly loyal to the Party which in both cases had led and organized them; both had strong indigenous leaders who were with their people throughout the "war of liberation", unlike the Dimitrovs and Paukers and Ulbrichts of Europe, so that these leaders had considerably greater popularity; both countries had a population consisting predominantly of peasants who had been mobilized by the Communist Party and were the base of its rule[133].

In 1948, however, the Communists in China had not yet defeated the Nationalist forces. Moreover, the Chinese Communist Party (CCP) followed the Cominform in its condemnation of the Yugoslavs, with a slight delay that was doubtless caused by the time it took for the message to be relayed to China[134]. Wu Xiuquan, the first Chinese Ambassador to Yugoslavia (May 1955-October 1958) during the first period of Sino-Yugoslav friendship, coincident with his Ambassadorship, also admitted that "China in fact had much in common with Yugoslavia" which the Yugoslavs had always claimed[135]. Before the Khrushchev-Tito reconciliation in 1955, however, according to Wu, the Chinese, "did not know much about Yugoslavia . . . because there was little ready information at home for our reference." They therefore accepted the Cominform's views about Yugoslavia, and prior to 1955 never conceived of regarding Tito as an example[136].

Nevertheless, the parallels struck Western foreign policy-makers. The first to see them in the British Foreign Office was the head of the Far Eastern Department, Scott, who noted on 11 August 1948, that he saw the possibility of China developing in the way Yugoslavia did[137]. As we have seen, the Southern Department's minute of 6 October 1948 mentioned the CCP as possibly susceptible to Yugoslav influence[138]. The American National Security Council in their paper NSC 34 of 13 October 1948, drafted by Kennan's Policy Planning Staff, dwelt on the similarities between the Chinese and Yugoslav Communist Parties:

> to the old conspirators of the Kremlin the questions to ask about any foreign Communist party are: who controls the party apparatus; who controls the secret police; who controls ... the armed forces; and does the foreign leader love power more than he fears the Kremlin? If the answers to these questions as applied to China are as unsatisfactory to the Kremlin as they turned out to be in the case of Yugoslavia, Moscow faces a considerable task in seeking to bring the Chinese Communists under its complete control, if for no other reason than that Mao Tse-tung has been entrenched in power for nearly ten times the length of time that Tito has.

Even if Mao were "fearfully loyal", China's sheer size would tempt the CCP, once it were in control, to shake off the Kremlin's domination, "especially as they would have, in part, risen to power on the heady wine of nationalism". This, not the victory or defeat of the CCP as opposed to the nationalist forces, was thought to be the Kremlin's major worry[139].

The Yugoslavs indulged in the same sort of wishful thinking, and they said so on many occasions over the next few years, even after the Chinese alignment with the Cominform countries in their joint condemnation of Yugoslavia, and after the Chinese intervention in Korea and its condemnation by Yugoslavia[140]. Similarly, until the Korean War the Western foreign ministries never dismissed this possibility. NSC 18/2 of February 1949 stated rather over-optimistically:

> Nationalist tendencies in communist parties which have only unwillingly accepted the iron discipline and control of Moscow have been given hope by virtue of Tito's successful challenge. His revolt may well condition or even bring about a crisis between the Chinese Communist Party and the Kremlin. Mao Tse-tung appears to be capturing power in China without dependence upon the Red Army and Mao himself might already be infected with the Tito virus.[141]

At a meeting of the British Russia Committee on 12 April 1949, R.M.A. Hankey mentioned it to his colleagues[142]. At a meeting on 21 June 1949, Adam Watson of the Southern Department expressed his view that the USSR might choose to give China more freedom than it had given Yugoslavia, but the majority consensus at this meeting was that the USSR would want China subdued[143]. Towards the end of the year it was reported at a Russia Committee meeting that anti-Soviet factions could be discerned within the CCP[144]. French diplomats also considered the likelihood of a Communist "defection" in the Far East[145], and they were aware of Anglo-American interests in this matter[146].

Even if Kennan conceived of the possibility of a Sino-Soviet split before the Yugoslav-Cominform dispute, it can probably be argued that there would not have been any majority consensus in the State Department and the Foreign Office on the recognition of this possibility as a factor in foreign policy-making. Nancy Tucker, examining Sino-American relations, has only one example of a Western diplomat observing tensions between the USSR and the CCP before the Tito-Cominform rift, while her examples of such observation after June 1948 and especially in 1949 abound. This was also the impression in the French Foreign Ministry, where it was said in a memorandum of 30 November 1953 that "le précédent yougoslave est à la base de toutes spéculations occidentales sur un divorce entre Moscou et Pékin." The events in Yugoslavia also gave Westerners, diplomats and journalists alike, a better idea of what signs to look out for that might reflect tensions[147].

There was thus in the West the hope that an estrangement between Moscow and Peking would take place, a hope that grew out of the perceived potential of China to rebel against Soviet domination following the same pattern that Western diplomats thought they had observed in Yugoslavia. The impact of the supposed Yugoslav "precedent" on Western policy towards Communist China has probably not been given sufficient emphasis in the existing works on this topic, apart from Tucker's[148]. But even a rough survey of the documentation of Western policy-making towards the Chinese Communists reveals that this Western hope was a major factor conditioning their policies, until the outbreak of the Korean War.

For once the possibility of a rift in these relations was acknowledged, the policies adopted in Britain and the US towards the CCP changed, and a less hostile attitude was adopted. Dean Acheson found the argument convincing that everything should be done to prevent the CCP from aligning itself permanently with the USSR. Consequently in early 1949 he advocated that American trade with Communist China should continue[149]. This found its recognition in the policy statement NSC 48/2 of 30 December 1949, approved by Truman:

> The United States should exploit, through appropriate political, psychological and economic means, any rifts between the Chinese Communists and the USSR and between Stalinists and other elements in China, while scrupulously avoiding the appearance of intervention. Where appropriate, covert as well as overt means should be utilized to achieve these objectives.[150]

Beyond this, Acheson favoured a gradual withdrawal from the obligations the US had incurred in the Far East, such as the support for Chiang Kai-shek's Taiwan. As Acheson had convinced Truman of the validity of his argument[151], the State Department under him was set on a course towards the recognition of Communist China which was only altered by the Korean War[152]. In spite of the failure on the part of the US to take advantage of certain opportunities to improve relations with Mao, the United States had indeed advanced so far on the course of recognition that the British Far Eastern Department was for a while under the impression that they were acting in full accord with the United States when they themselves prepared to extend recognition to Mao. When they realized that the Americans were not quite as ready as the British to do so early in January 1950, Bevin decided to urge his government to go ahead nonetheless. Britain thus recognized Mao's régime on 6 January 1950[153]. The French also favoured a recognition of the Chinese Communists, despite their own involvement in Indochina where they were bound sooner or later to clash with the Peking government who had interests in that area[154]. Acheson and Truman, however, under considerable pressure from the China lobby in Congress and from the military establishment, ultimately did not dare abandon their old policy of backing Chiang to recognize Mao in view of the changed situation in China[155].

Admittedly, the hope that Mao would "follow Tito" was not the only factor in British decisions and American near-decisions: the disillusionment with the Kuomintang forces of Chiang Kai-shek, Indian pressure for the recognition of the CCP's victory, and trade were other factors of importance[156]. Trade, however, always has two sides: the British hoped not only to profit from the trade with China, but also to give China economic ties with the "Free World", so as not to strengthen her links with the USSR more than necessary. This policy was founded on the belief that a "foot in the door" of China would be of economic and of political benefit to the West[157].

Although Mao might have laughed had it been suggested to him in 1949 that he could become "another Tito", especially if it had been put in these words, this was not merely something that the Yugoslavs hoped and that the Westerners tried in a modest way to bring about. Stalin was also afraid of it, and it was on his mind when he invited the new ruler of China to Moscow in the winter of 1949-50, as Mao himself stated later[158]. At the time Mao seems to have been loyally committed to solidarity with the USSR, and an important faction within the CCP was strongly opposed to any dealings with the West[159]. Yet Mao, unlike Tito, was to develop political concepts challenging the Kremlin's supremacy within the Communist world, and within a decade after the expulsion of Yugoslavia from the Cominform, the Chinese, unlike the Yugoslavs, were consciously heading for a dispute with Moscow. What had been mistaken assumptions on the part of the Western powers about the Yugoslav and a potential satellite drive for independence would have been much closer to the truth in China; in forgoing the possibility of helping Britain keep a foot or even just a toe in the door to China, the Americans contributed to Mao's decision of 1949 to lean only on the Soviet Union for help and assistance[160].

Western Policy Towards Albania
British Adoption of a Liberation Policy

Until June 1948 Albania was virtually a client state of

Yugoslavia[161]; thereafter the Tito-Cominform split left Albania cut off geographically from the Soviet bloc. Yet she came down on the side of the Cominform and against Tito in 1948. Because of her sudden geographical isolation, the British and the Americans thought her the most obvious target for their liberation policy. The British had not had any such policy prior to the Tito-Stalin split. In July 1948 the Bastion Paper still advocated that a purely defensive policy should be used to counter the Soviet threat[162]. On 25 November 1948, however, the 16th meeting of the Russia Committee under the chairmanship of Gladwyn Jebb, an Assistant Under-Secretary of State and expert on Soviet Affairs, considered a reversal of this policy. The Committee had before them a paper on "British Policy towards the Soviet Orbit in Europe" drafted by Robert Hankey, also an Assistant Under-Secretary. He proposed that British policy should no longer be purely defensive but should become offensive, stopping short only of a "hot war". In the discussion,

> Sir Ivone Kirkpatrick said that, in the present state of our finances and in view of public opinion, he thought that it would be best to start any kind of offensive operations in a small area and suggested for consideration in this regard Albania. Would it not be possible to start a civil war behind the Iron Curtain and by careful assistance to produce a state of affairs in Albania similar to the state of affairs the Russians had produced in Greece[163]? Mr. Jebb pointed out that United Nations observers in Greece would certainly come to hear of any operations we were undertaking and would complain to the United Nations with possibly unpleasant consequences. Mr. Bateman suggested that though Albania was a very weak point in the Soviet orbit there might be some advantage in allowing the rift there to widen without our interference especially as the Russians were in Albania in some force. Sir Ivone Kirkpatrick enquired whether it would not be possible to arrange that the operation should be undertaken by the forces of resistance in Albania. We knew that there was opposition to the present régime and it should be possible to make use of it.

Three other members of the Committee pointed out the

difficulties of working with underground movements, but there was agreement that "any action we undertook must be co-ordinated with the Americans". Then Frank Roberts, Bevin's private secretary and on this occasion his spokesman,

> pointed out that the most helpful development from our point of view in the Soviet orbit had been the quarrel between Tito and the Cominform. It owed nothing to us and if we went for too much activity on the lines suggested it would only have the effect of consolidating the orbit. . . . We must be very careful in anything that is done not to prevent developments like the Tito-Cominform dispute.

The meeting then set up a subcommittee to consider Hankey's proposal in view of its implications. But before the next point was discussed at the meeting, the Chief of Staff of the Royal Air Force, Lord Tedder, "said that he thought we should aim at winning the 'cold war' (by which he meant the overthrow of the Soviet régime) [*sic*] in five years time". Frank Roberts opposed him on this point, but this statement is an indication of the peak temperatures reached in some of the fierier minds in the Committee[164].

By mid-February 1949, Bevin had decided to go ahead with the project "to detach Albania from the orbit"[165]. The method chosen was an anti-Communist (and therefore not a "Titoist") insurrection sparked off by infiltrated Albanian exiles. The scheme would have been unthinkable, however, if Tito's country had still been a member of the Soviet orbit.

It is not clear whether the British planted the idea into the minds of the Americans. At any rate, by the end of March 1949 they were involved in "une opération indirecte sur l'Albanie", which the Greek Minister of War knew about, in response to the Cominform's threat to Yugoslavia (see Chapter 4); the Greek Minister thought that this operation was meant to deprive the Cominform of part of its leverage on the Yugoslav Eastern borders. "Cette opération serait basée sur un changement intérieur [du] régime que les services secrets Américains jugent aisément réalisables." Although the Minister liked the idea, he "craint que les services Américains ne se fassent des illusions sur leurs possibilités Albanaises. Ces possibilités diminueront d'ailleurs chaque jour à mesure que l'emprise Russe sur l'Albanie s'accroitra."[166]

The first US record of an American discussion of the topic dates from 1 April 1949; by then they had certainly been consulted by the British, as originally agreed by the Russia Committee. On that day Kennan's Policy Planning Staff met in his presence, and after restating the necessity of stimulating Titoism as a disintegrating force regarding Communist movements in general, the "Albanian situation" was discussed:

> it was generally agreed that something very definitely might be accomplished now in the way of (a) assisting in the over-throw of the present pro-Kremlin regime by a pro-Tito gang, or (b) by assisting in the setting up of a new regime which would be anti-Communist and therefore pro-western.

It was concluded that US policy should be to make

> Full use ... of the refugee organizations representing the various free movements within the satellite countries. Assistance and, wherever possible, support should be given to elements within the captured countries which represent a weakness in the political control within the Russian orbit.[167]

This policy was implemented in at least one other instance, in the Ukraine in 1951; it was equally unsuccessful[168]. The Albanian plan was discussed formally at a meeting between Bevin and Acheson on 14 September 1949 in Washington, when Bevin asked whether the Americans agreed "that we try to bring down the Hoxha government when the occasion arises", rather than inciting it to become a Titoist-type deviationist government. Acheson replied in the affirmative[169]. On the French side, the scheme had the support of the French ambassador in Moscow in mid-1949, but what the Foreign Ministry thought of it is not clear[170].

For the period in which these operations were going on[171], references continue to be found in Anglo-American correspondence to the Western aim of freeing Albania "from Communist control"[172]. The American National Security Council in their policy statement NSC 162/2 of 30 October

1953 admitted that "the detachment of any *major* European satellite from the Soviet bloc does not now appear feasible except by Soviet acquiescence or war."[173] This, however, did not imply an abandonment of the hope for the detachment of a *minor* satellite such as Albania, as they pointed out in mid-December 1953 in NSC 174 on "United States Policy Toward the Soviet Satellites in Eastern Europe"[174].

The Americans and the British were thus, in the case of Albania, guilty of all the sins of subversion and interference, disregard for national sovereignty and war-mongering, of which they always accused their Cold War enemy, the Soviet Union. This might be passed as *Realpolitik*, but it is embarrassing in view of the high ideals of a moral superiority of Western democracy and the hope to win the Cold War contest with the Soviet Union by means of the moral righteousness of the cause of the Free World, as put forward in the highfaluting concepts of Kennan and the National Security Council.

The operation was a tragic failure as most of the men who had been infiltrated were killed. This was partly due to dilettantism in regard to the execution of the scheme[175], partly to Anglo-American rivalry which so often seems to have got in the way of effective co-ordination[176], but mainly to the fact that one of the quartet of men conducting the operation was the Soviet agent Kim Philby, representing the British Secret Service. He obviously notified his Soviet contacts of the operations, so that the Albanian émigrés who had been trained by the CIA and the SIS for guerrilla warfare were all killed in action, or arrested and subsequently executed. The operations dragged on until the end of 1953 and were followed by purges and show-trials in Albania, which stamped out any further hopes for future defections[177].

A comment of Kim Philby's shines a light on one of the gravest errors of the whole scheme: in his opinion the presence of infiltrated exiles "would have been useful only if the country was seething with revolt. That, perhaps, was the unspoken assumption behind the whole venture." The Albanians sent into their native country by the CIA and the SIS, however, "had nowhere found arms open to welcome them"[178]. It can of course be argued that this was a particularly malicious comment to make, as Philby himself had seen to it that there would not be any arms open to welcome the dissidents; nevertheless, there is no indication of any real interest in a mass upheaval on the part of the Albanians. The mistaken assumptions made about this by the two Western intelligence services were due to some extent to the absence of first-hand information about that country, as neither the British nor the Americans had a diplomatic mission there, and relied on French information and dubious second-hand reports. The expectation of lively discontent within Albania, however, of an anti-Communist fifth column, consisting of a large proportion or even the majority of the population, was rooted deeply in the Western perception of the world, in an unwritten set of assumptions that for most people Communist tyranny was worse than death. It is this notion that Philby put his finger on; Western policy-makers were mistaken in clinging to it.

As noted previously, the Albanian episode was not in the end a Western plan to encourage "Titoism" in an East European country. It was thought possible, however, because of Yugoslavia's amputation from the Soviet orbit, which in turn left Albania isolated geographically. Although the Anglo-American operation in the last instance aimed at the overthrow of the Communist government in Tirana and its replacement by a royalist, pro-Western régime[179], the interchangeable interest of American and British policy-makers in the two options of a "pro-Tito gang" and an "anti-Communist and therefore pro-Western" régime was demonstrated in the deliberations of the Russia Committee and the American Policy Planning Staff.

3

Driving the Wedge: Western Policies Towards Yugoslavia

Economic Policies

Already before the drought of 1950 Tito's government had severe economic problems to contend with. Yugoslavia had a mainly agricultural economy, acutely underdeveloped industrially, and the wounds left by the Second World War had not yet healed in mid-1948 when the countries of the Soviet bloc imposed an economic blockade, bringing down imports from Cominform countries to Yugoslavia from 43% in 1948 to 13% in 1949[1]. Stalin's criticism of Yugoslavia's Five Year Plan of industrialization as unrealistic had been justified[2], and on top of this came the doubling of the defence expenditure between 1948 and 1950[3], and the external debt[4].

If the Western powers wanted Tito to survive as a wedge or disruptive force in the Communist movement, they had to "keep him afloat", that is, help to prevent his economy from collapsing. As early as 30 June 1948 the American National Security Council (NSC) accepted the advice given by Kennan and his Policy Planning Staff (PPS), encapsulated in the policy statement NSC 18, which was to support Tito if he wished it[5]. The underlying reasoning was always, until the Korean War, the effect "Titoism" was expected to have on other Communists[6] (see Chapter 2).

The phrase "keeping Tito afloat", dating from the autumn of 1948, stemmed from British Foreign Secretary Bevin[7]. It reflected the British distaste for the Communist régime of Belgrade: the British government were willing to help it survive, as proof that it was possible for a Communist government to exist without the Kremlin's blessing, but they did not wish to pamper the Yugoslavs. Indeed, they never quite ceased to hope for some gains for the British economy from economic relations with Yugoslavia. At least, they did not want to have too obvious losses in their dealings with Belgrade[8].

The Americans, however, saw quite a different reason for co-operating with Tito in economic matters: they wanted to make the Yugoslav economy a show-piece to demonstrate how prosperous a Communist-governed country could become if only it were willing to trade peacefully with the West[9]. On 1 September 1949 a State Department policy statement concerning Yugoslavia read:

> Our present immediate objective, in the light of Tito's defiance of Stalin, and our view that Titoism should continue to exist as an erosive and disintegrating force within the Russian sphere, is to extract the maximum political advantage from this quarrel within the Communist family. Accordingly, we are permitting Tito to purchase, to the extent his own funds and small credits will allow, urgently needed foods now required by Yugoslav civilian economy and which can no longer be obtained from the Soviet bloc because of the economic embargo. In this way, we hope to foster his independence of the USSR, strengthen his resistance to Soviet pressure, and provide an example to those dissatisfied elements in the Communist Parties of the Cominform countries of what they too might have if they embark on Tito's course.[10]

The earliest example of Western help for Tito was the unfreezing on 19 July 1948 by the Americans of the gold of the Kingdom of Yugoslavia which had been frozen at the German invasion of Yugoslavia in the spring of 1941[11]. This measure was in accordance with the guidelines of NSC 18, as was the sale by Britain and the US of 50,000-60,000 tons of crude oil to Yugoslavia in July 1948[12].

The American policy of "containment" (see Chapter 1) included restrictions on trade with Eastern Europe. In late 1947 and early 1948 the NSC had decided that they would in future export no arms or military equipment, nor any other commodity of military potential or in short supply in the West, to the Soviet Union or any of the satellite countries, including, of course, Yugoslavia. The granting of export licences for such goods to Eastern European countries was prohibited[13]. This rule was applied by the US from March 1948 onwards[14], but it only became official policy as NSC 15/1 in July 1948[15]. In this they had some co-operation from other member-states of the Organisation for European Economic Co-operation[16].

From September 1948 the American embassy in Belgrade recommended that Yugoslavia should be exempted from these export restrictions[17]. The American Chargé d'Affaires in the Soviet Union, Kohler, backed this proposal, arguing that "US and western Europe should extend trade relations with Yugoslavs, ... for sake of prolonging and aggravating Tito-Cominform break, encouraging non-Communist elements [in the] Soviet satellite states and securing useful contribution [to] European recovery."[18] On 20 May 1949 Kohler reiterated this recommendation, agreeing with the Belgrade embassy about the view that there was the possibility, as Cannon had said, of "Titoism" appearing elsewhere. In Kohler's words,

> postwar satellite developments to date suggest serious defects and shortcomings in Moscow's 'management of empire' which Soviet mentality and methods are as yet incapable of solving. Embassy continues to feel that vigorous coordinated western policies in fields of propaganda and trade regulations may help [to] exacerbate this situation.[19]

Containing once again the leitmotiv of the policy of supporting Yugoslavia until the Korean War, this recommendation was adopted by the NSC and President Truman in their second paper on Yugoslavia, NSC 18/2, of 17 February 1949, drafted by the Policy Planning Staff[20].

Meanwhile, the British were gradually abandoning their policy of "masterly inactivity"[21] in favour of the American approach. At the UN on 5 October 1948, the Yugoslav Vice-Minister of Foreign Affairs, Dr. Aleš Bebler, moaned to the British Minister of State, Hector McNeil, about the economic problems of Yugoslavia, "[any] assistance which [Britain] could give towards improving their economic position would be of most vital importance". He added, however, that all publicity given to aid measures would be embarrassing.

When Bevin was informed of this, he summoned Geoffrey

Wallinger and Charles Bateman, the top men from the Southern Department, and it was decided to "keep Tito afloat". He should also remain "balanced on the wall as long as possible"[22] (i.e. "sitting on the fence", cf. Chapter 2). This new policy of "keeping Tito afloat" was endorsed by the Cabinet in their Economic Policy Committee on 2 November 1948; it was agreed "that every effort should be made to avoid unnecessary delay in the trade negotiations with Yugoslavia"[23]. These had started long before the Tito-Stalin split, and its conclusion had been delayed in part by the British determination to secure favourable terms[24]. A one-year trade agreement was signed on 23 December 1948 [25].

Only afterwards were the real dimensions of the economic blockade imposed on Yugoslavia by the Soviet orbit recognized by the British[26]: exports to Yugoslavia were cut to one-eighth of what they had been in 1948. Bevin therefore suggested to Attlee that consideration should be given to what further supplies could be given to Yugoslavia (as part of a long-term trade agreement), if the Yugoslavs should request them.

> It is of great importance to HM government in their defensive struggle against Soviet Communism that Yugoslavia should not be re-absorbed into the Soviet bloc. Not only would her total defection make an important breach in Eastern European solidarity, but, as nothing is so potentially dangerous to an ideology or religion as a flourishing heresy, Tito's mere continuance to hold out in opposition to the orthodox Communist line works greatly to our advantage.[27]

He recommended a continuation of the policy of "masterly inactivity" until the British were explicitly asked for help; yet they should be ready to act at once when the request came. Bevin recommended this "masterly inactivity" as he was concerned to avoid "compromising Tito with his own supporters before he has had time to convince them of the inevitability of a change of front". This, he thought, would be playing into Stalin's hand[28]. "Masterly inactivity" was thus seen as a form of discretion, while formerly it had been a sign of British distrust (see Chapter 2).

On 17 January 1949 a meeting of ministers took place in 10 Downing Street, chaired by Attlee. Here it was agreed that the long-term trade negotiations which were likely to start soon, should be speeded up by Peake in Belgrade, if necessary. In case the Yugoslavs should ask for any goods on the list of export restrictions, the question of a relaxation of the ban on these individual items should be discussed with the US[29]. Thus by the beginning of 1949, both the British and the Americans had decided in principle to help Tito by increasing their trade with him and giving him access to strategic raw materials, not because he was regarded as a friend or an ally, but because his existence was seen as a thorn in the flesh of Communist unity, a potential incentive for other satellites to break with the Kremlin, a wedge in the Soviet bloc.

The French had more flexibility in their policy towards Yugoslavia, as they had not yet committed themselves to the observation of the export ban on strategic goods. On the one hand they resented and resisted American interference and prescriptions regarding goods which the French were allowed to export to Yugoslavia, when the Yugoslavs asked the French for an export licence for a cartridge plant[30]. For like the British, they were interested in trade relations and advantageous exports to Yugoslavia. But on the other hand their political attitude towards the Tito régime remained much more reserved than that of the "Anglo-Saxons".

During Anglo-Yugoslav negotiations for a long-term trade agreement in the first half of 1949 the Yugoslav government made a formal request for a credit of about £11 million[31]. This gave the British the opportunity to enact their policy of "keeping Tito afloat" by giving him "a shot in the arm", another expression of Bevin's. On 1 June 1949 the Cabinet's Economic Policy Committee, chaired by Attlee, decided a credit could be granted to Yugoslavia, even if it were justified only by political, and not by commercial considerations[32].

In the following months Bevin defended this decision staunchly against attempts by Sir Stafford Cripps of the Treasury to keep the credit's total sum down[33], and against the military's hesitations about exporting strategic goods to Yugoslavia[34]. On 24-25 August 1949 agreement was finally reached within an inner Cabinet consisting of Attlee, Harold Wilson of the Board of Trade, and Bevin, that the Yugoslavs should be given a medium-term credit of £8 million plus a short-term credit of 5 million[35]. The trade agreement was eventually signed on 26 December 1949[36].

The Yugoslavs also sought to expand their trade relations with the US[37]. Again they tried to obtain capital equipment which they had originally expected to receive from the Soviet bloc. At the end of 1948 the Yugoslavs were refused export licences for oil-well equipment they wanted to buy, because "Yugoslav actions at the Danube Conference and in the Security Council [had] indicated that they are still faithful supporters of Soviet foreign policy."[38] Yet the Yugoslavs were told that they could make requests for other equipment, which indeed they proceeded to do[39]. While between March 1948 and December 1948 $12 million worth of goods had been approved for export by the United States to Yugoslavia, between January 1949 and 25 March 1949 alone approval was given to the export of items worth $11 million[40].

NSC 18/2 had relaxed export controls regarding Yugoslavia for the very purpose of aiding her to obtain such capital equipment. There was some renewed discussion of the wisdom of this decision when a new Secretary of Defense was appointed in the person of Louis Johnson[41], who was opposed to the issuing of a licence to export a blooming mill to Yugoslavia[42]. He had the backing of the military establishment, and some haggling ensued, which in the end resulted in the sale and export of the mill with Truman's approval[43].

The argument winning the day was once more that the State Department regarded this export as being in the national interest of the United States. To the Yugoslavs, approval of the application would be evidence that they could turn to the West for help. Further, "Approval will also show the other satellites, whose five-year industrialization plans are failing, due to the unavailability of equipment from either the USSR or the West, how they can make them succeed."[44] So here again, the rationale was one of helping the Yugoslavs *pour encourager les autres*.

Western Credits for Yugoslavia

On 16 May 1949 the Yugoslavs began to urge the Americans to give them a $25 million credit from their Export-Import Bank (ExImBank)[45]. A State Department policy statement of 1 September 1949 said that, apart from a relaxation of export controls, "it is in our interest to see that Tito has such credits as are necessary to keep his regime from foundering". Also, the diversion of Yugoslav trade to the West was in the interest of the European Recovery Scheme, and gave the United States "opportunities to draw Yugoslavia toward the west politically as well as economically" even though "the US should not make political concessions [a] *sine qua non* of economic aid"[46]. This was in line with the long-term policy of working for the liberalization of Yugoslavia, while allowing Tito to sit on the fence. On 8 September 1949 the ExImBank therefore extended a credit of $20 million (as opposed to $25 million applied for) to Yugoslavia[47].

Because of the dollar deficit or gap in Europe as a whole[48], the International Bank for Reconstruction and Development (IBRD) was reluctant to give Yugoslavia dollars. Bevin and Schuman discussed the matter briefly at the first meeting of the Council of Europe in Strasbourg[49]. When Acheson, Bevin and Schuman met in Washington in September 1949, Bevin advocated a loan given jointly by the European countries: "This might have some over-all advantage as an outgrowth of the Strasbourg talks [the first meeting of the Council of Europe] and give a pan-European concept to the loan."[50] No decision was made at this conference[51], perhaps because Schuman was more worried than either his British or his American colleagues that aid given to Yugoslavia would be aid wasted if Tito were assassinated[52].

Nevertheless, the problem of credits for Yugoslavia was henceforth an Anglo-Franco-American project, due to Bevin's interest in involving the West European countries or at least France on the Anglo-American side in the smaller battles of the Cold War, as well as in the major projects such as NATO. As he explained to his Cabinet in a paper of 24 October 1949, he wanted to enlist the European countries in the task of preventing another world war by deterring the aggressor through an atmosphere of high spirits in Europe. Joint economic measures for this end, short of actual political and economic integration, should be supported most strongly by Britain[53]. This, then, for once, was an opportunity where the European countries in acting together would help Britain carry the burden of a commitment, instead of merely infringing on British rights. Bevin's mixed feelings about European co-operation and American pressure for European integration, to which on the whole he was not prepared to yield, have to be seen as the background to Bevin's sudden enthusiasm for the wider involvement of other European powers in this particular project of giving aid to Yugoslavia.

At the end of September 1949, the International Monetary Fund approved a $3 million drawing by Yugoslavia, and several European countries, among them Britain, France, Italy and the Netherlands agreed to participate[54]. At their meeting in Paris on 11 November 1949, Acheson told Bevin and Schuman that in addition to the ExImBank loan, the American government had given the Yugoslavs another $13 million credit, partly for the purchase of raw materials. The IBRD had in the meantime also given Belgrade two loans of $3 and $6 million. On 1 March 1950 the ExImBank approved the $20 million credit to Yugoslavia[55]. This then was the second ExImBank credit, following the $20 million of September 1949.

Conditional Aid? The End of Yugoslav Involvement in the Greek Civil War

The British rejected the notion that political "strings" should be attached to a credit to Yugoslavia, being acutely aware of Tito's touchiness on interference in the conducting of his country's foreign and domestic policy. Not only had this been one of the major points of disagreement with the Communist Party of the Soviet Union[56], but the British also felt that any evidence of Yugoslav yielding to political pressure from the West "could only make things more difficult for Tito" in the context of Cominform propaganda and his domestic credibility[57].

This is not to say, however, that the British made any bones about letting the Yugoslavs know what they disliked about their policies. Thus on 18 February 1949 Bevin talked to Dr. Bebler, who was in London attending a conference; Bevin told Bebler that he "wished the Yugoslavs would leave Greece alone". He also tried to dissuade Bebler from being adamant about Yugoslav claims to parts of Carinthia and their interest in Northern Epirus[58]. In this conversation, however, credits or economic relations were not mentioned.

According to Western information, Yugoslav aid to the

Greek guerrilla forces had not ceased. Although the United Nations Special Committee on the Balkans (UNSCOB) had reported that Yugoslav deliveries to the Greek rebels had decreased, it still had proof on 20 April 1949 "that Yugoslavia as well as Albania and Bulgaria" were helping them[59]. And this was a point of great concern to both the British and the Americans, who from the first days after the split were interested in the possibility of "clear[ing] up the situation in Greece"[60], as Bevin stated at a Cabinet meeting on 8 July 1948.

The closest the British ever got to exerting economic pressure, in the form of the "carrot" of credits rather than any "stick", was the visit to Yugoslavia of Fitzroy Maclean, who had been a British liaison officer with Tito's Partisans in the war and had become a personal friend of Tito. Unofficial though it was (the visit had been proposed by Maclean), Bevin telegraphed to Peake on 26 April 1949 that

> advantage might be taken of Mr. Maclean's visit . . . to hint to Tito that, if he still wished to receive economic support, it will be in his interest to give us some help in return; that there are ways in which he could help us without prejudicing his position among his Communist followers or vis-à-vis the Russians; and that one obvious example is the adoption of a policy of 'go slow' or complete unco-operativeness towards the Greek rebels.[61]

Yet already before the Tito-Maclean interview Bevin had stated that his government was "prepared in principle to the grant of a credit if political considerations warrant it"[62].

On 5 May 1949, Maclean explained to Tito that the West had regarded Yugoslavia "as a not unimportant part in the machinery of Soviet aggression and expansion", describing which Yugoslav actions had given them this impression. But he stated that the United Kingdom had no intention of luring Yugoslavia into the Western camp, or of interfering with Yugoslavia's internal affairs[63]. When the subject of Greece was brought up, Tito gave Maclean "an undertaking that the Yugoslav government would not in future allow rebels who crossed the frontier to return to Greece to fight, and no other help would be given to the rebels"[64]. Soon afterwards, Bevin had evidence that Tito was keeping his word[65].

Although Truman had approved NSC 18's advocacy of extreme circumspection in trying to effect changes in Yugoslav policies[66] (see Chapter 2), this decision was not always adhered to. Admittedly, the Americans were led to expect a change in Yugoslav policies in respect of Greece as early as 6 July 1948, when a Yugoslav official wandered into the US embassy and simply stated that his government "was extremely anxious to liquidate the Greek situation as soon as possible"[67]. When the US Special Representative in Europe, Averell Harriman, in July 1948 advocated that the US should offer aid to Yugoslavia, he thought that this should be done in exchange for a cessation of Yugoslav aid to Greece[68]. This condition was also urged by the American Ambassador in London, Douglas[69]. Cannon in Belgrade and Kohler in Moscow, however, advised against any attempt to use economic help to bargain for political concessions, as they expected this would create resentment on the side of the Yugoslavs[70].

NSC 18/2 of 17 February 1949 confirmed that US policy should continue to be one of not attempting to extract specific political commitments from Tito. And yet it was decided that Cannon should "exert sufficient pressure on [Tito] to the end that he shall abandon his assistance to the Greek guerillas", making it clear that this was the condition for US help to sanitize his economy[71]. Mainly because of this Llewellyn Thompson, the Deputy Director of the Office for European Affairs in the State Department, expressed his concern at the British plan of concluding a long-term trade agreement: he thought the Western powers should not commit themselves in the long term so that they could threaten to cut off aid if the Yugoslavs decided not to leave Greece alone[72]. Anthony Rumbold of the British Foreign Office observed that "the State Department have been slower than we have in coming round to the view that Tito must be given economic help without the exaction of absolutely binding assurances about his behaviour towards Greece"[73]. The British embassy in Washington knew that the State Department had instructed Cannon in Belgrade to

> do his best to keep up continual pressure on Jugoslav authorities in order to secure the implementation of the new policy [towards Greece]. In addition they suggest that Mr Cannon should take such opportunities as occur

to him to stress to the Jugoslavs the advantages of a Jugoslav-Greek rapprochement.[74]

In spite of NSC 18 and NSC 18/2, the State Department thus favoured a policy that made the linkage between aid and political conditions much more explicit than the British regarded as wise[75].

Western Mediation Between Greece and Yugoslavia

In 1949 the Western powers regarded as a matter of urgency the lasting conclusion of the Greek Civil War and the pacification of the area of South East Europe, the Balkan tinderbox. As we have seen, the Yugoslavs were still helping the Greek rebels at the beginning of that year. But the Greek rebel forces were led by pro-Cominformist Zachariades and no longer by pro-Titoist Markos; therefore the Yugoslavs had every reason to withdraw their support. If they were slow to notice this, Western diplomats certainly pointed it out to them[76]. On 25 January 1949 Peake, who was on increasingly good terms with Bebler, asked him whether his government intended to establish contact with the Greek government. Bebler explained that there had indeed been some thoughts in this direction, but he gave Peake to understand that internal pressures within the Communist Party of Yugoslavia had forced them to abandon this project[77]. Possibly at Peake's instigation, the Yugoslavs did attempt a secret *prise de contact* with the Greeks some time in March 1949[78].

Nothing came of it, however, as the Greek Foreign Minister, Tsaldaris, blew the gaff in a talk with the correspondent of the Daily Mail, Alexander Clifford, claiming "that Greece might be allied with Marshal Tito within a year". This of course played into the hands of the Cominform propagandists: they immediately interpreted this episode as a sign that Yugoslavia had gone over to the Western camp entirely[79]. This lack of discretion on the part of Tsaldaris led the Yugoslavs to distrust him subsequently[80]. Tsaldaris added insult to injury when later that year he gave a dinner in New York for the exiled King of Yugoslavia[81]. Yet as we have seen Tito had told Fitzroy Maclean in private in May[82], and stated publicly on 10 July

1949 in Pula that the Graeco-Yugoslav frontier was closed. Bebler admitted to Peake that "his government was sick and tired of supporting a rabble of Greek refugees of whom they were only too anxious to be rid"[83].

Following the announcement at Pula, Acheson ordered his ambassador in Belgrade to tell the Yugoslavs that his government hoped this would be followed by the re-establishment of "good-neighborly relations" with Greece, this "traditionally friendly State"[84]. Cannon was also given directives to sound out Yugoslav interest in the re-opening of the Graeco-Yugoslav railway line to Salonika, and the Yugoslav free port at its head. The Greeks liked the idea[85]. Cannon and his British colleague, Peake, did indeed take the matter up with various members of the Yugoslav Foreign Ministry[86], but without applying quite as much pressure as Acheson recommended — the Foreign Office in their instructions to Peake had pointed out the dangers of pushing the Yugoslavs too hard. They argued that the Yugoslavs had already gone a long way towards meeting Western demands[87].

In the early spring of 1949 the Athens and Belgrade governments shared a fear that trouble might arise from a possible proclamation of an independent Macedonia[88], but the issue of Macedonia suddenly turned into a dividing factor towards the end of the year. The problem arose from criticism in the Yugoslav press and radio of the treatment the Aegean (Greek) Macedonians received at the hands of the Greek government. Sir Clifford Norton, the British Ambassador in Athens, explained that "in order to defend his position in Vardar [Yugoslav] Macedonia against Bulgarian propaganda, Marshal Tito has to represent himself as the champion of all Macedonians elsewhere." Tito therefore had to tolerate the nationalist outbursts of the Yugoslav Macedonian Communist leaders that were reponsible for the press statements[89]. But these people dealt with refugees from Greek Macedonia, people who had left their own country because they felt persecuted, and consequently they must have been convinced that their countrymen in Greece were being ill-treated[90].

Yugoslav protests naturally alienated the Greek government and throughout the next year and a half provided the greatest obstacle on the road to a normalization of Graeco-Yugoslav relations. The re-opening of the railway line to Salonika was therefore delayed, much to the disadvantage of Yugoslavia, even though there were reports that it was technically intact as early as 16 December 1949[91].

Another unsolved consequence of the Greek Civil War was that some Greek children were still in Yugoslavia (and in many other satellite countries). They had been abducted or taken there by their parents. This was a rather emotional issue for the Greeks, but after some initial uncertainty as to how to proceed, and after some Western efforts to mediate[92], the Yugoslav government showed their willingness to co-operate.

Thus next to the Macedonian problem, the major stumbling-block on Yugoslavia's road to an *entente* with Greece remained the Yugoslav aversion to Tsaldaris[93]. In late 1949 the Greek Ambassador in London, Melas, talked to Bateman in the Foreign Office, and asked him to let the British Ambassador in Belgrade mediate between Greece and Yugoslavia. Melas indicated that his own government was not yet ready to make the first step itself[94]. At the same time the Greeks asked the French to act as go-between, claiming that France was "mieux placé que les Etats-Unis et l'Angleterre pour jouer le rôle d'intermédiaire"[95]. Conscious of the Yugoslav dislike of Tsaldaris, the Foreign Office thought the time to act had come when in early January 1950 a caretaker government with Pipinellis at the Ministry of Foreign Affairs replaced the Tsaldaris government for a month before general elections were to take place. On 18 January 1950 Hector McNeil therefore authorized a proposal addressed to the Americans and the French concerning mediation between Belgrade and Athens, to be undertaken by the British ambassadors[96]. This time it was the Americans who proved to be opposed to any further pressure on Yugoslavia. Nor were the French enthusiastic[97]: their Ambassador in Belgrade, Jean Payart, was under the impression that the Yugoslavs did not want to move before the next Greek election, regardless of its possible outcome[98]. Although no specific *démarche* was thus made, a certain amount of pressure was kept up by the Western powers, and the matter of Graeco-Yugoslav relations was taken up informally on various occasions[99]. As a result both the Greeks and the Yugoslavs madesome half-hearted, unsuccessful attempts to start talks[100].

Then between 19 and 22 March 1950 George Allen, Cannon's successor in Belgrade, visited Athens[101], and talked to officials and politicians of various political parties. He was handicapped by the great uncertainty as to whose word counted in Athens, due to the frequent changes in government[102]. Therefore Allen's visit bore little fruit, while giving rise to a *Pravda* article of 28 March 1950 on an "Athens-Belgrade 'axis', i.e. . . . a military-political alliance between Tito's police-gestapo Yugoslavia and monarcho-Fascist Greece"[103], at a time when Yugoslavia and Greece had not even exchanged ministers. Allen's initiative therefore earned him some criticism within the State Department[104].

But Western pressure did seem to have some measure of success: by 11 April 1950 Tito had made a confidential approach to General Plastiras, the Yugoslav favourite among the candidates for the Greek Prime Ministry. Plastiras indeed became Prime Minister on 20 April, and a large sector of the Greek press claimed that this was due to Western pressure[105], which probably was the case[106]. On 22 April 1950 the Yugoslavs even proposed the exchange of Ministers[107].

In mid-May the rapprochement experienced another crucial setback, however, again over the Macedonian issue[108]. Once more the Belgrade government could not risk an attempt to restrain the Yugoslav Macedonians, whose critical statements were angering the Greeks. Proof that the Yugoslav Federal government was keen on better co-operation with Athens was the announcement of 21 May of the name of a Yugoslav Minister to Greece[109]. In the view of the British embassy in Belgrade, there were

> two main reasons why the [Yugoslav] propaganda cannot now drop all the ancient Slav claims on the Macedonian issues. To do so would, in the first place, leave the field wide open to Bulgarian propagandists. . . . In the second place it would undoubtedly cause discontent among the leaders of the Macedonian Republic, and might well encourage them in the suspicion that Marshal Tito had indeed sold out to the West.[110]

This was also explained by Kardelj and Tito to Philip Noel Baker, the British Cabinet Minister, who visited Yugoslavia in August 1950: they said that Yugoslav failure to stand up for Macedonian rights would be used by the Cominform "to make all the Slav speaking people in Greece look to Bulgaria. . . .

Moreover, the Cominform would have strongly attacked the Yugoslav government if its spokesmen had kept silent on the subject in the foreign affairs committee [of the National Assembly]."[111] The issue delayed the exchange of Ministers, while the British and the Americans urged both sides to put the Macedonian question on ice[112].

The outbreak of the Korean War gave added strength to already existing fears of Communist aggression in the Balkans (see Chapter 5). This probably led to a shift in Yugoslav priorities: after the attack on South Korea, no mention of the Greek-Macedonian problem was found for a while in the Yugoslav press[113]. But pride and the considerations of domestic politics still prevented both sides from taking the first step. Now it was once more the Britsh who endeavoured to break the impasse urging both governments to overcome their reserve[114]; and some stumbling-blocks were certainly overcome due to Sir Charles Peake's relentless efforts[115]. Further attempts to talk reason to both sides were marked during the visit to Greece and Yugoslavia of Noel Baker, whose family's long and distinguished tradition as Hellenophiles gave him a special concern for this area. Tito and Kardelj told him that they wished to re-establish normal relations. Beyond desiring economic and traffic links, they thought that "with a potential danger of war it was desirable that they should be relieved of anxiety about their frontier with one of their neighbours"[116].

Then followed a visit by the Parliamentary Under-Secretary of State in the House of Commons, Ernest Davies. Bevin's instructions were now that in the matter of the Yugoslav-Greek rapprochement, "we should try to bring things to a head"[117]. Davies therefore set out on his tour of Italy, Greece, Yugoslavia and Austria, hoping to facilitate the resolution of the differences between these countries. He hoped to help align them "with the Western democracies to preserve their independence and participation in the Western alliance, of which Rome alone was at the time a member. The closer their relations could be soldered the better would they be able to resist Russian expansionism."[118]

Davies went to Athens before he went on to Belgrade. On 16 August 1950 he talked to the Greek Prime Minister, General Plastiras, and to the Under-Secretary of State for Foreign Affairs, Politis. Both expressed their anxiety to improve relations with Yugoslavia. Davies agreed to act as a courier carrying a secret proposal from Politis to the Yugoslav government regarding a Yugoslav declaration of disinterest in Greek Macedonia. With Bevin's approval[119] he took up the problem with Kardelj two days later in Belgrade. But in the meantime the Plastiras government had fallen, much to the regret of the Yugoslavs[120]. They were now less willing to be conciliatory: Kardelj refused to consider any statement of Yugoslav disinterest. Peake speculated that the presence at the interview of Vukmanović-Tempo, who was the most anti-Western member of the Yugoslav government, and of Vladimir Dedijer, equally considered as a hard-liner, had forced Kardelj into this uncompromising stance[121]. Forcing the issue, Davies made a statement at a press conference, saying that the present Yugoslav-Greek quarrel over Macedonia had arisen from a Greek misunderstanding of Yugoslav utterances. Unfortunately, Politis, who had survived in office the demise of the Plastiras government, made a public denial of this[122]. Therefore Davies failed to obtain any concessions on the issue of Macedonia in Belgrade[123], other than the agreement that both countries might make a statement of non-interference in each other's affairs once Ministers had been exchanged[124].

These British efforts were being watched with some jealousy by the French Ambassador in Athens, de Vaux St. Cyr, who told the Quai d'Orsay that the US Chargé d'Affaires, Minor, called all the visiting British Ministers "'busy bodies', à savoir les gens qui éprouvent le besoin irrésistible de toujours faire quelquechose, fût-ce à tort et à travers, et ne comprennent pas qu'il peut y avoir avantage à laisser mûrir une question dans la silence"[125].

There were further bickerings between the Greeks and the Yugoslavs, such as the vote cast by the Yugoslav representative at the UN on 30 August 1950 in favour of the Soviet motion condemning the "reign of terror" in Greece[126]. The British continued to take advantage of every talk in Belgrade or Athens or London with either the Yugoslavs or the Greeks to try to persuade them to swallow their pride and go ahead with the exchange of Ministers[127], and the American Ambassador, Allen, likewise did not cease to urge his government to try to act as a catalyst for a Graeco-Yugoslav *entent*. He thought that "If Cominform should attack either Greece or Yugoslavia, absence of even telegraphic communications between these two neighbouring countries will be tragic"[128].

Nevertheless, the impasse between Greece and Yugoslavia only became unstuck in November 1950, when the Yugoslavs returned some Greek prisoners of war, and some of the Greek children. On 30 November Venizelos, the head of the Greek government, announced the imminent exchange of Ministers[129]. Yugoslav-Greek postal services were only resumed on 15 February 1951, and the first Simplon-Orient express, re-routed to avoid Bulgaria, passed through Greece to Yugoslavia on 17 March 1951[130].

Although the story of Western attempts to reconcile Greece and Yugoslavia does not sound very successful, one must bear in mind that in spite of all the setbacks mentioned here, it only took a total of a year and a half from the closure of the frontier until the exchange of Ministers, which cleared the way for the defence co-operation (see Chapter 6). After seven years of enmity, the transformation to normal diplomatic relations thus took comparatively little time. The reconciliation was certainly hastened by the efforts of the Western powers, and in this case particularly, of Ernest Davies and Sir Charles Peake.

Political Issues between the Western Powers and Yugoslavia

The Recognition of Ho Chi Minh

Although there was thus a linkage between the end of Yugoslav involvement in the Greek Civil War and Western aid, this was never explicitly made a condition by the Western powers. In the opinion of Reams in Belgrade, any improvement in the Yugoslav attitude towards the US had been made possible largely "by our policy of not demanding political concessions while [the] Yugoslav government has [its] back against the wall."[131]

The Western powers' determination to continue with this policy was shaken when they found out in early February 1950 that Yugoslavia was considering the recognition of Ho Chi Minh, following the USSR's recognition on 31 January 1950. This alienated the French and had effects on their attitude towards extending credits to Yugoslavia[132]. Acheson was also taken aback: "Sov recognition of Ho in present circumstances [is] clearly designed [to] further Commie expansionist aims. Recognition by Yugo wld [*sic*] strengthen [the] very forces against which it is fighting for its own independence." Such a gratuitous gesture on the part of Yugoslavia only served to offend the Western powers. "We do not wish [to] make direct threats [against] Yugo Govt but you should use as much of foregoing [arguments] as necessary to ensure they clearly understand seriousness of obstacles which Yugo recognition of Ho wld [*sic*] create."[133]

A different view was held by John Paton Davies, an expert on the Far East and a member of the Policy Planning Staff. In a memorandum of 8 February 1950 to the new Director of the PPS, Paul Nitze, he argued that it might actually be in the interest of the US if Yugoslavia established contacts with Ho's régime, while recognition of Bao Dai would put Yugoslavia further into the "imperialist camp"[134]. Davies was one of the principal advocates of establishing diplomatic relations with Communist China, hoping that this would make possible the political distancing of China from the USSR[135].

Yet Acheson continued to take the line that a Yugoslav recognition of Ho Chi Minh would have nothing but disadvantageous consequences[136], and on his instructions the American embassy's First Secretary, Fowler, was sent to the Yugoslavs to explain "that recognition [of] Ho would not fail to affect attitude of many Americans toward economic assistance to Yugoslavia". But this move did not go down well with the Yugoslavs:

> Tito clearly interpreted this to be pressure on Yugoslav government and he took [the] occasion to let us know that he would not countenance pressure from US. . . . It is obvious that Tito has been angered by [the] implication that US attitude toward economic assistance will be affected by Yugoslav action re [*sic*] recognition [of] Ho Chi Minh. He has taken this occasion to let us and Cominform know forcefully that he will not allow interference from any quarter.

Tito vented his anger publicly at a speech at Uzice on 18 February 1950[137].

Yet Acheson and the State Department decided in the end that this should not affect American relations with Yugoslavia. As Acheson explained: "While we strongly disapprove Yugo [*sic*] recognition of Ho and so informed them in advance, we consider [that our] policy toward Tito must be realistic based on advantage we can derive from his heresy and not on approval or disapproval." He therefore tactfully delayed the announcement of the ExImBank credit of $ 20 million, but did not cancel it[138]. On 16 March 1950 Tito explained to George Allen that as Ho had requested Yugoslav recognition, the Yugoslav government had had no alternative but to extend it, as "it hoped to maintain its position with the 'progressive forces of the world'"[139]. Edvard Kardelj, the Yugoslav Minister of Foreign Affairs, warned Allen that if US political conditions were accepted by the Yugoslavs, this would be a victory for the USSR who could then show evidence that Yugoslavia, by leaving the Socialist camp, had been forced to submit to Western dictates[140]. On the issue of the recognition of Ho Chi Minh, and on the closing of the frontier to the Greek rebels, which will be discussed again presently, we thus find that Stephen Markovich's analysis holds: the Yugoslavs acted according to American wishes only if they had their own particular reasons for also aiming at the American goal. On the other hand, "when[ever] Yugoslav and American goals or interpretations differed, the United States had little success in using aid to restrain Yugoslavia from following a policy opposed by the United States"[141]. This was true for the Yugoslav attitude over Carinthia.

Carinthia

Yugoslavia's claims to Austrian Carinthia dated back from the end of the Second World War and had constantly been opposed by the Western powers, while Tito had had some rather lukewarm support from the USSR in this matter[142]. The Yugoslav claims were based on ethnic grounds and concerned an area of 210 square kilometres with a population of about 9,000, who were mostly Slovenes. The Yugoslav government was particularly interested in two power stations on the River Drava that had been constructed in the National Socialist era. The negotiations about these Yugoslav claims had been interrupted in May 1948 and were only resumed early in 1949. On 18 February 1949 Dr. Bebler, who was in London for the talks concerning the Austrian Peace Treaty, called on Bevin to obtain from him a promise to support Yugoslav claims in principle, but Bevin very firmly refused to comply. On his instructions, however, Bebler was later told that the UK would support Yugoslavia in pressing for certain rights for the Slovenes short of autonomy[143].

Bebler made a similarly unsuccessful approach to the US Deputy for Austria on the Council of Foreign Ministers, Reber[144]. Like Bevin, Acheson was opposed to any agreement in principle on a plebiscite or territorial concessions[145]. The French were mainly interested in a swift settlement of the Austrian peace treaty[146]. Surprisingly, the Soviet delegate, Zarubin, was backing the Yugoslav claim[147]: this was interpreted by Reber and by Bevin as a ploy "to attempt further to increase breach between Tito and West", knowing full well that the Western powers opposed any frontier changes[148]. In June 1949, however, with the Paris preliminary agreement on Austria, the Soviets gave up their support for the Yugoslav claim, in return for Western concessions in the question of ex-German property in Austria, which was settled mainly in the interest of the USSR[149].

By mid-1949 the Yugoslavs found that the problem of Carinthia had become irrelevant in comparison with the threat posed to their country by the Soviet Union, as they perceived it, as Dr. Bebler admitted to Reber on 3 October 1949: the Yugoslavs were simply anxious to effect the "withdrawal of Soviet troops from Austria and consequently from Hungary and Rumania" where Soviet troops were only allowed, under the peace treaty regulations, as long as they were necessary for the supply of troops in Austria[150]. The growth of Soviet-Yugoslav tensions will be discussed in the following chapter; it is thus clear that the Yugoslav backing down on the issue of Carinthia was not a result of Western pressure, but due solely to separate Yugoslav interests.

Stepinac

In questions concerning Yugoslav domestic affairs, the Western governments were more reluctant to make their own wishes a condition of an improvement of their relations with Belgrade. Alois Stepinac, the Archbishop of Zagreb, had been imprisoned by the Yugoslav Communist government in 1947 for collaborating with the Italians and Fascist Croats during the Second World War. The American House of Representatives was reminded of this in the context of the arrest, trial and conviction of Jósef Cardinal Mindszenty in Hungary in 1949, and it passed a condemnation of both governments, regarding the sentences as evidence of anti-religious measures. Acheson thought that if the Yugoslav government now were to make the gesture of releasing Stepinac, this would show them in a better light than the Hungarians and help to make Congress aware of the differences between Yugoslavia and the Soviet orbit[151]. When asked to comment, Cannon advised against such a suggestion, explaining that the roots of the conflict between the Communist government and Stepinac lay deep in the wartime fratricidal feuds and were such that it was most inadvisable to meddle in this affair. Besides offending Belgrade, forcing Tito to give in on this issue at this particular time would weaken his position internally[152]. Gowen, the US representative in the Vatican City, thought that nothing less than freedom and the right to resume his work in Zagreb would satisfy Stepinac and the Vatican[153].

The Roman Catholic Church was at this stage so bitterly opposed to Tito's government that this would have meant allowing Stepinac to use his archiepiscopacy as a platform for anti-Communist diatribes. It is difficult to see which side was more to be blamed in this period for the poor relations between the Catholic Church and the Belgrade government, the Catholic clergy, or the Communist régime. Nevertheless, the question of Stepinac's fate and similar issues continued to be raised with Tito on various occasions by the Western ambassadors[154].

Trieste

Throughout this six-year period, the most important obstacle to closer relations between the Western powers (and Italy) on the one hand and Yugoslavia on the other was the issue of Trieste. The fate of this city and its hinterland was of concern not only to the Italians, but also to the British and the Americans, who had had their forces stationed there since 1945. The city had acquired potential importance for the defence of Western Europe against the Soviet bloc; but now that Yugoslavia was no longer an integral member of this bloc, it had become more promising to negotiate an agreement with the Rome and Belgrade governments on this issue, so as to remove this stumbling-block on the way to a reconciliation of these two Adriatic neighbours.

The same complex diplomatic games were played by the Soviet Union's foreign policy-makers when it came to negotiating the solution of this problem[155], as we have found in the Carinthian question, and could be observed in other cases[156]. Immediately before the Cominform-Tito split, Britain, France and the United States had approached the governments of the USSR and Italy to suggest that the Free Territory of Trieste (i.e. the area occupied by Anglo-American forces) should be placed under Italian sovereignty. By making this proposal, the Western powers wanted to anticipate a similar suggestion from the USSR, which seemed to be in the offing: both the Western powers and the Soviet Union were fighting for the Italian electorate in view of the elections of the spring of 1948, in which the coalition between the Communists and Nenni-Socialists stood a very real chance to win an overall majority[157]. Yugoslav objections, however, made an outright Soviet acceptance of the scheme impossible[158]. The Soviet government could not appeal to the Yugoslav population to overthrow Tito and his friends[159] if at the same time it betrayed Yugoslav national interest and pride by advocating a settlement of Trieste in favour of Italy.

The controversy cooled for some time after the Tito-Stalin split. Throughout the period of 1945 to 1953, very little changed regarding the two sides' claims, except that measures on both sides deepened the political and administrative division of the territory. Nevertheless, it clearly remained a Western aim to persuade the Yugoslavs to give up their claims to the city of Trieste, as an Italo-Yugoslav reconciliation was impossible without a settlement.

4

The Perceived Threat to Yugoslavia in the Context of her Importance for Western Military Planning before Korea

Yugoslavia Threatened by War?

When Yugoslavia was expelled from the Cominform, it was feared in Washington and London[1], that this excommunication would be followed by an invasion by the Soviet Union. Between April and June 1948 the Yugoslav government took defensive measures which seem to indicate that they, too, feared an attack; for example, the army was kept in a state of alert from early April onwards[2]. On the day of the publication of the Cominform communiqué, the American Chargé in Belgrade, Reams, and the Military and Naval Attachés pointed out to their government that "Tito could not, of course, withstand Soviet invasion" unless he received "major help from West"[3]. American Army intelligence thought an outbreak of war fairly likely[4]. This raised the question of how the Western powers should react if this happened.

US embassy officials in Belgrade assumed prematurely that their government would send troops to help Yugoslavia if she were attacked by the Red Army[5]. The American Special Representative in Europe, Averell Harriman, argued in July 1948 that Yugoslavia should be given military supplies if attacked, and perhaps two shiploads of arms should be sent straight away[6]. But when no invasion of Yugoslavia materialized in the following months, the question of a Western response remained undecided.

Until the eve of the Korean War Western estimates as to the likelihood of an attack on Yugoslavia varied considerably, depending on rumours, planted disinformation and guesses about Soviet intentions. They all agreed, however, that the

103

Soviet Union was extremely unlikely to launch a global war; nor was Stalin thought to plan anything that would obviously entail the risk of war with the West[7]. A CIA report to the US President, dating from 3 May 1949, concluded that the USSR was "unlikely . . . to resort to even localized direct military action, except possibly with respect to Finland and Yugoslavia"[8]. Because the British and the Americans were convinced "that the Russians are determined one way or another to liquidate the Tito régime"[9], it could never be ruled out that this might take the form of military action.

The British and the Americans hoped that the Yugoslavs would take the whole issue to the UN to give it a public airing[10]. This proposal was put to the Yugoslav Vice-Minister of Foreign Affairs, Dr. Aleš Bebler, by Sir Charles Peake, on 28 August 1949[11]. It is possible that this sparked off the Yugoslav wish to be elected into the Security Council although this was not what the British had in mind. Both plans, however, were derived from the fear of Soviet intentions regarding Yugoslavia.

The Macedonian Problem

Beyond exerting economic pressure, beyond encouraging the Yugoslav population to overthrow the government, and short of a full-scale invasion, the most important option for Stalin in his attempt to bring down the "Tito clique" in late 1948 and early 1949, was to use Macedonia as a lever to break up the Yugoslav federal state. The Macedonians, whose territory was divided into three parts now respectively belonging to Yugoslavia, Bulgaria and Greece, had been given hopes for a united Macedonian state within the Balkan Federation planned in 1947-48 by Tito and Dimitrov. These had been disappointed when the Yugoslav-Cominform dispute made such a federation impossible, and when the end of the Greek Civil War consolidated the northern frontiers of Greece.

In the "period of diversity" (1945-47), Stalin had allowed the Communist parties of the satellites a considerable amount of leeway (see Chapter 1). This had also been true, as Elisabeth Barker has argued, for Stalin's attitude towards the various Macedonian Communist parties[12]. For this reason Tito and Dimitrov had been able to further their own plans for a federation in this area. After June 1948, however, the Communist Party (CP) of Bulgaria meekly followed Stalin's line, and influenced the Pirin (Bulgarian) Macedonians to join the rest of the satellite CPs in their campaign against Tito. At the 5th Congress of the Bulgarian CP, on 19 December 1948, Dimitrov denounced what he described as Yugoslav attempts to incorporate Pirin Macedonia into Yugoslavia[13].

The Greek aspect of the Macedonian problem was complex. In return for Yugoslav aid to the Greek rebels, the latter had been forced to allow Tito's Vardar Macedonian Communists to work among the Greek Macedonians in the areas close to the Yugoslav borders. But then the pro-Titoist Greek rebel leader Markos Vaphiades was replaced by pro-Cominformist Zachariades, and from March 1949 the Greek Macedonian Communists, at the behest of the Cominform[14], advocated the establishment of a united, independent Macedonia[15]. On the one hand they thus tried to appear as the representatives of all Macedonians; and by proclaiming that it was in the national interest of all Macedonians to be united, they challenged the loyalty of the Vardar (Yugoslav) Macedonians to the Belgrade government, which could no longer hold out this possibility. On the other hand, the Greek Macedonian Communists made their own position within Greece very difficult with this separatist stance; the Greek CP lost a considerable amount of support by advocating the cession of parts of their country to such a new state[16], particularly as this was associated by their enemies with efforts "to reconstitute 'greater Bulgaria'" by placing Greek Macedonia "under Bulgarian rule"[17].

The sole aim of this policy of the Bulgarian, the Greek Macedonian and the Greek Communists, in the opinion of Western observers, was to create trouble for the Belgrade government[18], or even to break up the Yugoslav federation, aided by the staging of frontier incidents on Yugoslavia's Hungarian and Albanian borders, as directed by Cominform. "Our thinking on [the] basis [of] evidence available here inclines to theory that major Cominform political effort could come through Macedonia and that reorganized Greek guerillas and Slavo-Macedonians have been selected as primary agents," as the American Ambassador, Cavendish Cannon, wrote on 8 March 1949[19]. The proclamation of an independent Macedonian state was thought possible by many, and according to some rumours it was planned for 15 March[20].

The Greek Ministry of Foreign Affairs considered asking the Western powers to protest officially in Sofia and Tirana, should this proclamation be made[21]. Cannon proposed a pact between Greece and her northern neighbours in recognition of all frontiers as they stood then[22], which would have made it very difficult for the Bulgarian government to recognize a self-proclaimed Macedonian state afterwards. Moreover, it would have drawn the attention of the United Nations to this area, and it would have prevented the Soviet leaders from making the erroneous assumption that Macedonia was an area of no concern to other powers[23]. It is worth noting that in the following year a similar erroneous assumption on the part of some Communist leaders about a Western lack of interest in certain areas of the world resulted in the Korean War.

These propositions were not followed up, but the British and the American governments tried to help the Yugoslavs in a different way. It was thought that the "tranquillisation of Greece's northern frontier would tend to alleviate the threat to Tito from Macedonia and enable him better to meet Eastern pressure". Therefore, in negotiations between Rusk (for the US), McNeil (for the United Kingdom) and Gromyko (for the Soviet Union) in the spring of 1949, the two Western statesmen pressed Gromyko to work for the ending of the Greek Civil War[24] (neither the State Department nor the Foreign Office had as yet understood that Stalin had never given the Greek Communists any real support).

But the Yugoslav leaders themselves strove to prevent a separatist movement from gaining ground among the Yugoslav Macedonians: they were granted more privileges than the populations of any other region. The Belgrade government let the Macedonians get away with severe propaganda attacks on the Greek government, even though Tito wanted a rapprochement with Greece (cf. Chapter 3). Another measure was the establishment, soon after the split with the Cominform, of a separate (Yugoslav) Macedonian CP, which held its own congress at Skopje in December 1948. Hilary King, the British Consul in Skopje, explained that this "took the wind out of the sails of the Bulgarian Communists, who until then had been in a good position to play on the anti-Serb, and therefore anti-Jugoslav feelings by declaring that the Partisan Movement in Macedonia was 'run by the Serbs'"[25]. At this congress, all opposition to the Yugoslav central government was denounced as reactionary or else as inspired by the Sofia government's ambitions to create a Greater Bulgaria[26]. It seems that these measures were successful as there was no serious uprising[27]. Indeed, by 20 June 1949 the CIA thought the proclamation of an independent Macedonia highly unlikely in the immediate future, and they estimated that it would have but little support among Macedonian Yugoslavs[28].

Nevertheless, the CIA continued to regard the initiation of a guerrilla war under the pretext of a nationalist Macedonian uprising as possible, as we shall see. It was thus Western concern about this possibility (perhaps due more to pessimistic appreciations of Balkan affairs made in Western capitals, than to observations made locally) that kept the question of Western reactions open. All three Western powers showed their concern at the highest level. The French President, Vincent Auriol, recorded in his diary on 19 February 1949 some information he had received about a Soviet plan to create a corridor between Cominformist Bulgaria and Albania by proclaiming a Cominformist independent Macedonia[29]. On 23 March 1949 the Policy Planning Staff (PPS) agreed to a suggestion by Dean Rusk, Deputy Under-Secretary of State, that a review of NSC 18/2 should be undertaken: "In view of this potentially explosive situation in Macedonia it is believed urgent consideration should be given to the position which the U.S. should assume if such events materialize, especially with respect to what arms and munitions Tito might need from outside under various contingencies."[30] On 1 July 1949 a new State Department policy statement recommended that the "Macedonian question, which has now emerged through Kremlin instigation as a trouble spot of importance involving Bulgaria, Greece and Yugoslavia", should be watched carefully[31]. Until the end of the year, Western diplomats and intelligence services continued to see a "threat to Tito's position" in the form of "a Stalinist coup or Macedonian insurrection", if it was thought in the Kremlin that there would be no risk of Western intervention[32].

Western Public Statements to Deter Aggression

On top of this, in July and August 1949, a war of diplomatic notes broke out for trivial reasons between the Yugoslav and Soviet governments, resulting in a considerable increase in tensions[33]. One of the Soviet notes, that of 11 August 1949, ominously threatened that the Soviet Union would proceed to "other more effective means" if they were not satisfied on various points (such as the question of the arrest of former Soviet citizens)[34]. This ambiguous wording, together with troop movements in the Soviet satellite area[35] could either be interpreted as a further aspect of the war of nerves, or else as the threat of action. This could mean anything, in the opinion of the Foreign Office, from the support for guerrilla warfare, to a full-scale invasion[36] — an estimate reflecting just the uncertainty Stalin doubtlessly wanted to create at least in the minds of the Yugoslavs.

The latter, it was thought in the West[37], would not take place as long as the Soviets were aware that they might seriously risk precipitating a world war. In order to create this awareness, the British Ambassador in Moscow, Kelly, suggested a démarche to the Soviet government by the "United Kingdom, United States and French governments seeking elucidation of the phrase [in the Soviet note] 'more effective means'"[38]. His American colleague, Kirk, would have preferred a declaration by the US Secretary of State, or the raising of the matter in the UN Security Council[39].

Their French colleague, Chataigneau, told Kelly that "he felt Russians must have some definite plan of action and that present situation was 'turning point'". He urged that the Western powers should do something as soon as possible[40]. His apprehensions were shared by members of his Foreign Ministry in Paris; Jacques Dumaine, the head of Protocol in the Quai d'Orsay, wondered whether disaster was imminent. "[A]lways on the same spot" he mused in his diary, obviously thinking of 1914, "the inevitable scene of conflict. . . . Will the Soviets continue to watch their struggling prey, or will they now fall on her?"[41]

The Yugoslav government did not want a Western démarche at the Security Council, nor in Moscow, as that would have given the Cominformists reason to claim that Yugoslavia had become the protégé of the imperialists[42]. The proposals made by the Ambassadors in Moscow were therefore dismissed. Even so, neither Robert Schuman nor Bevin believed that the existence of the possibility of a Soviet attack on Yugoslavia could be ignored, and both felt that some action was called for[43].

At this point the British Joint Intelligence Committee reports seem to have been particularly alarmist[44], as Ernest Bevin wrote on the margin of a report of late 27 August 1949: "Unless we and U.S. say something soon I am afraid Russians will resort to arms."[45] He authorized the Minister of State, Hector McNeil, to make a statement. The opportunity arose on 28 August 1949: at a talk in his constituency in Greenock, he expressed his government's concern about what they regarded as a danger to Yugoslavia; this was publicized by the press[46].

The British embassy in Washington received instructions to suggest to the State Department that a similar statement should be made by a high-ranking American official[47]. While Kirk advised against this, Acheson asked the Assistant Secretary of State, George Perkins, whether there was any alarming news about Yugoslavia, as "Chip [Charles Bohlen, a Soviet expert] is worried that the Russians may be intending to use the armoured divisions sent to the border in Hungary and Rumania."[48] Within the following week, however, the Foreign Office and the State Department decided that the Soviet troop movements were probably part of the war of nerves against Yugoslavia[49]; nevertheless Acheson thought it right to say at a press conference on 31 August 1949 that reported movements of Soviet forces in the Balkans were being watched closely by the US[50].

Acheson's and McNeil's statements were measures taken by the Western powers to deter the Soviet Union from any action against Yugoslavia. It is difficult to say whether such action was contemplated for 1949 (see Chapter 5). But if indeed it was, these statements probably had a deterrent effect, i.e. they probably contributed to the change of heart on the part of the Soviet Union, as no attack or uprising occurred in 1949. In that case they were successfully applied Western policy decisions.

The Threat to Yugoslavia and her Election to the Security Council

On 20 September 1949 the Yugoslavs informed various

Western delegations of their decision to stand for election to one of the three Security Council seats[51] which rotated among the smaller member-states of the United Nations. They hoped that their membership of the Security Council (and the expression of world-wide support implicit in an election) would deter the Soviet attack they lived in fear of[52].

For the Western powers, this created a problem: this seat had by tacit agreement gone to one of the Soviet Union's Eastern European satellites since January 1946; on the other hand, one other seat always went to a Commonwealth country[53]. Webb, the Acting Secretary of State in the State Department, wanted to avoid any provocation of the USSR. On the following day he therefore gave the US delegation instructions to vote for Yugoslavia only if she were likely to get a majority even without the US vote; in either case they should seek to avoid giving the impression that the Americans had suggested to the Yugoslavs that they should apply for the seat[54].

On the British side, McNeil, who first dealt with the matter, was also unhappy about the Yugoslav plan, and even told Bebler as much. But the Southern Department in the Foreign Office under Sir Anthony Rumbold, the Head of the Northern Department, Sir Maurice Hankey, and the Permanent Under-Secretary, Sir William Strang, disagreed with him: in their view there *was* "a strong possibility of the Russians actually going to war"; for this reason anything that could serve as a deterrent, even Yugoslav membership of the Security Council, was desirable. Further, the Yugoslavs could make an "important contribution" on the Western side in the "propaganda war" waged in the Council, even if they might prove embarrassing on other issues. They thought the unwritten rule of electing one East European Communist country annually would be fulfilled with the election of Yugoslavia, and would not jeopardize the other Commonwealth seat. In addition, as Hankey pointed out, "China will sooner or later be a Communist member of the Security Council with a veto & it is unreasonable that Soviets bloc [*sic*] should have three votes & 2 vetoes on that body."

Peake in Belgrade came to share their view[55], but Sir Gladwyn Jebb, Assistant Under-Secretary, took McNeil's side. In his eyes, the rejection of the Eastern bloc candidate, Czechoslovakia, "would in present circumstances be a political gesture of the first magnitude and would be in the nature of sticking a large pin into the Soviet bull". Only if a large majority of UN members were to vote for Yugoslavia would he agree that it would be in the interest of Britain to jump on the bandwagon[56]. It was Jebb and McNeil who won the support of Bevin, who wanted to avoid a provocation of the Soviet Union because of "a passing event such as this dispute between two powers". He, too, feared for the second Commonwealth seat, but would not raise any objections to American support for Yugoslavia, as long as the US did not canvass for her[57].

Strang raised the issue with Attlee behind Bevin's back, but the Prime Minister thought Bevin's decision had been wise[58]. The Cabinet, consulted three weeks later, agreed with Bevin that Britain should vote for Czechoslovakia. The Yugoslavs, it was thought, should not be encouraged by Britain's support to think that they would have British backing if they embarked upon some adventurous policy in the Balkans. Bevin was prepared to compromise only if Czechoslovakia should fail to obtain the necessary two-thirds majority, in which case the British should reconsider[59].

Robert Schuman also urged caution when asked about the French attitude towards the Yugoslav candidature[60]. Initially he did not want his own government to support Yugoslavia, as he felt much like Bevin on this issue. Meanwhile, however, the Americans decided to support Yugoslavia, come what might. Disregarding the views of Bevin and Schuman, Rusk put forward the clinching argument that the lack of American support for Yugoslavia would be interpreted as weakness, following the announcement of the first atomic explosion effected by the USSR. Truman agreed with Rusk[61], although he must have been aware that this meant a conscious provocation of the Soviets: Vyshinskij, the head of the Soviet delegation, had privately warned Acheson that his government would see it in that way[62]. The American delegation thus proceeded to vote for Yugoslavia. John Hickerson, one of its members, told the Yugoslav Ambassador, Sava Kosanovic, on 27 September 1949, that although not a condition for support, the Americans would appreciate Yugoslav compliance over Greece. Kosanovic happily promised this[63].

Gradually the US delegation began to exert influence on other countries. While they continued to say that US prestige was not involved, they began lobbying and hinting at the embarrassment it would cause if Yugoslavia did not get the seat[64]. At the same time, Vyshinskij used heavy-handed methods to rally other countries to the support of Czechoslovakia, by giving a big press conference in which he denounced the Yugoslav candidature as illegal and threatened that his country would cease supporting the UN if Yugoslavia were elected[65]. Displeasure with his methods, coupled with American lobbying, eventually resulted in the election of Yugoslavia. In the first ballot she obtained 37 votes and Czechoslovakia 20. As 37 was less than the required two-thirds majority, a second ballot was held, Yugoslavia eventually winning the seat with 39 to 19 votes[66]. Whether or not the British switched votes in the end is not clear, but likely[67]. Both Australia and Canada voted for Yugoslavia in both ballots, as did France, whose government had changed their opinion[68], and, of course, the United States. Thus Yugoslavia was elected to the Security Council for the period which saw the outbreak of the Korean war.

In this case Western decision-making was influenced not only by the consideration of encouraging the Yugoslav régime in its independent stance, but a variety of other factors as well. In this example various Western policies were in conflict, and for once, the support for Yugoslavia was not the most important consideration. Nor was it thought, however, that Yugoslavia's survival depended primarily on Western support for her election to the Security Council.

Western Defence Strategy 1948-1950

Credits and trade, public statements of a mildly deterrent sort, and the Yugoslav election to the Security Council would not have been enough to stop aggression against Yugoslavia, once it had occurred. The Yugoslavs were short of arms to defend themselves, and the only potential source for them was the West. But Western decisions regarding this point cannot be considered on the basis of Western perceptions of the political benefit of Yugoslavia's survival alone: the other aspect of the importance of Yugoslavia to the West was her strategic value. This in turn can only be understood in the context of Western defence strategy at the time.

Yugoslavia's new position in world affairs directly

influenced Western defence strategy. The impact was increased by its timing: these years witnessed the most important developments in the formation of the present Western defensive system. When Yugoslavia was expelled from the Cominform, the negotiations concerning the North Atlantic Treaty, which gave the Western Union its vital backing by the US, had not yet been concluded; it was not even certain yet who the member states were going to be, apart from the Western Union countries, the US and Canada. The establishment of military organization of the North Atlantic Pact was not begun until about the time of the outbreak of the Korean War in June 1950; Greece and Turkey were not admitted as members of NATO until 1952. This was a period of considerable flux, which preceded a very lasting crystallization and factors influencing the development of the defence structure in this period had a more lasting impact than they might have had a few years earlier or later.

Italian membership of the North Atlantic Pact was initially hotly debated by the Western powers. The Americans wished it[69]. So did the French[70], who thought that the wider the geographic distribution of NATO membership, the less France would be the main battlefield[71]. The French at one point considered the question of whether the entry of Italy into NATO (or the Western Union) might have an adverse effect on Yugoslavia, but it was concluded that it was more likely to strengthen her position vis-à-vis the Soviet Union[72]. The British, however, were opposed to the inclusion of Italy in NATO, strongly doubting her ability to resist aggression; but they were overruled[73].

Yugoslavia came to play an important rôle in the issue of the defence of Italy. For although Italy signed the Atlantic Pact on 4 April 1949 as a founding member, she was not immediately integrated into Western military planning. In the absence of accessible NATO documents, our information comes only from various British and American plans. American-British-Canadian plans of 1948 did not envisage any commitment of troops to the defence of any part of Continental Europe, which had to be undertaken by local forces alone. British forces were to be withdrawn from Greece at the outbreak of any hostilities[74]. The British doubted very much whether Italy would come into a war on the side of the Allies; therefore British forces stationed in Austria were to be withdrawn to the Rhine to fight along with the (retreating) Allied occupation forces from Germany; Austria itself was considered totally indefensible. The British forces in Trieste were to be evacuated by sea and re-deployed in the Middle East, the defence of which was Britain's main priority immediately after the defence of the homeland[75]. After the initial phase of fighting withdrawal from Europe, which was expected to last a year, it was hoped that there would be a strategic counter-offensive to liberate the Continent and defeat the Soviet Union[76].

The defence aims of the first Western Union plan of 1 September 1948 were very similar. One of the assumptions was that Trieste could not be defended against aggression from Yugoslavia, which, it was thought, would take advantage of the outbreak of war to capture the city. The Italians were to be encouraged to defend at least the south of their country and sicily, if attacked, as Soviet domination of these areas would pose a threat to the Mediterranean lines of communication. The British Joint Planning Staff did not believe the Italian forces capable of more[77].

It was assumed in any case in late 1948 that Trieste could not be held against the Yugoslav attack which was still expected on the outbreak of a general war. Field Marshal Montgomery seems to have been the only one at the time who thought it could be held and turned into a bridgehead for the counter-offensive for a liberation of Europe[78], although this seems to have been a development of a strategy favoured by Churchill during the Second World War[79]. Connected with this idea of holding Trieste was that of holding on to a mountain redoubt in Tyrol in Austria. Apart from Montgomery, this idea was favoured by the French. Their High Commissioner in Austria, General Béthouard, thought that "he holds Europe who has his hands on the Austrian Alps". General Descour, Commanding General of the French occupation forces in Austria, was opposed to the evacuation of Austria in case of a Soviet attack on the West[80]. The matter was discussed at the 7th Meeting of the Western Union Chiefs of Staff Committee in London on 15 December 1948, but it was agreed that it was premature to adopt this policy; whether or not the time would be ripe for it in the following two years "would depend a good deal on political developments with regard to Italy" (i.e. whether Italy would become part of the

Western Union or the Atlantic Pact)[81]. This project was to become very important later.

Ramadier, the French Minister of War, was in favour of bringing the Italians into further defence arrangements, but Bevin squashed his proposal on 26 October 1948, protesting that it was better to operate within the small nucleus of the Brussels Treaty Powers to start with[82]. Equally, Montgomery as chairman of the Western Union Chiefs of Staff Committee, would not allow the deployment of any Western Union troops to defend Italy[83].

The American strategic planners, however, disagreed with this. In talks held in October 1948 with their British colleagues, it emerged that

> The Americans put the withdrawal of Allied Troops into Italy as first priority in order to bolster up the Italians. . .
> [A] campaign involving British and U.S. troops in Italy was regarded as a wasted effort [by the British]; to the Americans, [however] Italy was a worthwhile ally to be backed up by forces from Austria and Trieste.[84]

The Americans were "prepared to stockpile [arms] in Italy to assist in the wartime maintenance of their forces. They had not seriously considered the possibility of Italy trying to remain neutral even for the first few days of a war."[85] A compromise was found: separate plans were drawn up for the case of Italy remaining neutral and of Italy declaring her intention of joining the Allies, in which case the Allied forces from Austria and Trieste were to withdraw to Italy and to fight alongside the Italians[86].

In all these plans Greece was considered entirely indefensible. Its long northern frontier was exposed to the Soviet bloc, and the civil war was still being waged within Greece; this would have worked to the advantage of any invading Eastern bloc army. In December 1948 Yugoslavia was still listed among the allies of the USSR, and therefore Italy and *sicily* would fall, it was thought, within three months of the first attack[87]. This was also the British estimate of January and April 1949[88].

An American long-term plan of January 1949 included Italy in the line of defence. This would therefore run from the North Sea along the Rhine to the Alps and along the Piave

River in northeast Italy, then down the Adriatic, turning east above Crete, continuing due east to include the "Iskenderun Pocket" on the south coast of Turkey, following the Turco-Syrian border to include as much of Iran as possible and thence to the Himalayas. It recommended as peacetime policy the "fostering of political and economic co-operation between Yugoslavia and the non-communist nations of Western Europe, particularly Italy, with a view toward encouraging a complete break militarily from the Soviet orbit, and, as a minimum, obtaining her neutrality in case of war". Yugoslavia was considered the only one of the Communist-governed countries that *might* remain neutral[89].

It was only on 8 June 1949 that the British planners were prepared to include possible Yugoslav neutrality in their defensive strategy[90]. This was done in connection with a theatre-defence plan for the Mediterranean, as prepared by the Americans, which also laid down that the Italians should be persuaded to defend at least sicily. Allied forces from Austria and Trieste "should fight defensively alongside the Italian forces as long as possible"[91]. The British Joint Planning Staff, however, were still not prepared to divert any troops or logistic support from the Middle East, to which they gave almost absolute priority[92]. On 25 July 1949 the British Joint Planning Staff reiterated their view that "Italy can make no worthwhile contribution to Allied strategy in a war in 1951/52."[93] In August 1949 they grudgingly conceded that their garrison in Trieste should help defend Italy, but nothing more; nor were they willing to give Turkey or Greece any aid other than air coverage[94].

Thus by September 1949 the Americans and the British agreed that a Soviet-cum-satellite onslaught on Europe could not be stopped by the occupation forces in Western Germany or Austria, and probably not even in France, although the Americans hoped to keep a foothold in southern Spain for their counter-offensive for the liberation of Europe. The withdrawal from the Rhine to Spain should, however, be a fighting withdrawal[95]. The Americans continued to advocate that the withdrawal from Italy be just as much a joint Allied enterprise as the withdrawal from France[96]. This became the accepted NATO plan; the British, however, pessimistically held on to a separate set of orders for Italy's non-belligerency.

Then the increasing conviction that Tito would not allow

Eastern bloc troops to pass through his country, mitigated British pessimism. A revised British plan, completed in March 1950, assumed that "unless the present régime has been overthrown, the Soviet leaders will have to employ force to utilize Yugoslav territory". Therefore the defence of Italy (and the withdrawal of occupation forces from Austria and Trieste) depended solely on the Italian commitment to her treaty obligations, and was not dismissed as impossible[97].

Yugoslavia was thus regarded as a shield to protect Italy from an onslaught from the northeast, and it was a pillar propping up both the mountain redoubt that might be held in Austria, and the northern frontier of Greece, which was so much exposed to a satellite attack. The preservation of the independence of Yugoslavia now had significant strategic implications for the West. This new development was reflected in Western decisions to give Yugoslavia arms aid in an emergency.

Policy Decisions Regarding Arms Aid for Yugoslavia

With the adoption of their third policy paper on Yugoslavia, NSC 18/4, on 17 November 1949, the National Security Council of the US decided to give arms to Tito if he needed them. Only thus could "the political and military advantages accruing to the United States from the USSR-Yugoslavia conflict" be safeguarded against Soviet-engineered action against Tito. A Soviet success in overthrowing Tito and in replacing his régime by a puppet government would result in a renewed Communist threat to Italy and Greece (both in a military and a political sense), which would be contrary to American security interests. It was thought in view of the Soviet note of 11 August 1949 that the USSR was contemplating "drastic action against Yugoslavia". Yugoslavia's determination to resist aggression could be strengthened considerably if she could expect some military support from the West. "Hence it is important that the U.S. immediately be in a position to give Yugoslavia a general assurance as to the availability of limited military supplies in the event of an attack." What military supplies should be given would be decided at the time when the Yugoslavs requested aid, and it should not cut into the reserves which the US considered necessary to implement emergency war plans for the North Atlantic Treaty area[98].

Four different contingencies were conceived:

(a) The "continuation and intensification of present pressures" on Yugoslavia, including a possible assassination of Tito and insurrections;

(b) The most likely scenario: guerrilla operations in Yugoslavia directed and supported from the outside, centering on Macedonia;

(c) An armed attack by satellite armed forces, This, it was thought, would fail unless they were given considerable logistic support by the Soviet Union, for "in number, quality and morale the Yugoslav forces are stronger than the combined forces of the four satellites [Albania, Bulgaria, Rumania and Hungary]."[99]

(d) An armed attack by Soviet forces, presumably in co-ordination with satellite forces; this was regarded as unlikely, as it might develop into a general (East-West) conflict.

While possibility (b) was modelled on the experiences of the Greek Civil War, possibility (c) was unprecedented in the post-World War II era[100]. In addition, contrary to Robert Jervis's argument, it shows that the PPS did conceive of the possibility of "limited war" (a local war which was not necessarily expected to turn into a global war) prior to the Korean conflict[101]. Even if a satellite attack on Yugoslavia were backed by the USSR, it would not have been regarded by Kennan's Policy Planning Staff as *necessarily* connected with a world war. Admittedly, there was no unanimity in the State Department about this point, but Kennan's belief "that an attack by the Soviets on Tito would be a local affair", rather than "the beginning of a chain of events which would lead toward a major war"[102] became the basis of the estimates of NSC 18/4, at least regarding a satellite attack.

The following American reactions to these contingencies were envisaged:

(a) If pressure on Yugoslavia continued or grew, the US should equally continue the limited economic support given to Yugoslavia according to the decisions of NSC 18/2.

If the Yugoslavs asked to buy arms, the US should help them do so. The US should avoid being the one to take the issue to the United Nations.

(b) Should there be guerrilla activities in Yugoslavia with foreign support, the US should still not take the initiative in calling on the United Nations to take action, but should support such action as decided on by the General Assembly.

(c and d) In case of a pure satellite attack or a combined Soviet/satellite attack, the US should take the problem to the United Nations, if the Yugoslavs themselves failed to do so, and consult with Britain, France and other interested states such as Greece about interim measures they could take, pending the outcome of UN deliberations (which it was assumed would be delayed by the Soviet veto on the Security Council). These measures could include taking action against the offending powers, e.g. the severance of diplomatic relations with the satellite governments, on the grounds of the terms of the peace treaties.

In any case the US should be prepared to give military aid to Yugoslavia and "even if Yugoslav resistance is reduced to guerrilla operations, [the US should] consider providing material support to those operations with the object of keeping the Soviets occupied in Yugoslavia". NSC 18/4 therefore amounted to a "major policy decision", as the US Joint Chiefs of Staff called it, regarding "the extent to which we are willing to back Tito against the Kremlin"[103]. The President had enough powers to authorize an emergency transfer of funds for arms aid as was envisaged in NSC 18/4[104]. This policy decision was finally approved by Truman on 18 November 1949.

But prior to this, a press leak had already occurred. On 5 October 1949 Joseph and Stewart Alsop of the *Washington Post* and *New York Herald Tribune* and on 6 October Eric Bourne of the British *Daily Graphic* reported on governmental decisions to give Tito "full arms aid", "short of war". This meant that even before the US Administration had agreed *in principle* to inform the Yugoslavs that *if the situation warranted it,* they would be given arms, the Yugoslav (and the Soviet) Ambassador could read about it in the papers; this press leak deprived the Americans of any bargaining-counters in dealing with the Belgrade government.

Perhaps the leak was meant as an answer to an informal enquiry made some time in October 1949 by the Yugoslav Assistant Minister for Foreign Trade, Kopčok, to the US Commercial Attaché in Belgrade about the possibility of supplying arms and ammunition to Yugoslavia[105]. In their concern not to be compromised as stooges of Wall Street, however, the Yugoslavs took more than a year before they called on the Americans to stand by the implicit promise contained in these articles. Yet there is evidence that the Yugoslavs chose to approach the French government with requests for arms sales at just this time, albeit on a very modest scale[106].

These premature press reports were presumably news not only to the Yugoslavs and the Soviets, but also to America's closest allies, who had not yet been consulted on the issue. Embarrassingly enough, the Deputy Assistant Secretary for European Affairs, Llewellyn Thompson, had to answer a British enquiry by admitting that the NSC had not yet decided the matter[107]. It was only later that the British Chiefs of Staff were asked by the Foreign Office to make a study of Yugoslav arms requirements[108]. His Majesty's government was informed officially of the main conclusions of NSC 18/4 only on 20 December 1949; the French and the Canadians were informed even later, on the occasion of a further press leak in January 1950, Britain and France were then asked to co-ordinate their policies towards Yugoslavia with America[109].

Just after the British had been told about NSC 18/4, another diplomatic anomaly occurred. After a routine visit to the White House on the eve of his departure for Europe, the new American Ambassador to Belgrade, George Allen, was asked by journalists to comment on the information that had come out of the recent press leaks. He affirmed the President's opposition to aggression, wherever it might occur, mentioning Yugoslavia in particular[110]. Truman was confronted with this statement at a press conference on 22 December 1949, and was forced to endorse it. Although he denied that this marked a change in US policy, the press saw it as such[111]. When the British embassy in Washington queried the State Department about this, the latter were forced to admit that neither Allen's nor Truman's statements had been premeditated[112].

The State Department intimated, however, that they

were by no means concerned at the way in which both. . . statements were played up in the foreign press. . . . [S]ome Italian papers . . . had suggested that the President's statement was almost equivalent to a United States military guarantee to Yugoslavia. The State Department had not denied this misstatement since they felt that it was all to the good that the Soviet government should be led to believe that the United States would react strongly to any overt Soviet aggression against Yugoslavia. [113]

The same stance was taken when further leaks occurred. There were still no plans for concrete measures, no estimates of Yugoslav needs or available Western supplies, when the *New York Times* proclaimed on 12 January 1950 that "limited United States military aid to help Yugoslavia resist attack by the Soviet Union or its satellites is made possible under a strategic plan . . .recently cleared by the National Security Council". Thompson of the State Department told the British embassy that "the leak was purely accidental. He explained that the report was sent to one of the State Department press officers for his purely background information in briefing correspondents. The new press officer, however, took it upon himself to show it to one or two correspondents, with the inevitable result."[114] This leak occurred at a time when the Americans still expected their closest allies to treat this information as "top secret". One French Ambassador commented wryly on receipt of the official American communication that this confirmed what the publicist Walter Lippmann had said to him some months ago[115].

Apart from vexations caused among America's closest allies by the tactless handling of the matter, the State Department was also faced with objections from other North Atlantic Treaty partners. For example, they had to answer anxious enquiries by the Dutch, explaining that the US had so far only relaxed export controls, and was not as yet giving the Yugoslavs any real military aid[116]. Like other small NATO powers, the Dutch were concerned about the further extension of US military commitments to non-NATO powers in Europe, lest American involvement in hostilities might be regarded as *casus foederis* and drag other Atlantic Treaty powers into defensive action they had not consciously committed themselves to. This concern was to be an important factor in Western rapprochement with Yugoslavia in the military sphere, as it was in the admission of Greece and Turkey into NATO.

Meanwhile, the Western powers had asked their military advisers to make suggestions as to how the Yugoslavs could be helped to defend their country. Reporting in early 1950[117], they recommended that the defence of Yugoslavia should take the form of a fighting withdrawal into the mountain region, which should be held with guerrilla techniques, which the Yugoslavs had practised successfully in the Second World War. Accordingly, the Yugoslavs should not be given any heavy weapons, but only such arms as would be useful for mountain warfare.

They regarded the rôle of the Yugoslav navy as insignificant. In view of the fact "that the majority of the Yugoslav airfields [situated mainly in the northern plains] would soon be overrun" in case of aggression, the British Joint Planning Staff recommended against the sale of piston-engined fighters, let alone jet aircraft[118], which the Yugoslavs had unsuccessfully asked to buy from Britain and France[119].

The question was still whether the risks of Western arms falling into Soviet hands in case of a Soviet or satellite invasion, or in case of an overthrow of the Tito régime, would be outweighed by the foreseeable advantages. The Quai d'Orsay and the British Chiefs of Staff agreed with the conclusions of NSC 18/4 that the "pros" seemed to outweigh the "cons". They urged restraint, however, in the allotment of priority to the Yugoslavs. As the French communiqué stated; "Il faut ... éviter toute action qui serait de nature à réduire les moyens de défense des pays occidentaux."[120] The British Joint Planning Staff suggested to the Chiefs of Staff that Yugoslavia should be placed in Class III (i.e. with fairly low priority), as "a country of strategic and political importance whose armed forces would be likely to make a significant contribution to allied strategy"[121].

Neither the British nor the French felt that they could give the Yugoslavs much themselves. They had little to spare, and they also felt greater reserve than the Americans with their tendency "to open their arms rather wider towards Yugoslavia than the Foreign Office thought politic"[122]. The British Chiefs of Staff, in agreement with the Foreign Office, admonished the Americans not to force arms aid upon the Yugoslavs, but to await an explicit request for aid; only if the worst came to the worst should the American and British Ambassadors hint to the Belgrade government that help would be theirs for the asking.

Although the British arms aid contribution was likely to be small, they emphasized that they did not want to be left out of discussions with the Yugoslavs if that stage should be reached. They proposed that Yugoslav needs should be established by an Anglo-American military mission to Yugoslavia[123].

The topic was also discussed in a tripartite meeting of officials in late April 1950. They agreed that "the likelihood of a Soviet attack on Yugoslavia now appeared considerably less than 6 months ago, but the *Americans* considered that the situation should be kept in mind and reverted to if necessary". It was apparent from remarks made at this meeting that the Americans were particularly willing to give arms to Yugoslavia and that they were monitoring the situation carefully. It seems that Donald Maclean attended this meeting, and we may assume that whomever he reported to in Moscow was aware of Western readiness to come to the defence of Yugoslavia if she were attacked[124].

It was not until 10 July and thus after the outbreak of the Korean War on 25 June 1950, that the American government issued an invitation to France and Britain to send representatives to Washington to discuss technical aspects of arms aid for Yugoslavia[125]. In the spring of 1950, the perception of a danger to Yugoslavia was less strong than in 1949. Reporting to the NSC on 11 May 1950, the CIA restated its view of the previous year that the Soviet Union was going to step up pressure on Yugoslavia throughout 1950 even to the extent of "limited guerrilla warfare but not direct attack"[126]. On 17 May 1950 the CIA was optimistic about the Tito régime's chances of survival, stating that "Yugoslavia appears to be in a stronger position than at any time since the break with the Cominform", and in their opinion there was nothing to suggest that the Soviet Union was planning an invasion[127].

On the eve of the Korean War, there was thus still a sense of danger but not of particular urgency in the minds of most Western decision-makers, regarding aid for Yugoslavia. When George Allen, impatient with the lack of momentum of his mission, suggested to his government in mid-June 1950 that they should offer military aid to the Yugoslavs, he was rebuffed. In the view of the State Department, this would have "a compromising effect . . . from the standpoint of the moral integrity of the United States policy"[128]. Giving arms to a Communist dictator was one thing, but offering them to him was another.

While the three Western powers thus agreed in principle that they would give arms to Yugoslavia if these were asked for in an emergency, preparatory measures were far from complete at the end of June 1950. Without a Yugoslav request for aid, the British and the French at any rate were determined not to discuss the matter with the Belgrade government, and without such a discussion, no clear estimate of Yugoslav needs was feasible. All action therefore hinged on the Yugoslavs overcoming their pride and their distrust of the West and taking the plunge to ask for aid.

5

The Impact of the Korean War

Stalin's Foreign Policy and the Origins of the Korean War

On 25 June 1950 North Korean troops crossed the 38th Parallel into South Korea. According to Khrushchev's memoirs, the attack had been conceived by Kim Il-Sung, the North Korean leader, who proposed it to Stalin. He in turn approved of Kim's plan, after consultation with Mao, who agreed with Kim's verdict that the US were not likely to intervene in such an "internal matter" as a Korean civil war[1]. Indeed, there was reason to believe this, as the Americans had recently withdrawn their occupation forces from South Korea, and statements made by US officials, including Dean Acheson, had indicated that the Americans did not regard South Korea as vital for their own security interest[2].

Until the outbreak of war in Korea, Stalin's foreign policy seems to have been in a phase in which he sought to avoid outright clashes with the West. He was consolidating his grip on the areas under his domination through extensive purges, treaties, economic co-ordination, and the reshaping of many institutions and organizations in the satellite states in the image of those in the Soviet Union. Two of his efforts to affirm his grip on his empire had miscarried: Yugoslavia had not been forced into submission, and West Berlin had not been wrested away from the Western powers. Direct military clashes over Berlin had only narrowly been avoided, and the blockade had only increased tension between East and West, instead of giving Russia more security. To reverse this trend, Stalin in 1948 launched the Peace Movement, a propaganda campaign designed to rob the Western governments of the support of their populations. It sought to equate Socialism of the Eastern variety with peaceful intentions, and efforts to consolidate and strengthen the West with war-mongering[3].

In this context it is perfectly comprehensible that Stalin would have tried to avoid exposing himself once more to the threat of direct armed clashes with American forces, particularly if the potential gain that could accrue to him from taking such a risk was small. Khrushchev recorded,

> when Kim Il-Sung was preparing for his march [the invasion of South Korea], Stalin called back all [Soviet] advisors who were with the North Korean divisions and regiments, . . . I asked Stalin about this, and he snapped back at me, "It's too dangerous to keep our advisors there. They might be taken prisoner. We don't want there to be evidence for accusing us of taking part in this business. It's Kim Il-Sung's affair."[4]

The most recent discussion of the controversy surrounding this issue[5] concludes that it is unlikely, on balance, that Stalin "manipulated North Korea in June 1950 but it is still a possibility"[6].

The question of whether Stalin approved of the Korean War, regarding it as an in all ways insignificant side-show, or whether it was an important element in his foreign policy-making, is crucial. If Stalin wanted a war to take place in the Far East, if he even counted on it to involve and tie down Western forces and distract the attention of the North Atlantic Treaty powers from Europe to Asia, possibly even in order to have a free hand for action on his western front, this would be a contradiction of his policy of peaceful co-existence, which was to give the Soviet Union the time to recover from the Second World War. Both before and during the Korean War Stalin made crucial contributions to its limitation to the local theatre of Korea, helping to prevent global escalation[7]. And yet it seems that in connection with the Korean War, Stalin was contemplating an attack in Europe.

Given that a government's intentions in foreign policy are necessarily limited by the options available to it, military intelligence services will study the potential adversary's capabilities. While it is often a fallacy to argue that because the opponent has the arms and the troops, he plans to use them, it is reasonable to assume that if he does not have the weapons and the manpower, he will try to avoid war. Looking at the Soviet Union and the satellites between 1948 and 1950, we find that the conclusive negative test does *not* apply: Stalin did indeed start a major rearmament programme, expanding the satellite armed forces very considerably (see Appendix C), and effecting in them a process of *Gleichschaltung*. They were permeated with Soviet military advisors and political officers, who controlled the local military apparatus[8].

This military centralization may have been a defensive reaction on the part of Stalin to the consolidation of the West, which he perceived as threatening, as Vojtech Mastny implies: the process started in mid-1948[9], that is after the signing of the Brussels Treaty. The Soviets were also kept well informed about the negotiations between the British and the Americans in preparation of the Atlantic alliance through Donald Maclean[10]. Also, Soviet *Existenzangst* was nurtured by the offensive sides of the Anglo-American policy of "containment" with all its elements of subversion, liberation propaganda and incitement to rebellion, as John Yurechko has demonstrated so ably[11]. In connection with the Western liberation policy, the purely defensive measures of rearmament and consolidation on the part of the West necessarily came across as threatening and offensive.

Nevertheless, a possibly purely defensive policy (if Stalin's remilitarization programme can be described as such) can be turned into a pre-emptive strategy, and the threat into a self-fulfilling prophecy, if an attack by the enemy is felt to be imminent. Moreover, the populations of totalitarian systems can be manipulated to believe that this is so, as the supposed attack by the Poles on the German broadcasting station Gleiwitz in 1939, and the Communist account of the outbreak of the Korean War prove[12].

There is indeed evidence that Stalin considered staging a preventive strike against Western Europe. Chepichka, the Czech Minister of Defence, attended an extraordinary conference in the Kremlin in January 1951. He explained to Karel Kaplan:

Dans les années 1950-1951, la direction soviétique était arrivée à la conclusion que pendant les seules trois ou quatre années à venir, les conditions resteraient encore

127

favorables à la réalisation des objectifs politiques qu'elle s'était fixés après la guerre, et qui constataient à étendre et à consolider l'influence de l'URSS dans l'Europe tout entière.

This the Soviets had originally hoped to do by filling the power-vacuum left by the decline of Britain and France, using the Communist parties in Western Europe, but the United States had beat them to it and was now the predominant power in that area.

En perte de vitesse sur le plan idéologique, sans résultats probants dans le domaine économique, l'U.R.S.S. n'avait plus comme atout que sa supériorité militaire. Même celle-ci était limitée dans le temps et, selon des calculs de tous les experts militaires soviétiques, le délai ne devait pas dépasser quatre ans. Dans ces conditions, il était urgent de le mettre à profit pour multiplier et perfectionner le potentiel militaire du bloc soviétique, de manière à pouvoir lancer une opération éclaire aboutissant à l'occupation de toute l'Europe.

Such a *Blitzkrieg* action would not give the local forces time to organise their defence, nor would the Americans have time to come in on their side. Stalin's estimation of American capabilities was so low, in the view of Kaplan, because of the lack of success of the American-led forces in Korea at the turn of the year 1950-51. This was the project Stalin is supposed to have outlined at the conference in the Kremlin[13].

Béla Király, a top officer in the Hungarian Army, also alleges that Stalin was planning a strike in Europe. According to Király, this would have been a lightning attack on Yugoslavia by the forces of her satellite neighbours, together with Soviet divisions, which he claims was planned from 1949 onwards, the preparations being concluded by the summer of 1950[14]. This tallies with an article which Philip Windsor claims to have found in the *Pravda* of 13 February 1957[15]. In early 1950 the Quai d'Orsay had information, also emanating from the Chiefs of Staff of the Hungarian Army, that "des préparatifs militaires dirigés contre la Yougoslavie seraient poursuivis actuellement en Hongrie"[16]. Király gives the date of the planned operation as autumn 1950 or spring 1951[17]. Király's evidence seems corroborated by further information from Chepichka: he was supposedly told by the Soviet Marshal Zhukov that there had been concrete plans for military intervention in Yugoslavia, favoured by all the Soviet marshals. Both Hungary and Romania were promised large parts of Yugoslavia if the country were defeated. On a visit to Belgrade in 1957, Zhukov is supposed to have bragged to Tito, "Did you know, Comrade, that we wanted to do you in in 1951?" to which Tito allegedly answered, "You know, Comrade, so did Hitler." The project is supposed to have been called off by Stalin at the eleventh hour[18], presumably in the autumn of 1950. Király speculates that Stalin may have acted thus because he was impressed by the initial success of the American forces in their reaction to the invasion of South Korea[19], which would tally with the date of Stalin's decision to cancel the operations against Yugoslavia if that had been taken before the Chinese entered the war in the Far East.

Examining the likelihood of this plan, one should again look at capabilities. It was Soviet military doctrine not to launch an attack unless Soviet forces were at least in a 3:1 position of superiority[20]. Yet a comparison of Soviet, satellite and Yugoslav force strengths for 1950-51 (only counting Soviet and satellite forces in the countries bordering on Yugoslavia) shows that this superiority was not quite reached even in early 1951, if the Yugoslav army indeed had 400,000 men; Király's claim that in the summer of 1950 the Hungarian People's Army had 250,000 men, *excluding* reserves, is not confirmed by other sources (see Appendix C).

It also seems that an attempt to seize Yugoslavia with a lightning attack would have come to grief in any case. Yugoslavia had two great strategic assets, her large army and her virtually impenetrable mountain regions. Western military experts considered that the Yugoslavs would be able to hold them almost indefinitely against any conventional attack especially if they were given arms by the West[21]. An attack on Yugoslavia would therefore in all probability have tied down Soviet and satellite troops in an inconclusive war, drawing the world's attention to the hypocrisy of Stalin's peace-talk.

It is, of course, possible to argue that these plans for military action were mere contingency planning, of the sort that military planners would draw up for all eventualities; it is noteworthy, however, that the Soviet Union was in that case thinking very much in terms of preventive strikes, as both plans clearly dealt with territory outside the Soviet orbit. Even as contingency plans, therefore, these Soviet projects, if they really existed, have an unpleasantly aggressive ring to them.

Western Perceptions of Soviet Intentions

The Western governments could only infer Soviet intentions from Soviet bloc force strengths, other bits of intelligence (which are not always accessible to the researcher), and public utterances of Soviet leaders or articles in the press. On 21 April 1950, the Cominform journal published an article by M. Mitin on the "International Significance of Leninism". The first point made here concerned the likelihood or even inevitability of war between the Socialist countries and the "imperialist" powers. While mentioning Lenin's thesis, often quoted by Stalin, that the peaceful co-existence of the Socialist and capitalist systems was possible, Mitin also stated that imperialism, the mature form of capitalism, was inseparable from unjust wars of conquest: "It is natural, therefore, that the Communist Parties fighting against capitalism are, simultaneously, combating aggressive wars."

Yves Chataigneau, the French Ambassador in Moscow and one of the most gifted Sovietologists of the period, drew his Ministry's attention to this contradiction, and to the implications of Mitin's statement that the Western powers were set on the path of war[22]. If Soviet foreign policy-makers assumed that the imperialists were by nature aggressive and planned to attack the Soviet bloc, it would be irrelevant whether the intentions of the Soviet Union towards the West were peaceful[23]. Given that Communist doctrine supplied the Soviets with this explanation of the causes of a potential future war, Western foreign policy-makers felt compelled to take into consideration the possibility of a Soviet first strike[24].

Secondly, Mitin's article quoted Stalin as saying that "Leninism is . . . . suitable and essential for all countries without exception, including the developed capitalist countries." Chataigneau took this to mean that the Soviet Union should actively encourage revolutions elsewhere. He pointed out that Mitin was thus at odds with Stalin's famous statement of 1936, which denied that the Revolution could be exported; this statement had only recently been repeated in *Pravda*[25].

As the Western powers regarded all Communist subversive activities as led by the Soviet Union and thus as inimical and warlike actions, this issue was related in the minds of Westerners to the question of whether the Soviet Union was prepared to start a war against the "free world". Thus the US National Security Council (NSC) in April 1950, two months before the Korean War broke out, agreed that "our free society finds itself mortally challenged by the Soviet System"; "the cold war is in fact a real war in which the survival of the free world is at stake."[26] Kennan's and Roberts's view of 1946, that the Soviet Union wanted to see Communism established world-wide (see Chapter 1), and not Kennan's later-held conviction that Stalin sought to avoid an all-out confrontation, had taken root in the minds of Western defence and foreign policy planners[27].

This view was reiterated on the first page of the new American overall policy statement NSC 68, drafted in April 1950: "The Soviet Union ... seeks to impose its absolute authority over the rest of the world."[28] Bohlen later commented that in NSC 68, "Soviet policy was represented as nothing more than an absolute determination to spread the Communist system throughout the world. . . . NSC 68's misconception of Soviet aims misled ... Dean Acheson and others in interpreting the Korean war."[29] This conviction about Soviet aims remained a fundamental Western belief throughout the period of this study[30].

In Western perceptions this contest between the two systems had become more dangerous in 1949 through the victory of the Chinese Communist forces and the first explosion of a Soviet nuclear bomb. Increasing the strength of the adversary, these two events caused the American administration to consider a programme of massive rearmament, outlined in NSC 68[31], and they prompted Truman in early 1950 to order the development and construction of the hydrogen bomb[32]. These events would not have sufficed, however, to persuade Western parliaments to approve of the extremely costly new policy of massive rearmament: what could be seen by the West as proof of the warlike intentions of the Soviet Union was necessary to convince the parliaments that rearmament was vital.

This proof was supplied by the invasion of South Korea[33], for it was assumed by the Americans, the British[34] and the French governments alike that the Soviet Union had "décidé de pousser le Gouvernement de Corée du Nord dans une aventure dont l'issue militaire est incertaine et dont les conséquences sont difficilement limitables", in the words of Chataigneau[35]. No serious doubt about Soviet direction of the war arose in the minds of Western decision-makers because it tallied perfectly with their predictions of Soviet aggressive action. For example, at the ministerial talks in London in mid-May 1950, Bevin and Acheson estimated that the Soviets did not plan a major war in the near future, but might

> adopt increasingly aggressive policies at key peripheral points . . . which the West would be obliged to accept or to counter with force, and they might be inclined now generally to take greater risks than hitherto in areas where they think the West may be likely to acquiesce in a Soviet advance.[36]

It is remarkable how well this prophecy fitted Korea; it could equally well have fitted Yugoslavia. The main American conceptual response to the Korean War, NSC 73/4, therefore stated: "The Korean war is only an additional and more acute manifestation of the chronic world situation resulting from the Kremlin design [*sic*] for world domination through the international communist conspiracy."[37] The invasion of South Korea thus served to confirm and strengthen certain suspicions that Western governments already harboured about the Soviet Union[38].

Yet the Korean War also brought about a change in Western perceptions: it could now be argued (in the words of NSC 73/4) that "it is a tenet of communism that war between communist and non-communist countries is inevitable."[39] Indeed, the incident seemed to be proof that the Soviet Union was prepared to bring it on. In Acheson's view, "the profound lesson of Korea is that . . . the USSR took a step which risked — however remotely — general war."[40] Bohlen recalls, "The Korean war was interpreted by Acheson and most others in the State Department, as well as the Joint Chiefs of Staff, as ushering in a new phase of Soviet foreign policy."[41] In the late 1940s the Soviet Union had been seen as ultimately expansionist, but economically too weak to want a world war in the short term. But now it was considered possible that the Soviet Union might launch a preventive strike against the West as the odds would become even less favourable once the North Atlantic Pact had become a military organization, and once Western Europe had fully recovered economically.

This fear was expressed repeatedly in British and American intelligence appreciations in the second half of 1950, and one went as far as naming 1952 as the peak danger period[42]. In December 1950 Truman warned US Congressional leaders that "the Kremlin may . . . have decided that the time was in fact ripe for a general war with the United States."[43] If Kaplan and his source, Chepichka, can be trusted, the Western powers thus guessed correctly at Stalin's thoughts.

As time went by, however, it became clear that the crossing of the 38th parallel was, in the words of Kennan, *not* "a first step in a world war"[44]. The foreign ministers of the US, Britain and France agreed on this point when they met in Washington in early September 1950[45]. Yet Kennan tried in vain to dissuade his colleagues from upholding the notion that Korea was "the first of a series of local operations designed to drain U.S. strength in peripheral theatres"[46]. Bohlen rightly recalls that he and Kennan were virtually on their own, while Acheson and the rest of the State Department including the Policy Planning Staff[47], and the Joint Chiefs of Staff[48] thought differently until 1951 at least: "Their view, which Truman accepted, was that having launched an attack in Korea — the first case of Communist open use of naked military force to expand the system — the Soviet Union was likely to call on satellite armies elsewhere . . . to spread Communist control."[49]

President Truman therefore gave orders to the American "strategic intelligence" gatherers to pay special attention to "Soviet activities in the vicinity of Yugoslavia, in Bulgaria especially, and in the vicinity of Northern Europe"[50]. On 18 July 1950 the Quai d'Orsay also expressed to Whitehall their fear "of a new Soviet initiative at some other point of the immense arc from Europe to Asia". They regarded "two points in Europe" as "particularly threatened: the city of Berlin . . . and Yugoslavia"[51]. This apprehension was expressed frequently by Western intelligence services and diplomats; moreover, it was thought that such a move could happen very quickly, because the Soviet "régime could produce a war psychosis [among its citizens] . . . within a fortnight"[52].

The Korean War had one other crucially important effect: it did away with Kennan's policy of strongpoint defence (see Chapter 1). It exposed the contradiction between his advocacy of a psychological ("moral") strengthening of the West, and the commitment to the defence of a limited number of areas only. The United States had to come to the defence of South Korea because its loss to the Communist bloc, however insignificant in strategic or economic terms, could have engendered a feeling of defeatism not only in Asia, but also in Western Europe[53]. This would have undermined concerted Western efforts to strengthen this area in view of the Soviet ideological and the potential military threat. This problem of the psychological effect of the fall of one country on all the others[54], which later became known as "domino effect", had already led to the Truman Doctrine over Greece and Turkey, the first step away from the Kennan doctrine of strongpoint defence.

NSC 68 was a further step in this direction, vastly increasing "the number and variety of interests deemed relevant to the national security [of the US]", and blurring the distinctions between them, in Gaddis's words[55]. But it was the Korean War that marked the acceptance by the US of a commitment to the defence of any part of the "free world" (which in this context included Yugoslavia) against Communist aggression, taking NSC 68 down from the drawing board into reality; this "global commitment" in turn would lead to America's involvement in the Vietnam War. It meant that an attack by Communist-led forces on any part of the world that had hitherto been outside the Soviet orbit would be regarded as a threat to American national security. In the words of the historian Robert Osgood, "'National security policy', in common parlance, became equivalent to the management of all facets of U.S. power to contain international communism on a global scale."[56]

Western Reactions following the Korean Invasion

The commitment to perimeter defence together with the realization that local, non-nuclear (i.e. "limited") wars could happen and had to be fought with conventional forces, necessarily entailed the shift towards conventional rearmament, as epitomized by NSC 68 and NSC 74. Acheson explained to Congressional leaders that "we had only one choice open to us, and that was the greatest possible build-up of our own military strength and that of our allies."[57] He had the support of the Joint Chiefs of Staff[58] and the National Security Council[59]. The Korean War was thus the main catalyst for the realization of pre-existing American plans for Western rearmament, both conventional and nuclear. It was a unique and possibly irreplaceable catalyst, as Robert Jervis argues, in the sense that the realization of the US Administration's previously conceived plans (particularly NSC 68) would not have been possible to such a degree and such a speed without Korea[60]. This also meant, of course, that there was no prospect of disarmament. At a conference of foreign ministers in Paris on 6 November 1951, Acheson told his colleagues Robert Schuman and Anthony Eden that he was against Western troop reductions, as these would weaken the Allied position in the Far and Middle East, "as well as, for example, more specifically in Indochina and Yugoslavia[61]".

Korea was clearly the cause for the increase in the defence expenditure of France[62], where no equivalent of NSC 68 had existed prior to the outbreak of war in the Far East. The British Chiefs of Staff had produced a Defence White Paper in March 1950, which like NSC 68 recommended rearmament: this, too, was only acted upon after the outbreak of the Korean War[63]. As for the other NATO powers, the Korean War stood at the beginning of their rearmament programmes, which were fixed by the Lisbon Conference force goals of 1952, and entailed a massive increase in conventional forces. The plan for an integrated European Army, including hitherto untapped West German manpower, was born out of the fear of a repetition of Korea in Europe, and resulted in the admission of Western Germany into NATO in 1955. The North Atlantic Treaty was strengthened through a military organization, charged with the co-ordination of defence plans, ready at any moment to assume a wartime command over the forces of the Treaty powers[64]. New efforts were made to extend security arrangements to other parts of the "free world": Greece and Turkey were integrated into NATO (see Chapter 6), and defence arrangements were made in Asia (the ANZUS and SEATO pacts).

There was thus unanimity in the West regarding the necessity of building up defences against the Soviet bloc. There was also agreement between London and Washington on the concept of peripheral defence, which the British had already accepted in the Bastion Paper of 1948. There was, however, a difference in ba*sic* perceptions. When in December 1951 representatives of the US, Britain and France, in the framework of the NATO standing group, assessed tendencies of Soviet foreign policy, the US delegation wanted a clause included which called for NATO rearmament to meet the Soviet threat. The British and French delegations resisted this suggestion, reluctant to permit this shift towards the confusion of Soviet capabilities and Soviet intentions about which there could be no certainty[65].

Disagreements also arose between the Western powers over the way in which the Korean War should be fought, and what risks should be incurred. The British and the French foreign ministers obtained consensus on their view that all Western measures should be entirely defensive, when they met with their American colleague in Washington in early September 1950[66]. The French in particular were resolutely opposed to all offensive, adventurist measures[67]. Therefore the positioning of American naval forces in the Straits between Formosa and mainland China, the decision of the American General MacArthur to let the UN forces under his command cross the 38th parallel into North Korea, thereby provoking Chinese intervention, and Truman's statement that he might order the use of the atomic bomb, aroused British and French disapproval of what they saw as excessively provocative behaviour on the part of the Americans[68].

American action without prior consultation of her main NATO partners added to their concern about effects on the Soviet Union. In March 1951 Chataigneau in Moscow felt that the Kremlin was suspicious about "la ténacité des Etats Unis dans l'armement". The Soviets seemed to think the Americans would rearm to a point where they could use their forces "pour amener les Soviétiques à composition par la négociation *ou pour les contraindre à soumission par recours aux armes*"[69]. Chataigneau continued to point out to his government how nervous the Soviet Union was becoming in consequence of what it perceived as Western encirclement[70].

In the British Foreign Office, the Permanent

Under-Secretary of State, Sir William Strang, minuted on 3 January 1951 regarding Anglo-American differences over policies in the Far East:

> The United States has come out of two great wars stronger than it went in to [*sic*] them, and can think and talk of a Third World War more light-heartedly than we Europeans can.... Our problem is to deflect the Americans from unwise or dangerous courses without making a breach in the united front.[71]

This view was shared by the key British decision-makers. Even the staunchest supporters of America among the West European nations, Bevin and Attlee, who had been prime movers in bringing the Americans into Western European defence arrangements, talked "about the dangers inherent in the policies now followed by the United States Government". Attlee thought it necessary to "put the brakes on the bleachers [the Americans]"[72]. In mid-January 1951, Bevin sent him a note, saying "It is not, I think, in the character of the American people to provoke a war, or to commit an act of aggression, nor does their constitution lend itself to action of this nature." But he conceded that "there is a risk that the United States Government by some ill-considered or impulsive action, or series of actions, might find themselves in an exposed position from which they might drift into hostilities, especially in the East." Yet in Bevin's opinion Britain could not do without America. The US must not be driven to retreat "into a kind of armed isolation". Britain had to help "build up the strength of the free world, morally, economically, militarily with the United States, and at the same time to exert sufficient control over the well-intentioned but inexperienced colossus on whose co-operation our safety depends"[73].

Thus the differences between the allies did not concern the necessity of joint defence efforts, but the conduct of the war in the Far East and the aggressive sides of "containment", such as the liberation policy regarding the Communist-ruled countries.

Western Disagreements Regarding the Policy of Liberation

The Americans reacted to the Korean War not only by expanding their defensive capacities, but also with an extension of their offensive liberation policy. On 15 January 1951 the American Joint Chiefs of Staff called not only for rearmament, but also for

> A coordinated and integrated crusade against Kremlin-dominated communism everywhere; . . .
> An even more rapid and more resolute build-up of the intangible resources favorable to our objectives which live in the minds and hearts of men both within and without the iron curtain; and . . .
> A large-scale program of psychological warfare, including special operations . . .

It was explained that "crusade is used in the sense of a vigorous and *aggressive* movement for the advancement of an idea or cause."[74] The chairman of the National Security Resources Board, Stuart Symington, at about the same time submitted a hysterically worded report to the NSC: "The United States is now in a war for survival; the United States is losing that war." Like the Joint Chiefs of Staff, he advocated a rigorous stepping up of the tempo of what Kennan had called "containment", both defensive and offensive[75].

This proposal was adopted by the NSC (as NSC 100) and approved by the President. The subversive policies initiated before Korea were expanded: in addition to the Voice of America broadcasts, Radio Free Europe was introduced in October 1951, organized by a Committee for a Free Europe. Its president, C. D. Jackson, explained that "what we wanted to do was to create conditions of turmoil in the countries our broadcasts reached." General Lucius Clay described the aim of its broadcasts as to "help those trapped behind the curtain to prepare the day of liberation"[76]. In July 1951 a Psychological Strategy Board was set up in the US Administration to co-ordinate propaganda and other activities more efficiently. The Mutual Security Act, passed in May 1951, provided for further funds to help opposition groups within the Soviet orbit; also, with the help of these funds, émigré groups were organized into military units[77]. The most important of these, under General Anders, claimed that they could mobilize a total of 6,250,000 men behind the Iron Curtain; the actual émigré strengths themselves were about 239,000, consisting of Poles, Balts, Bulgarians, Hungarians, Romanians and Czechs[78].

The rationale of the liberation policy is summarized very well in January 1952 by an interdepartmental steering committee:

> The Soviet Union . . . is endeavouring to create disunity, tensions and weakness in the free world. In the face of this massive attack, we believe we cannot adopt a defensive and passive position but rather must counter attack by political warfare activities directed against the USSR itself and against the Soviet satellites of Eastern Europe with the objective of increasing the discontent, tension and division known to exist in the Soviet orbit. The Iron Curtain must be pierced to bring home to the Kremlin's subject peoples the fact that they have friends and allies in the free world. In addition, such activities are designed to form the political basis and operational nuclei for resistance groups which, we hope, would weaken the Soviet regime in case of armed conflict.[79]

The last NSC policy statements of the Truman Administration temporarily introduced a note of caution regarding the liberation policy, in view of its possibly provocative consequences; NSC 141 of January 1953 even put a temporary halt to the constant increase of funds allotted to clandestine operations designed to "weaken Soviet control over the satellites and the military potential of the Soviet system"[80].

The French were none too pleased about the stepping up of the liberation policy in 1951-52. The Sous-Direction d'Europe Orientale of the Quai d'Orsay commented on 31 August 1951 on the revival of hopes for a liberation of Eastern Europe:

> Il ne s'en suit pas pour autant que nous devions accroître les dispositions de rebelles qui se font jour; elles comportent, dans l'état présent des choses, de trop

grands risques pour ceux qui viendraient à se révolter. Dans ce sens, les récentes interventions ... de [Radio]"Free Europe" peuvent être considérées comme néfastes, inutiles et dangereuses. Lancer, sur un pays asservi, des tracts qui proclament que l'heure de la déliverance est proche, est en quelque sorte, à l'heure actuelle, une malhonnêteté. ... Or, nous ne sommes prêts ni moralement ni matériellement à déclencher, dans les mois qui viennent, la 'croisade anti-stalinienne' que semble prophétiser "Free Europe".

It was recommended that the French government draw the Americans' attention "sur l'inutile danger auquel nous exposons les peuples des pays vassaux de l'Union Soviétique, en les incitant prématurément à secouer le joug qui les opprime". After all, the North Atlantic Alliance "a été fondée sur des bases *défensives*, elle doit rester fidèle à sa mission"[81]. The Direction d'Europe under François Seydoux agreed, arguing that it was of primary importance for the security of the North Atlantic Treaty area that the populations in Western Europe should have the will to resist Soviet aggression, which would only be the case if they identified entirely with what NATO stood for, and if "l'opinion publique soit convaincue que Moscou porte la pleine responsabilité de la guerre".

The Direction d'Europe recognized that "le gouvernement des Etats Unis ... assume les responsabilités principales dans la détermination de la politique de la coalition [NATO]...". Therefore public support in Western Europe, that area of "importance essentielle en cas de conflit" for the Western alliance, depended not only on the disposition of NATO, but also on the integrity of the foreign policy of the United States[82]. It did not help inter-Allied relations that the Republican presidential candidate, Eisenhower, and his Secretary-of-State-designate, Dulles, made the issue of the liberation of Eastern Europe from Soviet oppression one of the primary issues of their election campaign in 1952. That in practice their policies differed very little from those of the Truman Administration mattered very little in this context[83]. In mid-February 1953, the Sous-Direction d'Europe Orientale in the Quai d'Orsay once more complained about US policy:

Jusqu'ici [la nouvelle politique américaine] paraît plus

verbale que réelle. Elle n'en est pas moins dangereuse. Ses effets s'exercent beaucoup plus sûrement sur l'opinion des pays atlantiques que sur celle des satellites de l'URSS. Le refoulement ["roll-back"], si ... il pouvait se faire sans guerre, serait peut-être bon, s'il ne se fait pas et qu'on en parle sans cesse, l'unité de l'alliance sera profondément atteinte.[84]

Also referring to the liberation policy (which came to be known as "roll-back"), Sir William Strang in January 1951 stressed the necessity to "deflect the Americans from unwise and dangerous courses"[85]. Like the French, the British were now anxious "to avoid any action which might convince the Soviet Government that an attack from the West was inevitable". Although (unlike the French) they had adopted a liberation policy themselves in 1948 (see Chapter 2), they now ceased to be in favour of Secret Service operations in the Soviet orbit. The turning point may have been the return to power of Churchill and Eden at the end of 1951, but it was preceded by a change of heart in the Foreign Office, which now feared the consequences of high-risk policies[86]. On the eve of Churchill's and Eden's visit to Washington in January 1952, a US interdepartmental steering committee warned of differences that might arise between the new British Conservative government and the Truman Administration: the British might regard "arrangements with the soviet bloc in the 'spheres of influence' tradition" as desirable, while being more optimistic in their interpretation of Soviet intentions. The committee prophesied that

> The British will tend to question the necessity or desirability of political warfare operations. They are inclined to accept the present *status quo* in Eastern Europe and do not desire to engage in activities which they consider not only to be calculated to increase East-West tension, but which might even provoke the Kremlin to acts of aggression. The British, in short, appear to believe that the immediate dangers of provocation over-balance the long-term deterrent results of political warfare carried on within Moscow's own orbit.[87]

It is not clear whether Churchill and Eden raised this point on the occasion of this visit, but the Foreign Office continued to feel uneasy about the US policy of liberation. Commenting on an Eisenhower campaign speech on the "liberation of Eastern Europe" on 25 August 1952, a Foreign Office brief for Eden stated that such utterances "are calculated to raise false hopes among the peoples concerned while we would not at the same time wish to discourage them by the appearance of ready acquiescence in the maintenance of dominated régimes". At the time, however, British ideas on this were somewhat fluid[88]. They crystallized after the death of Stalin, when the British feared the foreclosure of an improvement in relations between the Western powers and the new Soviet leaders. This was brought to the attention of the Cabinet on 3 July 1953 by the Acting Secretary of State, the Marquess of Salisbury, who expressed concern about the

> dangerous American tendency, . . . to interpret the situation behind the Iron Curtain as already very shaky and therefore to advocate the early liberation of the satellite countries. The last thing we want to do is to bait the Russian and satellite Governments into taking measures against them. . . . We must of course keep the spirit of freedom alive in Eastern Europe, but we should also counsel prudence and restraint.

Therefore, in consonance with Churchill's wishes, he wanted to persuade Dulles to accept high-level talks with the Russians[89]. On 6 July 1953 the Cabinet agreed with the memorandum[90]. In the subsequent meeting with Dulles and Bidault in Washington, Lord Salisbury took up this point with them, hoping "to prevent any embarrassing initiatives by Mr. Dulles"; as he told the Cabinet afterwards, "Mr. Dulles had been extremely helpful."[91] This was not, however, the end of European-American disagreements over US policies. Under Eisenhower and Dulles, "United States Policy Toward the Soviet Satellites in Eastern Europe" as approved on 11 December 1953 (NSC 174) bluntly re-introduced the Truman Administration's NSC 58/2 of December 1949: the American aim was to counter, or possibly even to remove, Soviet influence from the European satellites, by all means available, short of war. NSC 174, however, also contained the first

American recognition that "Titoism" had failed to become a precedent for other Communist parties or governments[92].

No Further Spread of "Titoism"?

Between the outbreak of the Korean War and NSC 174 at the end of 1953, the rôle of Yugoslavia in US liberation policy changed but little. After his visit to Europe in February 1951, George Perkins told his colleagues in the State Department at the Under-Secretary's meeting on 26 February that there were "many Spanish Civil War veterans around Tito who feel that they were let down by Stalin. This is a cause for their personal defection and may be the cause for others within the satellites."[93] The Economic Cooperation Administration asserted, "Titoism tends to weaken the Communist regimes in the Soviet satellite states, even if there is little prospect of their following the Yugoslav example, and also to cause splits and sow confusion in the Communist parties of Western Europe."[94] The French Ambassador in Washington at the end of 1951 explained that the Truman government saw the liberation policy primarily as aimed at breaking the bonds between the satellites and Moscow, with the perceived "defection" of Yugoslavia as prime model of this process[95]. In Eisenhower's election campaign of 1952 and afterwards as Secretary of State, Dulles adopted this policy and presented it as his own. In spite of his belligerent rhetoric of 1952, designed to win over the traditionally pro-Democrat Slavic-ethnic communities[96], he was soon talking about "peaceful liberation" in public statements. Yugoslavia for him was the prime example of peaceful separation of countries from the Soviet Bloc. He frequently referred to the encouragement of Titoism as the main aim of his liberation policy[97].

Meanwhile, the British began to see Yugoslavia differently. Admittedly there is the occasional (but rare) reference to the Tito-Stalin split as the "first crack in the [Communist] monolith"[98], but the British did not, on the whole, stake anything on what they regarded at most as a very remote possibility of a further satellite "defection". The French Ambassador in London observed in early 1952, les Anglais ne voient dans le soutien économique ou militaire accordé à Tito qu'une mesure *défensive* dans le cadre de la guerre froide et non pas, pour le moment tout au moins, l'organisation d'un tremplin psychologique permettant de gagner progressivement par l'intérieur les satellites de l'U.R.S.S. impressionées par le succès du premier dissident. Cette conception moins dynamique de l'aide à la Yougoslavie prévalait déjà auprès du Gouvernement Travailliste.[99]

Indeed, by 1952 the Foreign Office had become wary of the dangers of the spread of national Communism ("Titoism") to Africa and Asia, where they regarded it as a greater threat to British interests than elsewhere, because it might have been more popular than Stalinism in these areas[100].

The new French Ambassador in Belgrade, Philippe Baudet, was infected with American optimism about possible satellite defections (see Chapter 7), but the Quai d'Orsay did not go along with his expectations[101]. The French Foreign Ministry was more preoccupied with Soviet anxieties and feelings than its transatlantic ally; it was informed by Chataigneau that according to Soviet newspaper articles, there was much concern that Yugoslavia was becoming an airbase for the supply of guerrilla forces within the Soviet orbit with arms and provisions, and was thus being turned into a springboard for US offensive activities[102].

In any case no other "defection" from the Soviet bloc followed within our period. Earlier the purges in Eastern Europe had been taken as evidence of the existence of "Titoism" (see Chapter 2). Now the other side of the coin was seen more clearly; as the Sous-Direction d'Europe Orientale stated on 31 August 1951,

Les épurations successives ont évidemment rendu fort improbables les chances d'un nouveau titisme, et le degré de servitude atteint par les divers dirigeants des démocraties populaires ne permet guère d'imaginer qu'un d'entre eux puisse actuellement marcher sur les traces du Chef yougoslave.[103]

The Foreign Office's Russia Committee's report on anti-Stalinist Communism as approved on 14 February 1950 had concluded "there is nothing to show that the hold of international communism has been appreciably weakened" by Titoism[104]. Surprisingly, the one explicit statement of British hopes for an effect of Communist Yugoslavia's independence can be found in a document dating from the following day[105]. But the main tendency of British thinking about further "defections" was increasingly pessimistic. As we have seen (Chapter 2), the survey on the "Effects of Titoism on Communist Parties in Other Countries", commissioned by the Russia Committee in the British Foreign Office in August 1948, proved, in its ultimate form, that these had been disappointingly slight[106]. Accordingly, the Foreign Office's Research Department, on 16 June 1950, remarked that while

> there is no doubt that the vast majority of adults living behind the Iron Curtain loathe the system, . . . [t]here is however no possibility of revolt against Communism in the present circumstances, and no indication that any new Tito is arising to challenge Soviet leadership.[107]

American analyses also pointed in this pessimistic direction, particularly when wishful thinking did not dominate their perceptions. The survey of "Communist Defections and Dissensions in the Postwar Period", completed on 22 June 1951 by the State Department's Office of Intelligence Research, read:

> Tito's defection . . . presented disaffected Communists with the opportunity of uniting ideologically around Yugoslavia into an anti-Stalinist Communist force. Yet, in spite of efforts by Tito to gain support in various Communist and fellow-traveling quarters, the number of pro-Titoists has remained small, and no international Titoist organization has materialized.[108]

In November 1952, the CIA agreed that "Soviet control over the satellites is virtually complete. . . . The popular discontent now current in each satellite will persist and perhaps increase. However, we estimate that no issue will develop into more than a nuisance or minor impediment to the Communist program" until the end of 1953[109]. At the end of 1952 the CIA even concluded that "the European satellites will probably remain under control of the Kremlin" for the following decade at least[110].

These pessimistic analyses did not deflect American decision-makers from indulging in wishful thinking when it came to dealing with the USSR's European satellites. Yet the opposite was the case when it came to the perception of China. In both cases, the elected politicians were more sensitive to Congressional opinion (such as the China lobby) and to the interests of minority groups (such as the Slav émigrés). This was reflected clearly by Attlee's talks with Truman and Acheson in Washington in December 1950, after the Chinese Communists had come into the Korean War on the side of the North Koreans. Acheson opposed any attempts to negotiate with Peking, arguing that "the American people" could not be expected to understand a policy which tolerated Chinese Communist aggression in the Far East, but would be unwilling to tolerate Soviet Communist aggression in Europe. Truman agreed that "it was important to realize that the United States could do nothing abroad without solid backing at home." Attlee found no support for his view that "the Chinese Communists were potentially ripe for 'Titoism'" and that the Western "aim ought to be to divide the Russians and the Chinese" by preventing the Chinese from "thinking that Russia is their only friend"[111].

In addition to public opinion, the US military establishment put pressure on Truman and Acheson, and after them on Eisenhower and Dulles, to treat Mao as an enemy. The assumption that the Soviet Union had ordered the invasion of South Korea led the American Secretaries of the Army, Navy, Air Force and Defence to regard this as evidence "that the Soviet movement is monolithic. Satellite troops are just as much Soviet in this sense as if they were members of the Red Army."[112] This dictum was applied to China in particular.

Thus the United States abandoned the hope that Mao might turn into a second Tito, and instead of following a course of coaxing the young Communist régime in Peking away from Stalin, the American relationship with the Chinese leaders grew worse, if possible, than that between Washington and Moscow[113]. The State Department concluded about China in June 1951 that two factors militated *against* a defection of the Chinese Communist Party (CCP) as a whole: the CCP's identification with the interests of the USSR, whence they received their material aid, and Stalin's realization that he needed China, and his consequent willingness to make concessions. Thus the defection of the CCP was not thought likely in the near future[114]. The CIA confirmed this view in November 1952[115]. A month later the CIA speculated that within the next decade, "the Chinese Communist will probably develop a Soviet-type state and society, which will continue to work in close accord with the USSR" although it was thought possible "that conflicts of aim and interest between Peiping and Moscow may cause Communist China to attempt to play a role increasingly independent of Kremlin direction. These potential weaknesses may be exploitable by the West."[116] Yet in March 1953 the State Department's Bureau of Chinese Affairs warned against the dangers of drawing parallels between the Chinese and the Yugoslav situations, which they felt were "often exaggerated".

> Yugoslavia was in the uncomfortable position of being a real satellite and of having no ready alternative to that menial role aside from a complete break away from the Soviet Union. Communist China on the other hand has been able to assume the role, at least to a significant extent, of Far Eastern leadership in world Communism. Far from being a helpless satellite, Communist China probably considers that it has gained considerable stature and importance through its ties in [*sic*] the Soviet camp. Furthermore, the Soviets themselves doubtless learned a lesson from the Yugoslav experience, and are dealing with China in the light of it.[117]

This was still the view of the CIA on 23 October 1953[118].

The Yugoslavs, however, clung to their belief that the Chinese would break with Stalin throughout the time of the Korean War. They were very interested in China and talked about it frequently in interviews with Westerners[119]. They maintained their cautious optimism regarding the future of Sino-Soviet relations although they had little concrete evidence of early dissonances[120], warning the Western powers not to foreclose possibilities of future good relations with China[121].

The Foreign Office brief for Eden's visit to Yugoslavia in

1952 spoke of excessive Yugoslav optimism in this matter, while summing up the British approach:

> Our policy certainly takes into account potential points of difference between the Communist states and we always have in mind to avoid actions likely to force them more closely into each others arms, but we believe that at present there is close harmony between their national interests and policies. Our China policy is on the one hand to take measures to prevent any further Chinese act of aggression, and on the other hand to seek reasonable means of living on good terms with China as a neighbour.[122]

Under Churchill and Eden, who took office in late 1951, there thus continued to be disagreements with the US over the treatment of Communist China, which had previously revolved around a series of issues from that of recognition[123] to the UN's condemnation of China as aggressor in the Korean War[124]. Under Eisenhower and Acheson, the US continued to have a more rigorously hostile attitude than that of the British towards the Peking government.

Ironically, as Adam Ulam put it, the Korean War "contributed to that psychological emancipation of the Chinese Communists which otherwise might have taken a long time and a different form"[125]. The British and the Yugoslavs were making accurate predictions and the American decision-makers were mistaken in the one instance where the power-political argument, and speculations regarding Mao's ultimate interest in being the master in his own house, were fully applicable, unlike the instance of Western interpretations of the origins of the Tito-Stalin split. For while the Soviet Union was practising restraint, China's successful involvement in the Korean War led the Chinese gradually to think of themselves as chief defenders of Communism in Asia; out of this grew their belief that Asian Communism should take the Chinese Revolution as an example, not the Russian Revolution. This paved the way for the Sino-Soviet rift[126].

Korea and the Perceived Threat to Yugoslavia

While in the three years after the outbreak of the Korean War the Western powers had differing views regarding Yugoslavia's value as a wedge or spearhead to break up the Soviet monolith, there was unanimity regarding her strategic importance. Indeed, this aspect became the major reason for Western support for Tito's régime, while her importance as an *offensive* weapon in "political warfare" of the Cold War receded into the background (see Chapter 7). Yugoslavia's strategic importance had already been recognized before 1950 (see Chapter 4). Now it became even greater in the context of increased Western fears of Soviet aggression, whether on a local or a global scale. Correspondingly, a threat to Yugoslavia was also of more direct concern to the Western powers.

Whatever Stalin's plans regarding Yugoslavia, the war of nerves which had been started by the Cominformist governments was stepped up every spring and every autumn, at the time of manoeuvres. As we have seen, the danger of an internal uprising in Yugoslav Macedonia grew into the fear that "volunteers" from the neighbouring countries might turn a civil war in Yugoslavia into a war on an international scale; and out of this, in turn, grew the perception of a danger of clashes between the satellite armed forces and the Yugoslavs. It was nurtured on the one hand by the gradual rearmament of the satellites bordering on Yugoslavia: in early 1950 these had still been deemed too weak to take on Yugoslavia's 30 divisions[127], but the ratio was changing rapidly (see Appendix C). On the other hand, the steady increase of incidents along Yugoslavia's borders provided ample opportunities to put a spark to the Balkan tinderbox. According to the Yugoslav *White Book*, published and presented to the UN to draw attention to the threat, the number of frontier incidents between 1 July 1948 and 30 September 1950 had increased almost seven-fold (see Appendix C).

In addition, propaganda in Cominformist press and radio broadcasts denounced Yugoslavia as a base for Western aggression against the Soviet bloc. While in April and May 1950 the North Korean radio advocated a "peaceful unification of Korea", other Communist broadcasting stations in Europe and Asia simultaneously talked about aggressive preparations on the part of the Western powers, among which were mentioned the forging of an "Athens-Belgrade axis" as part of a "Mediterranean pact to supplement the Atlantic Treaty", also described as an "aggressive Mediterranean bloc"[128]. The references in the Communist media to the military alliance which the "Anglo-American imperialists" were trying to force upon the "Titoists" and the "monarcho-fascists" of Yugoslavia and Greece were repeated from April 1950 onwards until the actual establishment of military links between these countries, anticipating real developments by almost two years[129]. The frequency of allegations regarding Graeco-Yugoslav aggressive intentions increased towards the date given by Király as the planned date for a Soviet-satellite attack on Yugoslavia, the spring of 1951. Thus the *Literaturnaya Gazeta* of 29 March 1951 claimed that the "Singman Rhees" of Athens and Belgrade were calling for American support to form armies capable of advancing towards the Danube on the flank of the enemy, and simultaneously the Greek Communists maintained that the Athens government was preparing for an attack on Tirana[130]. The psychological climate, at least in the Communist-governed countries, was thus certainly prepared for war on Yugoslavia (and possibly Greece), just as it had been prepared for the outbreak of war in Korea. But irrespective of Stalin's real intentions, anti-Yugoslav propaganda increased the psychological pressure on the Yugoslav leaders and on those elements in the Communist Party of Yugoslavia who still felt uneasy about supporting Tito against Stalin.

We have seen how the Western powers had feared for Yugoslavia's security since June 1948, and with a sense of alarm by the second half of 1949. The relative calm of the end of that year was succeeded by new waves of rumours in early 1950, which gave some Western decision-makers concern[131]. Prior to the outbreak of war in Korea, a Soviet move by proxy was anticipated by Bevin and Acheson, as we have noted. At the end of May 1950, Kennan also suspected that the Soviets might be "looking for an opportunity for a 'limited fracas'", and he asked the State Department "to consider the possibility that the Soviets might arrange to have the satellites engage in military action with Yugoslavia. . . . [I]t would be quite possible for the Soviet Union itself to remain untainted in it."[132] Accordingly, the occurrence of such a "limited fracas" in Korea, in confirming one part of the prediction of Kennan and others, seemed to make more likely the other part of the forecast, namely a satellite attack on Yugoslavia on Korean lines. Sir David Kelly, the British Ambassador in Moscow, also thought the Soviet Union might stage "a major incident elsewhere (e.g. in Berlin, Yugoslavia or Persia)"[133]. The Foreign Office's Russia Committee took note of the similarity between Cominformist propaganda efforts against Yugoslavia and anti-South Korean propaganda prior to the invasion[134]. Observers on the spot also felt uneasy. "Since the attack on Korea," wrote George Allen, a fortnight after it had occurred, "we've become more alert to the possibility that the Soviets might do something here."[135] Anything that could hitherto be dismissed as part of a war of nerves was henceforth regarded with new suspicion.

Truman wanted to know "at what other points the USSR or its satellites might attack", and at a meeting of the NSC on 29 June 1950, Kennan "thought the chief danger spots were Yugoslavia, Iran and Eastern Germany". The Director of the CIA, Admiral Hillenkoetter, agreed. An attack on Yugoslavia was something the Soviets might feel they could get away with[136]. The NSC based its policy-making on CIA reports which were decidedly alarmist after the invasion of South Korea, while they had been more optimistic about the Balkans in the earlier months of 1950 (see Chapter 4). The first post-Korean review, in line with other CIA and Joint Intelligence Committee reports[137] noted the

acceleration of Soviet and satellite troop movements in the Balkan area. Soviet military equipment and supplies have been flowing into the Balkans for several months in quantities that appear to be in excess of the needs of Soviet forces available there. . . . While it is still possible that Soviet-satellite troops in the Balkans are inadequate to mount a successful armed offensive against Yugoslavia, it would be possible for puppet troops with covert Soviet support at least to start a local war on considerable scale by moving across the borders of Yugoslavia, Greece and Turkey. Soviet propaganda is emphasizing the imminence of hostilities in this area (through Greek and Yugoslav "aggression" of course). The initiation of any kind of armed aggression in this area by Soviet puppet troops would present the basic issues of the Korean incident all over again, forcing the US either to abandon some of its commitments or to disperse its military strength.[138]

The report of the following month drew attention to Yugoslavia's vulnerability as she

> could be attacked virtually without warning by the armed forces of the nearby Soviet satellites, Bulgaria, Rumania, Hungary and Albania [that have been] . . . substantially strengthened by a steady increment of Soviet supplies and equipment during the past year. . . . The importance the USSR attaches to Tito's heresy against Moscow-controlled Communism suggests strongly that Yugoslavia eventually will be target for attack if the USSR proceeds to sponsor further local aggression through the medium of non-Soviet military forces.
> Other European and Near Eastern border areas are less likely targets than Yugoslavia for the immediate future.[139]

The danger to Yugoslavia was also perceived by the Secretaries representing the American Military Establishment[140] and the US Ambassador to the Soviet Union, Kirk[141].

Kennan, however, had changed his mind about the danger to Yugoslavia as early as 29 June 1950. At the NSC's second meeting that day, he argued that the Soviet Union would only attack Yugoslavia either as a prelude to World War III, or else if they became "jittery", of which he saw no signs[142]. His view is reflected in the passage of NSC 73 of 1 July 1950 that deals with Yugoslavia: a Soviet or satellite attack on Yugoslavia was not regarded as very likely as for the Soviet Union it would mean wasting resources and energy in an area peripheral to her main interests[143].

NSC 73/4 of 25 August 1950, tied together the more alarmist views of the military establishment and the intelligence services with those of Kennan. Here Yugoslavia was listed among the most endangered areas, together with Iran, Turkey, Greece, Afghanistan, Pakistan and Finland. A direct Soviet attack on Yugoslavia was not regarded as very likely, because it was assumed that the Soviet Union was trying to avoid a third world war, while a "direct USSR attack on

Yugoslavia would include a risk of involving the Western powers", which, it was thought, would mean a world war. A satellite attack, however, (without direct Soviet participation) was regarded as a real possibility[144].

At the beginning of the following year the perception of danger increased once more. In the Policy Planning Staff, Ferguson and Tufts, still fearing that the Korean War might be the overture for a global "*Götterdämmerung*", even had concrete ideas as to how the USSR would go about starting World War III:

> It must first assure the continued and increasing involvement of the U.S. in the Far East where no decision is possible, and second, during such involvement, the Soviet Union must neutralize and/or destroy the Yugoslav-Greek-Turkish forces on its flank and acquire the rest of Europe. In the European aspect of this strategy, the first move should be the invasion of Yugoslavia.[145]

In a memorandum also of late January 1951 John Paton Davies, the China expert on the Policy Planning Staff, expressed the fear that the Kremlin might proceed "to turn the heat on Yugoslavia", counting on the apathy of the Europeans[146].

Davies was mistaken if he assumed that the West Europeans felt less concern for the fate of Yugoslavia than the US. The members of the Western Union also monitored developments in the Balkans. In July 1950 their Military Committee's discussion corresponded closely to American thinking: while a Soviet/satellite surprise attack on Western Europe was thought less likely, satellite forces "might be employed without warning, simultaneously or in succession, at a series of vulnerable points along the Soviet periphery, for example Yugoslavia, Greece, Turkey and Iran"[147]. Intelligence reports of the most disquieting kind continued to flow into the Western foreign policy-making and defence establishments; for example, the Quai d'Orsay's Sous-Direction d'Europe Orientale recorded in late November 1950:

> Depuis quelques jours, des rumeurs de guerre analogues à celles qui se répandissent après le déclenchement du

conflit Coréen circulent dans toute l'Europe de l'Est. Il s'agit là d'un phénomène cyclique dont l'importance ne doit pas être surestimée, mais qu'on ne saurait pourtant entièrement négliger.

... En même temps, la campagne anti-titiste se dévelope dans la plupart des pays kominformistes et atteint un degré de violence jusqu'ici rarement dépassé.[148]

At the meeting of the North Atlantic Council Deputies on 26 January 1951, the UK representative pointed out that his government regarded Yugoslavia as one of the chief danger points for 1951. The other NATO members held the same view[149].

Yugoslavia's neighbour, Greece, was particularly nervous. Because of the similarity to the propaganda surrounding the North Korean attack, a nonsensical statement such as that made by the Greek Communist Party (KKE) on 7 July 1950 put the Greek government into a state of near-hysteria: the KKE claimed that US imperialism was using Greece to prepare for aggression against Albania or Bulgaria, in collaboration with the Tito clique, in order to turn the Balkans into another Korea[150]. Yugoslav statements on the subject varied. While Tito retained his cold blood[151], some of his countrymen, such as Bebler at the UN, showed signs of panic[152].

But irrespective of Yugoslav comments, the Western powers showed great concern for Tito's position. A memorandum of the Quai d'Orsay of 6 September 1950 sums up the effects of the events in Korea on Western attitudes towards Yugoslavia:

Le problème d'une aide occidentale à la Yougoslavie apparaît depuis les évènements de Corée sous un jour nouveau. En démontrant que le Kremlin ne répugne pas à lancer dans un conflit armée un état satellite, la guerre en Extrême-Orient dissipe les illusions que l'on pouvait encore entretenir sur la résolution pacifique de Staline. Elle incite en même temps à penser que la Yougoslavie, ceinturée par la chaîne des démocraties populaires, n'est pas à l'abri d'une aggression.

The memorandum concluded with an exhortation to get military aid talks started as soon as possible[153].

6

Strengthening the Shield — Military Relations 1950-1955

As we have seen, the Korean War gave new urgency to the question of the Western attitude in case of an attack on Yugoslavia. At the first NSC meeting on 29 June 1950, the question was raised whether an attack on Yugoslavia by the Soviets (and/or satellites) would vitally affect US interests and whether it would call for US military assistance[1]. At the second NSC meeting that day Kennan restated the American position of NSC 18/4, which was that they "ought to keep out" if Yugoslavia were attacked, "except for limited assistance to Tito", and the Council agreed with him[2]. This stance was confirmed in the policy paper NSC 73: the US government were not yet prepared to make a commitment to the defence of Yugoslavia[3]. Soon afterwards, however, in the context of the efforts to build up Western defences, Yugoslavia's importance for the West grew.

Yugoslavia in Defence Plans for Austria, Italy and the Adriatic

When the American Ambassador to Belgrade, George Allen, was interviewed on the US National Broadcasting system on 24 February 1951 about US aid measures for Yugoslavia, he said that

Yugoslavia is a shield for Italy and Greece. She also has a vital strategic position on the Adriatic Sea. It is not difficult to see how she protects the southern flank of a defense system that runs from the North Sea down

155

through the Netherlands, Belgium, Luxembourg, France, Western Germany, Austria, Italy, Greece and Turkey.

Yugoslavia had become important to Western military planners from the moment it was clear that she would not allow the USSR or any satellites to march through her territory in order to attack Italy or the Adriatic[4]. But it was still another step to assume that she would fight on the side of the West if there were a Soviet attack through Austrian territory on Italy, Greece or Germany, as Tito publicly implied he would on 22 February 1951[5]. Western military planners remained sceptical of Tito's promise[6], but it was enough that they could count on Yugoslavia's refusal to let Soviet troops or satellite forces pass through her territory.

Thus in December 1950 the American Joint Chiefs of Staff stated that "Yugoslavia['s] . . . strategic location makes it of direct importance to the defense of the North Atlantic area. . . . [T]he denial of Yugoslavia to the Soviets [is considered] vital in the sense that it is highly important to the security of the United States."[7] This estimate was shared in the State Department: in a memorandum of 23 January 1951, John Paton Davies of the Policy Planning Staff expressed his fear that the Soviets would resort to some action in Yugoslavia. "[I]f we do not go to the aid of Yugoslavia, the collapse in Europe and the Middle East will be . . . certain."[8] The Deputy Director of the Policy Planning Staff, Fergusson, and his colleague Tufts thought that failure to come to the defence of Yugoslavia might "effectively paralyze the infant defense efforts in Western Europe"[9]. The North Atlantic Council's Deputies also agreed in late January 1951, that the strategic advantages derived from the breach between Yugoslavia and the Soviet Union were "considerable"[10].

Meanwhile, the British Chiefs of Staff had taken up Field Marshal Montgomery's idea that an Italo-Austrian bridgehead should be held for the re-conquest of Europe[11]. Having once opposed the idea of holding Italy, the British now advocated it[12]: if Yugoslavia delayed the Soviet advance by waging a guerrilla war against the occupying forces, Austria could be given logistic support via Italy for at least as long as it would take the Soviets to secure an unbroken supply-line across

Yugoslavia, which in Western estimations would take a month[13].

The Chiefs of Staff proposed in June 1951 that Italy should be defended along the line of the Isonzo River, part of which flows through Yugoslav territory, rather than along the Tagliamento further west[14]. In May 1951 members of the US Joint Intelligence Committee recommended early American-Yugoslav staff talks to co-ordinate the defence of the Ljubljana Gap in advance of the Julian Alps[15]. The Supreme Allied Commander in Europe (SACEUR) had approved this by 21 September 1951, recommending an agreement with Belgrade that Yugoslavia should defend the Ljubljana Gap, also blocking the access to the Villach area through the Sava valley. Soviet troops would in that case be unable to circumvent the Italian defensive line along the Isonzo (and the Gorizia Gap) and invade from a more northerly point[16].

In mid-1952 the Yugoslavs announced their willingness to defend the Ljubljana Gap with three Army Corps of four divisions each[17]. This only became co-ordinated Yugoslav-Western policy in the military talks of August 1953[18]. Yet no formal commitment was made to this policy, because that would have required Italo-Yugoslav exchanges of military information. But before the Trieste settlement the two countries were never friendly enough to take this step, and the Western powers did everything to avoid offending the Italians by giving away military secrets about them.

Although there was no detailed technical agreement on the methods, the defence of this area as such became NATO strategy. The American Chief of the Army Staff, General Lawton Collins, at Anglo-American meetings in Washington in November 1951 obtained general agreement that any "action by Communist forces against the Ljubljana area would be a threat of general war", because it was the gateway to Italy and the back door to Austria[19]. In December 1952 the Yugoslavs stated their recognition of this strategic connection between the Julian Alps and the defence of Italy and Austria[20]. This tied in with NATO strategy, which now included the holding of parts of Austria, at least a certain Alpine redoubt, rather than its complete evacuation at the outbreak of war[21].

As long as Yugoslav defence co-operation could be ensured, Western military planning could be changed to a new NATO best-case-scenario, whereby forces under SACEUR's command (including Yugoslavia) should defend

> the Ijssel-Rhine line and ... the line of the Alps. The United States support this concept. However, the USCINCEUR [US Commander-in-Chief for all American forces in Europe] will prepare emergency plans to allow for the possibility of being forced back as far as ... United Kingdom — Spain — French-Italian-Austrian Alps — Denaric [*sic*] Alps[22].

So even this fall-back line included the defence of part of the Julian Alps by the Yugoslavs, who, with Allied logistic support, were thought to be able to hold that area, and the Dinaric Alps, indefinitely. Thus Western defence plans, mainly as a result of Yugoslavia's changed position in military strategy, now provided for the holding of an Austro-Italian bridgehead, shielded in the northwest by a neutral Switzerland and in the east by Yugoslavia[23].

Western Measures to Counter the Threat to Yugoslavia

Further Deterrent Statements and Measures

Yugoslavia's increased importance to the West led to a greater urgency for the Western powers to adopt policies to counter any Soviet threat to Belgrade. At the beginning of 1951, corresponding to the date for the planned invasion of Yugoslavia given by Király, there was another increase in intelligence reports warning of acute danger for Yugoslavia (cf. Chapter 5[24]). Feelings of unease were also recorded by Western diplomats in Belgrade. On New Year's Day George Allen wrote from Belgrade to his relations in the US: "The threat of war, unfortunately, has not diminished, but ... [w]e've at last become fully aware of the Russian menace and are doing something about it."[25] Sir Charles Peake, who had hitherto been anything but alarmist, showed his concern about the growth of the satellite armed forces (see Appendix C); he regarded it as "quite possible that by the spring of this year the tables will have been turned" on Yugoslavia, which had so far been stronger than its satellite neighbours taken together[26].

The winter of 1950-51 also saw an increase in the attention given to the threat to Yugoslavia in the press: from August 1950 the Alsop brothers wrote articles in the *Washington Post* and the *New York Herald Tribune* on the danger to Yugoslavia[27]. As a result of this there was some pressure on the Western governments to make statements along the lines of those that had been made in late 1949.

On 12 February 1951 Anthony Eden, the Shadow Foreign Secretary, made a Commons appeal to the government to make a statement in respect of the threat to Yugoslavia, which he described "as a Balkan-Korean problem"[28]. There was support for this proposal from the floor of the House, and it was suggested that Britain should consult with the US and other NATO powers regarding a joint declaration "that any attack on Yugoslavia would be resisted by us. A declaration of that sort . . . would prevent an attack or the likelihood of such an attack."[29] On St. Valentine's Day, the Minister of Labour, Aneurin Bevan, urged his Cabinet colleagues to take this proposal up; the Cabinet agreed in the absence of Bevin, who was already terminally ill[30]. It was thus at the request of the Commons that the British government made the statement which was read out by Aneurin Bevan that day:

> His Majesty's Government are alive to the potential threat to Yugoslavia from the swollen armed forces of the satellites which has been emphasized by hostile Soviet and satellite propaganda. Any threat to Yugoslavia, who played a heroic part in the resistance to Hitler's aggression, is naturally a concern to His Majesty's Government, and we are in touch with other Governments on this.[31]

The American Secretary of State made a similar statement on the same day. In this case the proposal originated in the State Department, where on 31 January 1951 Robert Joyce had suggested this as a measure the US could adopt, if it appeared "in the spring or summer of 1951 that Yugoslavia was on the point of being invaded"[32]. Acheson therefore mentioned Yugoslavia in a press conference, referring to Truman's report to Congress of 19 July 1950 that stated America's determination to resist aggression[33]. Soviet press and radio commentaries interpreted this as a warning against the launching of a campaign against Yugoslavia, which the American Ambassador in Moscow, Kirk, noted with relish[34]. In addition, the Americans may have strengthened their Mediterranean (6th) Fleet by delaying the departure of vessels and crew whose replacements had already arrived in early 1951. At the same time these forces were prepared for shore intervention at short notice, which, Philip Windsor observes, was most likely to be necessary in Yugoslavia at the time[35]. This show of force may well have had a deterrent effect.

There was consensus at the meetings of the North Atlantic Council Deputies on 22 and 26 January and on 13 February 1951 about the perception of a danger to Yugoslavia and about the importance she had for NATO[36]. The three Western governments in their dealings with Yugoslavia thus had the backing of their NATO partners. Bevan's and Acheson's statements were not, however, followed by a similar French public declaration. Although the head of the European Affairs Bureau, François Seydoux[37], was strongly in favour of making one, the Secretary General of the Quai d'Orsay, Parodi, only authorized a vague expression of concern, made to Tito by the French Ambassador on 26 February 1951[38]. Once again, France was falling behind Britain and America in her response.

Yugoslav Requests for Arms Aid

Apart from statements and gestures of support, the Yugoslavs needed arms. In view of their financial difficulties, they also needed credits or even gifts. Tito first asked the French for credit-sales of arms in an interview with their Ambassador on 28 October 1950[39]. Subsequent misunderstandings[40], combined with the French tendency to put narrow financial interests above strategic considerations[41], resulted in the loss of their opportunity to become Yugoslavia's main supplier of arms, and her main negotiating partner in the West.

Tito had to turn elsewhere: on 6 November 1950 he told the journalist Cyrus Sulzberger that he would buy arms from whoever made the best offer[42]. Tito was obviously waiting for the next move to be made by the Western powers, while these were determined to wait for a concrete request from him. They agreed, however, that he deserved arms aid[43]. The Yugoslavs were very hesitant to ask for arms openly, even denying any interest publicly until the spring of 1951[44]. They were afraid of Cominformist charges regarding aggressive intentions under Western leadership[45], which they feared would provide the Soviet bloc with an excuse for an invasion[46]. At last, at the end of January 1951, Milovan Djilas, one of Tito's closest associates, made the first official request for aid on a visit to London. He met Attlee secretly, who recorded Djilas' view that "it was undesirable that arms should be supplied through N.A.T.O. or indeed officially by the Western powers. Arms were needed but should be supplied unobtrusively. He asked how matters stood. I said I would . . . find out what the position was."[47] On 10 February 1951 the Yugoslavs gave the British a list of their arms and ammunition requirements[48].

General Velebit made a similar request for arms from the US on 3 February 1951[49]. This required a conscious American departure from the previous policy of not handing over arms to the Yugoslavs prior to an attack[50], as contained in NSC 18/4[51]. But the estimates of Soviet intentions and capabilities on which NSC 18/4 had been based were outdated, as the Joint Chiefs of Staff pointed out on 7 December 1950[52] and again on 2 February 1951; they no longer saw any objection to "deliveries of military items in a covert manner to Yugoslavia"[53]. The new policy statement on Yugoslavia, NSC 18/6[54], adopted their recommendations[55]; it was approved by the NSC on 7 March and by the US President on 12 March 1951[56].

On 5 March 1951, Ernest Bevin, resurfacing briefly during his final illness, recommended that the Cabinet "agree in principle to supply [the Yugoslavs] with arms and equipment subject to availabilities". Speed was essential, as "the threat to Yugoslavia may become actual during this summer"[57]. The Chiefs of Staff and the Cabinet's Defence Committee agreed that "as it was strategically desirable for Yugoslavia to be well armed", the United Kingdom "should not let purely financial considerations stand in the way"[58]. Nor was the French Conseil des Ministres opposed to the actual handing over of arms[59]. The US also obtained the agreement of the other NATO powers in the second half of March 1951[60]. These decisions were the basis of all Western arms aid to Yugoslavia.

While they were being made and long before they had been implemented, further press-leaks occurred[61] which created the impression that the Yugoslavs were receiving military aid from the West, at a time when they had not received a single cartridge. Should Stalin have had any plans of sending his satellite's troops into Yugoslavia, he may have been deflected by the Western statements in conjunction with these press reports[62]. If so, the West had won a victory of deterrence by bluffing.

Arms Aid For Yugoslavia 1951-1953

Disappointed with the reactions of the French, Tito tried to establish military relations with the West through Britain as chief mediator[63]. Once again he was disappointed, because Whitehall had little to offer and was unwilling to act without consultation with the Americans[64]. These, however, did not think it necessary to inform the British and the French before promising General Velebit on 2 March 1951 that they would make arms available immediately. A first shipload was picked up by the Yugoslavs in mid-May[65], and a second, larger delivery was promised[66].

It was only after this that the French became fully aware of the fact that the Americans expected military aid to be given on a grant basis; on 27 June 1951 the Conseil des Ministres decided at last, at the urgent request of Robert Schuman, to cede captured German arms to Yugoslavia "à titre gratuit"[67]. The Americans told their two partners soon afterwards that they had provisionally earmarked $75,000,000 for military equipment for Yugoslavia[68]. The British saw that their contribution (£4,000,000 or about $11,200,000) would be embarrassingly small by comparison. They were very keen to keep up with the US and not to let it "push us into the background"[69]. The bitter truth was, however, in the words of an official in the Ministry of Defence, that "quite obviously we cannot hope to compete with the Americans."[70] This weighty sentence sums up not just this individual case but the slow and painful process of realization that Britain was no longer America's equal.

In early May 1951 the Americans informed their partners that they would prefer bilateral talks with the Yugoslavs about the technicalities of military aid. Although the British and the French were not happy about this, the Americans now called the tune[71]. The Yugoslavs were told that they had to make a formal, public request for aid, in accordance with the requirements of the Mutual Defence Assistance Program (MDAP)[72], and that they had to accept the presence of an American military advisory group[73]. In return they were given the assurance that the US would "provide both logistic and operational support in [the] event of Soviet aggression"[74]. The Yugoslavs complied, and a Mutual Security Agreement between the US and Yugoslavia was signed in Belgrade on 14 November 1951 [75].

On 26 January 1951 Harriman, the director of the Mutual Security Program, suggested that in certain categories, arms supplies to Yugoslavia should have "a priority superior to those of our allies"[76]. The Joint Chiefs of Staff had recommended that Yugoslavia should be given "a priority equal to that of the NATO countries"[77]. The North Atlantic Council Deputies at the end of January 1951 agreed that in case of an emergency, equipment should be delivered to Yugoslavia by NATO members, "even if this might result in some delay in the completion of their own rearmament plans, provided that the overall defence plan of [NATO] was not thereby in jeopardy"[78]. This concession was later also applied to the direct arms deliveries at Yugoslavia's request[79].

A Joint Chiefs of Staff document of mid-March 1951 shows that Yugoslavia was given priority over Greece and Turkey as it was "considered that the build-up of Soviet-satellite forces constitutes primarily an increased threat to Yugoslavia, rather than to Turkey or Greece"[80]. Although not committed in any way to the defence of the West, Yugoslavia was thus treated in the same way as the United States' closest allies of the North Atlantic Treaty[81]. This was the order of priorities in peace or local war in Yugoslavia; in case of a global conflict, however, it was agreed by the Americans and the British that other demands on their arsenal would be so great that it would be well-nigh impossible for them to spare any modern equipment for Yugoslavia, let alone send them any troops or give more than minimal air-coverage[82]. The British put Yugoslavia's requirements below their own and those of the "Old Commonwealth Countries" (the official euphemism for "white Commonwealth Countries"), next to India and Pakistan[83].

At the end of the American budget-year 1951/1952 ("Fiscal 1952"), there were still some $63,000,000 unallotted. These, Harriman proposed, should be used as a supplementary programme for Yugoslavia; he obtained the consent of the rest of the government[84]. By the end of December 1952 Yugoslavia had thus received a proportion of equipment which in relation to the total Mutual Defence Assistance Program was "as high as that for any North Atlantic Treaty Organisation nation", as the US Joint Chiefs of Staff commented[85]. The reason given was Yugoslavia's importance in the overall Western rearmament effort[86]. Thus Yugoslavia received $156,360,000 under the Mutual Security Program for fiscal year 1952, totalling $ 4,818,850,000 US military aid (excluding Spain). The United Kingdom received $297,150,000, or not quite twice as much as Yugoslavia; France received a staggering $2,121,400,000; Italy $458,690,000, and Portugal $83,220,000. Greece, not yet in NATO, obtained $116,250,000; Turkey $225,160,000, and Iran $225,160,000[87]. For fiscal year 1953, Yugoslavia was scheduled to receive between $400,000,000 and $500,000,000[88].

Although initially arms aid for Yugoslavia had been a tripartite enterprise, in the end the Americans on their own provided by far the greatest amount, just as they were the main suppliers for all the other NATO powers. The French did not give on a grant basis anything other than the old German equipment. The British representative on the Working Group in Washington had rightly predicted that whoever provided the aid would in the end dominate all military relations[89]. The British had also harmed their relations with Tito by failing to sell him jets, although he was very keen on such a deal, in spite of having given him a promise to do so[90]. They went back on their word because of objections raised by the British Chiefs of Staff and by the Americans[91].

Localized Conflict in Yugoslavia?

When the priority of Yugoslavia in Western arms deliveries was discussed, the distinction was made between aid that could be given in peacetime, in a localized war, and in a global war. The possibility of a localized attack on Yugoslavia was considered in NSC 18/4 (and see Chapter 4). Although the Korean War did not create this concept in American thinking, it drew attention to it. Accordingly, the action proposed by NSC 73/4 in case of an attack on Yugoslavia was to "make every effort . . . to localize the action, to stop the aggression by political measures and to ensure the unity of the free world if war nevertheless follows"[92].

Yet in the age of superpower confrontation on a global scale, even with the achievement of nuclear parity, the hope that war could be localized could never be a certain factor in strategic calculations. The American Joint Strategic Planning Committee remained concerned about "the inherent and ever present possibility that any conflict in this area [Yugoslavia] . . . might well be the prelude to a global war"[93]. The British never accepted the view that a war that broke out in and around Yugoslavia would be "localized". The Chiefs of Staff and Sir Andrew Noble, the Under-Secretary in charge of the Southern Department, were convinced that it "would inevitably spill over the Yugoslav frontier" and "would lead to world war"; Noble therefore protested against the use of the term "second Korea" for Yugoslavia[94]. For this reason the Chiefs of Staff argued that the Western powers must not commit themselves irrevocably to diverting forces to Yugoslavia in case of an attack on her[95]. They obtained American agreement at military-political talks in Washington on 16 April 1952 "that it would be unrealistic to differentiate between planning for a localized war between Yugoslavia and the satellites and a general war"[96].

Nevertheless, the possibility of an isolated attack on Yugoslavia was not ignored. On 5 February 1951 the British Chiefs of Staff considered what action should be taken in this case. Even assuming that Yugoslavia would appeal to the UN, swift UN action was thought highly unlikely: the Soviets were back in the Security Council and could veto action; a reference to the General Assembly would take time; and Western forces were not stationed nearby, as had been the case in Korea. The Chiefs of Staff thought that

U.N. military action is only possible through some form of Agency Power, with an effective command organization already in being. The problem reduces itself to a Great Power decision as to whether or not to take military action, followed in the affirmative case by

U.N. action to give the necessary cover to satisfy the non-communist world.

The great powers should, therefore, take interim measures: this would later facilitate UN action, and influence positively the voting of wavering states in the General Assembly, something that would be difficult once Tito were overthrown and replaced by a puppet régime[97]. The British wanted to co-ordinate plans for such interim measures in advance with the Americans[98].

In early March 1951 at Anglo-American military-political discussions the British suggestion was approved and "it was generally agreed that the most effective action open to the Allies to assist Yugoslavia would be the provision of strategic and tactical air support."[99] Like other statements in the American documents[100], this instance reflects how little store the Western powers set by UN action and decisions in spite of the success of concerted action in Korea.

The Yugoslavs themselves strongly resisted any reference to a local war in their country. They wished to be seen as an asset to the West, not as a liability[101]. Accordingly, they did not wish to talk about a war-scenario in which they would be the petitioners; they obviously doubted that the Western powers would be prepared to back them if the West was not directly threatened by the Soviet bloc at the same time[102].

Two further issues were brought to the fore at the Anglo-American military-political discussions of March 1951, which were to remain unresolved for several months if not years. One concerned the dispatch of troops if Yugoslavia were attacked. The British Ambassador expressed his government's opposition to this idea in case of an attack by satellites only, while General Bradley, the chairman of the American Joint Chiefs of Staff, said that "for political reasons token land forces should be introduced"[103]. This view was also stated in the American Joint Chiefs of Staff's Joint Strategic Planning Committee on 7 April 1951. They emphasized, however, that numbers should be kept down "[s]ince ground forces once committed could not readily be extricated". NATO's emergency plans for global war must not be prejudiced[104]. The British Chiefs of Staff remained firmly opposed to the idea of sending any troops, even with these limitations[105]. Although the American Joint Chiefs of Staff had some agreement with their British colleagues' view[106], they insisted on keeping open the option of sending ground forces[107].

The other issue raised at the discussions of early March 1951 concerned nuclear strategy. The US military representatives proposed the use of nuclear weapons against satellites attacking Yugoslavia, as part of their "strategic air support"[108]. The British again had reservations about this point[109]. The American Joint Chiefs of Staff, however, considered that

> Final decisions should not be made now on the employment of atomic weapons against the satellite states. However, in view of the existence of suitable and highly profitable target complexes, and for the psychological advantages that would be obtained thereby, the United States should, after an attack occurs, and in the light of the conditions then existing, give serious consideration to the use of atomic weapons against the satellite states. Plans for such use should be prepared.[110]

The atomic bomb had, of course, not been used since the end of the Second World War. In spite of the explosion of the first Soviet atomic device in 1949, the United States could still count on the absence of a stockpile of nuclear bombs in the USSR. Taking into account American bombs and delivery systems, the Soviet Union was not likely to use the few bombs she might have had by 1950-51 in retaliation for American use of nuclear weapons against her satellites, whether in the Far East or in Europe. At the dawn of the age of an East-West nuclear stalemate, it was this reasoning that still allowed the concept of the (first and one-sided) use of atomic bombs to linger.

The public mention of the possibility of such use of the atomic bomb by Truman in a press conference on 30 November 1950 was merely a reflection of current American military strategy, and the President's determination to make use of it, if that were in the national interest of the United States, cannot be doubted[111]. But it horrified the Europeans who lived in what Truman in cold blood viewed as an appropriate theatre for such a nuclear "showdown". Truman's press statement provoked Attlee's hurried visit to Washington, where, on behalf also of the French, he pleaded for prior consultation before deciding to employ nuclear power[112]. But the use of the atomic bomb was the jealously guarded prerogative of the United States, and they were not willing to make this decision conditional upon agreement or even last-minute consultation with Britain, France or Canada. Nevertheless, Truman promised to Attlee on 8 December 1950 that Britain and Canada would be kept "informed at all times of developments which might call for the use of atomic weapons", particularly as British and Canadian bases might have to be used[113].

On 23 May 1951 a member of the State Department's Policy Planning Staff drew up a list of such potential developments:

A satellite attack on Yugoslavia would clearly increase the likelihood of global war. We would furnish military equipment to Yugoslavia and possibly military (air) support. In case of a satellite attack alone or with covert Soviet assistance, the conflict might be kept localized. We would probably not make atomic or other attacks on Soviet territory. Although there would be appropriate targets in Czechoslovakia and Rumania, we might, but probably would not, use atomic weapons against them. In case of a Soviet and satellite attack on Yugoslavia global war would probably eventuate. Thereupon we would use atomic weapons on Soviet, and probably satellite targets. The important question in these instances would be localization or generalization of conflict; the use of atomic weapons would depend largely on the answer to this question.

If Greece were attacked, "the situation would be similar to that arising from an attack on Yugoslavia." As Greece was a non-Communist country, albeit not yet a member of NATO, the West would have more of a moral obligation to come to her assistance[114].

Yugoslavia was mentioned in the subsequent discussions in June 1951 between Acheson and the Canadian Foreign Minister, Pearson, and his Ambassador, Wrong. Wrong tried to pin down the Americans with the formulation

that the fundamental assumption, one with which the

Canadian Government was in full accord, was that atomic weapons would be used only in the event of war with the Soviet Union. Mr. Nitze [director of the Policy Planning Staff] said that was the fundamental assumption; however, there might be certain exceptions, specifically Yugoslavia. In the case of Yugoslavia, the United States felt it would not foreclose the possibility of the use of atomic weapons, for there was some basis for believing that quick atomic retaliation might quickly localize and abort aggression in that area. Mr. Wrong thereupon said that the ba*sic* assumption might be reframed to say that atomic weapons will be used only in the event of war with the Soviet Union except in situations where the use of such weapons might serve to localize the conflict.[115]

Yugoslavia thus introduced a justification for a concept of an atomic strike against a non-nuclear power, which was the hope of localizing a conflict[116]. This is reflected in an interdepartmental paper of 3 August 1951, dealing with the "United States Position on Considerations Under Which the United States Will Accept War and on Atomic Warfare". It insisted that

> if a conflict which can be localized arises as a result of Soviet or Soviet-inspired aggression and United States armed forces are involved, the United States must retain its freedom of action to employ atomic weapons in such a localized conflict if the military situation dictates.

Although no specific reference to Yugoslavia is made in this paper[117], coming after the American-Canadian talks in June 1951, it shows that the problem of Yugoslavia had contributed, along with Korea, to the creation of a new principle for the employment of nuclear weapons in war.

This point was mentioned to British representatives at an Anglo-American military-political meeting in Washington on 13 September 1951. Before talking about general war, Nitze reminded his British interlocutors of a previous session (March 1951?) where they had examined

> the use of atomic weapons in local situations. We had discussed this possibility in connection with Yugoslavia

and had both expressed the view that it was conceivable that the use of atomic weapons in connection with aggression against Yugoslavia might be better calculated to localize it rather than spread it.

In September 1951, however, according to Nitze, American strategists thought that the use of nuclear weapons would not *necessarily* recommend itself in this case. Agreement was reached "that the issue should not be foreclosed but left open for consideration in the light of the circumstances existing at the time"[118]. There is no evidence to suggest, however, that the option of using nuclear weapons in case of an attack on Yugoslavia was discarded within the period under consideration.

Western Strategic Talks with Yugoslavia

After the decision to supply the Yugoslavs with arms had been taken, both the Americans and the Yugoslavs wanted to hold talks about strategic questions[119]. Preliminary talks were held in June 1951 between the Yugoslav Army Chief of Staff, General Koča Popović, and the American military planners, headed by General Eddleman[120]. But over a year lapsed before further talks took place, the delays being due to Italian sensibilities[121], British determination to be involved[122] and obstinate refusal to approve of the American choice of a head of mission[123].

Finally, the talks between an essentially American mission under General Handy and Yugoslav military and political leaders took place in Belgrade in the second half of November 1952. Like the Popović-Eddleman talks a year and a half earlier, these discussions were treated as preliminary by the Western powers, to the great disappointment of the Yugoslavs, who had awaited them impatiently[124]. The British Military Attaché, Colonel Bird, commented:

> The fact that General Handy came with absolutely nothing to offer except co-operation, and could make no commitments, soon made the Yugoslavs realise that they were likely to get the worst of a bad bargain and that they

were giving away their precious military secrets with nothing tangible in return.[125]

The Yugoslavs declared that they were unwilling to divulge any further information unless the West were prepared to say more. As General Handy had no authorization to comply, the talks came to an end on 20 November 1952. Both sides were frustrated at the meagre outcome, but agreed that more concrete talks should follow soon[126].

The follow-up talks once again took almost a year to materialize. They were held in Washington between 24 and 28 August 1953, this time with representatives from the US, Britain, France and Yugoslavia. With the Trieste question still undecided the Western powers promised not to disclose any of the information they were given by the Yugoslavs to any of their NATO partners including Italy[127]. These talks did indeed take the degree of involvement some steps further, as we shall see presently. It was agreed that "arrangements [should] be made for appropriate NATO Commanders to conduct operational discussions with the Yugoslavs"[128].

When these were about to be initiated[129], the storm broke over Trieste and the planned talks were prevented. Only in late 1954 had matters calmed down sufficiently for the West to give thought to a resumption of the military talks[130]. By March-April 1955 the Yugoslavs had begun to lose interest. The American Joint Chiefs of Staff in turn decided that if the West could not involve the Yugoslavs in talks any longer, further military aid to them would be unwarranted, as the West could not know what use it would be put to[131]. Consequently, from June 1956 onwards the US military assistance programme for Yugoslavia was gradually wound up: between mid-1956 and 1983 Yugoslavia received $5.9 million worth of military aid, while between 1951 and mid-1956 she had received $717.2 million worth of military aid[132].

Western military contacts with Yugoslavia thus ceased only six months after the American Joint Chiefs of Staff had asserted that "Defense of Italy is vital in the U.S. interest. Coordination of Yugoslavia defense plans and Italian defense effort is essential."[133] The great time-lags between the negotiations, caused by Western indecision and by the wish not to give away NATO information while Italy and Yugoslavia were still at loggerheads thus discouraged the Yugoslavs from ever entering into binding commitments towards the West. Only much later, after the settlement of the Trieste question and the normalization of Italo-Yugoslav relations, was the loss of this opportunity of involving the Yugoslavs in Western defences made up by direct negotiations between Rome and Belgrade.

NATO and Yugoslavia

The Western commitment not to divulge NATO secrets without the consent of other NATO partners and the opposition of Italy, had made defence co-ordination between NATO and Yugoslavia an impossibility. Tito's aversion to direct dealings with what the Communist-ruled countries referred to as the chief instrument of imperialist aggressive designs was also a major factor[134]. His attitude on this point had become modified by 1953, however, and he seems to have wished for a closer association with NATO[135]. The Balkan Pact (see below) and the Yugoslavs' temporary interest in joining the Western Union demonstrate their keenness although Tito denied any such interest earlier[136].

The Western powers gave the possibility of Yugoslavia's membership a good deal of consideration after 1950. This would have solved the problem of sharing information and of the defence of the Balkans. For this reason Generals Eisenhower and Collins wanted all planning with Yugoslavia to be conducted under the auspices of NATO[137]. The Western powers agreed that this was ultimately desirable[138].

The question was whether Yugoslavia should not become a member of NATO. At a Hearing of the Joint Senate Committee in the spring of 1951 the Americans Joint Chiefs of Staff and General Eisenhower spoke in favour of the admission of Yugoslavia[139]. The possibility of a gradual integration was established in the Yugoslav-American agreement on military aid signed on 14 November 1951: article VI.1 recorded the undertaking that Yugoslavia would contribute to the defensive strength of the "free world", which was interpreted as a bridge to membership of NATO in the Foreign Office[140]. This was indeed wished for by many within the US Administration[141].

Nevertheless, important ethical considerations stood

against the admission of Yugoslavia. For example, the influential journalist Cyrus Sulzberger, who at this time had much contact with the top officers of the Supreme Headquarters of the Allied Forces in Europe (SHAPE)[142], wrote in the *New York Times* on 20 February 1951 that

> Philosophical morality is vitally important to any allied cause whether in a hot or cold war. . . . In that connection it is always necessary to remember that the North Atlantic Treaty is conceived as a defensive alliance of democratic powers. Should it become an anti-Communist catchall it would lose much of its spiritual vitality and popular backing. . . . In seeking to relate such undemocratic countries as Spain and Yugoslavia to the treaty defense requirements it might indeed be well to attempt working out a 'co-belligerent' basis in cold war parlance, rather than one of full Allied equality.

This was his warning in view of the fact that "shape [*sic*] planners will obviously consider ways of relating Yugoslavia's potential to Graeco-Turkish defense".

The British government on the whole, and above all, Eden, were strongly opposed to the admission of Yugoslavia on these grounds: in Eden's words, "Yugoslavia surely cannot come in to NATO while existing internal conditions exist [*sic*]. We have our standards in NATO & should keep to them. If Jugo why not Spain?"[143] Robert Schuman, too, seems to have been opposed to Yugoslavia's admission[144]. After Schuman had been succeeded by Georges Bidault, however, the French began to be suspicious about the way in which Yugoslavia, in their view, was reaping all the benefits of an association with NATO without giving a reciprocal commitment: they therefore suggested that Yugoslavia should become a full member of NATO, or that a system of reciprocal guarantees should be established between the Balkan Pact powers (Yugoslavia, Greece and Turkey) on the one hand and NATO on the other, modelled on the planned European Defence Community[145].

Owing to the Trieste crisis and the early demise of the Balkan Pact, the occasion for any further consideration of the problem did not arise. It is of interest to note, however, how ready the Americans at any rate would have been to accept Tito's Communist dictatorship into the fold of NATO; this appears as a clas*sic* example of "national security interest" prevailing over moral considerations.

Yugoslav Defence Strategies

We have seen that by 1951 the Western powers saw the main function of Yugoslavia as one of a shield for Italy and Greece, an obstacle and a lasting embarrassment for invading Soviet troops, which would cause at least a considerable delay in their march south and south-west. In the defence talks with the Yugoslavs, the Western powers sought to persuade them to adopt strategies which would fit in with these plans.

Western defence planners were worried about evidence of Yugoslav determination to defend every inch of their territory[146]. Yet Tito himself had said as early as the winter of 1950 that he would abandon the Danubian plain and retreat to the Bosnian mountains, leaving Belgrade undefended if the worst came to the worst; the Yugoslav army would then be divided up into groups of 50 men to conduct partisan warfare[147]. Popović told Eddleman in the spring of 1951 that "the Yugoslavs are thinking mainly in terms of guerrilla warfare"[148].

General Collins, who visited Yugoslavia in October 1951, was told by Popović about Yugoslav expectations regarding an invasion from the north: they thought they would be able to defend the line along the Danube and Belgrade for 15 days. On D + 20 days they expected this line to be lost, and with it the capital. On D + 35 days they would find themselves at a "line from the junction point of the Austro/Hungarian/Yugoslav frontier — south of Zagreb — the line of the River Sava — South of Kragujevac — Kraljevo." The Yugoslavs planned to divide their 38 divisions into three army groups (*oblast*), each of three corps, based on Zagreb, Belgrade and Skopje. They were expecting to fight a combined satellite force of 85 divisions, which in their estimate would have Soviet air coverage. Finally Popović added "that there would be no aggressive action against Albania at this stage"[149]. The Handy talks of November 1952 confirmed that the Yugoslav "general plan seems to be as we had hoped, namely a fighting withdrawal from the frontier to successive lines of defence from where a counter offensive could be launched". In the final phase of their withdrawal they would retreat to the "bastion" defence area, the Dinaric Alps: "They do not appear to intend putting a major defence effort into the VOJVODINA, but they have allocated strong forces to the Ljubljana Gap area."[150]

Finally at the quadripartite talks in Washington in late August 1953, certain strategic concepts were agreed upon:

(a) *Northwest Yugoslavia*
The Yugoslavs should "Initially hold the mountain massif as far to the north and east as possible with a fighting withdrawal as necessary to final defensive positions for defense of the Ljubljana area".

(b) *Central Yugoslavia*
This area should be defended "keeping contact with the forces to the Northwest and Southeast and preventing Soviet satellite forces from obtaining a foothold on the Adriatic or linking up with Albania. (This portion of the concept was adopted primarily in the interest of harmony, and the United States attaches less importance to this area than to Northwestern and Southeastern Yugoslavia.)"

(c) *Southeast Yugoslavia*
The Yugoslavs should "Conduct an active defense as far to the north and east as feasible, tying in with Greek forces so as to prevent the exploitation of Greek and Yugoslav areas, to defend the Struma Valley approaches, and to block the Vardar-Morava [*sic*] corridor".

(d) *Albania*
Yugoslavia should stop an Albanian invasion, but "decisions concerning subsequent actions with respect to Albania should be made in the light of circumstances then existing"[151].

It was either during these talks or during the subsequent talks on logistics that the US committed itself to equip and continue to support nine Yugoslav infantry divisions, to be stationed at the Ljubljana Gap[152]. But the operational talks with NATO commanders, which should have followed, were not held; it therefore cannot be said how binding this agreement was for the Yugoslavs.

Yugoslavia's Rôle in Eastern Mediterranean Defence Strategy

When asked to justify American aid measures for Yugoslavia before the House of Representatives' Committee on Foreign Affairs, General Olmsted, the Director of the Office of Military Assistance, explained on 27 March 1952:

> Yugoslavia is at the hinge between Western Europe, the western flank and the southern flank, and through Yugoslavia are the terrain features through which access could be gained either to the Upper Adriatic and the northern plains of Greece, or to the eastern Mediterranean through Greece and Istanbul.[153]

There are two main themes which reflect the importance of Yugoslavia in the defence of the Balkans in this period: Yugoslavia's rôle in the admission of Greece and Turkey to NATO; and military talks between Yugoslavia, Greece and Turkey, in the context of the Balkan Treaty leading to the Balkan Pact.

Yugoslavia and the Admission of Greece and Turkey to NATO

As we have seen, Anglo-American defence plans of the late 1940s provided for the defence by Allied forces of a line running down the Adriatic, then eastwards passing between the Greek mainland in the north and Crete in the south, including also Cyprus and the Iskenderun pocket in Turkey, but not Greece or Turkey as such. The only foreign forces in either country were British troops in Greece, and these had specific orders to withdraw from the Greek mainland in case of an invasion of Greece at the outbreak of general war[154].

Yet through the Anglo-Franco-Turkish Treaty of Mutual Assistance of 1939 and the Truman Doctrine the Western powers were obliged to varying degrees to go to war if Turkey or Greece were attacked. The Turks, however, wanted a more binding commitment on the part of the Americans and asked to be admitted to NATO[155]. The Greeks followed suit. Ernest Bevin was opposed to this[156]. The British insisted that Turkey was of far greater importance for the defence of the Middle

East and the Mediterranean than for the defence of what was then NATO area[157]. Consequently Bevin tried to channel all Turco-Greek enthusiasm for defensive arrangements into a Mediterranean pact which he hoped to create[158]. The Greeks and Turks were not content with a military associateship which they were offered as a compromise[159], but were determined to acquire full membership[160].

Meanwhile, the American perception of the strategic geography of the northern and eastern Mediterranean was changing. Greece and Turkey were still part of the State Department's "Near Eastern Affairs" Bureau, and they were categorized with the Middle Eastern countries for the purposes of Mutual Security Aid. But while the Americans in 1950 still acknowledged the importance of Turkey for the defence of the Middle East, the "Northern Tier", which in American terminology used to refer to Greece, Turkey and Iran, now contained a new element: Yugoslavia. On 8 February 1951, the Deputy Director of the Policy Planning Staff, Fergusson, drew attention to the importance of these *four* countries in strategic considerations, in view of their force strengths and their geographical key position, which he described as a potential "bridge to Eurasia in the event the USSR occupies Western Europe". Yugoslavia and Greece, he thought, were of crucial importance to the formation of an effective resistance in Western Europe[161]. In joint State Department/Joint Chiefs of Staff discussions of 30 January 1951, Admiral Sherman, Chief of the US Navy Staff, said:

> We should start thinking about the Balkans as an entity and not link them up with the Middle East. It may be wise to group Italy, Yugoslavia, Greece and Turkey for planning purposes. . . . [W]e have to regard Greece and Yugoslavia as an area which can furnish couverture for Italy.[162]

The Middle East was less vital to the West than Western Europe, a point which the British, whose task it would be to defend the Middle East, were forced to concede grudgingly at staff talks on 26 October 1950[163]. Therefore, if Turkey and Greece were of importance to both Western Europe and the Middle East, it was preferable from the American point of view that Turkey and Greece should be linked with Western

Europe. Therefore the US Chiefs of Mission in Middle Eastern countries, meeting in Istanbul between 14 and 21 February 1951, recommended the acceptance of Greece and Turkey into NATO. While Turkey should be encouraged to continue to seek defensive arrangements with the Middle East, Greece should "be considered as belonging to a Western or Mediterranean region rather than the Middle East . . . and . . . be encouraged to seek appropriate arrangements for military cooperation with Yugoslavia and Turkey"[164]. The Senate's Committee on Foreign Relations raised this point with representatives of the military establishment. There was

> remarkable unanimity in opinion that Turkey and Greece (also Spain and possibly Yugoslavia) should be admitted to the Atlantic Pact. These views were expressed in strong terms by Generals Eisenhower, Bradley, Clay, Spaatz and George and by Admiral Sherman. General Eisenhower said: 'You do not have to be a soldier to know the great value which would accrue to freedom within the US by including these countries: Spain, Turkey, Greece and Yugoslavia'.[165]

Admiral Sherman, an ardent proponent of the linking of Greece and Turkey with the defence of southwestern Europe, explained to Lord Tedder, the British Chief of the Air Staff, that it was his greatest concern "to secure General Eisenhower's right flank; and that he regards Greece and Thrace as inevitably linked with Yugoslavia and Southern Europe under General Eisenhower"[166]. On 15 May 1951 the US Ambassador finally informed Whitehall "that the United States Government favoured the adherence of Greece and Turkey to the North Atlantic Treaty"[167].

The French head of the EMMO of the Western Union (Europe Méridionale, Méditerranée Occidentale) Command was at that point still opposed to Greece's, Turkey's and Yugoslavia's integration into either NATO or the British Middle East Command. He did not think that the national differences and peculiarities of these countries could be overcome effectively so as to integrate their defences but thought co-ordination of planning viable to some extent and suggested that there should be a planning group with representatives from these three countries, and from EMMO, with the exception of the Italians[168].

In the end the British felt obliged to agree to the admission of Turkey and Greece, because they did not want to antagonize the Americans and the Turks: Britain had little to offer Turkey in return for Turkish involvement in the defence arrangements for the Middle East, to compensate for forgoing the advantages of NATO membership[169]. Objections were raised when the Cabinet met on 22 May 1951, as the extension of NATO "might lead to demands that countries like Spain and Yugoslavia should also be included". But Attlee secured agreement that Britain should consent, to please the Americans, who in turn should make a greater effort to help create a Middle East defensive organization. Britain should point out that the admission of Greece and Turkey should not lead to the admission of Spain. By design or by accident, Attlee did not mention the admission of Yugoslavia as undesirable[170]. Consensus was at last achieved at the Ottawa Conference of the North Atlantic Council, which followed the Anglo-Franco-American meeting of foreign ministers in the autumn of 1951: Greece and Turkey were to be admitted to full NATO membership[171].

In mid-June 1951 command arrangements were discussed by the British and the Americans in Washington. General Collins remarked

> that the position of Yugoslavia played an important part in this. We might well in the future wish to associate Yugoslavia with NATO or even to include her in it. . . . In his view, Greece belonged to the Balkans which in turn hinged upon Yugoslavia. Both were vital to the defence of Europe. Therefore Greece should be under SACEUR.[172]

An alternative creation of a Supreme Allied Command, Eastern Mediterranean and Middle East, partly integrated with NATO, was proposed by the British Chiefs of Staff[173], but was opposed by the Americans, the French and the Greeks and Turks[174]. The two Aegean countries were eventually admitted to full membership of NATO under CINCSOUTH, on 25 February 1952.

Defence Co-ordination Between Yugoslavia, Greece and Turkey

Yugoslavia's defence involvement with Greece and Turkey followed a precipitate political rapprochement (see Chapter 3) caused solely by the quest for common defence. Like the close co-operation between Greece and Turkey at the time, it was a *mariage de convenance* without even a hint of love. A mere five months after the Yugoslavs stopped helping the Greek rebels, the Greek General Kitrilakis encouraged the Americans to discuss a defensive arrangement "immediately east of the countries included in the North Atlantic Pact". NATO had just been formed without Greece, but as the Greek Civil War had come to an end, Greece could also contribute to the defence of the free world. Kitrilakis argued:

> It is unquestionable that the Balkan peninsula can play a very important role for the Western powers in the event of a Russian aggression against them. And the greater the number of Balkan Nations assuming the above role, the more effective their contribution. . . . Consequently, cooperation of Yugoslavia with Greece and Turkey ensures great probabilities of success.

The concerted defence of these three states, he argued, would act as a deterrent, would slow down aggression once it occurred, and the area might ultimately be used as a base for a strategic counter-offensive. Therefore, "creation . . . of a Balkan bloc consisting of Turkey, Greece and Yugoslavia will greatly contribute to the maintenance of peace." He therefore wanted friendly relations with Yugoslavia[175].

As we have seen, the Western powers actively encouraged the political rapprochement between Greece and Yugoslavia. Ernest Davies (whose travels have been described in Chapter 3) thought that

> The objective of the West is to muster the maximum resistance to Russian expansion in order to preserve the independence of the Western countries and of the rest of the free world. . . . The problem . . . is to find some way of consolidating the countries of Eastern Europe and the Mediterranean without bringing them into the

Atlantic Pact, and taking into account the peculiar position of Yugoslavia.[176]

The American State Department's Bureau of Near Eastern Affairs was also interested in "military cooperation, as soon as political conditions permit, of Yugoslavia with Greece and Turkey"[177]. In the spring of 1951 Greece and Yugoslavia exchanged military attachés[178], and soon Turkey also began to show interest in Yugoslavia. Within the following eighteen months the three countries progressed from the establishment of diplomatic ties to the holding of staff talks[179].

The speed with which the rapprochement took place was connected with the common interest of Turkey, Greece and Yugoslavia in the defence of their frontiers against Bulgaria. As we have seen, the British had argued that Turkey should become part of the Middle East Command, concentrating on the defence of Anatolia, as Thrace could not be held. Turkey had not received any encouragement from the West to think that she would be given arms aid or troops to defend her European frontier. But in mid-1952, when Field Marshal Montgomery visited Greece and Turkey, he stated publicly that in the event of war, Thrace should and could be defended[180]. This idea pleased the Turks very much, and they quoted him on this on all suitable occasions[181]: after all, Thrace held the two most precious cities of their country's history, Edirne and Istanbul, the economic capital of Turkey.

Montgomery's statement, however, had not been cleared with the British strategic planners; and on 11 September 1952 the Chiefs of Staff restated their opinion that "any serious attempt by the Greeks and Turks to defend Thrace in the foreseeable future could only result in a military disaster."[182] The Chiefs of Staff could not disown Montgomery publicly, and it is not known whether the Turks and the Greeks were ever told frankly that his views were not shared by anybody else in the Western military establishments. Meanwhile politicians and officers in both Ankara and Athens took his statement as an encouragement to seek closer military relations with their neighbours along the Bulgarian border. Staff talks between Yugoslavs and Turks and Yugoslavs and Greeks followed very quickly, within six months after Montgomery's visit to Turkey[183], and the Balkan bloc which London and Washington had wished for took form.

Ironically it was at this point that the British, who had been encouraging this rapprochement for such a long time, began to show more caution: high-ranking officials in the Foreign Office thought military contacts would be premature[184]. The Americans were much more encouraging at this stage[185]. The self-help aspect of military co-ordination in the Balkans was regarded as an asset by them, as integrated planning in this region gave the NATO members Greece and Turkey a greater chance of successful defence without additional Western efforts to help them.

The military rapprochement was given another boost by the Yugoslavs at the end of November 1952, probably owing to the disappointment felt in Belgrade about the Handy talks[186]. In late December 1952 Turco-Yugoslav and Graeco-Yugoslav talks were held in Belgrade[187]. During these talks provisional agreements were concluded by the Greeks and the Yugoslavs that

(a) In the event of war, Yugoslav troops should freely enter Greece and Greek troops Yugoslavia. . . .

(c) Aim of both parties was defence. But if war came the object must become to pass to the offensive. To forestall possible stab in the back joint occupation of Albania should be undertaken at an early stage.[188]

Aware of Italian suspicions[189], the Turkish Minister of Foreign Affairs, Fuat Köprülü, proposed that either Yugoslavia should be admitted to NATO, or else a military pact should be concluded between his country, Greece and Yugoslavia, to which the Italians were welcome to adhere[190]. The Greek Prime Minister, General Papagos, shared his wishes[191]. As the British formally told the Turks that they opposed the admission of Yugoslavia to NATO[192], the Balkan military pact, framed in a treaty of friendship, became the obvious solution.

On 25 February 1953 the treaty was initialled in Athens. Its most important passage concerned military negotiations:

Art. 3: The General Staffs of the contracting parties will continue their collaboration with a view to submitting to their governments recommendations which they will draw up by mutual agreement concerning the question of defence with a view to co-ordinated decisions being taken.

The treaty took into consideration all obligations incurred by Greece and Turkey regarding the North Atlantic Treaty[193].

While the Americans initially maintained that it was up to the Greeks and Turks to make such arrangements for their defence[194], the British now gave Italian sensibilities foremost consideration[195], a view which was shared by Eisenhower, now US President (see Chapter 7). The transformation of the Balkan Treaty into a defensive alliance contained the danger that Yugoslavia might reap the benefit of NATO backing without reciprocal obligations unless Greece or Turkey were directly attacked. We have seen that this led the French to advocate the inclusion of Yugoslavia in NATO; together with the British[196], they persuaded the Americans to make a joint representation to Ankara to ask the Turkish government to slow down negotiations with the Yugoslavs[197].

Indeed, the Turks had lost much of their enthusiasm when they realized that the Americans would not make a similar commitment to the defence of Yugoslavia as they were about to take on[198]. But in early 1954 the negotiations between the Balkan powers, driven on by the Yugoslavs, had gathered a momentum which could no longer be stopped[199]. Finally, the Balkan Pact, a treaty of mutual defence in case of "any armed aggression against one, or several of them, at any part of their territories", was signed by Greece, Turkey and Yugoslavia at Bled on 9 August 1954. The treaty was stated to be valid for 20 years and renewable[200].

In spite of their scepticism, the joint planning of Yugoslavia, Greece and Turkey raised the hopes of Western planners regarding the defence of this area. This was reflected in NATO defence policy by March 1953: NATO planners now thought it conceivable that parts of both Greece and Turkey could be defended with Allied support, which in the case of Greece meant holding the Peloponnese. Thrace was still considered indefensible unless "the Soviets chose to conduct holding operations in Bulgaria, making their main effort elsewhere", in which case there would be "the possibility of a quick NATO seizure of Bulgarian territory to the line of the Balkan mountains". This presupposed that Yugoslavia defended her central mountain massif. So here too, NATO and American defence policy changed between 1949 and 1953, once again largely because of Yugoslavia's new position in European affairs[201].

7

Hopes and Disillusionment 1950-1953

Strengthening the Shield: Economic Aid

The increased strategic importance of Yugoslavia resulted in a shift of emphasis in the reason for giving her economic aid. With the waning hopes for further satellite "defections", the political advantages of preserving Yugoslav independence, although still mentioned frequently, receded into the background; military advantages became the key reason for supporting Tito.

Yugoslavia's economic situation in 1949 had already been so bad that her government was unable to manage without Western credits. In 1950 it became worse still when after a severe drought the harvest was too small to feed Yugoslavia's population, let alone fulfil Yugoslav export obligations incurred under the previous trade agreements. Another drought occurred in 1952, once more upsetting all hopes of balancing the Yugoslav budget. Yugoslavia urgently needed food aid to fend off a famine (see Appendix D).

The Western powers had been ready to give Tito economic support as early as 1948, and Yugoslavia's strategic importance by 1950 only added to the pressing need to give economic aid. In order to secure the approval of Congress, Truman on 24 November 1950 addressed letters to its foreign affairs and armed forces committees:

> The drought... and the imminence of famine in Yugoslavia is a development which seriously affects the security of the North Atlantic area. These events dangerously weaken the ability of Yugoslavia to defend

itself against aggression, for, among other consequences, it imperils the combat effectiveness of the Yugoslav armed forces.

Yugoslavia, moreover, is a nation whose strategic location makes it of direct importance to the defense of the North Atlantic area. This importance derives from Yugoslavia's geographic relationship to Austria . . . where the occupation forces of certain North Atlantic Treaty countries, including the United States, are on duty, Greece . . . , and Italy. . . .

As a result of these factors, an immediate increase in Yugoslavia's ability to defend itself over that which would exist if no assistance were supplied will contribute to the preservation of the peace and security of the North Atlantic area. . . . It is a settled premise of our foreign policy that the peace and security of the North Atlantic area is vital to the security of the United States.

Truman asked for the appropriation of funds under the Mutual Defense Assistance Act of 1949 "to provide food for Yugoslavia['s] . . . armed forces"[1]. On 29 November he used much the same reasoning in a special Message to Congress, urging legislation to authorize further food grants[2].

George Perkins, the US Assistant Secretary of State for European Affairs, addressing the Foreign Affairs Committee of the House of Representatives on 29 November 1950, called the drought "of such importance to the US and to world peace and security that the Congress is being asked to take emergency action to meet it". He pointed out that "the humanitarian appeal is reinforced by the hard factor of [US!] national interest". He then cited the same strategic arguments named by the President, adding: "Yugoslavia continues to be a significant factor weakening the power and influence of Stalinist Communism throughout the world" since it had "shown that the Soviet system has no place in it for independent nations, or even for independent Communist parties"[3]. The emphasis on Yugoslavia's importance to the national security interest of the United States is noteworthy: these were the magic words that usually passed budgets through Congress.

In a State Department "Program Statement" on food aid for Yugoslavia, circulated to congressional committees, it was argued that "the cost of United States economic support is small in relation to the important advantages gained." These were listed (the setback to Soviet expansionism, greater stability in Italy, the end of the Greek Civil War, Yugoslav trade flowing towards the West, Yugoslav co-operation with the UN), with the conclusion: "*Above all*, the existence of a strong Yugoslav army, willing to fight if attacked, is a deterrent to aggression, in the Balkans and elsewhere, and a force for peace and security."[4]

Accordingly, the State Department on 17 January 1951 urged the International Bank for Reconstruction and Development (IBRD), to give further loans to Yugoslavia, emphasizing her strategic importance, and that of Greece and Turkey to Western defence strategy[5]. According to the briefing of the US representative to the North Atlantic Council Deputies in January 1951, the basic American objective was to help Yugoslavia resist Soviet pressure as her loss would endanger Greece and Italy both psychologically and strategically. The importance of the survival of "Titoism" as an influence on the "internatl Commie movement [*sic*]" was also mentioned, but in a more negative way: while Tito's fall would discourage Communists in the Soviet orbit from harbouring hopes for greater independence from the Kremlin, it was not said that Tito's survival would encourage them to take action to gain more autonomy[6].

This shift of emphasis is also reflected in a State Department draft memorandum of 27 February 1951 by Walker of the East European Bureau. He first described the strategic significance of Yugoslavia, then added a paragraph about the effect that "Titoism" had on the Communist régimes in the satellites, "even if there is little prospect of their following the Yugoslav example". When Walker also called "national communism" a "decisive force" in the world, one of his superiors underlined "decisive" and added a question-mark to the margin of this note[7]. On 4 April 1951, S.H. Van Dyke of the Economic Policy Department in a memorandum still held that "The split between Yugoslavia and the Comintern [*sic*] has torn the Communist world apart", but then explained at length how important Yugoslavia was for "the security of the entire Eastern Mediterranean area"[8]. Thus even with the continued existence of the dream of a Yugoslav wedge in the Communist bloc, the emphasis of US discussions of aid was, in this period, to a greater extent on Yugoslavia's strategic value.

British views were similar. Bevin and Wilson, the President of the Board of Trade, persuaded the Cabinet in October 1950 to grant another loan to Yugoslavia to prevent a collapse of the Yugoslav régime in consequence of the food shortage: they feared that if the régime did fall, it could only be replaced by a Cominformist régime.

> It would be hard to over-estimate the gravity of such an event. The recapture of Yugoslavia by the Soviet Union would strike fresh fear into the hearts of the Italians, the French and the West Germans and by nourishing the myth of the inevitability of an ultimate Soviet dominion over Europe would do untold harm to the defence efforts of the Western powers. The threat to Greece would at once be revived. ... The Yugoslav army, which is not negligible in comparison with the armies of its neighbours, would be lost and the Russians would be able to dominate the Adriatic. The chance of Communist parties and fellow-travellers elsewhere being weaned from their allegiance to Moscow by the example of Tito would be gone.[9]

In mid-1951 Bevin's successor, Morrison, reiterated the arguments put forward by Bevin and Wilson, again recommending the granting of credits on the grounds that Yugoslavia had an army of thirty divisions "which can confidently be expected to fight if attacked, and which is hardly likely to remain indefinitely inactive in the event of a general war in Europe". He also listed the negative effects on the defence of Italy, Greece and Austria, if Yugoslavia were lost, and the weakening of "the anti-Stalinist forces in the world". More confidently expressed than elsewhere, Morrison also argued that

> Yugoslavia is an example and an encouragement to anti-Stalinist Communists on both sides of the Iron Curtain. In so far as its recent history proves that there are reasonable prospects for a Communist State to thrive without the protection of the Soviet Union, to live in harmony with its Western neighbours, and even to accept

187

capitalist economic assistance without sacrificing its independence, Yugoslavia has become a beacon for world peace.[10]

From late 1950 the French foreign ministry tried to transform their policy towards Tito fundamentally. They had approved the policy of "méfiance" recommended by the French Ambassador at the time of the Tito-Cominform split, Jean Payart[11]. His replacement by Philippe Baudet on 25 October 1950, however, symbolized the abandonment of this policy. His brief from the Direction d'Europe (under François Seydoux) at the start of his mission explained that after all the attempts of the Anglo-Saxon powers to persuade the Yugoslavs to adopt certain behaviour, it was the French, hitherto rarely associated with the pressure exerted by their two allies, who would now have the best chance to persuade Tito "des avantages qu'il pourrait retirer d'une harmonisation de son action avec les puissances atlantiques". The brief recommended helping the Yugoslavs soon in view of the threat to the Yugoslav régime posed by the drought and the danger of a satellite or Soviet attack. The Yugoslavs had asked the West for help, and the West had decided to give it, having judged "qu'une Yougoslavie anti-stalinienne, fût elle communisée, avait plus de chance de se ranger aux côtés des puissances atlantiques que dans les rangs de leurs ennemis"[12]. It was thus again the new emphasis on Yugoslavia's importance for the defence of the NATO area after the attack on South Korea that led the French to change their policy towards Tito.

Soon after his arrival in Belgrade, Baudet reported that as far as Franco-Yugoslav relations were concerned, "nous partons de bas". Yet in the future development of Yugoslav relations with the West,

> la France a . . . un rôle de première grandeur à jouer ici. C'est à elle qu'il appartient d'interpréter la pensée occidentale sans essayer de l'imposer et d'expliquer, en puissance continentale, les données nouvelles de la politique européenne. C'est à elle aussi à faire sentir son influence modératrice auprès de ceux qui voudraient aller trop vite en besogne. C'est en fonction de ces données que . . . je compte essayer d'orienter nos rapports avec la Yougoslavie nouvelle.[13]

Early in the following year, Baudet once again expressed his opinion that "notre pays devrait être en quelque sorte le pivot naturel des relations de la Yougoslavie nouvelle avec l'Occident."[14] Accordingly, the Sous-Direction d'Europe Orientale, headed by Jean Laloy, argued that France should be prepared to make a real, and not just a token contribution to Western economic aid to Yugoslavia, as all other French aid measures had been "dans la plupart des cas trop modestes par rapport à ceux de nos alliés ou trop tardifs pour nous valoir de réels avantages politiques"[15].

Yet for Robert Schuman and his successor, Georges Bidault, as for the French Assemblée Nationale, Yugoslavia came a long way behind most other foreign policy issues, and they did not give her as much attention as did their "Anglo-Saxon" partners. Moreover, French financial restraints made it impossible to make more than a modest contribution towards aid for Yugoslavia, however much the Quai d'Orsay would have wished otherwise.

In 1949 the Yugoslavs were given a credit of $55,000,000 from the American Export-Import Bank (ExImBank), and in 1950 they obtained a further $15,000,000[16]. After Western mediation, the Yugoslavs obtained a credit from West Germany of over $35,000,000 by September 1950[17]. When the effects of the drought of 1950 became clear, the Americans decided to furnish aid at Yugoslav request as part of Mutual Defence Assistance (MDA), which they regarded as justifiable because of the strategic importance of Yugoslavia[18]. For this, the approval of the National Security Council[19], the other NATO countries[20] and of Congress was sought and obtained[21].

On 20 October 1950 the British Cabinet agreed to grant credits of up to £5,000,000 to Yugoslavia[22], and on 5 April 1951 it approved another immediate credit of £4,000,000[23]. Meanwhile, the new American policy statement NSC 18/6 recommended granting further substantial aid, both economic and military. The main reasons put forward here were once again that Yugoslavia's "strategic location made it of direct importance to the defense of the North Atlantic Area"[24]. Congress allotted $60,000,000 to Yugoslavia under the Mutual Security Program (MSP, the successor of the MDA)[25].

To ensure a more concerted approach, the British, who had

not been informed in advance of this US decision, initiated Franco-Anglo-American talks to co-ordinate long-term aid[26]. In June 1951 the three delegations recommended to their governments the granting of a gift to the Yugoslavs of a total of up to £44,640,000 (or roughly $125,000,000) of which the US would give 65% (£29,010,000, or about $81,300,000), the UK 23% (£10,270,000), and the French 12% (£5,360,000, or about FF 5,500,000,000)[27].

The French contribution was sanctioned preliminarily by the French government by 5 July 1951. Baudet urged his government to hasten the final approval; on 19 September 1951 he told the President of the French Republic, Vincent Auriol, that if France did not decide to go along soon, "nous serions remplacés immédiatement par les pays anglo-saxons". France would lose her position among the two other great powers. But the French Assemblée Nationale only ratified the government's policy on 8 February 1952[28]. The British Cabinet had already approved their share in this grant aid project for the period of 1951 until the end of June 1952 in the Cabinet Meeting of 21 June 1951[29]. The US government also gave their preliminary approval by 5 July 1951, and the payment of their share was given congressional authorization at the end of the year[30]. In view of this grant, the Executive Board of the IBRD decided on 11 October 1951 to approve a loan to Yugoslavia of $28,000,000[31].

Yugoslav economic relations with the West were increasingly dominated by the US[32]. In February 1952 representatives of Britain, France and the US met once more to discuss the continuation of tripartite aid. There was serious dissent between the British and the Americans. The British thought that Yugoslavia should be persuaded to adopt policies which would allow her to balance her budgets as soon as possible[33]: this was in line with the aim of "keeping Tito afloat". At the same time the British wanted to reap economic benefits. The Americans were much more generous with their aid, giving the British the impression that

> The whole country is obsessed with the 'cold war' and the Mutual Security Association has been given [money] for foreign aid to fight it. If we tried to put the brake on Yugoslavia, we would be brushed aside. . . . If Yugoslavia

stood alone, things might be different, but it is only part of a very large programme.[34]

Ogilvy-Webb of the British economic mission in Belgrade observed that the Americans obviously wanted to make a political present to Yugoslavia. A member of the US embassy told him at the beginning of 1952 that his government was not interested in arguments about what form of aid would have best economic results in Yugoslavia.

> Their position was that for military reasons Yugoslavia must be supported both with military aid and with aid to the civil population to prevent unrest. Having entered into this commitment the United States could not escape from it and would probably be bound to continue aid for many years to come, just as they seemed bound to continue indefinite aid to Austria, Italy and Greece.[35]

Yet there was unanimity at the economic aid conference that Yugoslavia should continue to receive Western aid. The conference report of 21 April 1952 concluded that Yugoslavia would need about £35,000,000 (or about $99,000,000), of which the US should undertake to pay £28,000,000 (or $78,000,000), the British £4,500,000 (or $12,600,000) and the French £3,000,000 (or FF 2,940,000,000 or $8,400,000)[36]. The British Cabinet on 15 May 1952 approved of the Washington report[37]. By 3 July 1952 the French and the American governments had also given their *placet*[38]. Congress approved the decision[39], as did the Assemblée Nationale, albeit once more after a considerable delay[40].

The drought of 1952 then made further aid necessary, and already before the end of the year, the British government tentatively allocated £3,000,000 for Yugoslavia for 1953[41]. The Americans continued to want tripartite aid, as they found this easier to pass through Congress. The French had the same experience with the Assemblée Nationale[42]. They were in favour of extending aid to the amount of FF 2,000,000,000; they would only, however, give this aid if Britain were also willing to participate, at a rate of 3:2 in comparison with the French share[43]. After some to-ing and fro-ing the Americans allotted $45,000,000 to Yugoslavia by October 1953[44].

Although another series of tripartite aid talks did start in the summer of 1953, the Trieste crisis delayed any firm agreement with the Yugoslavs until January 1954[45].

As with the previous drought, extraordinary grant aid was given by the United States. At the beginning of January 1953 the government made available $20,000,000[46], which they topped with another grant of $11,000,000, announced in April 1953[47]. Yet a further American grant of $15,000,000 was announced in the summer of the year 1953[48]. But that was not the end of it; in October 1953 there were already proposals for the US Administration giving Yugoslavia a further $56,000,000 worth of extraordinary grant aid[49], and American aid proceeded to continue in that way.

The Western powers also continued to urge the IBRD to give Yugoslavia investment credits[50]. This resulted in a capital equipment loan of $30,000,000, approved on 11 February 1953[51].

Western Influence on Yugoslav Policies?

The Western powers again faced the question of whether they could use economic aid to influence the Yugoslav government to change certain policies. Bevin ensured that the Labour government's line was not to attach any conditions to credits[52]. Baudet received similar instructions from Alexandre Parodi, the Secretary General of the Quai d'Orsay[53]. The American attitude was much the same, although they pointed out their disapproval of Yugoslav policies more frequently and on more issues. Notes delivered to the Yugoslavs concerning the granting of a loan or gifts were accompanied by American statements, stressing their dislike of measures undertaken by the Belgrade government "suppressing or destroying religious, political or economic liberty in Yugoslavia"[54]. The US Administration was under greater pressure than the British or the French in these two years to justify their aid measures for Yugoslavia to "the public" and to Congress.

In late 1949-50 the Yugoslavs began to develop their own form of Socialism, which was almost diametrically opposed to the ultraleftist views they had held (at any rate in matters of foreign policy) until their expulsion from the Cominform[55]. This change of ideas was accompanied by reforms in the

Yugoslav Administration (ushering in decentralization, which became a major hallmark of Yugoslav Communism), in the judicial system (a reform of the lower law courts), and finally resulted in the constitution of 1953[56]. Starting in 1950, these changes were observed by Westerners with a mixture of hope and suspicion. While they might have been the first steps towards a liberalization and an eventual democratization of the régime[57], the measures could also be interpreted as "simples apparences destinées à faire illusion à l'opinion américaine", in the words of Baudet[58].

There were also changes in Yugoslav foreign policy, encouraged by the Western powers. The year 1951 finally saw the formalization of Yugoslav relations with Austria[59]. The visit of the Austrian Foreign Minister, Dr. Gruber, in June 1952, was the first by a top-level statesman in office from a non-Communist country since the war, and symbolized the acceptance of Yugoslavia among the independent, sovereign states of postwar Europe[60]. In Italo-Yugoslav relations, Trieste still remained the main obstacle to a reconciliation, but the question was largely kept on ice until October 1952 (see Chapter 7). The rapprochement with Greece and Turkey has been described in the previous chapter. While these countries had their own reasons to pursue this policy[61], it was also an objective of the Western powers; it is therefore not unwarranted to list this development among the positive achievements of Western policies towards the Balkans.

The Korean War created another issue between the Western powers and Yugoslavia. Although it increased the Yugoslavs' anxieties about a possible invasion, resulting in the stepping-up of their military preparations, they did not react in the way the Western powers would have desired in the political arena of the United Nations. The Security Council vote declaring a breach of peace and demanding an immediate cease-fire, was cast 9:0 in the absence of the Soviet representative, but Yugoslavia abstained[62]. This was a disappointment for the Western powers. While the British and the French had at first refrained from exerting any pressure on the Yugoslavs, George Allen called on Tito on 28 June 1950

and spoke to him about the great importance which the United States Government attached to the use made by the Yugoslav Government of its vote in the Security

Council. Tito replied that whilst his Government was solidly against aggression, it was necessary for him to be extremely cautious. If Yugoslavia was next on the list, Soviet tactics would probably be firstly to accuse the Yugoslav Government of allowing its country to be used as a base from which 'Western imperialists' were planning aggression against Russia, and any action taken against Yugoslavia would be represented as purely defensive. To this end action of Yugoslav delegate at Security Council might also be considered as a pretext for Soviet aggression.[63]

Tito made a similar remark to Ernest Davies[64]. He promised publicly to abide by the UN's decisions regarding the Korean incident[65]. Yet the Yugoslavs continued to vacillate[66], finding fault with Western policy, and adopting a policy of '"active neutrality' but opposed to North Korean-Chinese aggression", as Tito explained on 17 Feburary 1951 [67]. In May 1951, however, the Yugoslav leaders voted with the Western powers for the imposition of an arms and military materials embargo on China[68]. Whatever the Yugoslav motivation, their shift towards Western policies over the Korean question was in the interest of the Western powers, and this point can be counted among Western gains in dealings with Yugoslavia.

Continuity and Change in Western Governments and Policies

The end of 1951 saw the replacement of Attlee and Morrison and their Labour government by Churchill and Eden, while Truman and Acheson lost the 1952 US elections to Eisenhower and Dulles, who succeeded in January 1953. At virtually the same time, Robert Schuman in the Quai d'Orsay was replaced by his own predecessor, Georges Bidault, after he had weathered several changes of government. Yet the succeeding governments showed remarkable continuity in their attitude towards Yugoslavia. Bidault and Schuman did not differ much in their commitment to NATO and transatlantic co-operation, or in their criticism of US policies when those were deemed too aggressive (see Chapter 5). The more important of the points of disagreement between these two statesmen, such as over the European Defence Community (EDC), have little relevance in this context[69]. With regard to Britain, one could talk of "bipartisanship of foreign policy" when looking at Churchill's and Attlee's Cabinets[70]. The continuity in Eisenhower's and Dulles's foreign policy in relation to that of Truman's Democrat Administration has already been noted, although outward rhetoric seemed to indicate a stepping-up of the policy of liberation (soon to be known as "roll-back")[71].

With regard to Yugoslavia in particular, all three successor governments broadly maintained the policies of the previous administration based on the need to help Yugoslavia maintain her independence. The Yugoslav Dr. Bebler called on John Foster Dulles in June 1952 during the election campaign, and was assured by him that he was in favour of continued aid to Yugoslavia[72]. Chapter 6 discussed how Eisenhower had flirted with the idea of Yugoslavia's integration into NATO; he retained the conviction that Yugoslavia's independence from Moscow was of great importance to the West, and he was very concerned that Tito should not be driven back into complete reliance on the Soviet Union[73]. As Yugoslavia had low priority in French foreign policy, it was enough that the crucial top-level people in the French Foreign Ministry, who had more to do with Yugoslavia than the two Ministers, remained much the same during 1951-53. In Britain, Churchill and Eden had maintained a certain interest in and sympathy for Yugoslavia even whilst out of office[74].

There was, however, one departure from previous British policies towards Tito. Chapter 2 explained how Yugoslavia's function as a political spearhead in the ideological battle between East and West necessitated the Western decision not to interfere in Yugoslav affairs, so that the Western powers on the whole refrained from linking political conditions with aid, and from meddling in Yugoslav internal policies. Some notable exceptions have been discussed, but they mainly concerned issues of foreign policy. In July 1950 members of the Foreign Office's Southern Department still criticized the Americans for exerting pressure on the Yugoslav government to liberalize its régime, because they thought it wiser to pursue "our present policy of allowing Tito to sit on the fence"[75]. Yet unlike the British, the Americans never consciously departed from this policy.

The British embassy staff in Belgrade continued to point out that "however much we may welcome the Yugoslav Government's support for Western policy, e.g. in the UN, their prime value to the West at the moment is as a dissident and independent Communist state"[76]. The Quai d'Orsay's Direction d'Europe set down in October 1950 that the West should explain to Tito what they would like him to do in questions of foreign policy, and why, but that no pressure should be used[77]. Baudet agreed: the Western powers must not

> exercer sur le Maréchal Tito de trop lourdes pressions pour accélérer son alignement politique. . . . [S]i le Maréchal Tito cessait de faire figure de progressiste aux yeux des masses, à l'extérieur comme à l'intérieur, son Parti cesserait aussi de fournir l'exemple subversif et contagieux d'indépendance qu'il donne aujourd'hui à tant de communistes et de communisants qui ont tendance à se rebeller contre la dictature du Parti bolchevique. A vouloir aller trop vite nous risquerons de nous battre à notre propre jeu.[78]

Gradually, however, as the hope for further satellite "defections" waned, the British in particular began to hope that Yugoslavia might develop towards Western-type democracy[79]. Geoffrey Harrison, the head of the Foreign Office's Northern Department, commented on 20 January 1953 that in his view further improvement "can only be promoted if friendly relations between the régime and the West are maintained"[80]. It was therefore thought desirable to see as many contacts as possible develop between Yugoslavia and the West. On 4 September 1952, John Cheetham of the Foreign Office noted his Department's view (in view of Eden's proposed visit to Yugoslavia) "that the more closely and publicly Yugoslavia is associated with the West the better". Churchill agreed[81]. Sir Ivo Mallet in Belgrade reminded Eden that it was "by drawing Tito into our councils and our camp that we shall best advance the liberalisation of the régime"[82]. As a Foreign Office brief of 5 December 1952 put it, "HMG's policy towards Yugoslavia is . . . based on the assumption that it is to our interest to enable Yugoslavia to maintain her independence, and on the belief that increasing contact with her will cause the Yugoslav regime to shed some of its more objectionable features."[83]

Thus the liberalization of the Yugoslav régime was now increasingly in the foreground of British aspirations. Rather than "letting Tito sit on the fence", the British government now wanted to bring Tito over to their own side. They felt they no longer had to make allowances for the Yugoslav Communists' treatment of non-Communists, and they had fewer inhibitions about urging the Yugoslavs to grant greater religious freedoms, an approach for which Harrison obtained Eden's approval on 5 December 1952[84].

The Yugoslav government's conduct in the realm of church-state relations was particularly unsatisfactory by Western standards of human rights. Both in the US and in Britain, most popular opposition to aid for Tito focused on this issue, and in particular on the fate of Stepinac (see Chapter 3)[85]. The Vatican's relations with Belgrade deteriorated in 1952, culminating in Stepinac's elevation to the rank of Cardinal towards the end of the year; Tito reacted by severing diplomatic relations[86]. This came shortly before Tito's visit to the UK, which became a focus for an anti-Tito campaign by the Roman Catholic organizations of Britain[87]. Although the British government tried to assuage Catholic opinion[88], Eden and Churchill also raised the religious question with Tito[89].

The new Conservative government was less patient with Tito, surprising though this may sound in view of the Eden visit to Yugoslavia and the Tito visit to Britain. Thus on 27 February 1953 the Foreign Office's desk officer for Yugoslavia, J. Oliver Wright (now Sir Oliver Wright) proposed a new policy towards Yugoslavia; this is one of the rare examples of such a note rising from the bottom of the bureaucracy to the very top, finally being endorsed by both the Foreign Secretary and the Prime Minister. In view of the imminent visit of the Yugoslav leader, Wright suggested that the British might "try and cultivate in him some talent for compromise. . . . It is common interest in defence against the common danger that brings us together and not any sentimental ideas of friendship." Harrison added to this that British policy towards Tito might "involve an element of deflation of Tito but should aim above all to get him to . . . act as independent and equal member of the free community". Sir Pierson Dixon, one of the Deputy

Under-Secretaries of State, agreed that "Tito . . . wants all the advantages of friendship with the West without giving up a number of unpleasant totalitarian habits and practices. We should certainly educate him as much as we can when he comes to London."[90]

Among Tito's objectionable "totalitarian habits and practices" was the stance he took in the international arena of the United Nations and press statements on colonial issues with particular reference to British and French interests in North Africa and the Middle East; here he continued to irritate the British and the French[91]. Eden and Churchill raised the matter with Tito on various occasions in 1952 and 1953[92], but the Yugoslavs did not alter the tone of their statements[93].

Friendly Relations between the Western Powers and Yugoslavia; Rivalry among the Western Powers

Despite tensions over religious issues, a cautious rapprochement took place between Yugoslavia and the West in the period from the beginning of the Korean War until the end of 1951. In 1948, 1949 and early 1950, the Yugoslavs had been anxious to avoid contact with the West other than for the trade needed to replace that denied by the Cominformist countries. With the Korean War, however, Yugoslav relations with the West reached a watershed. Criticism of the West did not cease overnight, and, as the example of Yugoslav reactions in the UN over the Korean affairs demonstrates, they did not come into the "Western camp". But the revival of old friendships, the numerous visits to Yugoslavia by prominent Westerners, the social opening-up of Belgrade to the foreign diplomatic community (if not on a level known otherwise in the Western countries), the gradual shift of the Yugoslav stance to an open condemnation of China and North Korea — all these were great stepping-stones on the way to friendly relations.

The period of 1952-53, preceding the Trieste crisis, crowned the Yugoslav-Western rapprochement. It saw the Eden visit to Yugoslavia in the autumn of 1952[94], the conclusion of the Balkan Treaty with Greece and Turkey on 27

February 1953, the death of Stalin on 5 March 1953 and Tito's visit to England in mid-March 1953[95]. Relations between Yugoslavia and the West were probably at their friendliest since the Second World War and for a long time after. The number of visits of Yugoslavs to the West, and of Westerners to Yugoslavia even increased.

French relations with the Yugoslavs were decidedly better under Baudet than they had been under his predecessor. Yet Baudet himself was disappointed, seven months after his arrival in Belgrade, with the slow pace of the Franco-Yugoslav rapprochement which he intended to bring about. He thought France instead of Britain could have been the "godmother" of Yugoslav relations with the West[96]. The desire of Baudet and the Quai d'Orsay to improve relations with Yugoslavia was an attempt to outdo the other two Western powers in order to further the prestige of France, quite apart from encouraging a closer Yugoslav alignment with the West.

Each of the three Western powers sought to surpass the others in cordiality with the Yugoslavs, trying to win the confidence of high-ranking members of the ruling circles in Belgrade, hoping to influence them, to get more secrets out of them, thereby increasing the reputation of their own government. In the case of Britain, and even more so of France, these efforts also reflected the necessity to maintain or to re-establish, respectively, the reputation of these countries as Great Powers. Yet the proportions of the aid given to Yugoslavia by the three Western powers reflected their inequality, which ultimately determined their standing in world affairs. We have seen how the greater share in military aid given by the US allowed her virtually to monopolize Western aid negotiations and strategic talks with Yugoslavia.

But due to Yugoslav preferences for not dealing with the main leader of the Western "imperialist" bloc, and due to wartime relations, the other two powers, particularly Britain still had almost as strong a stance in Belgrade as the US, which occasionally evoked American jealousy (see, for example, Minor's remark, Chapter 3). These were reflections of inter-Allied rivalries on a larger scale. On the one hand there was French jealousy of the "Anglo-Saxons", who with their "special relationship" had been going behind the back of the French in many matters in the immediate postwar years[97]. On the other hand the "special relationship" had suffered since the US no longer saw much reason for treating Britain differently from the other members of NATO[98], and disagreements over the Far East had contributed to the demise of the English-speaking alliance[99]. Although Churchill on his return to power tried to revive it[100], Eden's antagonism to both Acheson and Dulles, and actions rooted in his inability to accept Britain's decline, undermined Churchill's efforts[101]. On a smaller scale, this situation was reflected by both the close collaboration and the envy in diplomatic circles[102]. Instead of giving in to feelings of rivalry and petty jealousy, the three Western powers should have rejoiced in any successful effort to strengthen the ties binding Tito to the West.

The Turn of the Tide

Tito's Détente with the Soviet Bloc and the Trieste Crisis

The death of Stalin on 5 March 1953 was a watershed in Yugoslav-Soviet relations. He was Tito's main adversary, and during his lifetime an amelioration of Yugoslav-Soviet relations was unthinkable. His death alone made a fundamental change in Soviet-Yugoslav relations possible. But the change took a long time to manifest itself. Although there were early conciliatory moves on the part of the Soviet Union[103], the frontier incidents on Yugoslavia's borders with the satellite countries continued unabated until the end of the year, as did the propaganda attacks from all the Cominform organs[104].

The rise of Khrushchev opened the road to a temporary reconciliation, but two years elapsed between the death of Stalin and Khrushchev's Canossa-pilgrimage to Belgrade. Even then, the Yugoslavs took care not to forgo the advantages of good contacts with the West, inviting the US Secretary of State, John Foster Dulles, to Belgrade in November 1955. He found Tito "extremely open and friendly" and was convinced that Tito wanted the best of both worlds, but had "no intention whatever of falling back into the clutches of Soviet [*sic*]"[105]. Yugoslavia would never again be willing to overstep a certain limit in dealings with Moscow, and the limit consisted of the clearly defined national sovereignty of the country, in which no interference was tolerated.

This interference was regarded as a threat by the Yugoslavs, whichever side it came from. In 1953 their leaders launched a campaign emphasizing Yugoslavia's independence from either bloc, and resistance to what was seen by a growing group within the leadership (particularly men like Vukmanović-Tempo) as an undesirable Westernization of their country. The growth of this reactionary feeling was decisively reinforced through the Trieste crisis[106]. The willingness on the part of the Yugoslav government to let the Trieste crisis escalate must be seen against the background of the gradual lessening of the previously acute Soviet threat.

The Trieste crisis of the autumn of 1953 owed its origins to the loss of patience by the Western powers, which after the eight-year impasse is only too understandable. Nevertheless, they made a mistake. Seeing that the Italo-Yugoslav conflict of interests was such that neither side could afford to give in in view of domestic opinion, Tito wanted the problem to be kept in cold storage[107], and made efforts to keep the temperature down[108]. Various proposals for a settlement were made by the Yugoslavs and the Western powers in 1951 and 1952; thus the British encouraged the Italians and the Yugoslavs to sort out the matter between themselves, but nothing came of it[109]. The three Western foreign ministers discussed the issue on several occasions in 1952; they even contemplated using financial aid "as lever for correctïng Yugoslavia recalcitrant [*sic*] on Trieste situation"[110]. Ultimately this was not done, however: Pierson Dixon of the Foreign Office explained to Eden and Acheson on 28 June 1952 that "because of other considerations, we cannot threaten to turn off the tap"[111].

The Western powers and the Italians continued to press for an early settlement. Further moves on their part left the Yugoslavs with the impression that the American and British governments were always backing the Italians. In the end the Yugoslavs felt justified in publicly accusing the Allied Military Government Zone A (which now included Italians) of not protecting the rights of the Slovene minority adequately. Yugoslav press statements of the end of August allowed the Italians to apply an interpretation implying that the Yugoslavs intended to annex Zone B (which they already administered); Italian troops were moved towards the frontier.

Dulles and Eisenhower were at the time much influenced by the pleas of the US Ambassador in Rome, Clare

Booth-Luce, who sympathized strongly with the Italian point of view. With a Blaise Pascalian train of deductions, she warned the US President that

> For the want of Trieste, an Issue was lost.
> For the want of an Issue, the Election was lost.
> For the want of an Election, De Gasperi was lost.
> For the want of De Gasperi, his NATO policies were lost.
> For the want of his NATO policies, Italy was lost.
> For the want of Italy, Europe was lost.
> For the want of Europe, America . . . ?[112]

Impressed with the logical force and sophistication of this argument, Eisenhower was left with the view that "the situation is jittery and the Italians are threatening to pull out of NATO". Although the President was keen to tie the Yugoslavs down in defensive arrangements, he was even more determined to use Italy as the rock on which the defence of the Southern Flank rested, having fought for the inclusion of Italy in NATO in 1948 and 1949. He remarked that given the choice between backing either of them (oblivious of the alignment of World War II), he considered that "the Italians have been our friends for a long time and the Jugs [*sic*] are Johnny-come-Latelies". On 8 September 1953, Eisenhower therefore told Dulles

> that he felt the Administration was swinging a little too far in favor of Yugoslavia. He indicated that military prejudice in favor of Yugoslavia was not justified. He remarked that Italy had not really had a chance in the last two wars to show what it could do when it was committed to a cause in which it really believed.

On top of all this the Western powers were very keen to see Italy ratify the treaty creating the European Defence Community, which was up for parliamentary consideration. They were therefore inclined to back the Italians, without any intention of offending the Yugoslavs[113].

In September 1953 Tito once more suggested the internationalization of Trieste; at the same time Western failure to urge Italy to call back her forces was interpreted by the Yugoslavs as a conspiracy to allow the Italians to obtain

Zone A. This was indeed what the British and the Americans tried to achieve by announcing on 8 October 1953 the imminent withdrawal of their forces, handing over the administration of Zone A to the Italians, giving a *de facto* solution to the problem[114].

Because they could not at the same time assure the Yugoslavs that they could keep Zone B, and because the Italians were tactless enough to state immediately that they did not intend to give up their claim to it, the Yugoslavs raised a hue and cry against what they saw as the revival of Italian expansionism, aided and abetted by the Western powers. Tito had not been given any warning of the Western intention to make the declaration (a clear diplomatic blunder on the part of the Western powers)[115], and his disappointment with his new partners was intense. Hostile demonstrations were staged in front of the British and American embassies, resulting in the damage of property; Tito made no attempt to dampen the outburst of leftist anti-Westernism[116].

The Yugoslav Foreign Minister was understood by Dulles to have threatened that Yugoslavia would "enter Zone A, despite the presence of US and British forces, if any Italian soldiers entered the Zone". The ex-soldier Eisenhower resorted to gunboat-diplomacy: he suggested "that it might be desirable at some point to move some of the 6th Fleet into the Adriatic area to indicate our readiness to deal with such a situation"[117]. On 14 October 1953, Eisenhower gave orders for several US warships to take position in the Adriatic without delay[118]. The suspension of arms deliveries to Yugoslavia and other measures of the same sort gave another blow to Yugoslavia's strained relationship with the Western powers.

The British Ambassador, Sir Ivo Mallet, feared that the Trieste crisis would "clearly have re-awakened the deep-rooted suspicions of the Western powers and of their attitude towards Yugoslavia. It will have seriously set back the growth of confidence in the West which Her Majesty's Government have been trying to foster in recent years."[119] The Trieste crisis destroyed much of the carefully cultivated common ground that existed.

The Western powers now tried very hard to find a compromise solution, and spent much time on efforts to make up for their previous tactless and ill-considered handling of it[120]. But there were also other examples of tactless behaviour on the part of the Western powers which exacerbated these tensions. Examples are the delay in and later the cancellation of British jet aircraft sales to Yugoslavia (cf. Chapter 6), and the American failure to replace George Allen when he had been moved from Belgrade at the end of March. After several Yugoslav enquiries, his successor, James Riddleberger, was only nominated at the beginning of July, so that there was no American Ambassador in Belgrade in the months immediately following Stalin's death when the Soviets were putting out first feelers regarding the re-establishment of normal diplomatic relations[121].

The Trieste affair was eventually settled in the following year after secret negotiations between the British, the Americans and the Yugoslavs in London. There seems to be no particular reason why the credit for this should go to Eden, as David Carlton argues[122], when, according to Eden's memoirs, it was the Yugoslavs who proposed further talks, and the Americans who suggested that they should be held in utter secrecy. The successful style in which they were conducted was praised by Eden in his memoirs: "The solution was a classic example of the true function of diplomacy, an open agreement secretly arrived at." Belying his own words, however, he continued to extol the virtues of risk-taking, and added that he would have thought the settlement impossible without the declaration of 8 October 1953 designed to bring about a *de facto* solution of the Trieste question, handing over the city to Italy[123]. This makes no sense as it is clear that only this untimely and ill-prepared declaration which so obviously favoured the Italians[124] caused Yugoslav relations with the West to take an irremediable turn for the worse. Even though the Trieste issue was sorted out in the following year, the opportunity for a firm commitment to common defence measures was lost, and with it the cautious work of many years (see Chapter 6).

The settlement itself was very much on the lines that had always seemed the most likely solution to the problem, Zone A going to Italy, Zone B to Yugoslavia, with minor frontier rectifications and various clauses for the protection of the minorities and political activists on either side; moreover, Trieste would continue to be a free port. The agreement was signed in London on 5 October 1954[125], and it initiated the relaxation of tensions between Yugoslavia and Italy, which eventually made possible the co-ordination of defensive measures between them[126].

Neither East nor West: Balkan Pact and Non-Alignment

The Yugoslavs' perception of their dependence on and their disappointment with both the Eastern and the Western camps, led them to seek a third option: this was to establish further contacts with peers, that is with states which were likely to have similar problems and aims in foreign policy. The most obvious choice was to build on the foundations which had already been laid: the Balkan Treaty with Greece and Turkey could be extended to provide for greater security in that area. This would be a partnership in which the Yugoslavs would not feel like a pawn in a greater game; instead, they might even assume the lead, as they had hoped to do with the planned Balkan Federation of the immediate postwar years.

Although the last phase of the Balkan Treaty's genesis and its metamorphosis into the Balkan Pact met with reserve and even opposition from the Western powers[127], they had to acknowledge, as was said in the Foreign Office brief for Eden in 1953, that "the last big gap [in Western defences] had now been closed"[128]. Yet their concern for Italian opinion outweighed their happiness about this[129].

The final impetus for the conclusion of the military alliance came from the Yugoslavs because the Trieste crisis set back the military rapprochement with the Western powers. Yet Yugoslavia showed goodwill by stating that Italy would be welcome to accede to the alliance[130]. The détente with the Soviet Union was still uncertain, so that Yugoslavia seemed once again isolated from both East and West[131]. For Yugoslavia the Balkan Pact was thus also an escape from complete isolation in 1954. The common aim of Yugoslavia, Greece and Turkey in concluding the Balkan Pact of mutual defence was the preservation of their independence through military co-operation. But beyond that, relations with Greece and Turkey were not satisfactory because there was no shared ideological basis or political sympathy. Tito had to look elsewhere for kindred spirits.

Tito had proclaimed his adoption of a position of "active neutrality" over the issue of the Korean War[132]. Although the

French Ambassador, Jean Payart, on 18 July 1950 observed that Tito was looking for "l'appui d'une 3ème force internationale rejetant à la fois l'hégémonie de l'URSS et celle des Etats Unis"[133], Tito for a long time dismissed the idea of a "third Bloc"[134], and he never had any sympathy for Nehru's and Gandhi's unarmed neutralism[135]. But the Yugoslav ideas on this were not yet fully matured. They increasingly wanted the co-operation of "progressive forces". This quest for friendship elsewhere indicates the Yugoslav leadership's dissatisfaction with the Western powers. The Eisenhower/Dulles condemnation in propaganda of all things Communist was perceived as threatening the very essence of the Yugoslav régime, even if they were at the same time bolstering it with economic and military aid. The search for co-operation with powers that had similar interests made Yugoslavia back anything that could lead to the creation of a Third Force: hence the Balkan Pact of 1954, and hence Yugoslav support for the European Defence Community, which Tito said he approved of, and to which he even wanted to link his country[136]. But then Tito was not pleased with the form the EDC was taking[137]. In late 1954, when the EDC began to bear the signs of defeat, Tito suddenly declared that it had always been "unviable"[138].

Then Tito turned his attention away from Europe, which marked the beginning of Yugoslavia's active involvement in what was to become the Non-Aligned Movement[139]. The roots of the friendly ties between Yugoslavia and various Third World countries went back to the immediate postwar period (Yugoslavia's contacts with Communist and Socialist parties in South and Southeast Asia have been discussed in Chapter 1). Some of these contacts outlasted the expulsion of Yugoslavia from the Cominform[140]; they were encouraged not only by the Yugoslavs[141], and partly took the form of exchange visits[142]. While Tito was declaring himself opposed to the idea of a "third Bloc", he thus still welcomed contacts with its proponents. The Belgrade government's attempts to woo Mao Tse Tung and Ho Chi Minh in 1949-50 met with no rewards, but Tito continued to forge links with Latin American states and with African countries[143]. Baudet in Belgrade observed Tito's emphasis on the United Nations and particularly on the principles of the equal treatment of all states and of the right of colonial peoples to independence. He thought this a policy "de rapprochement avec toutes les nations, peuples ou groupements, soucieux, à des titres et des degrés divers, d'éviter l'emprise de Washington comme de Moscou".

After the revival of strains in the Yugoslav relationship with the Soviet Union over the Hungarian invasion of 1956, Tito put his country's foreign policy firmly on the path of non-alignment, realizing that he could play a leading rôle in this movement, together with Nehru and Nasser. His involvement in the movement was fully recognized when the 1961 conference of the non-aligned countries was held in Belgrade[144]. Yugoslavia thus found a forum where she could assume a prominent position, without fear of interference in her affairs from the other powers she was dealing with, either her equals, or, in the cases of India and later China, not interested in meddling with Yugoslav politics.

Conclusions

In early 1948 the Western powers had a mistaken view of Stalin's foreign policy: they perceived him as expansionist and threatening, when he was trying to rein in the radical faction among the top leaders within the CPSU and the Communist movement. Tito was one of them: he, too, favoured a policy of total opposition to the Western powers, and of encouraging revolutions world-wide to spread Communism. Although the Western powers had noticed before 1948 how radical Tito was, they did not realize that his radicalism displeased Stalin. Nor did they see that Stalin's foreign policy had entered a period of retrenchment and consolidation within his orbit, while he (at least temporarily) shelved all expansionist ambitions, aiming at the avoidance of unnecessary provocation of the Western powers. For they in turn had reacted to the earlier phase of Stalin's postwar policy with intense suspicion. This had manifested itself in defensive coalitions and efforts to revive and consolidate the western and southern regions of Europe hitherto not under Soviet domination, and, in the case of the US, with a liberation policy aimed at the removal of Soviet influence from the European satellite states.

The Western powers also mistakenly assumed that the populations of those countries controlled by Communist régimes with the backing of the Red Army would be willing, after the exhausting effects of the Second World War, to rise up in arms, to shake off their totalitarian governments, and to risk their lives and those of their families for the sake of democratic and national freedom. Yet the populations of most of these countries had never experienced democracy. Further, in thinking (immediately after the expulsion of the Communist Party of Yugoslavia from the Cominform) that the Yugoslav leaders had themselves broken with the USSR for the sake of national self-determination, the Western powers mistakenly presupposed a strong nationalist opposition to the Kremlin among the satellite governments: the Communist régimes in Eastern Europe, however, owed their position to continuous backing by the Red Army, and even the two régimes for which this was not the case, those of Belgrade and Tirana, saw themselves as a prey for external enemies, with only the might of the Soviet Union behind them. The Western powers therefore mistook the Tito-Stalin split for a conscious bid for emancipation by the Yugoslavs, rather than seeing it as a desperate attempt by Stalin to rein in the most radical of his followers, who did not understand the subtleties of his foreign policy and who refused to believe that Stalin could abandon what seemed to them the obvious goal of the Communist movement, namely the spreading of the world revolution.

Because they assumed that the initiative for the split had lain on the side of the Yugoslavs, the Americans and the British initially hoped for similar "action" by other satellite governments. The US and Britain therefore adopted a policy designed to encourage other satellite leaders to "follow" Tito. There were other options: Policy One, the overthrow by means of force of the Yugoslav Communist régime and its replacement by a more liberal one, was tried by the CIA, and abandoned; its modified, non-violent version, aiming at the liberalization rather than the "liberation" of Yugoslavia, remained a long-term aim, but was not, for the time being, a priority. Policy Two, "masterly inactivity", was practised by the French and also, to start with, by the British.

The American NSC, however, from the beginning sought to follow a third policy, which blended in with their policy of liberation: this was to seek to exploit the Tito-Stalin split as a political advantage in the Cold War. This necessitated Yugoslavia's economic survival, her continued independence, and the continuation in power of her Communist leaders. Only thus could Yugoslavia serve as barrier between Albania and the Soviet orbit, while the Anglo-American secret services sought to effect the overthrow of Tirana's Communist government. More important still, only if Tito remained in power could Western propaganda point to him as to a Communist leader who could be master in his own house and withstand Soviet pressure. Policy Three was thus to help Tito survive without immediately forcing him to change his government to a Western-style one (by letting him "sit on the fence"). Moreover, the US wanted to turn Yugoslavia's economy into a show-case of how well an independent Communist-ruled country could fare at the hands of the West. Yugoslavia should thus serve as a spearhead or wedge to break up the Soviet bloc.

As this policy was based on mistaken assumptions, it did not have the desired results. Nothing leads us to believe that any leaders of the satellite states ever contemplated "following" Tito as long as Stalin was alive, or that Western treatment of Tito let them lose any of their fear of powers actively working for the liberation of Eastern Europe from Communism, for which they had positive evidence (e.g. Anglo-American activities in Albania). The Western liberation policy, seen in this context, was not only unsuccessful but also counterproductive: together with all the hostile anti-Communist (rather than anti-Russian imperialist, or anti-Stalinist) rhetoric, it outweighed the efforts to wean the Eastern European Communist régimes away from Stalin's control.

What was a mistaken assumption in the case of Yugoslavia, however, would have been a real possibility in the case of Mao's China, although even he had no intention of breaking with Stalin as long as Stalin was alive. The Western powers certainly had a chance of establishing reasonably co-operative relations with Mao, and gradually to draw Communist China away from its exclusive orientation towards Moscow by offering trade. The British government saw this and tried to pursue this policy. But by having educated US public opinion to recognize the Soviet (Communist) threat, the American government found themselves in the position of Goethe's "Zauberlehrling", the magician's apprentice, who, having conjured spirits is unable to control them, and the McCarthyite frenzies and the heated anti-Communism of the China-lobby made it impossible for the US to follow Britain. Moreover, General MacArthur's aggressive strategy provoked the Chinese Communists into lasting hostility towards the West precisely when the seeds of an equally lasting disillusionment with the Soviet Union took root in Peking.

Stalin, however, shared the Western view that Tito's insubordination after his expulsion from the Cominform might provoke centrifugal forces within the other satellite régimes and Communist China. This was in line with Stalin's paranoid fear of his subordinates. His measures to quell any potential opposition even of the most minor sort, taking the form of the purges, and his attempts to bring down Tito through pressure of various sorts, probably including plans to invade Yugoslavia with military force, strengthened the Western belief in its own misperception of the Tito-Stalin split and its significance.

Meanwhile, as Mastny has argued (see Chapter 5), Stalin was horrified by the defensive consolidation of western and southern Europe. Coupled with the Western powers' determination to bring western Germany into their orbit and the aggressive liberation policy pursued by the US and Britain, Western behaviour must have been seen as threatening. Stalin responded with a militarization of the satellite states and with the overall rearmament of the Soviet bloc. It is not impossible that he toyed with the idea of launching a preventive war in 1950-52. In this context also, the American liberation policy, featuring so prominently in Eisenhower's and Dulles's rhetoric, must have further fed Stalin's paranoia, and once more appears foolish and counterproductive. Stalin's precise reasoning in this period and his reactions to Western measures can only be speculated about, but the work of John Yurechko shows how important a factor the Western offensive liberation policy and rhetoric was in Communist thinking (see Chapter 5). This was noticed at the time by the French who were most sharply opposed to the liberation policy not only on account of the provocative effect it had on the Soviet leadership, but also because it challenged the integrity of the defensive spirit at the heart of the Atlantic Alliance.

The purely defensive measures of rearmament and consolidation on the part of the West necessarily came across as threatening and offensive if seen in connection with the liberation policy, and Stalin's decision to rearm his orbit is by no means unintelligible. One may conclude that defensive measures should never be accompanied by provocative, offensive measures, as one does not have to be a paranoid dictator to mistake the former for the latter. The Anglo-American (and later purely American) liberation policy, apart from making nonsense of Western talk about non-interference in other countries' internal affairs as upheld by the UN Charter, was in every respect dangerous and absurd: the Western powers were not ready to wage World War III for the sake of liberating Eastern Europe from Communism, yet at the same time they projected precisely that image. Meanwhile, the lives of exiles from the Eastern European countries were wasted in lukewarm attempts to overthrow their régimes, badly organized, planned without regard to political realities within the target countries, and betrayed by Kim Philby.

On the other hand the Western response to Communist foreign policies after the Second World War, and in particular to the Korean War, and the Western responses to the threat to Yugoslavia, in as far as they were defensive, seem to have been successful. The Soviets and satellites were probably deterred from attacking Yugoslavia. Although the rearmament of NATO worried and provoked Stalin, it also seems ultimately to have dissuaded him from starting a war against the West.

Focusing more narrowly on Western policies towards Yugoslavia, the Western powers were successful in mediating between Belgrade and Athens as well as between Belgrade and Vienna, which can be counted to their credit, even if it was also in the interest of Yugoslavia. Then the Korean War increased Yugoslavia's strategic importance in the eyes of the West. This was such that Western overall defence strategies were changed fundamentally: it became accepted policy that Italy and small parts of Austria should be held as a bridgehead in case of a Soviet onslaught on NATO territory. This would have been possible because Yugoslavia was now seen as a shield for the defence of Italy, a pillar propping up the Austrian mountain redoubt which was to be held, and the Greek northern line of defence. Moreover, the American doctrine regarding the employment of atomic bombs was changed in the context of defence plans for Yugoslavia. Accordingly, military aid was given to her primarily because this was seen as a means of reinforcing Western defences. The period of the Korean War also saw a shift of emphasis in economic and political relations: with the waning of the hope for further satellite "defections", the mention of political advantages of the preservation of Yugoslav independence, although still mentioned frequently, receded; military advantages became the key reason for supporting Tito. In turn, Yugoslavia's integration into Western defence strategy was of potentially great military advantage for NATO, and can be termed a temporary major gain for the Western powers.

Although by 1950 any real hope for further "Titoist defections" waned and it should have been clear to Western policy-makers that Yugoslavia had failed as a political wedge in the Soviet bloc, the policy of letting Tito "sit on the fence" (i.e.

of respecting Yugoslavia's political independence), was still applied more often than not, based on the reasoning that Tito should continue to be an example to other Communists. This was the case in the US and France, in spite of the differences in their attitudes towards various other Cold War policies after Korea. The British also shared this approach in 1950-51. But with the advent of the Conservative government in late 1951, doubts were raised about the wisdom of this policy, and the British became keen to draw Yugoslavia into the Western camp. This policy was entirely unsuccessful because Tito vowed that he would rather let his country starve than accept political conditions (a vow much easier to make once Stalin was dead and détente with the Soviet Union was possible for Tito). Also, the Americans in remaining unwilling to attach political conditions to the granting of economic aid (clinging to the pipe-dream of the effect an independent, prosperous, Communist government might have on other Communist régimes) neutralized the effect of British efforts. At the same time Tito might have had severe problems with the hard-liners within his government (such as Vukmanović-Tempo) if he had permitted any further "Westernization" of Yugoslavia at the request of the Western powers.

Having called the integration of Yugoslavia into Western defences a temporary major gain for the West, we should note that it was a major Western fault that the opportunity of securing a firm commitment from Yugoslavia to fight with the West was lost again so quickly. The Trieste crisis encouraged the Yugoslavs to seek detachment from the Western powers. They resented any dependent relationship with greater powers, and the feeling that they were at their mercy: this was their subjective impression of dealings with the US. This they felt even if historians might judge with hindsight that Yugoslavia, like many small powers caught between two rival poles, found herself in the advantageous position of being so precious to at least one of them, that it was she who could call the tune most of the time. This Yugoslav sensitivity was a factor which was ignored or underestimated by the Americans and British in the Trieste affair, and however much they needed to pacify Italian opinion, they must bear the blame for mishandling their relationship with the Yugoslavs. The effect was the ultimate defeat of Western aims relating to Yugoslavia, as she was neither "pulled off the fence" and into the Western camp, nor did her leaders ever commit her lastingly to the Western side to fight aggression — with the exception of the ephemeral Balkan Pact.

The main beneficiaries of Western policies towards Yugoslavia during this period were the Yugoslavs themselves. And yet there were temporary gains for the Western powers: the thought of a Yugoslavia aligned with the West in a potential war may well have played a part in deterring Stalin from launching a preventive war against NATO.

APPENDICES

Appendix A

1: Yugoslav investments (in thousand million dinars)

	1947	1948	1949*	1950
Industry and mining	15.3	15.0	24.4	19.1
Forestry	1.0	2.6	1.9	1.4
Transport and communication	8.9	8.1	10.6	9.0
Agriculture	1.7	5.7	8.2	6.7
Local investment*	1.4	5.0	*	5.0
Defence, etc.	7.0	13.4	9.6	13.9

*Included in 1949 figure in the individual sections.
Source: PRO, FO 371/102209, WY 1104/29 of August 1952.

2: Number of co-operatives in Yugoslavia

	1945	1946	1947	1948	1949	1950	1951
Number of co-operatives	31	545	779	1,381	6,625	6,968	6,694
Number of families in co-operatives (in 1,000)	—	25.1	49.6	60.2	340.7	418.7	429.8
total surface of co-operatives farms* (1,000 ha)	121.5	211.0	324.0	868.8	1,839.9	2,226.2	2,595.0

*Including private plots.
Source: C. Boborowski; La Yougoslavie Socialiste (Armand Colin; Paris, 1956), p. 106.

3: Crop production in Yugoslavia (in 1,000 metric tons)

	Prewar average	1946	1948	1949	1950	1951
Wheat	2,633	1,960	2,524	2,516	1,827	2,277
Maize	4,469	1,974	4,071	3,702	2,085	4,033
Other cereals	1,030	514	1,008	1,080	721	969
Sunflower seeds	16	n/a	121	130	69	94
Vegetables	2,255	n/a	2,675	3,616	1,692	2,776

Source: PRO, FO 371/102209, WY 1104/29 of August 1952.

Appendix B

	Yugoslav exports (%)					Yugoslav imports (%)				
	1938	1947	1948	1949	1950	1938	1947	1948	1949	1950
Sterling area	10	3	7	21	20	8	5	6	13	17
France	1	1	1	4	3	4	3	2	3	3
US	5	2	2	8	13	6	4	3	9	22
Austria	6	5	6	11	11	7	3	5	9	8
Greece	3	—	—	—	—	1	—	—	—	—
Netherlands	2	7	7	7	4	1	7	7	9	4
Italy	6	11	8	10	12	9	9	11	12	10
Belgium	7	1	2	2	3	1	2	5	5	2
W. Germany	36*	3	1	6	12	32	4	4	7	17
Switzerland	2	4	3	3	4	2	3	4	7	3
USSR and satellites	15	48	51	14	—	18	52	43	13	—
Others	7	15	12	14	18	11	8	10	13	14
Total	100	100	100	100	100	100	100	100	100	100

* 1938: all of Germany.   1938: USSR and Eastern European states.
Source: PRO, FO 371/102209, WY 1104/29 of August 1952.

Appendix C

1: Strength of Soviet and satellite armed forces

Country	Treaty	August 1950 (a)	Late 1950 (b)	Winter 1950-51 (c)	February 1951 (d)	March 1951 (e)	May 1952 (f)	August 1952 (g)	November 1952 (h)	November 1952 (i)
USSR										
Army										
Total Ground*		2,500,000							2,500,000	
Total†									2,900,000	
Romania										
Army	125,000	186,000								
Total Ground	125,000		250,000	263,000		323,000	240,000	240,000	267,000	482,000
Total	138,000				323,000		279,000	296,000	323,000	
Bulgaria										
Army	58,800	94,000								
Total Ground	58,800		130,000[2]	266,000	286,000		190,000[4]	205,000[4]	205,000[4]	
Total	65,500					291,500	238,000	258,000	272,000	
Hungary										
Army	65,500	38,500								
Total Ground	65,500		125,000[2]	117,000	175,000		150,000	185,000	185,000	
Total	70,000					142,000	185,000	220,000	220,000	
Albania										
Army		45,000								
Total Ground					41,000		40,000	40,000	40,000	
Total							50,000	50,000	50,000	
Yugoslavia										
Army		275,000[1]								
Total Ground					400,000[3]					
Total										

* Total Ground (Forces) includes various security forces, such as secret police, frontier guards, etc.
† Total Army, all security troops, Navy and Air Force

Appendices

1 PRO, FO 371/95549, RY 1201 of 17 February 1951: Annual Report on the Yugoslav Army.

2 May not include police and security troops.

3 This may be an exaggerated figure: cf. PRO, FO 371/95549, RY 1201/1, report by the British Military Attaché of 17 February 1951.
Perhaps the figure of 400,000 refers to the expected strength of the Yugoslav army five days after mobilization.

4 Includes 25,000 labour troops.

(a) US estimate: KCMF 62, JIC 530/3, Ad Hoc Committee of the Joint Intelligence Committee, report of 25 August 1950. At the same time the US had an army of 630,000; the UK had 358,000; France had 500,000; Italy had 170,000; Belgium and the Netherlands between them had 152,000; Canada had 21,600; and Denmark had 23,000, which makes a total of 1,854,600 for NATO ground forces.

(b) PRO, FO 371/95009, RY 1193/14 of 13 March 1951: Yugoslav Army Chief of Staff, General Popovic, gave these figures to C. Sulzberger of the *New York Times* in the presence of Tito.

(c) PRO, FO 371/95009, R 1193/14, Foreign Office brief for North Atlantic Council Deputy, early March 1951.

(d) PRO, FO 371/95548, 1194/5/51, British estimate: Peake dispatch to Bevin, 10 February 1951.

(e) PRO, FO 371/95009, R 1193/16, British estimate of 1 March 1951.

(f) KCMF 41, JIC 607/1 of 21 May 1952, US estimate, Part III table 9(a).

(g) KCMF 41, JIC 607/2 of 6 August 1952, US estimate, new table 9(a) of Part III.

(h) KCMF 42, JIC 607/3 of 21 November 1952, US estimate, new table 9(a) of Part III.

(i) PRO, FO 371/102168, WY 1022/94/G, Tito's estimate; it is not quite clear whether the two figures refer to total ground force strengths or only to army strengths.

Appendices

2: Soviet force strengths

Khrushchev in his speech of January 1960 gave the strength of the Soviet Army as follows:

1927	1937	1941	1945	1948	1955	1960
586,000	1,433,000	4,207,000	11,365,000	2,874,000	5,763,000	3,623,000

Thomas Wolfe assumes that the figures include the Navy and the Air Force, and thus argues that the figure for 1948 is generally regarded as too small by Western observers[1]. Yet if these figures are taken to exclude the Navy and Air Force, this figure tallies with various Western estimates dating from 1948 to 1951[2]. The Soviet security forces are in each case estimated at 400,000. The figure of 4,000,000[3] or even 4,600,000[4], which is quoted in some contemporary documents, presumably includes security forces, Navy and Air Force, which are thus estimated at 400,000, 800,000 and 800,000 respectively[5]. The dates for both the lower and the higher estimates (as made by Western observers) range from September 1947 to December 1952, so that it cannot be argued that there was either a gradual increase or decrease.

1 Thomas W. Wolfe, *Soviet Power and Europe, 1945-1970* (Baltimore; Johns Hopkins University Press, 1970), p. 10.

2 KCMF 62, JIC 435/12, "Soviet Intentions and Capabilities, 1949" of 30 November 1948; MAE, Z 459-2-3, vol. 16, no. 617-620 from Moscow, Catroux on 23 March 1948; KCMF 62, JIC 530/3 of 25 August 1950; *FRUS* 1951 I p. 193f of 24 September 1951.

3 PRO, FO 371/71695, Peterson, Moscow, no. 156; Roberts, telegram no. 2116 of September 1947; calculated Soviet armed forces including Navy, Air Force and security troops, as 4,000,000, a figure confirmed by the War Office.

4 British Minister of Defence, Emmanuel Shinwell, quoted this figure at a press conference in late July 1951: MAE, EU 31-4-2, vol. 15, no. 1369 from Massigli, London, of 30 July 1951.

5 TL, PSF, Central Intelligence Reports, Box 254, NIE-64 of 12 November 1952.

3: Incidents on Yugoslav frontiers according to Yugoslav findings

	1948	1949 (total)	1949 (Jan.-Sept.)	1950 (Jan.-Sept.)
Yug.-Hung. frontier	11	101	75	92
Yug.-Rum. frontier	0	37	26	147
Yug.-Bulg. frontier	23	139	93	132
Yug.-Alb. frontier	29	96	70	59
All frontiers of Yug.	63	—	264	430

Source: Ministère des Affaires Etrangères de la République Populaire Fédérative de la Yougoslavie: *Livre Blanc sur les Procédés Aggressifs des Gouvernements de l'URSS, de Pologne, de Tchéchoslovaquie, de Hongrie, de Roumanie, de Bulgarie et de l'Albanie envers la Yougoslavie* (Belgrade, 1951), Annex 16-19.

Appendix D

1: Aid for Yugoslavia

US grant aid to Yugoslavia		Year	$
Emergency civilian relief		1945-1946	6,500,000
UNRRA aid for Yugoslavia (US share)		1946-1947	299,100,000
MDAP food assistance		1950	15,200,000
Emergency Relief Assistance Act		1950	50,000,000
MDAP raw materials assistance		1951	29,000,000
UNICEF aid for Yug. (US share)		1951	10,600,000
US share in tripartite aid	(FY)	1952	78,000,000
US share in tripartite aid*	(FY)	1953	78,000,000
US special drought aid (total)*		1953	46,000,000

US loan aid to Yugoslavia	Year	$
Export-Import Bank	1949	20,000,000
Export-Import Bank	1950	35,000,000

*It seems that the given figure for "US share in tripartite aid" includes the three supplementary grants, which are not listed.
Source: USNA, RG 59, 768.5-MSP/10-2753.

British grant aid to Yugoslavia	Year	£	$
British share in tripartite aid	1951-June 1952	10,000,000	27,600,000
British share in tripartite aid	1952-1953	4,500,000	12,600,000

British loan aid to Yugoslavia	Year	£	$
	1949	13,000,000	36,400,000
	1950	3,000,000	8,280,000
	1951	6,000,000	16,560,000

Source: 513 H.C.DEB. col.40, 19 March 1953.

French grant aid to Yugoslavia	Year	FF	$
French grant for flour	1951	350,000,000	1,000,000
French share in tripartite aid	1951-June 1952	5,040,000,000	14,400,000
French share in tripartite aid	1952-1953	2,940,000,000	8,400,000
French loan aid to Yugoslavia	1951	5,600,000,000	16,000,000

Source: David D. Larson, *United States Foreign Policy towards Yugoslavia, 1943-1963* (Washington: University Press of America, 1979, originally 1965), p. 346.

2: Yugoslav agricultural production (estimate of 15 October 1952)

Production (in 1000 tons)	1950 (drought)	1951 (good harvest)	1952 (drought)
wheat and rye	2,045.1	2,554.0	1,903.5
barley	266.0	358.9	257.3
oats	194.5	292.7	215.8
maize	2,084.6	4,033.0	1,480.6
sunflowers	69.3	94.3	51.4
sugar beet	850.6	1,936.6	483.2
potatoes	1,018.8	1,621.3	1,007.5
beans	62.5	187.4	51.3

Source: US National Archives, Record Group 59, Box 5336, 868.03/10-1552 of 15 Oct 1952 from Belgrade.

Notes

Introduction

1. Robert M. Blum "Surprised by Tito: The Anatomy of an Intelligence Failure", *Diplomatic History XII* (Winter 1988) pp. 39-57; Henry Brands, "Redefining the Cold War: American Policy Towards Yugoslavia, 1948-1960", *Diplomatic History XI* (Winter 1987) pp. 41-54; John Campbell, *Tito's Separate Road—America and Yugoslavia in World Politics* (New York; Harper & Row, 1967); Harry Chase, "American-Yugoslav Relations, 1945-1956: A Study in the Motivations of U.S. Foreign Policy" (University of Syracuse, Social Science Ph.D. dissertation, 1957); Robert Hathaway, "Truman, Tito and the Politics of Hunger" in William Levantrosser (ed.) *Harry S. Truman: The Man from Independence* (Westport, Ct.: Greenwood Press, 1986); Robert Strausz-Hupé, "Yugoslav Counteroffensive in the Cold War", *The Yale Review* XL (December 1950), pp. 273-284; Strausz-Hupé, "The United States and Yugoslavia: A Reappraisal", *The Yale Review* XLV (December 1955), pp. 161-177; Novak Jankovic, "The Changing Role of the U.S. in Financing Yugoslav Economic Development since 1945", paper presented at the Symposium "Policy Options of American Governments" at the John F. Kennedy Institute, Free University, Berlin, July 1987; A. Ross Johnson, *The U.S. Stake in Yugoslavia, 1948-1968* (California: Southern California Arms Control and Foreign Policy Seminar, 1972); David Larson, *United States Foreign Policy towards Yugoslavia, 1943-1963* (Washington, D.C.: University Press of America, 1979, first edn., 1965); Lorraine Lees, "The American Decision to Assist Tito, 1948-1949", *Diplomatic History* 2 (1978), pp. 407-422; Lees, "American Foreign Policy Toward Yugoslavia, 1941-1949" (Pennsylvania State University, Ph.D. dissertation, 1976); Stephen Markovich, "American Foreign Policy and Yugoslav Foreign Policy" in Peter Potichnyj and Jane Shapiro (eds.), *From the Cold War to Detente* (New York: Praeger, 1976), pp. 78-96; Markovich, "The Influence of American Foreign Aid on Yugoslav Policies, 1948-1966" (University of Virginia, Ph.D. dissertation, 1968); Philip Windsor, "Yugoslavia, 1951, and Czechoslovakia, 1968" in Barry Blechman and Stephen Kaplan, *Force Without War: United States Armed Forces as a Political Instrument* (Washington, D.C.: Brookings Institution, 1978).

2. John Young, "Talking to Tito: the Eden Visit to Yugoslavia, September 1952", *Review of International Studies* XII 1 (January 1986), pp. 31-41; Joze Pirjevec, "Die Auseinandersetzung Tito-Stalin im Spiegel britischer diplomatischer Berichte", *Südostforschungen* XL (1981), pp. 164-174; for an earlier period, see Elisabeth Barker, *British*

Policy in South-East Europe in the Second World War (London: Macmillan, 1976).

3. Joze Pirjevec, *Tito, Stalin e l'Occidente* (Trieste: Editoriale Stampa Triestina, 1985) concerns the years 1945-48; Stevan Pavlovitch, "The Grey Zone in NATO's Balkan Flank", *Survey* XXV 3 (Summer 1980), pp. 20-42; for an earlier period, see Walter Roberts, *Tito, Mihailovic and the Allies, 1941-1945* (New Brunswick, N.J.: Rutgers University Press, 1973); Nora Beloff, *Tito's Flawed Legacy — Yugoslavia and the West, 1939-1984* (London: Victor Gollancz, 1985), however, is of little use for the researcher.

The works on Franco-Yugoslav relations are of limited value: Agence Yougoslave d'Information, *La Coopération Culturelle entre la France et la Yougoslavie* (Paris: Service de Presse et Documentation, 1956); Fadil Ekmecic, *La Présence Yougoslave en France depuis 100 Ans* (Paris: Yougofranc, 1981); for an earlier period, see Stevan Pavlovitch, *Unconventional Perceptions of Yugoslavia, 1940-1945* (New York: East European Monographs no. CLXXXVIII, Columbia University Press, 1985), on de Gaulle's relations with Tito.

4. In Britain, the 30-year rule is applied very rigorously and reliably; the release of material under the Freedom of Information Act in the US is more erratic and the last papers used here were released as late as March 1987. The French material from the Quai d'Orsay was theoretically not fully accessible in the summer of 1986, and the final "classement" may not have been completed even now; access was granted by special permission. An example of the crucial importance of such documents is Philip Windsor's mistaken assumption of 1978 that the US government did not take the Tito-Stalin split seriously until 1949; see "Yugoslavia, 1951, and Czechoslovakia, 1968" in Blechman and Kaplan (eds.), *Force*, pp. 445-448.

5. Of the works on Yugoslavia (see above), the following authors make use of archival material: Blum, Brands, Lees, Stefan, Young and Pirjevec.

6. See Bibliography, particularly works by Adomeit, Brzezinski, Deutscher, Geyer, Hammond, Hentsch, Hoensch, Hoffmann and Fleron, McCagg, Marcou, Mastny, Nogee and Donaldson, Porter, Ra'anan, Rubinstein, Shulman, Taubmann, Ulam, and Wolfe.

7. See, e.g. Chapter 1, the use of French archival material for the discussion of Soviet policy towards the Greek Civil War.

8. See, e.g. Graham Allison, *Essence of Decision* (Boston: Little, Brown and Company, 1971), pp. 67-100.

9. Nevertheless, Stephen Markovich, "The Influence" makes a convincing attempt to reconstruct Yugoslav policy in detail.

10. Harry Howe Ransom: "Secret Intelligence in the US, 1947-1982: The CIA's Search for Legitimacy" in Christopher Andrew and David Dilks (eds.), *The Missing Dimension* (London: Macmillan,

1984), p. 203.

11. Richard Snyder in Snyder, H.W. Bruck and Burton Sapin (eds.), *Foreign Policy Decision-Making* (New York: Free Press of Glencoe, 1962), p. 65.

12. Peter Richards, *Parliament and Foreign Affairs* (London: Allen & Unwin, 1967), pp. 32-35, 117-143, 158-164; and Richards, "Parliament and the Parties" in Robert Boardman and A.J.R. Groom (eds.), *The Management of Britain's External Relations* (London: Macmillan, 1973), pp. 245-262; H.G. Nicholas, "L'influence de l'opinion publique sur la politique étrangère de la Grande-Bretagne" in Jean-Baptiste Duroselle and André Siegfried (eds.), *La Politique Etrangère et ses Fondements* (Paris: Armand Colin, 1954), pp. 107-124, particularly 108f; Avi Shlaim, "The Foreign Secretary and the Making of British Foreign Policy", in Shlaim, Peter Jones and Keith Sainsbury(eds.), *British Foreign Secretaries since 1945* (Newton Abbot: David & Charles, 1977), p.19; Joseph Frankel, *British Foreign Policy, 1945-1973* (London: Oxford University Press, 1975), pp. 32-39; William Wallace, "The Role of Interest Groups" in Boardman and Groom, *Management*, pp. 263-288; and Wallace, *The Foreign Policy Making Process in Britain* (London: Allen & Unwin, 1976, 1977 edn), pp. 88-118; Peter Jones, "British Defence Policy: the Breakdown of Inter-Party Consensus", *Review of International Studies* vol. XIII (April 1987), pp. 111-113.

13. Pierre Gerbert, "L'influence de l'opinion publique et des partis sur la politique étrangère de la France", in Duroselle, *Politique*, pp.83-106; Philip Williams, *Crisis and Compromise* (London: Longmans, 1964), pp. 224-225; Alfred Grosser, *La IVe République et sa Politique Extérieure* (Paris: Armand Colin, 1961), pp. 79-189.

14. see Note 11.

15. Pierre Gerbert, "Opinion Publique"; Paul Courtier, *La Quatrième République* (Paris: Presses Universitaires de France, 3rd edn, 1983), p.52ff concerning predominating themes in French foreign policy.

16. see Harry Chase, "American-Yugoslav", particularly pp. 111-163, 190-250.

17. Zara Steiner, "Decision-making in American and British Foreign Policy: an Open and Shut Case", *Review of International Studies* (1987) vol. XIII 1pp. 1-18; H.B. Westerfield and Robert Osgood in Duroselle, *Politique*, pp. 125-142 and 179-201; and case-studies: Graham Allison, *Essence*; Thomas Etzold and John L. Gaddis (eds.), *Containment: Documents on American Policy and Strategy, 1945-1950* (New York: Columbia University Press, 1978), pp. 8-18; essays by Nye, Schneider, Dester, Bowie and May in Joseph Nye (ed.): *The Making of America's Soviet Policy* (New Haven, Yale University Press, 1984); Warner Schilling, Paul Hammond and Glenn Snyder, *Strategy, Politics and Defence Budgets* (New York: Columbia University Press, 1962); Avi Shlaim, *The United States and the Berlin Blockade, 1948-1949* (Berkeley:

University of California Press, 1983), particularly p. 73; Snyder and Paige, "The US Decision to Resist Aggression in Korea" in Snyder, Bruck and Sapin, *Foreign Policy*, pp. 206-249.

Regarding the importance of the NSC, Shlaim points out that Truman "was disinclined to allow it to play a major role in policymaking". In the case of Yugoslavia, however, the PPS and the NSC were clearly the main policy-formulators, and the President seemed merely to underwrite the policies proposed by them. It is the NSC's rôle in presenting proposals for basic policies and for wide-reaching policy changes, and the binding force of (presidentally approved) NSC decisions for the executive that made the NSC so important within the government apparatus.

18. The records of the meetings of the Permanent Under-Secretary's Committee are unfortunately not open to the researcher. Lord Strang, *The Diplomatic Career* (London: André Deutsch, 1962), pp. 110-111; Shlaim, "The Foreign Secretary", p. 34f; Anthony Adamthwaite, "Britain and the World, 1945-9: the View from the Foreign Office", *International Affairs* LXI no. 2 (Spring 1985), pp. 228-231, 232-234; Ray Merrick, "The Russia Committee of the British Foreign Office and the Cold War, 1946-1947", *Journal of Contemporary History* XX 3 (July 1985), pp. 453-468.

19. Articles by Larner, O'Leary, Bishop, Figges and Nailor in Boardmann and Groom, *Management*, pp. 31-74, 117-136, 137-160, 161-172, 221-224; Frankel, *British Foreign*, particularly pp. 112-150; Wallace, "Interest Groups", pp. 21-60; Shlaim, "The Foreign Secretary", pp. 13-26.

20. The Minutes of the Conseil des Ministres are published in excerpts in the diaries of Vincent Auriol, *Journal du Septennat, 1947-1954* vols. 1-6 (Paris: Armand Colin, 1977).

21. Alfred Grosser, *IVe République*, pp. 39-78; Raoul Girardet, "L'influence de la tradition sur la politique étrangère de la France", and Jacques Grunewald, "L'influence des facteurs économiques sur les décisions dans la politique étrangère de la France" in Duroselle, *Politique*, pp. 3-34 and 143-163.

22. Grunewald, "Facteurs économiques", *passim.*

Chapter 1

1. Elisabeth Barker, *Churchill and Eden at War* (London: Macmillan, 1978), part IV, particularly pp. 246-260; Julian M. Lewis, "British Military Planning for Post-War Strategic Defence, 1942-1947", Ms D.Phil. Oxford 1981), *passim*; Daniel Yergin, *The Shattered Peace* (London: André Deutsch, 1978), pp. 67-75 on the rôle of Admiral Leahy; Victor Rothwell, *Britain and the Cold War* (London: Jonathan Cape, 1982), p. 85ff, particularly p. 115.

2. Alan Bullock, *Ernest Bevin: Foreign Secretary* (London: Oxford University Press Paperback, 1985), p. 105; Kenneth Morgan, *Labour in Power, 1945-1951* (Oxford: Clarendon Press, 1984), p. 235.

3. Adam Ulam, *The Rivals* (New York: Viking Press, 1971), p. 61.

4. Elisabeth Barker, *The British Between the Superpowers 1945-1950* (London: Macmillan, 1983), pp. 1-13.

5. Lynn Davis, *The Cold War Begins* (Princeton, N.J., Princeton University Press, 1974), chapters 2-4, 7-8; A.W. DePorte, *Europe Between the Superpowers* (New Haven: Yale University Press, 1979), pp. 92-101.

6. DePorte, *Europe,* pp. 142-154; see also below, discussion of Marshall Aid; Frank Howley, *Berlin Command* (New York: Putnam, 1950), pp. 11-12.

7. Walter La Feber, *America, Russia, and the Cold War, 1945-1971* (2nd edn, New York: John Wiley & Sons, 1972), p.28; Yergin, *Shattered Peace,* p. 148f.

8. Barker, *The British,* p. 45.

9. *Foreign Relations of the United States* [henceforth *FRUS*]. 1946 VI, pp. 969-709, Moscow Embassy telegram of 22 February 1946.

10. For this much-quoted comment by Kennan's contemporary in the State Department, Louis Halle, see his *The Cold War as History* (London: Chatto & Windus, 1967), p. 105; see also John Gaddis, *Strategies of Containment* (New York: Oxford University Press, 1982) pp. 54-56. For some further examples of the acceptance of Kennan's ideas by key decision-makers, such as Dean Acheson (Secretary of State) and Dean Rusk (Deputy Under-Secretary of State), see e.g. discussion of Acheson's press conference by the British Cabinet, Public Records Office, London [henceforth PRO], FO 371/86751, NS 1052/14 G of 8 February 1950; or Rusk's talk with C. Sulzberger, *A Long Row of Candles* (London: Macdonald, 1969), p. 504.

11. Gaddis, *Strategies,* pp. 54-91, *passim.*

12. Kennan in his famous "X"-article in *Foreign Affairs,* July 1947: "The Sources of Soviet Conduct", p. 574.

13. Barker, *The British,* p. 44f; see also Rothwell, *Britain,* p. 247ff.

14. Rothwell, *Britain,* p. 251.

15. Ibid., p. 255ff.

16. Guy de Carmoy, *The Foreign Policy of France, 1944-1968* (Chicago: University of Chicago Press, 1970), p. 23.

17. Alfred Grosser, *The Western Alliance* (London: Macmillan, 1980), p. 62.

18. De Carmoy, *Foreign Policy,* pp. 4-6.

19. Philippe Robrieux, *Maurice Thorez* (Paris: Fayard, 1975), p. 360.

20. Rothwell, *Britain,* p. 285ff.

21. Barker, *The British,* p. 92.

22. Rothwell, *Britain,* p. 285ff.

23. Harry S. Truman Library, Independence, Missouri [henceforth TL], President's Secretary's Files [henceforth PSF], Box 203, CIA "Review of the World Situation", CIA 3-48, of 10 March 1948. See also Robert Garson, "The Role of Eastern Europe in America's Containment Policy, 1945-1948", *Journal of American Studies* XIII (1979), p. 80. For British reaction, see Bullock, *Bevin*, p. 526ff; for French reaction, see de Carmoy, *Foreign Policy*, p. 6ff.

24. *FRUS* 1948 I Pt. 2 p. 546.

25. Bevin urged his Cabinet to accept the Brussels Treaty quickly because of the events in Prague: PRO, CAB 128/12, CM(48)19th of 5 March 1948.

26. Cf. René Massigli, *Une Comédie des Erreurs* (Paris: Plon, 1978), p. 116f.

27. The reflection of this determination can still be found in a fictional construction of a scenario for nuclear war, made in the 1980s: see the American TV film *The Day After* of 1984, in which the conflict starts with another Berlin blockade.

28. H.M. Gladwyn Jebb, *The Memoirs of Lord Gladwyn* (London: Weidenfeld & Nicolson, 1972), p. 214; see also Michael Howard, "Introduction" in Olav Riste (ed.), *Western Security* (Oslo: Norwegian University Press, 1985), p. 14.

29. TL, PSF, Central Intelligence Reports, Box 256, ORE 58-48 of 30 July 1948; ORE 60-48 of 28 September 1948.

30. Gaddis: *Strategies*, p. 34f; *FRUS* 1950 I p. 128.

31. PRO, FO 371/72196, R 10197/8476/G, "Bastion Paper" of July/August 1948.

32. Gaddis, *Strategies*, p. 23f.

33. Lewis, "British Military", particularly p.102ff; Rothwell, *Britain*, p. 104ff.

34. Barker, *The British*, p. 47; Anthony Adamthwaite, "Britain and the World", *International Affairs* LXI no. 2 (Spring 1985), pp. 223-235 on internal organizational changes in response to the Cold War.

35. Thomas Etzold and John Gaddis, *Containment* (New York: Columbia University Press, 1978), pp. 8-18; cf. Avi Shlaim, *The United States and the Berlin Blockade, 1948-1949* (Berkeley: University of California Press, 1983), pp. 68-92.

36. Alfred Grosser: *La IVe République et sa Politique Extérieure* (Paris: Armand Colin, 1961), p. 73.

37. E.g. John Foster Dulles, who had also served under Truman, denounced "containment" as too passive when he fought under Eisenhower in the electoral campaign of 1952: cf. Michael Guhin, John Foster Dulles (New York: Columbia University Press, 1972), pp. 172-175. For the extensive literature on "containment" see: Halle, *Cold War*, pp. 105-109; George Kennan, *Memoirs 1925-1950* (London: Hutchinson, 1968), p. 365f, p. 463; John Gaddis, "Containment — A Reassessment", *Foreign Affairs* LV (1976-77); Edward Mark, "The

Question of Containment: A Reply to John L. Gaddis", *Foreign Affairs* LVI (1978); Gaddis's and Kennan's replies, ibid.; Gaddis, *Strategies,* pp. 19-88; Yergin, *Shattered Peace,* pp. 279, 321ff; John Yurechko, "From Containment to Counteroffensive" (Ms Ph.D., Berkeley, California, 1980), pp. 64-66. Earlier works, including Fleming, Kolko and Kolko, Hammond, Schlesinger etc., are largely outdated as their authors did not have access to crucial primary sources, such as the crucial NSC papers.

38. Gaddis, *Strategies,* p. 55ff.

39. Ibid., pp. 25-53.

40. Ibid., p. 30ff.

41. Kennan, "The Sources", p. 581.

42. Ibid., pp. 581-582.

43. Gaddis, "Containment: A Reassessment", p. 880.

44. E.g. NSC 14/1 of 1 July 1948: "The Position of the United States with Respect to Providing Military Assistance to Nations of the Non-Soviet World", in *FRUS* 1948 I Pt. 2 pp. 585-588.

45. Kenneth W. Condit, *The History of the Joint Chiefs of Staff, 1947-1949* vol. 2 (Wilmington: Glacier, 1979), pp. 275-280.

46. Bullock, *Bevin,* p. 473.

47. John Gaddis, "Was the Truman Doctrine a Real Turning Point?" *Foreign Affairs* LII 2 (January 1974), p. 384ff.

48. Paul Y. Hammond, *The Cold War Years* (New York: Harcourt, Brace & World, 1969), pp. 41-44.

49. Gaddis, "Was the Truman Doctrine", p. 389.

50. *FRUS* 1948 IV p. 312.

51. Bennett Kovrig, *The Myth of Liberation* (Baltimore: Johns Hopkins University Press, 1973), pp. 80-93.

52. *FRUS* 1948 I Pt. 2, pp. 546-550; cf. also Frank Ninkovich, *The Diplomacy of Ideas* (Cambridge: Cambridge University Press, 1981), pp. 139-167 on the world-wide cultural offensive; see also his pp. 168-180 on the contradictions between the American of freedom of thought advocacy abroad and narrow-minded McCarthyism internally.

53. Etzold and Gaddis, *Containment,* pp. 125-128.

54. Yurechko, "From Containment", pp. 134-135, 156-162, 299-309.

55. Quoted in Gaddis, "Containment", p. 878.

56. Gaddis, *Strategies,* p. 67.

57. Quoted in Geoffrey Warner, "Britain and Europe in 1948: The View from the Cabinet" in Josef Becker and Franz Knipping (eds.), *Power in Europe? Great Britain, France, Italy and Germany in a Postwar World, 1945-1950* (Berlin: De Gruyter, 1986), p. 34.

58. PRO, CAB 129/23, Bevin Memorandum to the Cabinet, CP(48)6 of 4 January 1948; see also Ray Merick, "The Russia Committee of the British Foreign Office and the Cold War,

1946-1947", *Journal of Contemporary History* XX 3 (1985), pp. 453-568; Bullock, *Bevin*, pp. 513-547; Barker, *The British*, pp. 112-120, 127-136; Cees Wiebes and Bert Zeeman, "The Pentagon Negotiations — March 1948", *International Affairs* LXI 3 (1983), p. 353ff; John Baylis, "Britain, the Brussels Pact and the Continental Commitment", *International Affairs* LX 4 (Autumn 1984).

    59. PRO, FO 371/72196, R 10197/847 b/G of July/August 1948.

    60. E.g. PRO, DEFE 5/12, COS(48)200(0) of 8 September 1948.

    61. Grosser, *The Western Alliance*, p. 62; de Carmoy, *Foreign Policy*, p. 23ff; Klaus Hänsch, *Frankreich zwischen Ost und West* (Berlin: de Gruyter, 1972), *passim*; cf. Michael Harrison, *The Reluctant Ally* (Baltimore: Johns Hopkins University Press, 1981), pp. 6-48, *passim*; and John Young, *Britain, France and the Unity of Europe* (Leicester: Leicester University Press, 1984), *passim*.

    62. DePorte, *Europe*, pp. 229-231.

    63. William Deakin, *The Embattled Mountain* (London: Oxford University Press, 1971), pp. 1-9; Fitzroy Maclean, *Eastern Approaches* (London: Jonathan Cape, 1949), pp. 279, 303-308; and agreement at Teheran Conference: Duncan Wilson, *Tito's Yugoslavia* (Cambridge: Cambridge University Press, 1979), p. 28f.

    64. Rothwell, *Britain*, p. 128f.

    65. E.g. Churchill's complaint about this to Stalin on 18 July 1945, PRO, FO 181/1009/6.

    66. Charles Stefan, "The Emergence of the Soviet-Yugoslav Break", *Diplomatic History* IV no. 4 (Fall 1982), p. 387.

    67. Barker, *The British*, p. 50, early 1946.

    68. Harry Chase, "American-Yugoslav Relations, 1944-1956" (Ph.D. Thesis, University of Syracuse, 1957), p. 131.

    69. Ministère des Affaires Etrangères, Archives, Paris [henceforth MAE], Z 499-34, 499-6 sd 4, no. 981 from Belgrade of 24 December 1947; no. 218 from Belgrade of 3 March 1948; Press report of 25 October 1948; nos. 1157 and 1186 from Belgrade of 24 November and 2 December 1948; ibid., no. 6880, Note by Ministry of Foreign Affairs to the Ministry of the Interior, 18 December 1948. For wartime relations, see Stevan Pavlovitch, *Unconventional Perceptions of Yugoslavia, 1940-1945* (New York: Columbia University Press, 1985), Ch.1, "General De Gaulle", pp. 1-32.

    70. Stefan, "Emergence", p. 387.

    71. PRO, FO 371/72578, minute of 12 January 1948.

    72. MAE, Z 492-1sd1, vol. 22, no. 595/EU.

    73. E.g. an instance recorded by James Byrnes, *Speaking Frankly* (London: William Heinemann, 1947), p. 145.

    74. Irena Reuter-Hendrichs, *Jugoslawische Aussenpolitik, 1948-68* (Cologne: Carl Heymanns Verlag, 1976), pp. 25-40.

    75. PRO, FO 371/72196, R 8476/8476/G 67.

    76. Kennan, *Memoirs 1925-1950*, p. 365; see also Avi Shlaim, *Berlin,*

p. 59.

77. Wilson, *Tito's Yugoslavia*, p. 27; see for example Vladimir Dedijer, *Tito Speaks* (London: Weidenfeld & Nicholson, 1953), pp. 233-235.

78. Dedijer, *Tito Speaks*, pp. 283f.,285; Westerners took note of this, see e.g. Walter Bedell Smith, *Mission to Moscow, 1946-1949* (London: Heinemann, 1950), p. 193.

79. George Hoffman and Fred Neal, *Yugoslavia and the New Communism* (New York: Twentieth Century Fund, 1962), pp. 95-97; Konni Zilliacus, *Tito of Yugoslavia* (London: Michael Joseph, 1952), p. 227.

80. Stalin and Molotov for the CPSU to Tito and Kardelj for the CPY, 4 May 1950, in Stephen Clissold (ed.), *Yugoslavia and the Soviet Union, 1939-1973* (London: Oxford University Press, 1975), p. 190; see also the Cominform communiqué of 28 June 1948, ibid., p. 202f.

81. Vladimir Dedijer, *The Battle Stalin Lost* (New York: The Universal Library, Grosset & Dunlap, 1971), p. 111; Clissold, *Yugoslavia*, p. 204.

82. Milovan Djilas, *Conversations with Stalin* (New York: Harcourt, Brace & World, 1962), pp. 133, 145-161.

83. Robert Bass and Elisabeth Marbury, *The Soviet-Yugoslav Controversy 1948-1958* (New York: Prospect Books, 1959), pp. 4-39; also in Royal Institute of International Affairs, *The Soviet-Yugoslav Dispute* (London: November 1948).

84. Clissold, *Yugoslavia*, p. 196, letter from Stalin, 4 May 1948.

85. State Department, Washington, document of 30 December 1948, declassified on 2 June 1986: Bebler to Czech diplomat.

86. Clissold, *Yugoslavia*, pp. 204-206, Cominform communiqué; and letters from the CC of the CPSU, pp. 172 and 195.

87. Ibid., p. 202; author's emphasis.

88. Ibid., pp. 172f, 187.

89. Ibid., p. 173; author's emphasis.

90. Zbigniev Brzezinski, *The Soviet Bloc — Unity and Conflict* (Cambridge, Mass.: Harvard University Press, 1967, reprinted 1969), pp. 41-64.

91. Louis Fischer, *The Road to Yalta* (New York: Harper & Row, 1972), p. 214f.

92. For the effect of the Marshall Plan on Stalin, see Othmar Nikola Haberl, "Die Sowjetische Aussenpolitik im Umbruchsjahr 1947", unpublished article, with the permission of Mr. Francis S. Wyman.

93. Vojtech Mastny, "Stalin and the Militarisation of the Cold War", *International Security* IX, no. 3 (Winter 1984/85), pp. 110-116.

94. William McCagg, *Stalin Embattled, 1943-1948* (Detroit: Wayne State University Press, 1978), p. 262ff.

95. Brzezinski, *Soviet Bloc*, p. 59; Mastny, "Militarisation", p. 119.

96. McCagg, *Stalin,* pp. 118-146, 266-273; Gavriel Ra'anan, *International Policy Formation in the USSR* (Hamden, Ct.: Archon Books, Shoe String Press, 1983) *passim.*

97. McCagg, *Stalin,* pp. 16ff, 118-146.

98. Ibid., p. 14f.

99. loc. cit. McCagg's analysis is identical with that of the Quai d'Orsay of 10 April 1953, submitted to the Foreign Minister, Bidault: see Archives Nationales [henceforth ANJ], Bidault Papers, file 457 AP 48, no. A 2332-430/21.

100. Fischer, *Road to Yalta,* p. 214.

101. McCagg, *Stalin,* pp. 205f, 266, 307, 379; Ra'anan, *International,* p. 162.

102. Dedijer, *The Battle,* p. 24f; Ra'anan, *International,* pp. 111-113.

103. Svetozar Vukmanovich-"Tempo", *How and Why the People's Liberation Struggle in Greece Met With Defeat* (London: Merlin Press, 1985), p. 4.

104. Djilas, *Conversations,* p. 182f.

105. Dedijer, *The Battle,* pp. 8f, 22f; and see Chapter 2.

106. Elisabeth Barker, "Yugoslav Policy towards Greece, 1947-1949" in Lars Baerentzen, John Iatridis and Ole Smith (eds) *Studies in the History of the Greek Civil War 1945-1949* (Copenhagen Museum: Tusculanum Press, 1987), p. 264.

107. Vladimir Dedijer, *Novi Prilozi za Biografiu J.B. Tita (Treci Tom)* (Belgrade, 1984), p. 226f. (The late Elisabeth Barker kindly allowed me to use her translation in excerpts of this work).

108. Vukmanovich, *How and Why,* p. 5f.

109. Dimitrios Kousoulas, "The Truman Doctrine and the Tito-Stalin Rift: A Reappraisal", *South Atlantic Quarterly* LXXII (Summer 1973) p. 428.

110. Dedijer, *Novi Prilozi,* p. 267.

111. Vukmanovich, *How and Why,* pp. 4-9; see also Djilas, *Conversations,* p. 131.

112. McCagg, *Stalin,* pp. 266-273; see also Ra'anan, *International,* p. 136.

113. McCagg, *Stalin,* pp. 273-284.

114. Ra'anan, *International,* p. 162.

115. Ibid., pp. 147-149.

116. MAE, Z 492-1sd1, vol. 23, no. 1879/EU from Berne of 11 August 1948; no. 1329 from Moscow of 27 July 1948 (Reports in *Pravda* and *Izvestiya*); no. 1617/EU and 1624/EU from Berne.

117. Pavel Tigrid, "The Prague Coup of 1948" in Thomas T. Hammond (ed.), *The Anatomy of Communist Takeovers* (New Haven: Yale University Press, 1975), pp. 399-432.

118. Hannes Adomeit, *Soviet Risk-Taking and Crisis Behaviour* (London: George Allen & Unwin, 1982), pp. 121-133.

119. *FRUS* 1947 V p. 477.

120. *House of Commons, Debates*, 22 January 1948, vol. 448. cols. 384-386.

121. Djilas, *Conversations*, p. 181f; see also Edvard Kardelj, *Reminiscences* (London: Summerfield Press, 1982) p. 108.

122. Service Historique de l'Armée de Terre, Château de Vincennes, Vincennes [henceforth SHAT], dossiers "Grèce", no. 169, Attaché Militaire, Athens, 19 June 1948. I have been unable to trace any record of the Bebler statement in the British files.

123. SHAT, Grèce, no. 138, Attaché Militaire, Athens, 18 May 1948.

124. Note the appearance here of Molotov as mediator, sympathizing with the Marcos faction. According to Ra'anan, Molotov is one of the members of the radical Zhdanovite faction (see above).

125. SHAT, Grèce, no. 169, Attaché Militaire, Athens, 19 June 1948.

126. Ibid., nos. 151 and 159 from A.M., Athens, of 2 June and 6 June 1948.

127. PRO, FO 371/78768, R 4224/1634/92 of 26 April 1949.

128. SHAT, Grèce, no. 180, Attaché Militaire, Athens, 29 June 1948.

129. State Department Document of 30 December 1948, declassified 2 June 1986.

130. Vukmanovich, *How and Why*, pp. 2-8.

131. McCagg, *Stalin*, p. 14f.

132. Clissold, *Yugoslavia*, p. 45; Dedijer, *The Battle*, pp. 202-212.

133. Ra'anan, *International*, p. 44f.

134. Stephen Peters, "Ingredients of the Communist Takeover in Albania" in Hammond, *Anatomy*; Peter Prifti, *Socialist Albania Since 1944* (Cambridge, Mass.: The MIT Press, 1978), pp. 9-19; Clissold, *Yugoslavia*, pp. 30,44,46.

135. Djilas, *Conversations*, pp. 133-136.

136. Ibid., p. 143.

137. Ibid., p. 179.

138. MAE, Z 3-4, vol. 14, *passim*.

139. Clissold, *Yugoslavia*, pp. 17f, 47; Dedijer, *Tito Speaks*, p. 330.

140. Elisabeth Barker, *Macedonia* (London: RIIA, 1950), p. 130ff.

141. Djilas, *Conversations*, pp. 176, 179.

142. Ibid., p. 171; Adam Ulam, *Titoism and the Cominform* (Cambridge, Mass.: Harvard University Press, 1952), p. 93f; Dedijer, *Tito Speaks*, p. 323.

143. Kardelj, *Reminiscences*, p. 105.

144. Djilas, *Conversations*, p. 177f; Dedijer, *Tito Speaks*, pp. 332, 336-338.

145. Dedijer, *Tito Speaks*, p. 333.

146. Djilas, *Conversations*, p. 167.

147. Clissold, *Yugoslavia*, p. 51.

148. PRO, FO 371/72580, R 7822/407/92 of 1 July 1948.

149. MAE, Z 542-1, vol. 45, no. 20 from Belgrade, 7 January 1948.

150. PRO, FO 371/72162, no. 162 from Moscow of 29 January, no. 179 from Sofia of 9 February 1948.

151. Clissold, *Yugoslavia*, p. 174; Le Figaro, 12 February 1948, p. 3; *FRUS* 1948 IV p. 1067, Memo by Hickerson of 23 April 1948; see also US Army Intelligence Report on this in USNA, RG 319, Box 298, 350.05 Yugoslavia, of 20 April 1948 which concluded that Yugoslavia might be about to make a military move into one of its neighbouring countries; Stefan, "Emergence", pp. 396, 403f; *FRUS* 1948 IV p. 1073.

152. PRO, FO 371/72578, Peake's telegram no. 477 from Belgrade, dispatch no. 118 and telegram no. 541, all May 1948; MAE, Z 492-1sd1, vol. 22, no. 315/EU, no. 447/EU, no. 99/EU from Belgrade and Zagreb, May and early June 1948; Stefan, "Emergence", p. 396; King's College, London University, Liddell Hart Archives, Microfilms [henceforth KCMF], no. 82, CIA 6-48, "Review of the World Situation" of 17 June 1948.

153. *FRUS* 1948 IV pp. 1070-1072.

154. Ibid., pp. 593-615, 1073-1074; see also Stefan, "Emergence", p. 391.

155. Interview with Sir Denis Wright, Aylesbury, Bucks., Spring 1986; and see private papers of Sir Denis Wright, which contain formulations very similar to those used by Reams.

156. PRO, FO 371/70229, W 3767/676/803 of 16 June 1948.

157. PRO, FO 371/72630, Peake's 614 of 18 June 1948.

158. Ibid., no. 615 from Belgrade, 18 June 1948.

159. Ibid., no. 837 from Paris, 23 June 1948.

160. Clissold, *Yugoslavia*, pp. 174, 181; Sir Charles Peake did indeed have close personal relations with him: PRO, FO 371/72579, letter from Peake to Wallinger, 29 June 1948.

161. PRO, FO 371/72578, Peake's letter to Wallinger of 22 May 1948.

162. MAE, Z 492-1sd1, vol. 22, no. 551/EU of 9 June 1948.

163. MAE, Z 492-1sd1, vol. 23, no. 545 from Budapest, 9 September 1948.

164. Vladimir Dedijer, *Tito Speaks*, p. 381.

165. Ibid., no. 595/EU of 22 June 1948.

166. W. Bedell Smith, *Mission*, p. 193f.; cf. Robert Blum, "Surprised by Tito: The Anatomy of an Intelligence Failure", *Diplomatic History* XII 1 (Winter 1988) pp. 39-57.

167. PRO, FO 371/72579, no. 656 from Belgrade of 29 June 1948.

168. MAE, Z 492-1sd1, vol. 22, no. 1521/EU from Bonnet, Washington, 6 July 1948.

169. MAE, Z 492-1sd1, vol. 22, no. 422/424 from Belgrade of 29 June 1948.

170. Ibid., no. 109/EU from Belgrade of 30 June 1948.

171. MAE, Z 492-1sd1, vol. 22, no. 1195-1203 from Moscow of 10 July 1948.

172. PRO, FO 371/72579, no. 887 from Paris of 30 June 1948.

173. MAE, Z 492-1sd1, vol. 22, no. 826-839 from Dejean, Prague, of 1 July 1948.

174. Ibid., e.g. letter no. 646 from Belgrade of 6 July 1948.

175. Ibid., no. 2578 from Massigli, London, of 7 July 1948.

176. E.g. PRO, FO 371/72580, R 7770/407/92 of 29 June 1948 from Warsaw.

177. E.g. Sterndale-Bennet's telegram from Sofia, ibid., R 7848/407/92 of 1 July 1948; Holman, Bucharest, R 7857/407/92 of 29 June 1948.

178. W. Bedell Smith, *Mission*, p. 193.

179. E.g. NSC 7 of 30 March 1948, *FRUS* 1948 I Pt. 2, pp. 546-550.

180. W. Bedell Smith, *Mission*, p. 179.

Chapter 2

1. See Chapter 1; MAE, Z 492-1sd1, vol. 22, *passim*.

2. *FRUS* 1948 IV pp. 1083 (Bedell Smith of 2 July 1948); 1088 (Reams of 7 July 1948); *per contra*: John Campbell, *Tito's Separate Road*, (New York: Harper & Row, 1967), p. 13f.

3. MAE, Z 492-1sd1, vol. 22, no. 2413-2418 from London, 29 June 1948.

4. PRO, FO 371/78582, R7994, Wallinger's comment of 9 July 1948; FO 371/72569, R 8790, Wallinger's comment of 6 July 1948; and FO 371/72579, King, Belgrade's no. 662 of 30 June 1948.

5. PRO, FO 371/78716, R 2168 of 15 February 1949.

6. *FRUS* 1949 V p. 857.

7. *FRUS* 1948 IV p. 1081, NSC 18.

8. MAE, Z 492-1sd1, vol. 22, no. 425-426 from Belgrade of 30 June 1948.

9. Ibid., no. 109/EU from Ljubljana of 30 June 1948 (italics in original).

10. Ibid., no. 826 from Prague of 1 July 1948; no. 2857 DN/2 of 25 August 1948.

11. PRO, FO 371/72579, G.T.C. Campbell minute of 30 June 1948 on no. 657 from Belgrade; FO 371/72583, G.T.C. Campbell minute of 5 July 1948.

12. PRO, FO 371/78715, R 2160, Bateman's minute of 17 February 1949.

13. SHAT, Yougoslavie, Relations Extérieures, no. 3 from Military Attaché, Belgrade, 14 January 1949.

14. *FRUS* 1949 V p. 858f.

15. PRO, FO 371/78715, R 2160/10345/92 G, minutes by

Bateman, Sargent, Roberts; and the FO's no. 2057 to Washington.

16. United States National Archives [henceforth USNA], NSC 18/2 of 17 February 1949; also in *FRUS* 1948 IV 1079-1081.

17. Hary Rositzke, "America's Secret Operations", *Foreign Affairs* LIII 2 (January 1975), pp. 335-336; John Prados, *The Soviet Estimate* (Princeton, N.J.: Princeton University Press, 1982), p. 25; Harry Howe Ransom, "Secret Intelligence in the United States, 1947-1982" in Christopher Andrew and David Dilks, *The Missing Dimension* (London: Macmillan, 1984), pp. 199-205.

18. PRO, CAB 129/22, CP(47)313 of 24 November 1947; see also CAB 129/23, CP(48)6 of 11 January 1948.

19. PRO, FO 371/72630, Belgrade's 615 of 18 June 1948; and FO 371/72576, R 12455 of 21 October 1948.

20. PRO, FO 371/72579, no. 887 from Paris of 30 June 1948.

21. PRO, FO 371/72579, Bevin's dispatch no. 936 to Washington, 30 June 1948.

22. *FRUS* 1948 IV p. 1076 of 29 June 1948.

23. PRO, FO 371/72579, Bevin's 936 to Washington, 30 June 1948.

24. *FRUS* 1948 IV p. 1078 of 30 June 1948.

25. Ibid., p. 1076 of 29 June 1948 to Belgrade (note); p. 1078 of 1 July 1948 to London (note).

26. PRO, FO 371/72576, R 12455, Bateman to Washington, 13 November 1948; and FO 371/74183, draft of 22 December 1948, AN 308/1053/45 G.

27. PRO, FO 371/72579, Franks's no. 3207 from Washington of 30 June 1948.

28. Frank Wisner was Deputy to the Assistant Secretary of State for Occupied Areas in 1948.

29. *FRUS* 1948 IV p. 1096 of 22 July 1948.

30. MAE, Z 492-1sd1, vol. 22, no. 3009-3011 of 1 July 1948.

31. *FRUS* 1948 IV p. 1079f.

32. MAE, Z 492-1sd1, vol. 22, no. 2857 DN/2 from the Ministry of Defence, 25 August 1948.

33. Ibid., no. (illegible) 1521/EU(?) of 6 July 1948.

34. PRO, FO 371/72579, Belgrade's 662 of 30 June 1948.

35. John Gaddis, *Strategies of Containment* (New York: Oxford University Press, 1982), p. 44.

36. PRO, FO 371/72579, no. 662 from Belgrade of 30 June 1948.

37. PRO, FO 371/72589, R 11401 of 6 October 1948.

38. Vladimir Dedijer, *The Battle Stalin Lost* (New York, Grosset & Dunlap, 1972), p. 172.

39. Ibid., pp. 167-186. See also the articles in the Communist paper edited by André Wurmser, *L'Humanité*; on the PCF's attitude towards Tito in 1948, see M. Andereth, *The French Communist Party* (Manchester, Manchester University Press, 1984).

40. Tito speech of 16 February 1951: MAE, EU 32-8-1, old vol. 25,

no. 239 from Belgrade, 18 February 1951; DD (79) 287 A, OIR Report no. 5483 of 22 June 1951, "Communist Defections and Dissensions in the Postwar World", pp. 16-21.

41. Dominique Desanti, *Masques et Visages de Tito et des Siens* (Paris: Eds. du Pavillon, 1949) with Preface by André Wurmser.

42. David Caute, *Communism and the French Intellectuals, 1914-1960* (London: André Deutsch, 1964), pp. 177-180; Irwin Wall, *French Communism in the Era of Stalin* (Westport, Ct.: Greenwood Press, 1983), pp. 76-77.

43. Louis Dalmas, *Le Communisme Yougoslave Depuis la Rupture avec Moscou* (Paris: Terre des Hommes, Documents, 1950).

44. Marcel-Edmond Naegelen, *Tito* (Paris, Eds. Flammarion, 1961).

45. Dalmas, *Le Communisme*, "Faux Savants ou Faux Lièvres", pp. I-XLIII.

46. Agnès Humbert, *Vu et Entendu en Yougoslavie* (Paris: Deux Rives, 1950).

47. "La Révolution et la Vérité" in *Esprit*, December 1949, and other articles, ibid.

48. E.g. "Réponses", *Esprit*, December 1949.

49. DD (79) 287 A, OIR Report no. 5483 of 22 June 1951, p. 8.

50. Caute, *Communism*, pp. 180-184; 232.

51. Cf. Philippe Robrieux, *Maurice Thorez* (Paris: Fayard, 1975), p. 401; Neil McInnes, *The Communist Parties of Western Europe* (London, the Oxford University Press for the RIIA, 1975), pp. 132-134.

52. DD (79) 287 A, OIR Report no. 5483, p. 3f.

53. Grant Amyot, *The Italian Communist Party* (London: Croom Helm, 1981), pp. 34-53; particularly 46f; Giuseppe Vacca, "The Eurocommunist Perspective: the Contribution of the Italian Communist Party" in Richard Kindersley (ed.), *In Search of Eurocommunism* (London: Macmillan, 1981), p. 134f.

54. Andrzej Korbonski, "The Impact of the Soviet-Yugoslav Rift on World Communism" in Wayne S. Vucinich (ed.), *At the Brink of War and Peace: The Tito-Stalin Split in a Historic Perspective* (New York: Columbia University Press, 1982), p. 1ff; Lilly Marcou, *Le Kominform* (Paris: Presses de la Fondation Nationale des Sciences Politiques, 1977), pp. 144-153

55. PRO, FO 371/86899, NS 2191/34/G of 14 February 1950, "Anti-Stalinist Communism".

56. DD (79) 287 A, OIR Report no. 5483, "Communist Defections and Dissensions in the Postwar World" of 22 June 1951.

57. PRO, FO 371/72580, R 7786 of 1 July 1948.

58. PRO, FO 371/78716, R 11684 of 23 November 1949; see also MAE, Z 3-4, vol. 14 no. 1127 from Belgrade of 22 November 1948.

59. PRO, FO 371/72580, R 7857 from Bucharest of 29 June 1948, and the following telegrams from Bucharest.

60. MAE, Z 492-1sd1, vol. 23, situation summary of 15 July 1948; Gauquie from Budapest, no. 453-454 of 16 July 1948.

61. Ibid., vol.22, no. 817-823, 840-843, 845, 853-856 from Prague; PRO, FO 371/72580, R 7798 of 1 July 1948.

62. PRO, FO 371/72630, Sofia's 706 of 21 June 1948.

63. Gavriel Ra'anan, *International Policy Formation in the USSR* (Hamden: Archon Books, 1983), pp. 144-147; Djilas quoted in Vladimir Dedijer, *The Battle*, p. 190; Milovan Djilas, *Conversations with Stalin* (New York: Harcourt, Brace & World, 1962), p. 182 — he even claims that Kostov was sympathetic on this occasion.

64. MAE, Z 492-1sd1, vol. 22, no. 3002-3008 from Washington, 1 July 1948; vol. 23, no. 243-246 from Sofia, 20 July 1948.

65. Zbigniev Brzezinski, *The Soviet Bloc — Unity and Conflict* (Cambridge, Mass.: Harvard University Press, 1967, reprinted 1969), p. 61; Franz Borkenau, *European Communism* (London: Faber & Faber, 1953), p. 508.

66. A. Ross Johnson, *The Transformation of Communist Ideology* (Cambridge, Ma.: MIT Press, 1972), p. 90.

67. Stephen Clissold, *Yugoslavia and the Soviet Union, 1939-1973* (Oxford: Oxford University Press, 1975), p. 203.

68. PRO, FO 371/72580, R 7832 and R 7833 from Warsaw of 2 July 1948.

69. PRO, FO 371/72581, R 7906 of 5 July 1948.

70. MAE, Z 492-1sd1, vol. 23, no. 635-642 of 10 July 1948.

71. E.g. PRO, FO 371/72588, R.A. Sykes's minute of 6 September 1948 on R 10242.

72. PRO, FO 371/72632 A, R 10425 of 6 September 1948.

73. PRO, FO 371/72589, R 11501 of 5 October 1948.

74. MAE, Z 492-1sd1, vol. 24, no. 976 from Warsaw, 21 October 1948.

75. Ibid., no. 36 from Warsaw of 11 January 1949.

76. *FRUS* 1948 IV p. 1109.

77. PRO, FO 371/72588, Wallinger's minute of 7 September 1948 on R 10071.

78. Ibid., Talbot minute of 21 September 1948 on R 10671.

79. Dedijer, *The Battle*, pp. 133-140; PRO, FO 371/72589, R 11402 of 27 September 1948.

80. PRO, FO 371/72588, R 10033 of 27 August 1948; see also R 10242 of 28 August 1948; MAE, Z 492-1sd1, vol.22, no. 2417/EU from Berne of 13 October 1948.

81. E.g. PRO, FO 371/88260, RY 1072/7 of 8 July 1950.

82. The words of a Hungarian victim of the show-trials, Béla Száz, *Volunteers for the Gallows* (London: Chatto & Windus, 1971), p. 160.

83. Brzezinski, *Soviet Bloc*, p. 97.

84. Articles by Jean Cassou, François Fejtö, and Vercors in *Esprit*, November and December 1949; see also Mosha Pijade, *Ce que révèle le*

procès Rajk (Belgrade: Le Livre Yougoslave, 1949).

85. Jörg Hoensch, *Sowjetische Osteuropa-Politik 1945-1975* (Düsseldorf: Athenäum/Droste, 1977), p. 57ff.

86. E.g. PRO, FO 371/78245, 78249-78251; 78521-78524, *passim.*

87. TL, PSF, NSC Meetings, Box 204, CIA 11-48, "Review of the World Situation" of 17 November 1948.

88. TL, PSF, NSC Meetings, Box 205, CIA 10-49, "Review of the World Situation" of 19 October 1949.

89. PRO, FO 371/71687, RC (16) 48 of 25 November 1948, p.5.

90. PRO, FO 371/77566, N 1225/1016/38 of 2 February 1949.

91. *FRUS* 1949 V pp. 886-889 of 25 April 1949.

92. A. Ross Johnson, *Transformation,* p. 241.

93. PRO, FO 371/72579, no. 662 from Belgrade, King on 30 June 1948.

94. PRO, FO 371/77594 *passim.*

95. PRO, FO 371/86751, RC/19/50 of 4 February 1950; see also CAB 129/29, CP(48)223 of 13 September 1948, and CAB 129/34, CP(49)72 of 24 March 1949.

96. PRO, FO 371/86899, approved by Russia Committee on 14 February 1950.

97. PRO, FO 371/72588, R 10071 of 28 August 1948.

98. PRO, FO 371/77622, PUSC(31) Final Approval, 28 July 1949.

99. MAE, EU 32-8-1, old vol. 24, Note of 9 November 1949.

100. *FRUS* 1949 V p. 941; see also PRO, FO 371/78715, R 2160/10345/92 G, Wallinger's minute of 17 February 1949.

101. *FRUS* 1948 IV, p. 1096 of 22 July 1948.

102. *FRUS* 1949 V p. 42ff: NSC 58/2 of 8 December 1949.

103. See footnote (1) in *FRUS* 1949 V p. 43.

104. *FRUS* 1949 V p. 941; and PRO, FO 371/78715, R 2160/10345/92 G, Wallinger's minute of 17 February 1949.

105. *FRUS* 1948 IV pp. 1079-1081 of 30 June 1948.

106. *FRUS* 1948 IV pp. 1079-1081 of 30 June 1948.

107. PRO, FO 371/74183, AN 308/1053/45 G, draft minute of 22 December 1948.

108. PRO, FO 371/77622, PUSC(31) Final Approval, 28 July 1949.

109. PRO, FO 371/78715, R 2160 of 17 February 1949.

110. *FRUS* 1948 IV p. 1104 of 31 August 1948.

111. PRO, FO 371/73105, minute of 8 October 1948.

112. PRO, FO 371/74183, AN 308/1053/45 G of 22 December 1948.

113. *FRUS* 1949 V p. 857.

114. *FRUS* 1949 V p. 858f.

115. USNA, NSC documents, NSC 18/2.

116. *FRUS* 1949 V p. 12.

117. *FRUS* 1949 V p. 29, Ambassadors' Meeting in London,

October 1949.

118. Thomas Etzold and John Gaddis (eds.), *Containment: Documents on American Policy and Strategy, 1945-1950* (New York: Columbia University Press, 1978), p. 182ff.

119. *FRUS* 1949 V pp. 886-889 of 25 April 1949; Etzold and Gaddis, *Containment*, p. 211ff.

120. Ibid.

121. PRO, FO 371/77622, PUSC(31) Final Approval, 28 July 1949.

122. PRO, FO 371/72579, no. 737 from Sofia, 30 June 1949; FO 371/72580, no. 7781 from Bucharest of 1 July 1949.

123. PRO, FO 371/78447, R 1953/10392/19 of 17 February 1949, McNeill to Noel Baker, citing Peake's view.

124. PRO, FO 371/87694, RG 10392/54 of 30 June 1950.

125. *FRUS* 1948 IV p. 1079, italics in original.

126. Ibid., pp. 1079-1081.

127. MAE, EU 32-8-1, old vol. 24, note of 9 November 1949.

128. *FRUS* 1948 IV p. 1075 of 18 June 1948; cf. Handler in the *New York Times* of 29 June 1948.

129. MAE, Z 499-8, vol. 42, no. 595 from Lisbon, 5 July 1948, France Presse.

130. *FRUS* 1949 V pp. 886-889 of 25 April 1949.

131. John Gaddis, "Containment: A Reassessment", *Foreign Affairs* LV (1976-1977), p. 878; Kennan's use of language was not only often obscure, but also lacking in taste in some instances such as this.

132. For the discussion of the Soviet contribution to the liberation of Yugoslavia, see Mosha Pijade, *About the Legend that the Yugoslav Uprising Owed its Existence to Soviet Assistance* (London: Yugoslav Information Service, 1950); Josip Broz Tito, "Political Report of the CC of the CPY at the Fifth Congress of the CPY", June 1948, in Mark Wheeler, "Yugoslavia's Contribution to Victory in the Second World War" (London: School of Slavonic and East European Studies, University of London, Background Briefings, 29 May 1985); both explain that the USSR only had a small share in the credit for the liberation of Yugoslavia, which was mainly achieved by Yugoslav partisan forces. For a statement to the contrary, see Michael Howard letter to *The Times*, 18 June 1983.

133. Chalmers A. Johnson, *Peasant Nationalism and Communist Power* (Stanford: Stanford University Press, 1962), particularly p. 157ff.

134. MAE, Z 492-1sd1, vol. 22, no. 622 from Prague of 14 July 1948; vol. 23, no. 578 from Nanking, 17 July 1948.

135. Wu Xiuquan, *Eight Years in the Ministry of Foreign Affairs* (Beijing: New World Press, 1985), p. 128.

136. Ibid., pp. 94-100.

137. PRO, FO 371/72588, R 10242, Watson to Belgrade, 30 September 1948; reference to Scott's F 11031/33/10 of 11 August

1948 — withheld?

138. PRO, FO 371/72589, R 11401 of 6 October 1948.

139. TL, PSF, NSC Meetings, NSC 34, p. 8ff.; see also *FRUS* 1948 I pp. 638-643: a memorandum on NSC 34 by the State Department. For further references to this see NSC 34/2: "United States Policy Toward China", 28 February 1949, *FRUS* 1949 IX pp. 491-495.

140. PRO, FO 371/72588, R 9969 from Belgrade, 21 August 1948 and R 10242 of 28 August 1948; MAE, Z 492-1sd1, vol. 22, no. 672-677 from Belgrade, 24 August 1948; *FRUS* 1950 IV p. 1357, footnote, of 22 January 1950; PRO, FO 371/95488, RY 1053/1 of 8 December 1950; MAE, EU 31-9-11 s/d1, vol. 74, no. 283-285 from Rangoon, 13 July 1953.

141. USNA, NSC 18/2, p. 4.

142. PRO, FO 371/77623, N 3583 of 12 April 1949.

143. PRO, FO 371/77624, N 5675 of 21 June 1949.

144. Ibid., N 10086 of 6 December 1949, Sir R. Stevenson.

145. MAE, Z 495-1, vol. 33, de Vaux St. Cyr, no. 306 from Athens, 9 April 1949.

146. MAE, Z 499-8, vol. 42, Armand Berard (Chargé d'Affaires), no. 1720 from Washington of 19 April 1949.

147. Nancy Tucker, *Patterns in the Dust* (New York: Columbia University Press, 1983), pp. 29-31; MAE, EU 31-9-1, vol. 51, note of 30 November 1953.

148. See Bibliography for other titles.

149. *FRUS* 1949 IX pp. 826-834: NSC 41, "United States Policy on Trade with China", and ibid., pp. 295-296; see also Gaddis, *Strategies*, p. 68.

150. Gaddis, *Strategies*, p. 69.

151. John Gaddis, "Was the Truman Doctrine a Real Turning Point?", *Foreign Affairs* (January 1974), pp. 392, 395.

152. Tucker, *Patterns*, pp. 193-207.

153. Ibid., p. 25; Elisabeth Barker, *The British Between the Superpowers* (London: Macmillan, 1983), p. 174.

154. Tucker, *Patterns*, p. 38.

155. William Stueck, *The Road to Confrontation* (Chapel Hill, N.C.: University of North Carolina Press, 1981), pp. 126-152.

156. Barker, *The British*, pp. 169-170; Stueck, *The Road*, p. 65.

157. Cf. James Tang, "Diplomatic Relations with a Revolutionary Power — Britain's Experience with China, 1949-1954" (Ms. Ph.D., University of London, 1987).

158. Mao in a speech in 1962, quoted in Jacques Guillermaz, *Le Parti Communiste Chinois au Pouvoir (1949-1972)* (Paris: Payot, 1972), p. 184.

159. François Fejtö, *Chine-URSS: La Fin d'une Hégémonie* (Paris: Plon, 1964), p. 65; Stueck, *The Road*, pp. 121f; Robert Blum, *Drawing the Line* (New York: W.W. Norton, 1982), p. 56.

160. Stueck, *The Road*, pp. 121-126; Blum, *Drawing*, pp. 56-59.

161. See Chapter 1; e.g. PRO, FO 371/72580, R 7786/407/92 of 1 July 1948; MAE, Z 3-4, vol. 14, no. 163-169 from Tirana of 3 July 1948; no. 1127 from Belgrade of 22 November 1948. See also Borkenau, *European Communism*, pp. 396-408.

162. See Chapter 1.

163. About the Western assumption that the USSR was involved in the Greek Civil War, see Chapter 1.

164. PRO, FO 371/71687, RC(16)48 of 25 November 1948.

165. Nicholas Bethell, *The Great Betrayal* (London: Hodder & Stoughton, 1984), p. 39.

166. SHAT, Grèce, no. 56, M.A. Athens, 26 March 1949.

167. *FRUS* 1949 V p. 12f.

168. John Yurechko, "From Containment to CounterOffensive" (Ms. Ph.D., 1980, University of Berkeley, California), pp. 80-90; Kim Philby, *My Silent War* (New York: Ballantine Books, 1968), p. 163f; AN, Archives Bidault, 457 AP 48, no no., Chataigneau's note for the President, 20 January 1953 concerning activities in the Ukraine and the Caucasus.

169. *FRUS* 1949 VI p. 415.

170. *FRUS* 1949 VI footnote 4 p. 365; MAE, EU 32-8-1, note of 9 November 1949.

171. MAE, EU 32-8-9, old vol. 41, *passim*.

172. PRO, FO 371/107295, WA 1051/3 G of 4 March 1953, H.M. Ambassador in Belgrade.

173. Gaddis, *Strategies*, p. 155, author's emphasis.

174. USNA, NSC 174 of 11 December 1953.

175. Bethell, *Great Betrayal*, pp. 127-201, *passim*.

176. Ibid., p. 99; Philby, *Silent War*, p. 161.

177. Bethell, loc. cit.

178. Philby, *Silent War*, p. 162.

179. Bethell, *Great Betrayal*, pp. 183-184.

Chapter 3

1. C. Boborowski, *La Yougoslavie Socialiste* (Paris: Librairie Armand Colin, 1956), p. 98, has the figures 46% (1948) and 14% (1949); for my figures, see Appendix B. For Western information on this, see, e.g. PRO, FO 371/72556, R 8046 and R 8550 of early July 1948; FO 371/72575, R 10283 of September 1948; FO 371/72576, R 13099 of November 1948 by Michael Kaser; and PREM 8/1573, R 14183 of 11 December 1948, by Denis Wright.

2. Boborowski, *Yougoslavie*, p. 85.

3. Boborowski, *Yougoslavie*, pp. 97-104.

4. PRO, FO 371/78730, R 1585; Parliamentary question, 461 HC

DEB 5s, col. 345ff of 9 February 1949; PRO, CAB 134/555, ON(48)10th of 16 January 1948, and following meetings.

5. Surprisingly, both Dr. Campbell (*Tito's Separate Road* (New York: Harper & Row, 1967)), pp. 15-18, and, following him, Philip Windsor ("Yugoslavia, 1951 and Czechoslovakia, 1968" in Barry Blechman and Stephen Kaplan (eds.), *Force Without War* (Washington, D.C.: the Brookings Institution, 1978), pp. 445-448) mistakenly assume that US policy did not take the split seriously until 1949. That this is not so is amply proved by NSC 18 of 30 June 1948.

6. *FRUS* 1949 V pp. 29 and 923; cf. Campbell, *Tito's*, p. 17.

7. *FRUS* 1949 V p. 903, Reams on British policy, 24 June 1949.

8. CAB 134/560, ON(48)281 of 20 July 1948; CAB 134/216, EPC(48)34 of 2 November 1948.

9. *FRUS* 1949 V p. 899; Lorraine Lees, "The American Decision to Assist Tito, 1948-1949", *Diplomatic History* II (1978), pp. 407-422.

10. *FRUS* 1949 V p. 941 of 1 September 1949.

11. *FRUS* 1948 IV p. 1093, editorial note.

12. *FRUS* 1948 IV p. 1095, Wisner on 1095.

13. Bennett Kovrig, *The Myth of Liberation* (Baltimore: Johns Hopkins University Press, 1973), pp. 92-93.

14. ... and not from 1949, as Lees wrote: "The American", p. 408.

15. USNA, NSC 15/1, see also *FRUS* 1949 V p. 208. As late as 12 April 1949 the US Assistant Secretary of State for Economic Affairs denied the existence of lists of restricted export items: ibid., pp. 881-883.

16. PRO, CAB 134/556, ON (48) 69th, Item 1; *FRUS* 1949 V p. 78.

17. *FRUS* 1948 IV p. 1106 of 16 September 1948; *FRUS* 1949 V. p. 855.

18. Ibid., p. 856.

19. Ibid., p. 892.

20. USNA, NSC 18/2.

21. PRO, FO 371/72579, Bevin's minute on no. 657 from Belgrade of 29 June 1948; the Foreign Office's 877 to Belgrade of 2 July 1948; Bevin's 936 to Washington of 30 June 1948; FO 371/72556, Watson etc. in R 8550/9/92 of 8 July and Wallinger's brief for Bevin R 8609/9/92 of 13 July 1948.

22. PRO, FO 371/72589, R 11501 of 5 October 1948, R 11791 and minutes.

23. PRO, CAB 134/216, EPC(48)37 of 2 November 1948, Item 2; see also PREM 8/1573; and CAB 134/221, EPC(49)1 note by Bevin to the Economic Policy Committee (EPC) of 1 January 1949.

24. CAB 134/560, ON(48)281 of 20 July 1948; CAB 134/216, EPC(48)34 of 2 November 1948.

25. Cmd.7600, Treaty Series no. 2(1949) and Cmd.7601, Treaty Series no. 3(1949).

26. PRO, PREM 8/1573, R 14183, report from Denis Wright, Belgrade, of 10 December 1948, and R 14406 of 18 December 1948.

27. PRO, PREM 8/1573, PM/49/6, 7 January 1949, Bevin's memo for Attlee.

28. See the same document in PRO, FO 371/78729, R 305/1152/92 G of 7 January 1949.

29. PRO, CAB 130/44, GEN 268, 1st meeting, 17 January 1949.

30. *FRUS* 1949 V p. 78 of 5 February 1949 from Paris.

31. PRO, FO 371/78729, R 5098/1152/96 G, G.T.C. Campbell on 14 May 1949.

32. PRO, PREM 8/1573, E.P. C.(49)20th of 1 June 1949.

33. PREM 8/1573, ON(49)181(Revise) of 26 May 1949; CAB 134/562, ON(49)44th of 24 May 1949.

34. CAB 134/562, ON(49)29th of 31 March 1949.

35. See PRO, PREM 8/1573 *passim*; CAB 134/566, ON(49)289 of 24 August 1949; CAB 134/563, ON(49)66th of 25 August 1949; CAB 134/563, ON(49)67th of 30 August 1949.

36. PRO, PREM 8/1573, ERP(49)168 of 19 December 1949; *FRUS* 1949 V pp. 946 and 984.

37. See Appendix B.

38. *FRUS* 1948 IV p. 1105.

39. Ibid., p. 1106, note.

40. *FRUS* 1949 V p. 883.

41. USNA, NSC 18/2.

42. Lees, "The American", pp. 407-422; *FRUS* 1949 V p. 909, 21 July 1949.

43. *FRUS* 1949 V p. 920f; *Public Papers of the President, Harry S. Truman, 1949* (Washington, D.C.: US Government Printing Office, 1964), p. 428, item 182; *New York Times* of 18 August 1949, "Truman Approves Mill for Belgrade".

44. *FRUS* 1949 V p. 898f, Thorp Memo of 9 June 1949.

45. Ibid., pp. 892-894.

46. Ibid., pp. 941-944, 1 September 1949.

47. Ibid., p. 946f, 12 September 1949.

48. For dollar-gap problems, see *FRUS* 1949 V pp. 976 and 977, 2 November 1949; Elisabeth Barker, *The British Between the Superpowers* (London: Macmillan, 1983), pp. 95-102, *passim.*

49. PRO, FO 371/78726, R 9000/1121/92 of 16 September 1949.

50. *FRUS* 1949 V p. 955f, 14 September 1949.

51. *FRUS* 1949 V p. 957f, 15 September 1949.

52. Ibid.

53. Barker, *The British,* p. 160.

54. PRO, FO 371/78726, R 9000/1121/92 of 16 September 1949.

55. *FRUS* 1950 IV, pp. 1373 and 1378.

56. See Chapter 1 on the origins of the Tito-Stalin quarrel.

57. PRO, FO 371/78716, R 3387/1051/92 G of 21 March 1949.

58. PRO, FO 800/522, C 1520/176/18 G of 18 February 1949.

59. PRO, CAB 129/35, CP(49)113 of 16 May 1949.

60. PRO, CAB 128/13, CM(48)48th of 8 July 1948.

61. PRO, FO 371/78768, R 4224/1634/92.

62. PRO, FO 371/78768, R 4460/1634/92 of 3 May 1949.

63. Ibid., R 5235, Maclean's letter of 7 May 1949. Sir Fitzroy Maclean sadly did not recall any details of this talk when I interviewed him on 7 February and 10 April 1985. *FRUS* 1949 VI p. 364 claims that all copies of this interview have been destroyed, but this is not so: see PRO, FO 371/78716, R 4734/1051/92 G of 6 May 1949.

64. *FRUS* 1949 VI p. 363.

65. PRO, CAB 128/15, CM(49)36 of 19 May 1949.

66. *FRUS* 1948 IV pp. 1079-1081 of 6 July 1948.

67. *FRUS* 1948 IV p. 1086.

68. Ibid., p. 1094, 22 July 1948.

69. Ibid., p. 1099, of 27 July 1948.

70. *FRUS* 1949 V p. 855, 10 January 1949; ibid., p. 856, 13 January 1949.

71. USNA, NSC 18/2.

72. ibid., p. 870 of 17 February 1949. When the Greek government were told that the US had decided not to insist on political concessions from Tito, this was probably done in order not to raise their hopes too high: ibid., p. 876, 2 March 1949.

73. PRO, FO 371/78448, R 6907/10392/19, Rumbold on 13 July 1949.

74. ibid., R 6890 of 16 July 1949.

75. See also Stephen Markovich, "American Foreign Policy and Yugoslav Foreign Policy" in Peter Potichnyj and Jane Shapiro (eds.), *From the Cold War to Detente* (New York: Praeger, 1976), pp. 78-96.

76. For Western concerns for the defence of this region, see Chapter 4.

77. PRO, FO 371/78716, R 1067 and R 1095/10392/19 G of 28 January 1949.

78. FO 371/78447, R 3959/10392/19 G, E.H. Peck letter of 8 April 1949; see also *FRUS* 1949 VI p. 267f of 18 March 1949.

79. FO 371/78447, R 3959/10392/19 G of 8 April 1949.

80. ibid., R 7069/10392/19 of 21 July and R 6595/10392/19 of 6 July 1949.

81. FO 371/78716, no. 2708 from New York, 25 November 1949.

82. ibid., R 4734/1051/92 G of 6 May 1949; this is the document which was not destroyed, as is claimed in *FRUS* 1949 VI p. 364, note.

83. PRO, FO 371/78716, R 1067/10392/19 G of 28 January 1949.

84. *FRUS* 1949 VI, p. 369 of 14 July 1949.

85. *FRUS* 1949 VI p. 374 of 27 July 1949.

86. ibid., p. 380 of 4 August 1949; PRO, FO 371/78448, R 7069/10392/19 of 21 July 1949.

87. ibid., R 6932/10392/19 of 20 July 1949.

88. See the following chapter on the Macedonian problem.

89. PRO, FO 371/78449, R 11392/10392/19 of 2 December 1949.

90. ibid.

91. PRO, FO 371/78716, no. 2708 from New York, 25 November 1949.

92. *FRUS* 1950 IV p. 1357f of 26 January 1950.

93. PRO, FO 371/78449, R 7589/10392/19 of 5 August 1949; R 7334 of 30 July 1949 from Peake; FO 371/87693, RG 10392/2 of 6 January 1950 from Norton.

94. FO 371/87688, RG 1022/1, 22 December 1949.

95. MAE, EU 13-8-10, Grèce 52, no. 1147 from Athens of 31 December 1949 and no. 13 to Belgrade from Quai d'Orsay, 5 January 1950.

96. PRO, FO 371/87693, RG 10392/6.

97. *FRUS* 1950 V p. 1356, and note 6; PRO, FO 371/87693, RG 10392/11, of 4 February 1950.

98. MAE, EU 13-8-10, vol. 52, no. 39-45 from Belgrade, 9 January 1950; PRO, FO 371/87693, RG 10392/7 from Athens of 25 January 1950; MAE, EU 13-8-10, vol. 52, no. 804/EU from Athens of 5 November 1949; no. 13 to Belgrade of 5 January 1950.

99. MAE, EU 13-8-10, vol. 52, no. 134/EU of 23 February 1950.

100. ibid., *passim.*

101. *FRUS* 1950 IV, p. 1394, note.

102. E.g. see Tito's interview with Rendel of *The Times* on 6 April 1950.

103. PRO, FO 371/87693, RG 10392/13.

104. *FRUS* 1950 IV p. 1400, note 1.

105. USNA, RG 59, no. 668.81/4-2250, of 22 April 1950.

106. Cf. French comments on the rôle of US Ambassador Grady, a "sorte de vice-roi occulte", MAE, EU 33-1-4, Généralités vol. 18, note of 20 April 1950; EU 13-4-1, Grèce vol.10, no. 881/EU from Athens of 20 November 1951; *FRUS* 1951 IV p. 1779 of 12 April 1951, Greek government asking for "advice".

107. PRO, FO 371/87693, RG 10392/16, note by R.C. Barnes; RG 10392/17 of 22 April 1950.

108. ibid., RG 10392/25 of 17 May 1950; RG 10392/27ff. FO 371/87694, RG 10392/35 of 31 May 1950; -/37 of 3 June 1950.

109. FO 371/ 87694, RG 10392/30 of 30 May 1950; see also the interpretation given by the Department of State: *FRUS* 1950 IV p. 1429.

110. PRO, FO 371/87694, RG 10392/37 of 3 June 1950.

111. FO 371/87695, RG 10392/72 of 11 August 1950.

112. ibid., *passim,* June 1950; *FRUS* 1950 IV p. 1420, note 5; p. 1426, of 21 June 1950.

113. PRO, FO 371/87695, RG 10392/61.

114. FO 371/87695, RG 10392/60 of 12 July 1950.

115. FO 371/87694, *passim*; FO 371/87697, RG 10392/127 of 2 December 1950, and Talbot minute.

116. FO 371/87695, RG 10392/72 of 11 August 1949.

117. FO 371/87695, RG 10392/66 of 10 August 1950.

118. Private papers of Mr. Ernest Davies [henceforth Davies Papers], Autobiographical Note.

119. PRO, FO 371/87695, RG 10392/75 of 16 August 1950, and FO to Davies, 17 August 1950.

120. Mates to Allen, *FRUS* 1950 IV p. 1440, of 23 August 1950.

121. PRO, FO 371/ 87695, RG 10392/77 of 19 August 1950.

122. ibid., RG 10392/81 of 22 August 1950.

123. Davies Papers, Savingram of 29 August and 1 September 1950.

124. ibid., brief for Secretary of State, 5 September 1950.

125. MAE, EU 13-8-10, vol. 53, no. 613/EU from Athens of 12 August 1950; cf. Chapter 7.

126. PRO, FO 371/87696, RG 10392/91 of 8 September 1950.

127. ibid., *passim.*

128. *FRUS* 1950 IV p. 1440 of 23 August 1950.

129. PRO, FO 371/87697, *passim.*

130. MAE, EU 13-8-10, vol. 53, *passim.*

131. *FRUS* 1950 IV p. 1350, 7 January 1950.

132. PRO, CAB 134/562, ON(49)137 and ON(49)34th of 20 and 21 April 1949.

133. ibid., p. 1365f. of 19 February 1950.

134. ibid., p. 1366, note.

135. Nancy Tucker, *Patterns in the Dust* (New York: Columbia University Press, 1983), p. 29f.

136. *FRUS* 1950 IV p. 1370, 11 February 1950.

137. *FRUS* 1950 IV p. 1370f., 19 February 1950.

138. ibid., p. 1373 of 22 February 1950

139. ibid., p. 1390 of 16 March 1950.

140. ibid., p. 1379 of 2 March 1950.

141. Markovich, "American", p. 94.

142. Robert Knight, "Die Kärter Grenzfrage und der Kalte Krieg", *Carinthia* I (1985), CLXXV, p. 325ff.

143. PRO, FO 371/76436, C 1520/176/18 G of 18 and 23 February 1949.

144. *FRUS* 1949 III p. 1073f.

145. ibid., p. 1075 of 23 February 1949.

146. ibid., p. 1080 of 10 March 1949.

147. See also *FRUS* 1949 III pp. 1093-1095 of 11 May 1949.

148. ibid., p. 1079ff of 10 March 1949; and PRO, FO 371/78716, R 2168/1051/92 G of 22 February 1949.

149. Robert Knight, "Die Kärtner".

150. *FRUS* 1949 V p. 967 of 3 October 1949.
151. *FRUS* 1949 V p. 868, 14 February 1949.
152. ibid., p. 869f, of 17 February 1949.
153. ibid., p. 871 of 19 February 1949.
154. E.g., *FRUS* 1950 IV p. 1362, 3 February 1950.
155. PRO, CAB 128/12, CM(48)24th of 22 March 1948; CAB 128/13, CM(48)54th of 26 July 1948.
156. Sebastian Siebel-Achenbach, "The Rôle of Lower Silesia in the Cold War", Ms. D. Phil. Oxon, 1987.
157. PRO, CAB 128/12, CM(48)24th of 22 March 1948.
158. CAB 128, CM(48)54th of 26 July 1948.
159. See Chapter 1, the Cominform communiqué of 28 June 1948.

Chapter 4

1. PRO, FO 371/72579, minute on no. 657 from Belgrade.
2. *FRUS* 1948 IV p. 1067; USNA, RG 319, Army Intelligence 1946-1948, Box 298; AN, Bidault Papers, 457 AP 97, 875-3 A Yougoslavie 1948, reports from Military Attaché, March-June 1948, particularly no. 36 of 20 May 1948.
3. *FRUS*, 1948 IV, pp. 1078 (Reams) and 1076f.
4. USNA, RG 319, Army Intelligence 1946-1948, Box 298.
5. MAE, Z 492-1sd1, vol. 22, no. 8296 from Belgrade, 30 June 1948; see also *FRUS* 1948 IV pp. 1076-1077.
6. *FRUS* 1948 IV p. 1094.
7. TL, PSF, Central Intelligence Reports, Box 256, of 3 May 1949; *FRUS* 1949 I p. 339, Staff Paper for NSC and National Security Resources Board, 1 June 1949; *FRUS* 1950 IV p. 1352; PRO, FO 371/78691, R 8046/1023/92 of 19 August 1949; DEFE 4/24, COS(49)117th of 31 August 1949; MAE, Z 492-1sd1, vol. 22, no. 826-839 of 1 July 1948.
8. TL, PSF, CI Reports, Box 256, ORE 46-49.
9. *FRUS* 1949 V p. 936, of 27 August 1949, Reams.
10. ibid., pp. 929-939; PRO, FO 371/78692, R 8189/1023/92 of 23 August 1949.
11. ibid., R 8309 of 28 August 1949.
12. Elisabeth Barker *Macedonia* (London: Royal Institute of International Affairs, 1950), p. 109.
13. ibid., pp. 103-108.
14. SHAT, dossier "Grèce", no. 19, M.A., Athens, 17 February 1949.
15. Barker, *Macedonia*, p. 117f.
16. MAE, Z 495-1sd1, vol. 33, no. 178 from Athens, 4 March 1949, and no. 1012 from Massigli, London, of 11 March 1949.
17. SHAT, dossier "Grèce", no. 19, M.A., Athens, 17 February

1949; USNA, RG 319, Army Intelligence, Box 289, 350.05 Yugoslavia, 16 March 1949, Memo for Chief of Staff: "Current Situation in Yugoslavia".

18. Loc. cit.

19. *FRUS* 1949 V p. 877.

20. *FRUS* 1949 VI p. 263 of 11 March 1949; MAE, Z 542-1, vol. 45, note of 22 March; no. 64 from Athens of 2 April; no. 1012 from London, 11 March 1949.

21. *FRUS* 1949 VI p. 263, note 1 to telegram of 16 March 1949.

22. ibid., p. 264 of 16 March 1949.

23. ibid., p. 292f. from Cannon of 8 April 1949.

24. ibid., p. 328, of early April 1949.

25. PRO, FO 371/78684, R 934/1011/92 of 16 January 1949.

26. ibid., and R 1047 of 21 January 1949.

27. Interviews with Mr. Hilary King in Glasgow, 29 September and 2 October 1986.

28. TL, PSF, CI Reports, Box 256, ORE 44-49 of June 1949, CIA Report.

29. Vincent Auriol, *Journal du Septennat*, vol. 3 (1949) (Paris: Armand Colin, 1977), p. 123.

30. 23 March 1949, George Butler, Acting Director, PPS, to Dean Rusk, State Department document declassified on 2 June 1986.

31. *FRUS* 1949 V p. 339, 1 July 1949.

32. King's College, London, Microfilms [henceforth KCMF] no. 82, CIA 9-49, "Review of the World Situation" of 14 September 1949; MAE, EU 32-8-7, old vol. 45, letter no. 5266/EU from Washington of 27 October 1949; TL, PSF, NSC Meetings, Box 205, CIA 10-49, "Review of the World Situation" of 19 October 1949; cf. discussion on NSC 18/4, below; MAE, EU 31-4-2, vol. 15, telegram no. 340/341 from Sofia, 5 November 1949; EU 32-6-8, vol. 21, no. 2590/91 of 15 December 1949.

33. PRO, FO 371/78712, R 9510/10338/92 of 28 September 1949.

34. PRO, FO 371/78708, R 8066/10338/92.

35. E.g. FO 371/78707, R 3752/10338/92 G of 5 April 1949; *FRUS* 1949 V p. 936 of 27 August 1949.

36. E.g. PRO, FO 371/78694, R 8684/1023/92 G of 3 September 1949 (State Dept. Paper) = *FRUS* 1949 V pp. 941-944.

37. PRO, FO 371/78695, R 9588/1023/939, Russia Committee Meeting on 27 September 1949; Stewart Alsop in the *New York Herald Tribune* of 5 October 1949; Fitzroy Maclean in the *Spectator* of 18 November 1949.

38. PRO, FO 371/78708, R 8066/10338/92 of 22 August 1949.

39. ibid., R 8068/10338/92 of 22 August; *FRUS* 1949 V p. 928.

40. PRO, FO 371/78708, R 8121/10338/92 of 23 August 1949.

41. Jacques Dumaine, *Quai d'Orsay (1945-1951)* (London, Chapman & Hall, 1958), p. 218.

42. PRO, FO 371/78708, R 8209/10338/92 of 27 August 1949.

43. ibid., R 8209/10338/92 and R 8121/-; FO 371/78709, R 8172/10338/92, FO 8095 to Washington of 26 August and R 8209/10338/92 of 25 August 1949.

44. American intelligence was less alarmist: TL, PSF, ORE 44-49 of 20 June 1949; DD(78)41G of 22 August 1949, and DD(78)42 A of 29 August 1949.

45. PRO, FO 371/78693, R 8537/1023/92 G, JIC memo not enclosed.

46. *The Times*, 29 August 1949.

47. *FRUS* 1949 V p. 939 of 30 August 1949.

48. ibid., p. 940, note, 31 August 1949.

49. ibid., p. 940f., and p. 944f. of 7 September 1949.

50. ibid., p. 932, note 2; PRO, FO 371/78710, R 8496/10338/92 of 1 September 1949.

51. *FRUS* 1949 II p. 245 footnote.

52. PRO, FO 371/78822, UN 1923/212/78, of 20 September 1949.

53. PRO, CAB 128/16, CM(49)60th of 20 October 1949, Bevin's statement. There was considerable uncertainty both in the State Department and in the FO as to whether a formal agreement on this had ever been made, or whether this was only the *de facto* outcome of past elections: FO 371/78822, UN 2232/212/78.

54. *FRUS* 1949 II p. 245f of 21 September 1949.

55. PRO, FO 371/78822 and 78823, FO 3014 and 3021 to Washington, UN 1988, UN 2021, of 29 September 1949 etc.

56. FO 371/78822, UN 1962 of 20 September 1949.

57. FO 371/78823, UN 2033 of 30 September 1949; *FRUS* 1949 II p. 247.

58. FO 371/78823, minute on UN 2033, 4 October 1949; the original decision was taken by Bevin alone: FO 371/78822, UN 1988 of 27 September 1949. See also announcement in *The Times*, 29 September 1949, prior to Cabinet discussion.

59. PRO, CAB 128/16, CM(49)60th of 20 October 1949. Only Nye Bevan dissented from this Cabinet decision. There is no indication that the Yugoslavs were planning any adventures in the Balkans, something that cannot be said of the Western Powers in view of their activities in Albania.

60. *FRUS* 1949 II p. 247 of 23 September 1949.

61. ibid., p. 248f of 26 September 1949.

62. USNA, RG 319, Army Staff, 091 Yugoslavia, Plans and Operations report of 20 October 1949.

63. *FRUS* 1949 II p. 254 of 27 September 1949.

64. ibid., p. 260f of 6 October 1949, Webb to US delegation; and pp. 262-275.

65. For the interview, see various summaries and transcripts, FO

371/78824 *passim*; and *Manchester Guardian* (20 October), *Daily Telegraph* (21 October). For the debate about the legality of Yugoslavia's candidature, see FO 371/78824, *passim*; it is worth noting that the British and the Americans were convinced that Yugoslavia's election was not in any way illegal, which seems confirmed by the absence of Soviet measures to challenge it afterwards.

66. PRO, FO 371/78824, UN 2234 of 20 October 1949.

67. PRO, FO 371/78823, filed with UN 2220, 20 October 1949; 470 H.C.DEB. 5s, col. 349-350, Parliamentary Question by Mr. Keeling, 23 November 1949.

68. PRO, FO 371/78824, UN 2275 and UN 2344.

69. Cees Wiebes and Bert Zeeman, "The Pentagon Negotiations — March 1948", *International Affairs* LIX no. 3 (1983), p. 353ff.

70. Alan Bullock, *Ernest Bevin, Foreign Secretary* (Oxford: Oxford University Press Paperback, 1985) pp. 643-646, 670.

71. Archives du Maréchal de Lattre, Paris, by the kind permission of the Maréchale de Lattre, Top Secret speech of Général de Lattre at Fontainebleau, 5 August 1949.

72. ibid., note M 217a of late January 1949.

73. Bullock, *Bevin*, pp. 643-646, 670; see also Martin Folly, "Britain and the Issue of Italian Membership of NATO, 1948-1949", *Review of International Studies*, XIII (1987), pp. 177-196; and see below.

74. PRO, DEFE 5/9, COS(48)210 of 16 December 1948: *Speedway* is a revised version of *Doublequick*. Cf. Kenneth Condit, *The History of the Joint Chiefs of Staff* vol. 2 (1947-49) (Historical Division, Joint Secretariat, Joint Chiefs of Staff; Wilmington: Glazier, 1979), p. 280ff.

75. PRO, DEFE 6/6, J.P. (48)92(Final) of 14 September 1948.

76. PRO, DEFE 5/9, COS(48)210.

77. PRO, DEFE 6/6, J.P. (48)91(Final); DEFE 5/12, COS(48)200(0).

78. PRO, DEFE 5/11, COS(48)156(0) of 19 July 1948.

79. John Wheeler-Bennet and Anthony Nicholls, *The Semblance of Peace* (London: Macmillan, 1972), p. 226.

80. Margit Sandner, *Die Französisch-Oesterreichischen Beziehungen während der Besatzungszeit von 1947 bis 1955* (Vienna: Verband der Wissenschaftlichen Gesellschaften Oesterreichs, 1983), pp. 260-265.

81. PRO, DG 1/10, File 53, F.C.(48)7th Meeting, 15 December 1948.

82. Bullock, *Bevin*, p. 623f.

83. PRO, DG 1/10, File 53, F.C.(48)7th Meeting, 15 December 1948; DEFE 5/8, COS(48)140 of 26 October 1948.

84. PRO, DEFE 6/7, J.P. (48)130(Final) of 4 November 1948.

85. PRO, DEFE 6/7, J.P. (48)134(Final) of 4 November 1948.

86. PRO, DEFE 4/18, COS(48)170th, Item 1, 26 November 1948; see also: USNA, RG 319, Operations and Planning (O & P), Box no. 85, 370.05, no. 4/32 of 16 November 1948; and see subsequent plans

for the defence/withdrawal from Austria, Trieste and Italy, *Pilgrim Able, Baker, Charlie, Dog*; and *Boniface, Bovey* and *Barnabas*.

87. PRO, DEFE 5/9, COS(48)210 of 16 December 1948: *Speedway*.

88. PRO, DEFE 4/22, COS(49)97th Meeting, Appendix to Item 3: J.P. (48)59(Final-Second Revise) of 6 July 1949; DEFE 6/8, J.P. (49)7(Final) of 4 April 1949.

89. KCMF no. 64, JCS 1920/1 of 31 January 1949: *Dropshot*

90. PRO, DEFE 6/9, J.P. (49)62(Final) of 8 June 1949. Yugoslavia's attitude was first regarded as an unknown in a memo by Montgomery of 26 October 1948: DEFE 5/8, COS(48)140.

91. PRO, DEFE 6/9, J.P. (49)83(Final) of 25 July 1949: *Smartweed.*

92. PRO, DEFE 6/9, J.P. (49)62(Final) of 8 June 1949.

93. PRO, DEFE 6/9, J.P. (49)83(Final) of 25 July 1949.

94. PRO, DEFE 4/23, COS(49)112th Meeting, Minute 5, Annex: J.P. (49)83(Final).

95. PRO, DEFE 6/9, J.P. (49)85(Final) of 5 September 1949; DEFE 6/11, J.P. (49)133(Final) of 14 October 1949: *Centre Strategy.*

96. See, e.g. priorities of *Pilgrim* plans: USNA, RG 319, Box 248, P&O 318 PIM TS, JSPC 790/49 of 29 June 1949.

97. PRO, DEFE 4/29, J.P. (49)134(Final), 1 March 1950: *Galloper.*

98. *FRUS* 1950 IV pp. 1341-1348; USNA, NSC Papers, NSC 18 Series, NSC 18/4 as declassified on 16 March 1987.

99. *FRUS* 1950 IV pp. 1341-1348.

100. Graham Allison, *Essence of Decision* (Boston: Little, Brown, 1971), pp. 67-100, particularly p. 84, explain that organizations mainly think in terms of "standard scenarios" which have occurred previously: our example is obviously an exception to Allison's rule.

101. Robert Jervis, "The Impact of the Korean War on the Cold War", *Journal of Conflict Resolution* vol. XXIV no. 4 (December 1980), pp. 571-572.

102. *FRUS* 1949 V p. 960 of 16 September 1949. The division in opinion persisted after the outbreak of the Korean War, which was seen by Kennan and Bohlen as a one-off event, while the majority in the State Department and in the other Western foreign ministries expected other moves elsewhere. Even when these did not occur, the question remained unanswered as to whether this was the result of deterrence, or because there had been no such plans on the Soviet side. Cf. Chapter 6.

103. DD(1982)001269 of 16 November 1949.

104. *FRUS* 1950 IV p. 1439f.

105. According to British information: PRO, FO 371/88259, RY 1071/5 of 27 January 1950.

106. MAE, EU 32-4-1/1,2 vol. 6, nos. 1520 and 1521 from Direction des Affaires Economiques et Financières of 10 December 1949; no. 1149-1151 from Belgrade, 19 December 1949.

107. PRO, DEFE 5/17, COS(49)371 Annex 1.

108. PRO, DEFE 5/17, COS(49)371, Rumbold to COS, 1 November 1949.

109. USNA, NSC Series, progress report on NSC 18/4 of 31 January 1950; *FRUS* 1950 IV p. 1353, aide-mémoire to the French Government of 13 January 1950; USNA, RG 59, 661.68/1-1850, J.C.Campbell's Memorandum of 18 January 1950. The French had been given unofficial information by 30 November 1949: MAE, EU 32-4-1/1,2 vol.6, no. 5746/EU; and see ibid., no. 182/183 from Washington of 12 January 1950, and following letters and telegrams.

110. *The Times*, 23 December 1949 and *New York Times*, 24 December 1949.

111. *Public Papers of the President of the U.S.: Harry S. Truman* (Washington D.C.: US Government Printing Office, 1964), Item 269, p. 585, 13]; *The Times*, 23 December 1949.

112. It is clear from a letter which George Allen wrote to his sister Zalene that he was perturbed at the press interpretation of his interview: he had obviously not intended to give cause for these speculations. Papers of G.V. Allen, TL.

113. PRO, FO 371/88245, RY 10345/1.

114. PRO, FO 371/88259, RY 1071/1 of 18 January 1950.

115. MAE, EU 32-4-1/1,2, no. 89/95, Fouques Duparc, Rome, 20 January 1950.

116. USNA, RG 59, 611.68/1-1250 of 12 January 1950.

117. USNA, RG 330, Box 33, CD 6-4-26 of 17 February 1950; PRO, DEFE 4/30, JP(50)10(Final) of 31 March 1950, and references to the closed JIC(49)104(Final); MAE, EU 32-4-1/1,2, no. 175-181 from London of 21 January 1950; no. 117/126 from Belgrade of 29 January 1950, and Communiqué of Quai d'Orsay to US embassy of 23 February 1950.

118. PRO, DEFE 4/30, JP(50)10(Final) and references to JIC(49)104(Final).

119. PRO, FO 371/72596, R 613/461/92 of 29 January 1948; *FRUS* 1949 V p. 116f of 27 May 1949; p. 132 of 27 June and 12 July 1949; see also Chapter 3.

120. MAE, EU 32-4-1/1,2, Communiqué of 23 February 1950.

121. PRO, DEFE 4/30, JP(50)10(Final).

122. USNA, NSC 18 series, progress report on NSC 18/4 of 16 May 1950; PRO, DEFE 5/15 Pt. II, COS(49)288 of 5 September 1949.

123. PRO, DEFE 4/30, COS(50)56th Meeting on 3 April 1950; official British answer given on 2 May 1950, *FRUS* 1950 IV p. 1411; MAE, EU 32-4-1/1,2, no. 1013'/EU from London of 26 June 1950.

124. PRO, FO 800/449 of 28 April 1950, italics in original. The list of British participants simply records the presence of "Maclean". There was only one Maclean (Donald) in the FO at the time.

125. MAE, EU 32-4-1/1,2 no. 2603/05 from Washington, 11 July 1950.

126. TL, PSF, ORE 8-50 of 11 May 1950.
127. KCMF 82, CIA 5-50 of 17 May 1950.
128. USNA, RG 59, 768.5-MAP/6-1450 of 14 June 1950.

Chapter 5

1. Nikita Khrushchev, *Khrushchev Remembers* (London: Sphere Books, 1971), p. 332f; see also Peter Lowe, *The Origins of the Korean War* (London: Longman, 1986), pp. 150-157; Karunker Gupta, "How did the Korean War Begin?", *China Quarterly*, VIII (1972), pp. 699-716.

2. Dean Acheson, *Present at the Creation* (London: Hamish Hamilton, 1969), p. 356f; William Stueck, "The Soviet Union and the Origins of the Korean War", *World Politics* (June 1976), p. 632. This is also reflected in US military planning assumptions, see for example KCMF 64, JCS 1920/1 of 31 January 1949, *Dropshot*.

3. Jörg Hoensch, *Sowjetische Osteuropa Politik, 1945-1975* (Düsseldorf: Athenäum/Droste, 1977), pp. 49-87 *passim*; Marshall Shulmann, *Stalin's Foreign Policy Reappraised* (Cambridge, Mass.: Harvard University Press, 1963), pp. 50-138; Joseph Nogee and Robert Donaldson, *Soviet Foreign Policy Since World War II* (Oxford: Pergamon Press, 1981), pp. 78f.

4. Khrushchev, *Remembers*, p. 335; concerning the reliability of his memoirs, see titles listed in note 5.

5. Robert Simmons, *The Strained Alliance* (New York: Free Press, 1975), pp. 117-124; Khrushchev, *Remembers*, p. 334; Stueck, "Soviet Union", pp. 622-635; Geoffrey Warner, "The Korean War", *International Affairs*, LVI (1980), p. 98ff; William Zimmermann, "The Korean and the Vietnam Wars", in Stephen Kaplan, *Diplomacy of Power* (Washington D.C., Brookings Institution, 1981), pp. 323-336; Lowe, *Origins*.

6. Lowe, *Origins*, p. 156f.

7. Zimmermann, "The Korean", pp. 328-336; Adam Ulam accepts the theory that Stalin must have ordered or approved the Korean War: *Expansion and Coexistence* (New York: Praeger, 2nd edn 1974), p. 518.

8. Béla Király, "The Aborted Soviet Military Plans against Tito's Yugoslavia" in Wayne Vucinich (ed.), *At the Brink of War and Peace* (New York: Columbia University Press, 1982), pp. 273-282; Hoensch, *Sowjetische*, p. 83f.

9. Király, "Soviet Plans", p. 273ff; Vojtech Mastny, "Stalin and the Militarization of the Cold War", *International Security*, IX 3 (1984/85), pp. 109-129.

10. Cf. Sheila Kerr, London School of Economics, unpublished manuscript: "A Breach of Security: Donald Maclean and the Development of the Cold War", to be submitted to the University of London as Ph.D. thesis.

11. John Yurechko, "From Containment to Counteroffensive: Soviet Vulnerabilities and American Policy Planning, 1946-1953" (Ms. Ph.D., University of Berkeley, California, 1980).

12. Cf. A.A. Gromyko and B.N. Ponomarev, *Soviet Foreign Policy* II (1945-1980) (Moscow: Progress, 1981), pp. 149-153.

13. Karel Kaplan, *Dans les Archives du Comité Central* (Paris: Eds. Albin Michel, 1978), p. 164f; this information is accepted by Mastny, "Militarization", p. 127.

14. Király, "Soviet Plans", pp. 286-288.

15. Philip Windsor, "Yugoslavia, 1951, and Czechoslovakia, 1968" in Barry Blechmann and Stephen Kaplan, *Force Without War* (Washington, D.C.: Brookings Institute, 1978), p. 451. This author could not find the statement referred to by Windsor in the *Pravda* of 13 February 1957.

16. MAE, EU 32-8-1, old vol.24, no. 139-140 from Quai d'Orsay to Belgrade of 2 February 1950.

17. Király, "Soviet Plans", pp. 286-288; Ulam agrees with the verdict that Stalin was surprised by the Western reaction: *Expansion*, p. 521.

18. Siegfried Kogelfranz, *Das Erbe von Jalta* (Hamburg: Spiegel-Verlag, 1985), pp. 175-176. This book contains no footnotes. According to Kogelfranz, the Zhukov quote comes from two sources, one being Chepichka in Prague, the other an unnamed person in Belgrade. Letter to the author of 8 February 1985; cf. also Windsor, "Yugoslavia, 1951".

19. Király, "Soviet Plans", p. 286.

20. USNA, Suitland Branch, RG 319, Army-Intelligence 1950-1952, Box 188, 350.05 Yugoslavia, Lt. Col. Kraus, 12 June 1952.

21. E.g. PRO, FO 371/95548, Peake to Bevin after consultation with Military Attachés, 1194/5/51 of 10 February 1951.

22. MAE, EU 31-9-1 vol. 47, no. 7191/EU, 8 May 1950; *For a Lasting Peace, for a People's Democracy*, 21 April 1951, p. 2.

23. Frederic Burin has argued that in Marxist/Leninist/Stalinist writings, there is no concept of the inevitability of war between the Socialist and the Imperialist systems: "The Communist Doctrine of the Inevitability of War", *American Political Science Review* 57 no. 2 (1963), pp. 334-354. In the example of Mitin's article of 21 April 1950, however, we find that there was some degree of inconsistency in Soviet utterances on this point. Further confusion was created by the Sino-Soviet debate about the inevitability of anti-colonial wars of national liberation, but this only came up in 1959ff.

24. TL, PSF, Intelligence File, Box 253, NIE-3 of 15 November 1950, "Soviet Capabilities and Intentions".

25. MAE, EU 31-9-1, vol.47, no. 7191/EU; *Pravda* of 28 March 1950.

26. Thomas Etzold and John Lewis Gaddis (eds.), *Containment*

(New York: Columbia University Press, 1978) pp. 389, 442.

27. Etzold and Gaddis, *Containment*, NSC 68, p. 434; see Chapter 1; NSC 7 of 30 March 1948 in *FRUS* 1948 I p. 545ff; Bastion Paper, FO 371/72196, R 8476/8476/G 67 of 17 July 1948.

28. Etzold and Gaddis, *Containment*, p. 385; see also Michael Cox: "The Rise and Fall of the 'Soviet Threat'", *Political Studies*, XXXIII (1985), p. 484f.

29. Charles Bohlen, *Witness to History, 1929-1969* (New York: W.W. Norton, 1973), pp. 290-291.

30. *FRUS* 1952-1954 II pp. 551-554 of 23 October 1953; see also TL, PSF, CI Reports, Box 258, SE-35 of 29 December 1952.

31. Warner Schilling, "The Politics of National Defense: Fiscal 1950"; and Paul Hammond, "NSC-68: Prologue to Rearmament" in Warner Schilling, Paul Hammond and Glenn Snyder, *Strategy, Politics, and Defence Budgets* (New York: Columbia University Press, 1962), p. 267ff.

32. John Lewis Gaddis, "Was the Truman Doctrine a Real Turning Point?", *Foreign Affairs* (January 1974), pp. 393-396.

33. Robert Jervis, "The Impact of the Korean War on the Cold War", *Journal of Conflict Resolution*, vol. 24, no. 4 (December 1980), p. 580.

34. PRO, FO 371/86756, NS 1052/68 of 1 July 1950, "The Soviet Union and Korea". For US opinion, see, e.g. Dean Acheson, *Present*, p. 405; Rosemary Foot, *The Wrong War* (Ithaca, N.Y.: Cornell University Press, 1985), p. 58f.

35. MAE, EU 31-9-1, vol.47, letter no. 718 from Moscow of 3 July 1950.

36. PRO, CAB 129/40, C.P. (50)114 of 19 May 1950.

37. *FRUS* 1950 I pp. 377 and 385.

38. Jervis, "The Impact", particularly pp. 584-590; see also Samuel Wells, "Sounding the Tocsin: NSC 68 and the Soviet Threat", *International Security*, IV 2 (Autumn 1979), particularly p. 140f; Paul Nitze, "NSC 68 and the Soviet Threat Reconsidered", ibid., IV 4 (Spring 1980), pp. 170-176.

39. *FRUS* 1950 I pp. 337 and 385.

40. *FRUS* 1950 I p. 293.

41. Bohlen, *Witness*, p. 292.

42. Jervis, "The Impact", p. 579; PRO, FO 371/86762, NS 1053/27/G of 26 September and NS 1053/26 of 12 September 1950; see also NSC Meeting of 29 June 1950, *FRUS* 1950 I pp. 327-330; TL, PSF, CI Reports, Box 254, NIE-64 PT II p. 1 of 11 December 1952; Box 258, CIA Special Estimate SE-35 of 29 December 1952, "The World Situation over the Next Decade".

43. Harry Truman, *Memoirs*, vol. 2: *Years of Trial and Hope* (London: Hodder & Stoughton, 1956), p. 446.

44. *FRUS* 1950 I p. 361, 8 August 1950; the US Ambassador in

Moscow, Kirk, agreed with Kennan: ibid., p. 367, 11 August 1950; see also NSC 73/4 of 25 August 1950, ibid., p. 378.

45. For account of Conference of Foreign Ministers, see MAE, EU 31-9-1, vol.47, no. 3527-3534 from Washington, telegram of 2 September 1950.

46. *FRUS* 1950 I p. 361, 8 August 1950.

47. *FRUS* 1951 I p. 40, PPS memorandum of 29 January 1951; Paul Nitze's memories are obviously not entirely accurate: "NSC 68 and the Soviet Threat", p. 172; cf., for example, the JCS statement of 7 December 1950, USNA, RG 330, Office of the Secretary of Defence, CD 091.3 Yugoslavia: "...the risk of global war is increasing".

48. *FRUS* 1951 I p. 63, JCS Study of 15 January 1951, approved 13 April 1951 the possibility of local attacks in stressed also by Carlton Savage of the PPS, 23 May 1951, *FRUS* 1951 I p. 840.

49. Bohlen, *Witness*, p. 292.

50. Truman, *Memoirs*, vol. 2, p. 359.

51. PRO, DEFE 7/743, Item 39 of 18 July 1950.

52. PRO, FO 371/86762, NS 1053/26 of 12 September 1950.

53. MAE, EU 31-9-1, vol. 47, no. 3527-3534 from Washington of 2 September 1950: the CFM's agreed memorandum read: "L'Europe occidentale demeure la zone cruciale pour la défense du Monde libre tout entier".

54. The degree of despondency which was sometimes felt in Europe, regarding the American readiness to come to the defence of other areas, is illustrated by a diary entry of Jacques Dumaine, *Quai d'Orsay* (London: Chapman & Hall, 1958) p. 268.

55. John Lewis Gaddis, *Strategies of Containment* (New York: Oxford University Press, 1982) pp. 90-92.

56. Robert Osgood, *Limited War Revisited* (Boulder, Co: Westview Press, 1979), p. 105.

57. Truman, *Memoirs*, vol. 2, p. 446.

58. Author's emphasis, *FRUS* 1951 I p. 63 of 15 January 1951, approved 13 April 1951.

59. NSC 100 of 11 January 1951, *FRUS* 1951 I p. 7; Bennett Kovrig, *The Myth of Liberation* (Baltimore: Johns Hopkins University Press, 1973), pp. 93-96; cf. also Samuel Wells, "The First Cold War Buildup" in Olav Riste (ed.), *Western Security, the Formative Years* (Oslo: Norwegian University Press, 1985), pp. 181-195.

60. See note 38.

61. *FRUS* 1951 I p. 580 of 6 November 1951.

62. MAE, EU 31-9-1, vol.49, no. 773 from Ministry to Moscow, 2 August 1952; PRO, FO 371/102180, WY 1052/38 G of 11 September 1952.

63. Kenneth Morgan, *Labour in Power 1945-1951* (Oxford, Clarendon Press, 1984), p. 424f; Robert Osgood, *NATO — The Entangling Alliance* (Chicago: University of Chicago Press, 1962), p. 70;

Kenneth Harris, *Attlee* (London: Weidenfeld & Nicolson, 1982), p. 455.

64. Osgood, *NATO*, pp. 68-87.

65. MAE, EU 31-9-1, vol. 49, no number, note by Foreign Minister, 24-25 January 1952.

66. MAE, EU 33-20-5, Généralités vol. 95, note de la Sous-Direction d'Europe Orientale, 31 August 1951.

67. MAE, EU 31-9-1, vol. 48, note of 31 August 1951.

68. Loc. cit., and see, for example Alan Bullock, *Ernest Bevin, Foreign Secretary* (Oxford: Oxford University Press, 1985), p. 791; Lowe, *Origins*, pp. 206-215.

69. MAE, EU 31-9-1, vol. 48, no. 796-800 from Moscow of 30 March 1951; author's emphasis.

70. Ibid., vol. 48, no. 2440-2448 from Moscow of 22 October 1951; vol. 49, letter no. 1242 from Moscow of 13 November 1951; author's emphasis.

71. PRO, FO 371/92067, F 10345/2 G of 3 January 1951; Michael Dockrill, "The Foreign Office, Anglo-American Relations and the Korean War", *International Affairs* LXII 3 (1986), pp. 459-476.

72. Harris, *Attlee*, p. 455.

73. PRO, PREM 8/1439, PM/51/4 of 12 January 1951.

74. Author's emphasis, *FRUS* 1951 I p. 63 of 15 January 1951, approved 13 April 1951.

75. NSC 100 of 11 January 1951, *FRUS* 1951 I p. 7.

76. Kovrig, *The Myth*, pp. 93-96.

77. Yurechko, "From Containment", pp. 65f, 90-95, 128, 300.

78. MAE, EU 33-20-5, Généralités. vol. 95, VII, note by François Seydoux of 20 August 1951.

79. Quoted in David Carlton, *Anthony Eden* (London: Allen Lane, 1981), p. 331.

80. *FRUS* 1952-1954 II pp. 82-83, 85 (NSC 135/1 of 15 August 1952); pp. 224-229.

81. MAE, EU 33-20-5, Généralités. vol. 95, VIII, note of 31 August 1951.

82. MAE, EU 31-9-1, vol. 48, note of 23 August 1951.

83. Yurechko, "From Containment", pp. 134-171; Michael Guhin, *John Foster Dulles* (New York: Columbia University Press, 1972), pp. 155-158.

84. MAE, EU 31-9-1, vol. 50, no number, 18 February 1953.

85. PRO, FO 371/92067, F 10345/2 G of 3 January 1951.

86. The British pulled out of the Albanian affair in early 1952 after the Conservatives were returned to power. There were other reasons as well, such as the CIA's suspicions about Philby, and the lack of success. Nicholas Bethell, *The Great Betrayal* (London: Hodder & Stoughton, 1984), p. 180ff.

87. Quoted in Carlton, *Eden*, p. 331.

88. PRO, FO 371/102180, WY 1052/38 G of 11 September 1952.

89. PRO, CAB 129/61, C(53)187 of 3 July 1953; Anthony Seldon, *Churchill's Indian Summer* (London: Hodder and Stoughton, 1981), pp. 396-409.

90. PRO, CAB 128/26, C.C.(53)39th of 6 July 1953, Item 3.

91. PRO, CAB 128/26, C.C.(53)44th of 21 July 1953, Item 4.

92. USNA, NSC 174 of 11 December 1953.

93. USNA, RG 59, Box 2, UM Minutes, UM M-311 of 26 February 1951.

94. USNA, RG 330, Box 83, OMA 319.1 Yugoslavia, March 1951.

95. MAE, EU 32-4-1sd1, vol. 9, no. 5582/EU of 14 December 1951.

96. Guhin, *Dulles*, p. 172.

97. Guhin, *Dulles*, p. 175, and Townsend Hoopes, *The Devil and John Foster Dulles* (London: André Deutsch, 1974), p. 128.

98. PRO, FO 371/107817, WY 1016/10(A) of late April 1953.

99. MAE, EU 32-8-6, old vol. 38, no. 84 EU, letter from London of 16 January 1952, author's emphasis.

100. PRO, FO 371/102180, WY 1052,38 G of 11 September 1952.

101. MAE, EU 32-8-1, old vol. 24, telegram no. 1212 from Belgrade of 22 November 1950; see below.

102. MAE, EU 32-8-7, old vol.45, no. 143/EU from Moscow of 23 January 1952.

103. MAE, EU 33-20-5 Généralités, vol. 95, note VII of 31 August 1951.

104. PRO, FO 371/86899, NS 2191/34 of 14 February 1950.

105. PRO, FO 371/88239, R 1032/9 of 15 February 1950.

106. PRO, FO 371/77594, *passim*; FO 371/86899, as approved by Russia Committee on 14 February 1950.

107. PRO, FO 371/86146, N 10112/1 of 16 June 1950.

108. DD(79)287 A, OIR Report 5483 of 22 June 1951.

109. TL, PSF, Central Intelligence Reports, Box 254, NIE-64 of 12 November 1952.

110. TL, PSF, CI Reports, Box 258, SE-35 of 29 December 1952.

111. Truman, *Memoirs*, vol. 2, pp. 427-428.

112. *FRUS* 1950 I p. 345 of 1 August 1950.

113. Foot, *Wrong War*, p. 27f.

114. DD(79)287 A, OIR Report no. 5483 of 22 June 1951, p. 52.

115. TL, PSF, CI Reports, Box 254, NIE-64 of 12 November 1952.

116. TL, PSF, CI Reports, Box 258, SE-35 of 29 December 1952.

117. USNA RG 59, 668.93/3-2653 of 26 March 1953.

118. *FRUS* 1952-1954 II p. 553.

119. E.g. PRO, FO 371/88238, RY 1022/18 of 8 August 1950; FO 371/88260 and -/88346 *passim*, -/95469, RY 1022/11 of 22 June 1951; -/102164, WY 10112/6 of 8 November 1952 etc.

120. MAE, EU 32-8-5, old vol. 32, no. 1610/EU, letter and

enclosure; USNA, RG 84, Belgrade, Yugoslavia 1950-54, Box 4, 320 Relations between states, letter no. 261 from Belgrade of 2 October 1953; ibid., Box no. 5, 340 Yugoslavia, no. 903 from Belgrade of 8 May 1953; MAE, EU 31-9-11 s/d 1, vol. 74, no. 283-285 from Rangoon, 13 July 1953.

121. USNA, RG 84, Belgrade, Box no. 5, 340 Yugoslavia, no. 903 from Belgrade of 8 May 1953.

122. PRO, FO 371/102180, WY 1052/38 G of 11 September 1952.

123. Ritchie Ovendale, *The English-Speaking Alliance* (London: George Allen & Unwin, 1985), pp. 185-210; Bullock, *Bevin*, pp. 825-828.

124. ibid., p. 226f; see also John Baylis, *Anglo-American Defence Relations — 1939-1984* (London: Macmillan, 2nd edn., 1984), p. 61; Morgan, *Labour*, p. 428f; see also statements in the Russia Committee, PRO, FO 371/86762, *passim*, for late 1950.

125. Ulam, *Expansion*, p. 531f; Joachim Glaubitz, *China und die Sowjetunion* (Hannover: Niedersächsische Landeszentrale für Politische Bildung, 1973), pp. 10-27. Alexander Metaxas thinks that Stalin planned Korea in order to keep Communist China in trouble and antagonistic towards the Western Powers, *Pékin contre Moscou* (Lausanne: Eds. Scriptar, 1959), p. 64f. According to Catherine Quirinal, China was indeed willing, prior to Korea, to have contact with any country, *La Politique Extérieure de la Chine* (Paris: Yenan Synthèses, Eds. François Maspero, 1975), p. 116f; for evidence of Sino-Soviet tensions at this early stage, see e.g. André Goral, *Où va la Chine?* (Paris: Eds. Renée Lacoste, 1956), pp. 173-203.

126. François Fejtö, *Chine-URSS* (Paris: Plon, 1964) pp. 57-69.

127. PRO, FO 371/88239, RY 1023/10, Peake to Foreign Office, 10 February 1950.

128. PRO, FO 371/86754, NS 1052/43 of 18 April and -/46 of 8 May 1950 MAE, EU 31-9-1, vol. 47, no. 548 of 18 May: reference to letter of 15 April 1950 (not enclosed); letter no. 70 from Luxembourg of 23 June 1950.

129. For examples of this, see e.g. MAE, EU 32-8-7, no. 2006/10 from Moscow of 27 August 1950; EU 13-8-10, Grèce, vol. 53, letter no. 669/EU from Bulgaria of 29 August 1950; EU 31-9-1, vol. 47 no. 271 from Moscow of 27 January 1951, vol. 48, letter no. 248 from Moscow of 21 February, no. 796-800 from Moscow of 30 March and letter no. 8165 of 21 April 1951.

130. MAE, EU 31-9-1, vol. 48, letter no. 8165 from Moscow of 21 April 1951

131. PRO, FO 371/88239, RY 1023/3 of 27 January 1950 and minutes: see for example Charles Bateman's minutes, and ibid., RY 1023/9 of 15 February 1950; cf. also report by British Military Attaché, Col. Dewhurst, in RY 1023/10 of 10 February 1950.

132. USNA, RG 59, 661.68/5-3150 of 31 May 1950.

133. PRO, FO 371/86756, NS 1052/70 of 30 June 1950.

134. ibid., and FO 371/86757, NS 1052/74 of 15 July 1950.

135. G.V. Allen to his family, 8 June 1950, Allen Papers, Duke University and Truman Library.

136. *FRUS* 1950 I p. 324ff.

137. KCMF 62, JCS 1924/15; TL, PSF, Intelligence File, Box 250 — weekly CIA situation summaries, of July 1950 — N.B. report of 20 July.

138. ibid., Box 350, CIA 7-50.

139. KCMF 82, CIA 8-50, Noted by NSC on 17 August 1950 at 65th Meeting.

140. *FRUS* 1950 I p. 354.

141. ibid., p. 367.

142. ibid., p. 327ff.

143. NSC 73, "The Position and Actions of the United States With Respect to Possible Future Moves in the Light of the Korean Situation", in *FRUS* 1950 I p. 331; and see Kennan's memo to Acheson, p. 364.

144. *FRUS* 1950 I pp. 376-389.

145. *FRUS* 1951 I p. 40 of 29 January 1951.

146. *FRUS* 1951 I p. 20 of 23 January 1951.

147. PRO, DEFE 5/22, COS(50)277 of 27 July 1950.

148. MAE, EU 31-4-2, vol. 15, no number 25 November 1950.

149. *FRUS* 1951 IV pp. 1704-1706 of 26 January 1951.

150. MAE, EU 13-4-1, Grèce, vol. 10, no. 573 from Athens of 4 July and letter no. 549/EU from Athens of 15 July 1950.

151. E.g. PRO, FO 371/88260, RY 1072/2 of 29 June 1950; MAE, EU 32-8-5, old vol. 32, no. 1248 from Den Haag of 12 September 1950.

152. PRO, FO 371/88240, RY 1023/37 of 22 July 1950.

153. MAE, EU 32-4-1/1,2 vol. 6, no number, RL/AL memo of 6 September 1950.

Chapter 6

1. *FRUS* 1950 I p. 324ff.

2. *FRUS* 1950 I p. 328, of 29 June 1950.

3. *FRUS* 1950 I p. 333ff of 1 July 1950.

4. E.g. USNA, RG 218, CCS 092 Yugoslavia (7-6-48) sec. 5, JIC 401/14 of 12 February 1951. US military intelligence estimates were that Yugoslavia would not let Soviet troops pass: sec. 14, JIC 501/22 of 4 January 1952.

5. E.g. PRO, DEFE 5/32, COS(51)408 of 10 July 1951 records Tito statement of 22 February 1951.

6. Department of State, NSC 18/6 declassified on 16 March 1987; RG 330, Box 54, CD 091.3(MDAP) Yugoslavia; same RG, Box 222, CD

091.3(MDAP)Yugoslavia; PRO, FO 371/95469, RY 1022/6 of 27 February 1951; DEFE 5/32, COS(51)408 of 10 July 1951.

7. USNA, RG 330, Office of the Secretary of Defense, CD 091.3 Yugoslavia, 7 December 1950.

8. *FRUS* 1951 I p. 19f of 23 January 1951.

9. *FRUS* 1951 I pp. 39, 47 of 29 January and 8 February 1951.

10. *FRUS* 1951 IV pp. 1704-1706 of 26 January 1951.

11. PRO, DEFE 6/16, J.P. (51)33(Final) of 17 May 1951.

12. PRO, DEFE 4/42, COS(51)83rd Meeting of 21 May 1951.

13. USNA, RG 218, Box 119, CCS 092 Yugoslavia(7-6-48) sec. 11, ALO 290 of 30 August 1951.

14. PRO, DEFE 5/31, COS(51)340, 5 June 1951, EMMO Short Term Plan.

15. USNA, RG 218, CCS 092 Yugoslavia(7-6-48) sec. 7.

16. PRO, DEFE 5/33, COS(51)546 of 21 September 1951.

17. USNA, RG 319, Army Intelligence 1950-1952, Box 188, of 12 June 1952.

18. USNA, RG 218, CCS 092 Yugoslavia(7-6-48) sec. 23, JSPC 969/47 of 25 October 1954.

19. PRO, DEFE 7/221, no. 3582, 13 November 1951.

20. PRO, DEFE 7/224, no. 64, of 10 December 1952.

21. USNA, RG 218, Box 119, CCS 092 Yugoslavia (7-6-48) sec. 11, ALO 290 of 30 August 1951; for British and French recommendation, cf. Chapter 4.

22. DD(76)161 C of 26 March 1953.

23. The US Joint Intelligence Group had reason to think the Yugoslavs would co-operate: USNA, RG 218, CCS 092 Yugoslavia(7-6-48) sec.15, JIC 501/23 of 25 January 1952.

24. For reports concerning the danger in 1949, see Chapter 4; for 1951 see: TL, PSF, Intelligence File, Box 250, CIA Situation Summary of 15 December 1950; USNA, RG 319, Mil. Intelligence 1950ff., Box 188, 350.05 Yugoslavia of 15 January 1951; PRO, DEFE 7/215 no. 29 of 19 January 1951, briefing of UK Deputy on NATO Council; US Joint Intelligence Committee Memorandum JIC 401/14 of 12 February 1951, in USNA, RG 218, CCS 092 Yugoslavia (7-6-48) sec. 5; and sec. 6, Air Intelligence Memorandum no. 3 of 23 February 1951; see also *FRUS* 1951 I p. 19f of 23 January 1951 by J.P. Davies. On the other hand JCS 1924/49 of 5 February 1951, which is DD(1976) 248 D, stressed that the Soviet Union was likely to do anything short of war to bring Yugoslavia back into the fold. The COS on 5 February 1951 once again came back to the 1949-idea of a possible guerrilla war erupting in Yugoslavia: PRO, DEFE 5/27, COS(51)52.

25. TL, Papers of George V. Allen, 1 January 1951.

26. PRO, FO 371/95538, RY 1102/13 of 16 January 1951 by Sir Charles Peake.

27. MAE, EU 31-4-2 vol. 15, no. 2658 from Berne, 28 December

1950; and see for example articles in *Washington Post* of 23 and 24 January 1951, "Matter of Fact: the Chance of War"; and cf. MAE, EU 32-4-1sd1, vol. 7, no. 179/187 from Belgrade of 8 February 1951.

28. House of Commons, 484 H.C.DEB, 5s, col. 45f of 12 February 1951.

29. Ibid., col. 126, 12 February 1951; col. 430, 14 February 1951; MPs for Aston and Norwood, ibid., cols. 711, 712.

30. PRO, CAB 128/19, CM(51)14 of 15 February 1951.

31. 484 H.C.DEB. 5s, col. 731 of 15 February 1951.

32. State Department document of 31 January 1951, declassified on 2 June 1986.

33. *FRUS* 1951 IV p. 1733f. of 14 February 1951.

34. USNA, RG 59, 768.5/2-2051 of 20 February 1951.

35. Philip Windsor, "Yugoslavia, 1951, and Czechoslovakia, 1968" in Barry Blechmann and Stephen Kaplan, *Force Without War* (Washington, D.C.: Brookings Institute, 1978), p. 460f.

36. *FRUS* 1951 IV pp. 1704-1706 of 26 January 1951; and p. 1729f. of 13 February 1951.

37. MAE, EU 32-8-1, old vol. 25, no. 3281, note of 17 February 1951.

38. MAE, EU 32-4-1sd1, vol. 7, no. 277/282 from Belgrade of 26 February 1951; EU 32-8-3, old vol. 34, no. 210 from Parodi to Belgrade of 25 February and no. 276 from Belgrade of 26 February 1951.

39. MAE, EU 32-4-1/1,2 vol. 6, no. 1085/87 of 28 October 1950.

40. ibid., no. 1088/1090 of same date; MAE, EU 32-4-1/1,2 vol. 6 *passim.*

41. MAE, EU 32-4-1sd1, vol. 7 no. 30-32 to Belgrade of 11 January 1951, and no number, memo by Seydoux of 23 January 1951; PRO, FO 371/95538, RY 1192/21 from Belgrade of 16 January 1951.

42. MAE, EU 32-4-1/1,2 vol. 6 no. 1219-1229 from Belgrade of 25 November 1950.

43. USNA, RG 330, Office of the Secretary of Defense, CD 091.3 Yugoslavia, 7 December 1950.

44. USNA, RG 330, Office of the Secretary of Defense, CD 091.3 Yugoslavia; RG 59, 661.68/1-1951 of 19 January 1951.

45. PRO, FO 371/95538, RY 1192/28 from Belgrade of 16 January 1951.

46. Private Papers of Mr. Ernest Davies [henceforth Davies Papers]. Record of conversation and FO Minute, both of 30 January 1951.

47. PRO, PREM 8/1574, 29 January 1951.

48. Davies Papers, FO Minute of 10 February 1951.

49. USNA, RG 59, 768.5/2-351 of 3 February 1951 — withheld.

50. USNA, RG 330, Box 82, 091.3 Yugoslavia, of 1 February 1950.

51. USNA, RG 59, Box 2, Office of the Executive Secretary, UM D-60a.

52. USNA, RG 330, Office of the Secretary of Defense, CD 091.3 Yugoslavia.

53. USNA, RG 330, Box 54, CD 091.3 (MDAP) Yugoslavia.

54. State Department, document declassified on 16 March 1987.

55. USNA, RG 330, Box 54, CD 091.3 (MDAP) Yugoslavia.

56. See footnote in *FRUS* 1951 I p. 374.

57. PRO, CAB 131/11, D.O.(51)23 of 5 March 1951.

58. PRO, CAB 131/10, D.O.(51)5th Meeting on 9 March 1951, Item 2.

59. MAE, EU 32-4-1/1,2 vol. 6, no number, Memo of 28 December 1950.

60. MAE, EU 32-4-1sd1 vol. 7, no. 38/39 from London of 22 March 1951, and no. 1468 to London of 24 March 1951; as NATO documents have been inaccessible to this author, this is only an extrapolation.

61. *New York Times* of 7 March 1951: "Allies may sell military aircraft to Tito to bolster Yugoslavia against aggression"; 9 April 1951: "Yugoslavs ask U.S., Britain and France for Armaments Aid" and 17 April 1951: "United States to send supplies to Yugoslav Army".

62. The Soviet decision-makers apparently regarded the Western press as organs of the respective governments, analogous to the situation in the USSR. Press leaks were therefore regarded as conscious government policy, and consequently Soviet observers read the Western press very carefully. See e.g. William Taubman, *Stalin's American Policy* (New York: W.W. Norton, 1982). Windsor is mistaken in thinking Yugoslavia might have received military aid in 1950: Windsor, op. cit., p. 454.

63. PRO, FO 371/95540, RY 1192/77 of 31 March 1951.

64. PRO, DEFE 4/41, COS(51)48th, JP(51)47(Final) of 12 March 1951; the Yugoslavs were equally disappointed at the outcome of the visit of General Todorovic to the UK: DEFE 4/43, COS(51)90th of 1 June 1951; FO 371/95542, RY 1192/136 G and *passim.*

65. *Survey of International Affairs, 1951,* Pt. IV sec. 3, p. 249.

66. USNA, RG 330, Box 54, CD 091.3(MDAP)Yugoslavia, enclosure to 9 April 1951.

67. Vincent Auriol, *Journal du Septennat* vol. 5 (1951) (Paris: Armand Colin, 1975) p. 24, 27 June 1951; MAE, EU 32-4-1sd1, no number, Note by Seydoux to Schuman of 29 May and no. 5568/69 Parodi to Washington, 7 June 1951.

68. PRO, FO 371/95541, RY 1192/95 G of 14 April 1951.

69. PRO, FO 371/95541, RY 1192/98 G of 16-29 April 1951.

70. PRO, DEFE 7/217, RY 1192/105 G of 1 May 1951.

71. USNA, RG 330, Box 222, 091.3(MDAP)Yugoslavia, 3 May 1951.

72. USNA, RG 218, CCS 092 Yugoslavia (7-6-48) sec. 8, 22 and 23 May 1951.

73. USNA, RG 330 Box 222, 091.3(MDAP)Yugoslavia, 14 July 1951.

74. USNA, RG 218, CJCS 1953-1947, 091 Yugoslavia, of 13 October 1954 [*sic*].

75. USNA, RG 330, Box 222, 091.3(MDAP)Yugoslavia, of 14 July 1951; the act was renewed on 31 August 1951 as Mutual Security Act [H.R.5113], which provided for US military aid to qualified countries totalling $4,818,850,000, cf. KCMF, JC 2099/158 of 3 January 1952; USNA, RG 218, CCS 092 Yugoslavia(7-6-48) sec. 14, Treaties Series 2349.

76. USNA, RG 59, 768.5/1-2951 of 29 January 1951.

77. State Department document of 26 January 1951, declassified on 2 June 1986; *FRUS* 1951 IV p. 1707 of 26 January 1951; this tallies with NSC 18/4 regarding Yugoslavia's priority: USNA, RG 330, Box 222, CD 091.3 (MDAP) Yugoslavia, 10 March 1951.

78. MAE EU 32-4-1sd1 vol. 7, no number, note of Sous-Direction d'Europe Orientale, of 27 January 1951; also, PRO, FO 371/95545, RY 1192/194 G of 18 July 1951.

79. USNA, RG 59, 768.5, memo from Higgs to Strauss, 7 March 1951.

80. KCMF 17, JCS 2099/84 of 2 March 1951.

81. PRO, FO 371/95541, RY 1192/106 G of 26 April 1951.

82. E.g. USNA, RG 218, CCS 092 Yugoslavia(7-6-48)sec. 6 of 7 April 1951.

83. PRO, DEFE 4/54, COS(52)67th Meeting of 15 May 1952.

84. USNA, RG 330, Box 311, CD 091.3 Yugoslavia, 25 June 1952; Box 83, 111 FY 1952, Yugoslavia of 11 August 1952.

85. KCMF 3, JCS 1901/100 of 19 February 1953.

86. *FRUS* 1952-1954 II p. 175, 5 November 1952: Yugoslav rearmament is seen as part of the conventional military build-up planned by the JCS.

87. KCMF 18, JCS 2099/158 of 3 January 1952; see also JCS 2099/168 of 29 January 1952, ibid.

88. KCMF 18, JCS 2099/216 of 17 July 1952.

89. PRO, FO 371/95541, RY 1192/98 G of 16 April 1951.

90. PRO, FO 371/95546, RY 1192/219 G of 24 August 1951.

91. PRO, DEFE 4/57, COS(52)143rd Meeting of 9 October 1952; FO 371/107874, WY 1224/5, -/6 G; CAB 131/13, D(53)10th Meeting of 28 May 1953, items 1 and 2.

92. *FRUS* 1950 I pp. 376-389.

93. USNA, RG 218, CCS 092 Yugoslavia (7-6-48) sec. 6, JSPC 969/2 of 7 April 1951.

94. PRO, FO 371/107842, WY 1076/4 of 7 January 1953 and minutes; DEFE 5/27, COS(51)52, "Implications of an Act of Aggression against Yugoslavia", 5 February 1951; DEFE 4/40, COS(51)37th Meeting on 27 February 1951.

95. PRO, DEFE 4/46, Annex to J.P. (51)139(Final) of 21 August 1951.

96. PRO, FO 371/102165, WY 1022/6 G of 16 April 1952.

97. PRO, DEFE 5/20, COS(51)52 of 5 February 1951.

98. PRO, DEFE 4/40, COS(51)31st Meeting, 14 February 1951, Item 2.

99. PRO, DEFE 5/29, e.g. COS(51)143, COS(51)148, COS(51)158; DEFE 4/46, JP(51)139(Final), Annex, 21 August 1951; cf. NSC 18/4 and NSC 18/6, State Department, declassified 16 March 1987.

100. PRO, DEFE 5/20, COS(51)37th Meeting, 27 February 1951.

101. Cf. Djilas visit to the UK in late January-early February 1951, Davies Papers.

102. Cf. Yugoslav statements on this: *FRUS* 1951 IV p. 1737, Tito on 17 February 1951; PRO, FO 371/95542, RY 1192/134 G of 16 May 1951, statement by General Todorović; *FRUS* 1951 IV p. 1843, Tito and Harriman agree, 27 August 1951; PRO, FO 371/107844, WY 1076/87 of 10 March 1953: disagreement between General Handy and the Yugoslavs.

103. PRO, DEFE 7/216, 7 March 1951, from BJSM Washington.

104. USNA, RG 218, CCS 092 Yugoslavia (7-6-48) sec. 6, JSPC 969/2 of 7 April 1951.

105. PRO, FO 371/95541, A. Noble's comment of 21 April 1951 on RY 1192/98 G; DEFE 7/217, RY 1192/105 G of 1 May 1951.

106. *FRUS* 1951 I p. 868

107. USNA, RG 330, Box 220, CD 091.3 (MDAP) Yugoslavia, 16 October 1951; cf. also *FRUS* 1951 I p. 580, Acheson to Eden and Schuman, 6 November 1951; PRO, DEFE 7/222, of 8 March 1952, Memo by K.C. Mclean for Minister of Defence; DEFE 4/53, COS(52)58th Meeting, Item 6, 28 April 1952; Admiral Carney denies that he proposed this: Interview in Washington, D.C., 8 August 1985.

108. PRO, DEFE 4/46, JP(51)139(Final), Annex, 21 August 1951.

109. PRO, DEFE 7/216 of 7 March 1951.

110. USNA, RG 218, CCS 092 Yugoslavia(7-6-48) sec. 6, JSPC 969/2 of 7 April 1951.

111. Alan Bullock, *Ernest Bevin, Foreign Secretary* (Oxford: Oxford University Press, 1985), p. 820f; Arthur Krock, *Memoirs* (London: Cassell, 1968), p. 260.

112. Kenneth Harris, *Attlee* (London: Weidenfeld & Nicolson, 1982), pp. 462-467; Roy Jenkins, *Truman* (London: Collins, 1986), p. 178; Harry Truman, *Memoirs — Years of Trial and Hope*, vol. 2 (London: Hodder & Stoughton, 1956), pp. 418-438.

113. *FRUS* 1951 I p. 835.

114. *FRUS* 1951 I p. 839, memo of 23 May 1951.

115. *FRUS* 1951 I p. 849, talks of 14 June 1951.

116. *FRUS* 1950 I pp. 376-389, see particularly p. 386, para. 36; see NSC 73/4 of 25 August 1950, *FRUS* 1950 I p. 376ff.

117. *FRUS* 1951 I pp. 866-874 of 3 August 1951.

118. *FRUS* 1951 I p. 887.

119. USNA, RG 218, CCS 092 Yugoslavia(7-6-48), sec. 7, JIC 501/10 of 3 May 1951; RG 59, 768.5/3-251 of 9 April 1951.

120. USNA, RG 218, CJCS 1953-1957, 091 Yugoslavia, 13 October 1954 [*sic*]; RG 330, Box 222, 091.3(MDAP)Yugoslavia of 13 June 1951.

121. PRO, DEFE 4/5, COS(51)119th Meeting of 23 July 1951, Item 3; MAE, EU 32-4-1sd1 vol. 8, various numbers, from Parodi, 14 July 1951; for French loyalty to Italy, see MAE, EU 33-9-3, Gen.44, note of 28 April 1950; PRO, FO 371/102167, WY 1022/70 G of 3 November 1952.

122. PRO, FO 371/102166, WY 1022/43 G of 1 October 1952.

123. See various marginal comments by Eden in documents in the PRO, FO 371/102165, particularly on WY 1022/6 G of 22 April 1952. Yugoslavia, the UK and France did not want NATO involvement.

124. E.g. PRO, DEFE 7/222, Memo by K.G. McLean of 8 March 1952; FO 371/102166, WY 1022/39 G at the Eden visit in September 1952.

125. PRO, FO 371/102168, WY 1022/94 G of 22 November 1952.

126. PRO, FO 371/102168, WY 1022/94 G and -/98 G; USNA, RG 218, CCS 092 Yugoslavia(7-6-48) sec.18, JCS 1901/95 of 11 December 1952; PRO, FO 371/102168, WY 1022/100 G; MAE EU 32-4-1sd3 vol. 11, PJP-337 of 6 December 1952.

127. USNA, RG 330, Box 55, 337 Yugoslavia of 25 September 1953.

128. DD(79)408 A.

129. USNA, RG 330, 337 Yugoslavia, 19 October 1953.

130. USNA, RG 218, CJCS 1953-57, 091 Yugoslavia, 13 October 1954.

131. USNA, RG 218, CJCS 1953-1957, 091 Yugoslavia, 1 March 1955; CCS 092 Yugoslavia(7-6-48), sec. 25, JCS 1901/132 of 18 April 1955.

132. USNA, RG 218, CCS 092 Yugoslavia(7-6-48) sec. 28, JCS 1901/142; A. Ross Johnson, *The U.S. Stake in Yugoslavia, 1948-1968* (California: Southern Californian Arms Control Seminar, 1972), pp. 8-9; Ivo Omrćanin, *Enigma Tito* (Washington, D.C.: Samizdat, 1984), tables pp. 401-413.

133. USNA, RG 218, CJCS 1953-1957, 091 Yugoslavia, 13 October 1954.

134. For Yugoslav statements, see e.g. PRO, FO 371/102173, WY 10319/6 of 24 May 1952; DEFE 5/44, COS(53)14 of 8 January 1953; FO 371/107827, WY 1023/11 of 15 June 1953.

135. PRO, FO 371/107843, WY 1076/27 of 31 January and -/42 of 13 February 1953; the Turks made this point on several occasions, see FO 371/107842, *passim*; but it is also clear that the Turks wanted NATO to share their own commitment to the defence of Yugoslavia, ibid. and following files, *passim*; PRO, DEFE 5/44, COS(53)14.

136. *FRUS* 1952-1954 V p. 1400 of 19 October 1954; Edvard Kardelj

later claimed that his government never intended to join NATO: *Reminiscences* (London: Blond & Briggs, Summerfield Press, 1982), p. 129.

137. PRO, DEFE 7/221, no. 3582, Washington to FO, 13 November 1951.

138. E.g. State Department Documents concerning Anglo-American Politico-Military talks of 16 April 1952, declassified 25 March 1986.

139. See below, and see PRO, CAB 129/45, CP(51)130 of 17 May 1951.

140. PRO, FO 371/95547, RY 1192/224 of 14 November 1951, note of 23 November 1951.

141. Cf. *FRUS* 1952-1954 II p. 557 of 23 October 1953; USNA, NSC 174 of 11 December 1953; *FRUS* 1951 I, p. 200 of 24 September 1951.

142. Cyrus L. Sulzberger, *A Long Row of Candles* (London: Macdonald, 1969), pp. 531-571, *passim*; see particularly pp. 531-532, conversation with Lt. Gen. Lauris Norstad on 15 February 1951.

143. PRO, FO 371/102165, WY 1022/1 G of 31 December 1951; the Labour government may have been less opposed to the idea of Yugoslav NATO membership, cf. CAB 128/19, CM(51)36th of 22 May 1951, and discussion above in discussion of NATO membership of Greece and Turkey; FO 371/107842, WY 1076/17 of 17 January 1953.

144. USNA, RG 330, Box 354, NYT, Mr. Lovett's Book, NYT D-4/2(Special) of 7 November 1952.

145. PRO, FO 371/113167, WY 1071/17 of 18 May 1954.

146. E.g. statement of General Todorović in Britain, PRO, FO 371/95542, RY 1192/134 G of 16 May 1951.

147. Anton Ciliga, *La Yougoslavie sous la Menace Intérieure et Extérieure* (Paris: Iles d'Or, 1951), p. 8.

148. PRO, FO 371/95542, RY 1192/143 G of 29 May 1951, from BJSM, Washington to F.O.

149. PRO, FO 371/954855, RY 10345/2 of 9 November 1951.

150. In the words of the British Military Attaché; PRO, FO 371/102168, WY 1022/94 G of 22 November 1952.

151. DD(79)408 A.

152. USNA, RG 218, CCS 092 Yugoslavia (7-6-48) sec. 24, JSPC 969/47 of 25 October 1954 [*sic*].

153. Harry Chase, "American-Yugoslav Relations, 1945-1956" (Social Science Ph.D. dissertation, University of Syracuse, 1957), p. 240.

154. PRO, DEFE 5/9, COS(48)210 of October 1948 (*Speedway*); DEFE 4/19, J.P. (48)117(Final) of 19 January 1949; KCMF 64, JCS 1920/1 of 31 January 1949 (*Dropshot*); KCMF 39, JCS 1868/136 "Strategic Guidance for ... Regional Planning", 25 October 1949; KCMF 65, JCS 1920/5 the revised *Dropshot* of 19 December 1949; USNA, RG 218, JCS 1951-53, 381(1-26-50)B.P. Part I, JCS 2143/6

(*Reaper*) of 7 December 1950.

155. *FRUS* 1951 V pp. 1110-1113 of 24 January 1951.

156. Bullock, *Bevin*, p. 643.

157. E.g. PRO, DEFE 5/42, COS(52)629 of 19 November 1952: far more importance is given to the defence of Anatolia than of Thrace.

158. PRO, FO 371/78328, R 1843/1972/67 G of 14 February 1949.

159. Walter Poole, *The History of the Joint Chiefs of Staff*, vol. 4 (Historical Division of the Joint Secretariat, Joint Chiefs of Staff, Washington, D.C., December 1979; Wilmington, Glazier), p. 238ff.

160. E.g. PRO, FO 371/87942, RK 1023/4 of 5 August 1950; CAB 21/1967, COS(51)147 of 19 March 1951.

161. *FRUS* 1951 I p. 46f.

162. *FRUS* 1951 V p. 42.

163. E.g. *FRUS* 1951 V p. 4ff, memo by McGhee; PRO, DEFE 4/23, J.P. (49)59(Final) of 11 July 1949, Annex, para. 1; *FRUS* 1950 V p. 188ff.

164. *FRUS* 1951 V pp. 50-61.

165. PRO, CAB 129/45, CP(51)130 of 17 May 1951; cf. also Eisenhower's advocacy of Yugoslav admission to the United States of Europe which he hoped for: Robert Ferrell (ed.), *The Eisenhower Diaries* (New York: W.W. Norton, 1981), p. 194, entry for 11 June 1951.

166. PRO, DEFE 6/11, JP(51)61(Final) of 27 March 1951.

167. PRO, CAB 129/45, CP(51)130 of 17 May 1951.

168. PRO, DEFE 5/31, COS(51)285 of 7 May 1951.

169. PRO, CAB 129/45, CP(51)130 of 17 May 1951.

170. PRO, CAB 131/11, D.O.(51)12th Meeting, Minute 4; see also CAB 129/45 CP(51)132 of 17 May 1951.

171. PRO, CAB 128/20, CM(51)60th of 27 September 1951.

172. PRO, DEFE 5/32, COS(51)391 of 27 June 1951; CAB 131/11, D.O.(51)81 of 28 June 1951; cf. also Ferrell, *Eisenhower Diaries*, entry of 16 November 1951, p. 205.

173. PRO, DEFE 5/34, COS(51)630 of 30 October 1951.

174. ibid. and DEFE 5/35, COS(51)751 of 13 December 1951.

175. USNA, RG 319, P & O 091, Greece TS 23/2, JCS 1868/152.

176. Davies Papers.

177. *FRUS* 1951 V p. 27 of January (?) 1951 (undated).

178. USNA, RG 59, 781.5 MAP/6-951 of 9 June 1951.

179. PRO, FO 371/102191, WY 1076/5; FO 371/102173, WY 10319/10 of 14 June 1952.

180. PRO, DEFE 5/40, COS(52)429 of 31 July 1952.

181. PRO, FO 371/102191, WY 1076/10 of 26 July 1952; WY 1076/19 of 30 September 1952; etc.; DEFE 5/40, WU 11921/9 (=COS(52)429) enclosure of 23 June 1952.

182. PRO, DEFE 5/41, COS(52)511 of 12 September 1952.

183. PRO, FO 371/102173, WY 10319/17 of 8 October and -/18

of 17 October 1952.

184. PRO, FO 371/102191, comments on WY 1076/2 of 30 April 1952; see also -/5 and -/7.

185. USNA, RG 84, Belgrade, Yugoslavia 1950-1954, Box 2, 350 Yugoslavia vol. 2 of 25 October 1952; TL, Acheson Papers, Box 67a of 27 November 1952.

186. PRO, FO 371/102191, WY 1076/24 G of 9 December 1952.

187. PRO, FO 371/107842, WY 1076/2 of 2 January and also -/5 of 9 January 1953.

188. PRO, FO 371/107842, WY 1076/4 of 7 January 1953; for discussion of policy towards Albania, see Chapter 4.

189. *The Times*, 8 January 1953: "Yugoslavia's Role in the Balkans — Signor de Gasperi's visit to Athens — Eyes on Trieste".

190. PRO, FO 371/107842, WY 1076/8 of 7 January 1953 and comments.

191. PRO, FO 371/107842, WY 1076/13 of 16 January 1953.

192. PRO, FO 371/107842, WY 1076/26 of 23 January 1953.

193. PRO, FO 371/107843, WY 1076/57 of 25 February 1953; FO 371/107844, WY 1076/95 of 18 March 1953.

194. PRO, FO 371/113166, WY 1071/13 of 11 May 1954.

195. PRO, FO 371/107845, WY 1071/15 of 14 May 1954.

196. PRO, FO 371/113167, WY 1071/17, and following, particularly WY 1071/28.

197. PRO, FO 371/113167, *passim.*

198. PRO, FO 371/107842, WY 1076/2 of 2 January 1953; USNA, RG 84, Belgrade Yugoslavia, 1950-1954, Box 4, 320 Relations between Countries, 30 September 1953; PRO, FO 371/107845, WY 1076/125 of 16 July 1953; WY 1076/135 and -/137.

199. PRO, FO 371/113168, WY 1071/74 of 12 June 1954; WY 1071/84 of 19 June 1954.

200. PRO, FO 371/112649, W 1071/11.

201. DD(76)161 C of 26 March 1953.

Chapter 7

1. *Public Papers of the President of the U.S.: Harry S. Truman 1950* (Washington, D.C.: US Government Printing Office, 1964), p. 718.

2. ibid., p. 718.

3. USNA, RG 59, Box 5334, 868.00 R/12-1150 of 29 November 1950.

4. USNA, GG 59, Box 5334, 868.00 R/12-1150, of 27 November 1950, author's emphasis.

5. *FRUS* 1951 IV p. 1689 of 17 January 1951.

6. *FRUS* 1951 IV p. 1694 of 20 January 1951.

Notes

7. USNA, RG 59, 611.68/2-2751, of 27 February 1951.

8. ibid., 611.68/4-451, of 4 April 1951.

9. PRO, CAB 129/42, C.P. (50)234 of 17 October 1950.

10. PRO, CAB 129/46, C.P. (51)160 of 18 June 1951.

11. MAE, EU 32-8-1, old vol. 24, no number, note of 9 November 1949.

12. MAE, EU 32-8-3, old vol. 34, no number, note of 13 October 1950.

13. ibid., no. 1116 from Belgrade of 1 November 1950, approved by Parodi, the Secretary General of the Quai d'Orsay in no. 1185-86 to Belgrade of 10 November 1950.

14. ibid., no. 101/105 from Belgrade of 19 January 1951.

15. ibid., no number, note pour le Secrétaire Générale, 11 May 1951.

16. *FRUS* 1950 IV p. 1438; USNA, RG 59, Box 5337, 868.10/8-1550 of 15 August 1950; for tables on US economic aid see John Campbell, *Tito's Separate Road* (New York: Harper & Row, 1967), p. 171; Novak Jankovic, "The Changing Role of the United States in Financing Yugoslav Economic Development since 1945" (Paper given at Symposium held at J.F. Kennedy Centre in Free University, Berlin, July 1987), pp. 2-4; *FRUS* 1950 IV p. 1445f of 5 September 1950.

17. USNA, RG 59, Box 5337, 868.10, *passim*, September 1950.

18. *FRUS* 1950 IV p. 1462f of 9 October 1950.

19. *FRUS* 1950 IV pp. 1471-1473 of 16 October 1950.

20. USNA, RG 59, 768.5 MAP/11-350 of 3 November 1950, and *passim*; *FRUS* 1950 IV p. 1489f of 31 October 1950; *FRUS* 1951 IV p. 1762f.

21. *FRUS* 1950 IV pp. 1480-1485 of 25-27 October 1950.

22. PRO, CAB 129/42, CP(50)234 of 17 October; CAB 128/18, CM(50)66th Meeting of 20 October 1950.

23. PRO, CAB 128/19, CM(51)24th Meeting of 5 April 1951.

24. *FRUS* 1951 IV pp. 1765-1768, of 23 March 1951; Truman, *Public Papers 1951*, p. 232 of 16 April 1951; TL, Acheson Papers, Box 66, Memoranda of meetings with the President, of 23 March; 2, 10 and 12 April 1951.

25. *FRUS* 1951 IV p. 1844.

26. *FRUS* 1951 IV pp. 1743-1745, *passim*; Vincent Auriol: *Journal du Septennat (1947-1954)* vol. 5, 1951 (Paris: Armand Collin, 1977), p. 184.

27. *FRUS* 1951 IV pp. 1743-1745, *passim*; pp. 1802-1814 of 18 June; PRO, CAB 129/46, CP(51)160 of 18 June; PRO, FO 371/95514, RY 1102/270 of 29 June 1951.

28. *Annales de l'Assemblée Nationale — Débats*, 1952 I (Paris: Imprimerie des Journaux Officiels, 1952), p. 548.

29. PRO, CAB 128/19, CM(51)45 of 21 June 1951; 489 H.C. DEB. 5s (1951), cols. 2500-2503 of 5 July 1951.

30. David Larson, *United States Foreign Policy toward Yugoslavia, 1943-1963* (Washington, D.C.: University Press of America, 1979), p. 246.

31. *FRUS* 1951 IV p. 1853f of 11 October 1951; p. 1688 of 17 January 1951 .

32. PRO, FO 371/102180, WY 1052/38 G of 11 September 1952.

33. PRO, FO 371/102201, WY 1103/21 and -/36 of 25 January and 21 February 1952; FO 371/102202, WY 1103/47 quoting WE 1015/23 and WY 1103/42 of 4 March 1952.

34. PRO, FO 371/102202, WY 1103/50 of 5 March 1952.

35. PRO, FO 371/102202, WY 1103/59 of 16 March 1952; FO 371/102211, WY 1106/11 of 4 January 1952.

36. PRO, FO 371/102203, 1103/83 of 21 April 1952, and CAB 129/51, C.(52)145 of 8 May 1952; USNA, RG 59, 768.5-MSP/4-1252 of 12 April 1952.

37. PRO, CAB 128/25 of C.C.(52)53rd of 15 May 1952, Item 9.

38. PRO, FO 371/102205 *passim*; USNA, RG 59, 768.5 MSP/7-1552 of 15 July 1952.

39. Truman, *Public Papers 1952/53*, Item 18 of 21 January 1952; Item 27 of 5 February 1952; Harry Chase, "American-Yugoslav Relations, 1945-1956" (University of Syracuse, Social Science Ph.D. dissertation, 1957), p. 238ff; see also U.S. Congress, Senate, Committee on Foreign Relations, *Hearings on Mutual Security Act of 1952 [for 1953]*, 82nd Congress, 2nd session, 1952, and U.S. Congress, House, Committee on Foreign Affairs, *Hearings, Mutual Security Act Extension*, 82nd Congress, 2nd Session, 1952.

40. *Annales de l'Assemblée Nationale – Débats* (Paris: Imprimerie des Journaux Officiels, 1953) vol. 1953 II, pp. 914-941, of 3 February 1953; USNA, RG 59, Box 5338, 868.10/3-1753 of 17 March 1953.

41. PRO, FO 371/102207, WY 1103/177 and -/185 of 12 November and 3 December 1952.

42. USNA, RG 59, Box 5338, 868.10/2-1053 letter of 10 February 1953.

43. USNA, RG 59, Box 5338, 868.10/3-1753 and -/3-1953 from Paris.

44. USNA, RG 59, 768.5-MSP/10-2753 of 27 October 1953.

45. USNA, RG 59, 768.5-MSP *passim.*

46. PRO, FO 371/107815, WY 1013/2 of 16 January 1953.

47. PRO, FO 371/107815, WY 1013/8 of 11 April 1953.

48. PRO, FO 371/107847, WY 1101/7 of 4 June 1953; FO 371/107853, WY 1103/63 of 4 June 1953; USNA, RG 59, Box 5338, 686.10, *passim*, Summer 1953.

49. USNA, RG 59, 768.5-MSP/10-2153 of 21 October 1953.

50. PRO, FO 371/102213, WY 1107/8, -/9 of 29 May and 25 June 1952.

51. USNA, RG 59, Box 5338, 868.10/2-1153 of 11 February 1953.

52. PRO, CAB 128/18, CM(50)66th Meeting of 20 October 1951.

53. MAE, EU 32-8-3, old vol. 34, no. 1185-86 to Belgrade, 10 November 1950.

54. E.g. *FRUS* 1951 IV p. 1758f.

55. A. Ross Johnson, *The Transformation of Communist Ideology* (Cambridge, Ma.: MIT Press, 1972), pp. 122-138.

56. PRO, FO 371/88240, RY 1023/29 of 28 June 1950, and comments; see Bibliography for works on Yugoslav ideology and economy.

57. PRO, FO 371/88231, RY 1017/22 of 27 October 1950; PRO, FO 371/95460, RY 1013/12 of 8 June 1951; FO 371/95462, RY 1015/31 of 1 December; comment of 5 December 1951.

58. MAE, EU 32-8-3, old vol. 34, no. 1116 of 1 November 1950; PRO, FO 371/88240, RY 1023/29 of 28 June 1950, and comments; PRO, FO 371/95462, RY 1015/33 of 1 December; -/37 of 14 December 1951.

59. *FRUS* 1951 IV p. 1719.

60. PRO, FO 371/102156 and -/102157, WY 1013/13, -/14 and -/23 of 21 June, 5 July and 7 November 1952.

61. Stephen Markovich, "American Foreign Policy and Yugoslav Foreign Policy" in Peter Potichnyj and Jane Shapiro (eds.), *From Cold War to Détente* (New York: Praeger, 1976), pp. 78-96.

62. Alan Bullock, *Ernest Bevin, Foreign Secretary* (Oxford: Oxford University Press, 1985), p. 790f.

63. PRO, FO 371/88248, RY 1072/2 of 29 June 1950, from Peake.

64. PRO, FO 371/88238, RY 1022/22 of 29 August 1950.

65. PRO, FO 371/88238, RY 1022/28 of 11 November; see also Sulzberger interview with Tito of 6 November 1950 in *New York Times*, cf. C.L. Sulzberger, *A Long Row of Candles* (London: Macdonald, 1969), p. 505f.

66. *FRUS* 1951 IV p. 1701 of 26 January 1951; FO 371/88238, RY 1022/17 of 7 August 1950; *FRUS* 1950 IV p. 1479 of 23 October 1950; *FRUS* 1951 IV p. 1712 of 29 January 1951.

67. MAE, EU 32-8-1, old vol. 25, no. 239 of 18 February 1951; *FRUS* 1951 IV p. 1737 of 19 February 1951.

68. MAE, EU 32-8-1, old vol. 25, no. 673 from Belgrade of 23 May.

69. Cf., e.g. in Herbert Tint, *French Foreign Policy since the Second World War* (London: Weidenfeld & Nicolson, 1972), p. 48ff; Alexander Werth, *France 1940-1955* (London: Robert Hale, 1956), p. 428ff; Alfred Grosser, *Affaires Extérieures* (St. Amand-Montrand (Cher): Flammarion, 1984), p. 87ff; Michael Harrison, *The Reluctant Ally* (Baltimore: Johns Hopkins University Press, 1981), pp. 12-45.

70. Frank Roberts, "Ernest Bevin as Foreign Secretary" in Ritchie Ovendale (ed.), *The Foreign Policy of the British Labour Governments, 1945-1951* (Bath: Leicester University Press, 1984), p. 23.

71. See description of the Eisenhower/Dulles concepts of

defence, etc. in John Lewis Gaddis, *Strategies of Containment* (New York: Oxford University Press, 1982), pp. 129-132; John Yurechko, "From Containment to Counter-Offensive: Soviet Vulnerabilities and American Policy Planning, 1946-1953" (Ms. Ph.D. thesis, University of Berkeley, California 1980), p. 134ff; William Schneider, "Public Opinion" in Joseph Nye, *The Making of America's Soviet Policy* (New Haven: Yale University Press, 1984), p. 11f.

72. USNA, RG 59, Box 5338, 868.10/6-2652 of 26 June 1952.

73. DD(78)457 C, Memorandum by Eisenhower of 22 October 1954; Stephen Ambrose, *Eisenhower, the President, 1952-1969* (London: Allen & Unwin, 1984), pp. 379-380 for 1957.

74. Milovan Djilas, *Rise and Fall* (London: Macmillan, 1985), p. 275f; e.g. 484 H.C.DEB. 5s, col. 45f of 12 February 1951; 489 H.C.DEB. 5s, col. 2501-2503 of 5 July 1951.

75. PRO, FO 371/88260, RY 1072/3 of 1 July 1950.

76. PRO, FO 371/88238, RY 1022/28 from Belgrade of 11 November 1950.

77. MAE, EU 32-8-3, old vol. 34, no number of 13 October 1950.

78. MAE, EU 32-8-1, old vol. 24, telegram no. 1212 from Belgrade of 22 November 1950; old vol. 25, telegram no. 645 of 16 May 1951.

79. PRO, FO 371/102156, WY 1013/1 and -/2 of 5 January and 19 January 1952; concerning Yugoslav press, see also FO 371/102246, WY 1451/1 of 15 February 1952; FO 371/102159, WY 1016/9 of 5 February 1952.

80. PRO, FO 371/107819, *passim*; FO 371/107837, WY 1053/3 of 20 January 1953.

81. PRO, FO 371/102179, WY 1052/26 of 4 September 1952; as the Eden visit occurred at Yugoslav suggestion, it is not clear why Sidney Aster implies that this was "an imaginative stroke" on the part of Eden: *Anthony Eden*, (London: Weidenfeld & Nicolson, 1976), p. 106.

82. PRO, FO 371/102181, WY 1052/51 of 26 September 1952.

83. PRO, FO 371/102160, WY 1016/31/52 of 5 December 1952.

84. PRO, FO 371/102164, WY 10112/11 of 18 November 1952.

85. TL, Office File 364, Miscellaneous, *passim.*

86. PRO, FO 371/102157, WY 1013/25 and -/26 of 6 and 19 December 1952; FO 371/102266, WY 1781/30 of 17 December 1952.

87. PRO, FO 371/102181ff.; FO 371/107836f *passim.*

88. PRO, FO 371/102184, WY 1053/82 of 26 November 1952ff; and particularly WY 1053/83 of 3 December 1952.

89. PRO, PREM 11/577, WY 1054/84 G of 17 March 1953.

90. PRO, FO 371/107843, WY 1076/51, J.O. Wright's minute of 27 February 1953 and subsequent minutes.

91. PRO, FO 371/102179, WY 1052/10 of 25 July 1952; FO 371/102180, WY 1052/38 G of 11 September 1952.

Notes

92. PRO, FO 371/102181, WY 1052/53 of 22 September 1952; FO 371/107880, WY 1511/3 of 18 March 1953; PREM 11/577, WY 1054/84 G, of 17 March 1953.

93. PRO, FO 371/102181, WY 1052/66 of 16 December 1952; PRO, FO 371/107880, *passim* and PRO, FO 371/107899 *passim* for mid-December 1953; MAE, EU 32-8-3, old vol. 36, no. 88/89 from Baudet of 19 January 1953; *Review of World Affairs* (Belgrade) of 1 October 1952.

94. The Eden visit and all its preparations are treated in great detail in John Young, "Eden's First Visit to Tito in 1952", *Review of International Studies*, XII (January 1986).

95. Cf., e.g. interview of Ambassador Joze Brilej with Lionel Bloch of the *Birmingham Post*, printed 15 October 1952; FO 371/107835 and -/107836, WY 1054/113 and -/114; statement in House of Commons, 1 April 1953.

96. MAE EU 32-8-6, old vol. 38, letter no. 617 EU from Belgrade, 29 May 1951.

97. Pierre Melandri, "France and the Atlantic Alliance, 1950-1954" in Olav Riste (ed.), *Western Security, the Formative Years* (Oslo: Norwegian University Press, 1985), pp. 266-279; R.B. Manderson-Jones, *The Special Relationship* (New York: Crane & Russak, 1972), pp. II, 1-15, 16-31, 65-81; Peter Boyle, "The British Foreign Office and American Foreign Policy, 1947-1948", *American Studies* XVI 3 (1982), pp. 373-389; Cees Wiebes and Bert Zeeman, "The Pentagon Negotiations, March 1948", *International Affairs* LIX 3 (1983) pp. 353ff; David Reynolds, "A 'Special relationship'?", *International Affairs*, LXII 1 (Winter 1985/1986), pp. 4-12.

98. Anthony Seldon, *Churchill's Indian Summer* (London: Hodder & Stoughton, 1981), pp. 389-392; Robert Ferrell (ed.), *The Eisenhower Diaries* (New York: W.W.Norton, 1981), p. 232.

99. Richie Ovendale, "Britain and the Cold War in Asia" in Ovendale, *Foreign Policy*, p. 122f; and Ovendale, *The English-Speaking Alliance* (London: Allen & Unwin, 1985), pp. 211-238.

100. Seldon, *Churchill*, pp. 30, 387-396.

101. Seldon, *Churchill*, p. 389ff; Robert Rh. James, *Anthony Eden* (London: Weidenfeld & Nicolson, 1986), p. 352f; Aster, *Eden*, pp. 100, 107ff.

102. MAE, EU 32-8-6, old vol. 38, letter no. 617 EU from Belgrade of 29 May 1951; no. 1327/EU from Belgrade of 30 September 1952; old vol. 39, no. 473/EU from London, of 25 March 1953; PRO, FO 371/102181, WY 1052/51 of 26 September 1952.

103. MAE, EU 32-8-7, old vol. 46, *passim.*

104. E.g. PRO, FO 371/107840, WY 1072/5 of 8 May 1953; FO 371/107815, *passim*; MAE, EU 31-9-1, vol. 51, no. 137, note pour le Président, 17 June 1953; PRO, FO 371/106233 on Bulgarian-Yugoslav détente; -/106273 on Hungarian-Yugoslav détente; -/106461 on

Rumanian-Yugoslav détente; -/107295 on Albanian-Yugoslav détente, *passim.*

105. DD(84)1954 of 7 November 1955; see also Henry William Brands, "Redefining the Cold War: American Policy toward Yugoslavia, 1948-60", *Diplomatic History*, XI 1 (Winter 1986/1987), pp. 48-51.

106. Jean-Baptiste Duroselle, *Le Conflit de Trieste, 1943-1954* (Brussels: Eds. de l'Institut de Sociologie de l'Université Libre de Bruxelles, 1966); Bogdan Novak, *Trieste, 1941-1954* (Chicago: University of Chicago Press, 1970); Diego de Castro, *La Questione di Trieste*, 2 vols. (Trieste: Lint, 1982); John Campbell (ed.), *Successful Negotiation: Trieste 1954* (Princeton, N.J.: Princeton University Press, 1976).

107. E.g. PRO, FO 371/107827, WY 1023/1/G of 2 January 1953.

108. PRO, FO 371/107827, WY 1023/1/G of 2 January 1953.

109. PRO, FO 371/107367, WE 1011/1 of 7 April 1953; FO 371/102156, WY 1013/5 of 1 March 1952; Yugoslav proposal for internationalization: e.g. TL, Acheson Papers, Box 67, 6 March 1952 and 18 March 1952.

110. *FRUS* 1952-1954 V, pp. 168, 171, Meeting of 26 February 1952; p. 173f, Meeting of 1 April 1952.

111. TL, Acheson Papers, Box 67, Meeting of 28 June 1952.

112. Dwight Eisenhower, *Mandate for Change* (London: Heinemann, 1963), p. 409; see also pp. 409, 415f.

113. Sully-Mudd Library, Princeton, Eisenhower Library Papers of John Foster Dulles, Chronological Series, Box 5, memorandum of telephone conversation of 5 September 1953; Box 1, telephone conversations of 12 and 30 September , and 10 November 1953; memo of conversation Eisenhower-Dulles of 6 October 1953; DD(1982) 001160, memo by J.F. Dulles of 8 September 1953; *FRUS* 1952-1954 V p. 817 of 5 October 1953. It is ironic to think that less than a decade earlier the Yugoslavs had fought on the side of the Western powers against Italy, the common enemy!

114. PRO, FO 371/113151, WY 1011/1 of 31 December 1953; CAB 129/63, C.(53)268 of 29 September 1953; CAB 128/26, C.C.(53)54th of 2 October and C.C.(53)56th of 8 October 1953.

115. Evelyn Shuckburgh, *Descent to Suez* (London: Weidenfeld & Nicolson, 1986), pp. 108-109: he calls this move "a bit of a mess".

116. PRO, CAB 128/26, C.C.(53)57th of 13 October 1953.

117. Sully-Mudd Library, Eisenhower Library Papers of J.F. Dulles, White House Correspondence, Box 1, memo of conversation, 14 October 1953 .

118. Eisenhower, *Mandate*, p. 414.

119. PRO, FO 371/113151, WY 1011/1 of 31 December 1953.

120. PRO, CAB 128/26, C.C.(53)57th, 59th, 60th and 61st of 13, 19, 22 and 27 October ; 64th, 65th, 67th and 70th of 9, 10, 17 and 24

November ; 77th of 8 December 1953, and Cabinet papers in CAB 129/64; CAB 128/27, CC(54)28th of 13 April 1954; CAB 129/68, C.(54)197 of 16 June 1954; *FRUS* 1952-1954 V p. 1744f of 4 December 1953; AN, Archives de Georges Bidault, 457 AP 48, records of Tripartite Conference of Foreign Ministers, London, 16-19 October 1953.

121. MAE, EU 32-8-5, old vol. 33, no. 709/EU of 29 May 1953 and *passim*; USNA, RG 59, 611.68/6-2053 of 20 June 1953; DD(1982) 001167 of 2 February-31 May 1954.

122. David Carlton, *Anthony Eden*, (London: Allen Lane, 1981), p. 360.

123. Anthony Eden, Earl of Avon, *Memoirs* vol. 3: *Full Circle* (London: Cassell, 1960), pp. 183, 188.

124. Shuckburgh, *Descent*, pp. 108-109: "our Trieste venture has been a major error".

125. PRO, CAB 129/68, C.(54)197 of 16 June 1954; CAB 128/27, C.C.(54)63rd of 5 October 1954; see also *FRUS* 1952-1954 V pp. 990-994 of June 1954. For an account of these negotiations in detail, see John Campbell (ed.), *Trieste 1954*, particularly pp. 3-22.

126. This defence co-ordination between Italy and Yugoslavia, backed by American troops stationed in Northern Italy, continues to this day.

127. PRO, FO 371/107843, *passim*; -/107844, WY 1076/73 of 5 March 1953ff.

128. PRO, FO 371/107845, WY 1076/104.

129. PRO, FO 371/113166, *passim*, particularly WY 1071/44 of 26 May 1954; FO 371/113167 and -/113168 *passim*.

130. PRO, FO 371/113168, WY 1071/74 of 12 June 1954; concerning invitation to Italy to join, see FO 371/107845, WY 1076/101 of 28 March 1953.

131. PRO, FO 371/113168, WY 1071/74 of 12 June 1954.

132. MAE, EU 32-8-1, old vol. 25, nos. 239 and 283-285 from Belgrade, 18 and 26 February 1951.

133. MAE, EU 38-8-1, old vol. 24, no. 730-735 of 18 July 1950.

134. PRO, FO 371/95483, RY 10322/2 of 18 January 1951.

135. MAE, EU 32-8-1, old vol. 25, 1519-21 from Belgrade of 2 November 1951.

136. *New York Times*, 13 May 1954; see also Sulzberger, *Long Row*, p. 843, entry for 7 May 1954, Bled; Veselin Djurdjevac, *La Yougoslavie Socialiste et Non-alignment* (Paris: Le Sycomore, 1983), pp. 43-46.

137. West Germany monitored Tito's opinion on this issue carefully: Auswärtiges Amt, Bonn, III 211-00/39, vol. 4, III 6986/54 of 16 March 1954, and other papers in this file.

138. MAE, EU 32-8-7, old vol. 47, *passim* for late 1954

139. Cf. Irena Reuter-Hendrichs, *Jugoslawische Aussenpolitik, 1948-1968* (Cologne: Carl Heymanns, 1976), pp. 130-140; Peter

Willets, *The Non-Aligned Movement* (London: Frances Pinter, 1978), pp. 2-11; Peter Lyon, *Neutralism* (Leicester: Leicester University Press, 1963), pp. 130-138.

140. PRO, FO 371/86898, NS 2191/20/G of 25 January 1950.

141. MAE, EU 31-9-1, vol. 47, letter no. 1207 from Moscow of 8 November 1950.

142. MAE, EU 32-8-1, old vol. 25, *passim*; EU 32-8-13 and 14, old vol. 43, July 1951 *passim*; PRO, FO 371/102156, WY 1013/1 of 5 January, -/3 of 1 February; -/11 of 24 May; FO 371/102157, WY 1013/14 and -/16 of 5 July and 2 August 1952; WY 1013/24 of 21 November 1952; see also MAE, EU 32-8-13 and 14, old vol. 43 *passim*; see also USNA, RG 85, Belgrade, Yugoslavia, 1950-1954, Box no. 4, *passim*; PRO, FO 371/107815, WY 1013/5 of 27 February 1953.

143. MAE, EU 32-8-1, old vol. 25, letter no. 1304/EU from Belgrade, 13 November 1951.

144. See also: Alvin Rubinstein, *Yugoslavia and the Non-aligned World* (Princeton, N.J.: Princeton University Press, 1970), p. 39ff.

Bibliography

Interviews

Mr. George V. Allen Jr., Washington, D.C., August 1985
M. Burin de Roziers, Paris, September 1986
Dr. John Campbell, Cohassett, Massachusetts, September 1985
Admiral Carney, Washington, D.C., August 1985
Mr. Ernest Davies, London, June 1984
Dr. Louis Dollot, Paris, August 1986
M. Jean Gueury, Pourville-sur-Mer, Normandy, September 1986
Admiral Irvin, Washington, D.C., September 1985
Mr. Hilary King, Glasgow, September 1986, and Oxford, June 1987
M. Jean Laloy, Meudon, September 1986
Dr. Le Breton, Paris, August 1986
Sir Fitzroy Maclean, London, February 1985, and Strachur, April 1985
Lady Peake, Hampton Court, November 1984
Général Renault, Paris, September 1986
Sir Denis Wright, Aylesbury, Buckinghamshire, June 1986

Archives and Private Papers

Public Records Office, Ruskin Avenue, Kew, Richmond, Surrey (referred to as **PRO** in Notes): British governmental papers and Western Union papers
Papers of Mr. Ernest Davies, London
Papers of Sir Denis Wright, Aylesbury, Buckinghamshire
United States, State Department, individual documents declassified at the author's request in 1986 and 1987
National Archives of the United States, Washington, D.C. (referred to as **USNA** in Notes): Diplomatic Branch, Military Branch, and NSC papers
National Archives of the United States, Suitland, Maryland (also referred to as **USNA**: N.B. different Record Groups [**RG**])
Harry S. Truman Library, Independence, Missouri (referred to as **TL** in Notes)
Sully Mudd Library, Princeton University, Princeton, New Jersey
Stirling Memorial Library, Yale University, New Haven, Connecticut
Archives Diplomatiques, Ministère des Affaires Etrangères, Quai d'Orsay, Paris (referred to as **MAE** in Notes)
Archives Nationales, Paris (referred to as **AN** in Notes)
Archives Economiques et Financières, Paris
Archives de l'Armée de Terre, Château de Vincennes, Vincennes
Archives du Maréchal de Lattre, c/o la Maréchale de Lattre, Paris
Archive des Auswärtigen Amts, Bonn

Bibliography

Unpublished Primary Sources

John C. Campbell, "Oral History", recorded by Richard D. McKenzie for the Harry S. Truman Library, 24 June 1974

Edvard Kardelj, "Le Vatican dans la Lutte contre la Yougoslavie" (Typescript, Bibliothèque Nationale, 18 December 1952)

Published Primary Sources

A. Government Documents

Assemblée Nationale, *Débats (Journal Officiel)* (Paris: Imprimerie des Journaux Officiels, 1948-1953)

Thomas Etzold and John L. Gaddis (eds.), *Containment — Documents on American Policy and Strategy, 1945-1950* (New York: Columbia University Press, 1978)

House of Commons Debates, 1948-1953, various volumes

Ministère des Affaires Etrangères de la République Populaire Féderative de la Yougoslavie: *Livre Blanc sur les Procédés Agressifs des Gouvernements de l'URSS, de Pologne, de Tchéchoslovaquie, de Hongrie, de Roumanie, de Bulgarie et de l'Albanie envers la Yougoslavie* (Belgrade, 1951)

United States, Department of State, *Foreign Relations of the United States* (Washington, D.C.: U.S. Government Printing Office, various years) referred to as *FRUS* in Notes

——Declassified documents, microfiches (various years)

——Joint Chiefs of Staff and NSC documents, on microfilms, available in University of London, King's College, Liddell Hart Archives

B. Other Contemporary Documents

Robert Bass and Elizabeth Marbury (eds.), *The Soviet-Yugoslav Controversy: A Documentary Record* (New York: Prospect Books for the East European Institute, 1952). These documents are also printed in *The Soviet-Yugoslav Dispute — Letters and Communiqués* (London: Royal Institute of International Affairs, November 1948)

Henry M. Christman (ed.), *The Essential Tito* (Newton Abbot, Devon: David & Charles, 1971)

Clark M. Clifford, "American Relations with the Soviet Union - A Report to the President by the Special Counsel to the President" (Reproduction Branch, Department of State, 24 September 1946); also in Arthur Krock's *Memoirs* (see below)

Stephen Clissold (ed.), *Yugoslavia and the Soviet Union, 1939-1973: A Documentary Survey* (London: Oxford University Press for the Royal Institute of International Affairs, 1975)

Bibliography

Vladimir Dedijer, *Tito Speaks — His Self-Portrait and Struggle with Stalin* (London: Weidenfeld & Nicolson, 1953)

——*Tito* (New York: Simon & Schuster, 1953)

Dominique Desanti, *Masques et Visages de Tito et des Siens* (Paris: Eds. du Pavillon, préf. d'André Wurmser, 1949)

Thomas H. Etzold and John L. Gaddis (eds.), *Containment — Documents on American Policy and Strategy, 1945-1950* (New York: Columbia University Press, 1978)

R. Barry Farrell, *Jugoslavia and the Soviet Union, 1948-1956: an Analysis With Documents* (Hamden, Ct.: Shoestring Press, 1956)

Agnès Humbert, *Vu et Entendu en Yougoslavie* (Paris: Deux Rives, 1950)

Jiri Pelikan, *The Czecholovak Political Trials, 1950-1954: the Suppressed Reports of the Dubcek Government Commission of Inquiry, 1968* (London: Macdonald, 1970)

Jean-Claude Servan Schreiber, *Retour de Yougoslavie* (Paris: Pamphlets les Echos, 105, December 1951)

The Soviet-Yugoslav Dispute (London: Royal Institute of International Affairs, London, November 1948)

Josip Broz Tito, *Le Front Populaire* (Paris: Eds. Sociales, May 1948)

Svetozar Vukmanović ("Tempo"), *How and Why the People's Liberation Struggle of Greece Met with Defeat* (London: originally 1949; Merlin Press, 1985)

C. Diaries, Letters, Memoirs

Dean Acheson, *Present at the Creation — My Years at the State Department* (New York: W.W. Norton, 1952)

——*Sketches from Life* (London: Hamish Hamilton, 1961)

Clement R. Attlee, *As It Happened* (London: Heinemann, 1954)

Vincent Auriol, *Journal du Septennat, 1947-1954*, 6 vols. (vol. 4 for 1950 does not exist) (Paris: Armand Colin, 1977)

The Earl of Avon (Anthony Eden), *The Eden Memoirs: Facing the Dictators* (London: Cassell, 1962) and *Full Circle* (London: Cassell, 1960)

Sir Rhoderick Barclay, *Ernest Bevin and the Foreign Office* (London: Butler & Tanner, 1975)

Charles Bohlen, *Witness to History, 1929-1969* (New York: W.W. Norton, 1973)

Arthur Bryant, *The Triumph in the West 1943-1946: Based on the Diaries and Autobiographical Notes of Field Marshal the Viscount Alanbrooke* (London: Collins, 1959)

James F. Byrnes, *Speaking Frankly* (London: William Heinemann, 1947)

Georges Catroux, *J'ai vu tomber le Rideau de Fer — Moscou 1945-1948, Récits et Souvenirs* (Paris: Hachette, 1952)

Hugh Dalton, *High Tide and After.* vol. 3 *of Memoirs (1945-1960)* (London: Frederick Muller, 1962)

Bibliography

F. William Deakin, *The Embattled Mountain* (London: Oxford University Press, 1971)

Vladimir Dedijer, *The Battle Stalin Lost — Memoirs of Yugoslavia 1948-1953* (New York: Universal Library, Grosset & Dunlap, 1972)

Milovan Djilas, *Conversations with Stalin* (London: Rupert Hart-Davis, 1962)

——*Tito — Eine Kritische Biographie* (Wien: Fritz Molden Verlag, 1980)

——*Rise and Fall* (London: Macmillan, 1983)

Jacques Dumaine, *Quai d'Orsay* (London: Chapman & Hall, 1958)

Lawrence Durrell, *Esprit de Corps* (London: Faber & Faber, 1957)

Dwight D. Eisenhower, *The White House Years: Mandate for Change, 1953-1956* (London: William Heinemann, 1963)

Robert H. Ferrell (ed.), *Off the Record: The Private Papers of Harry S. Truman* (New York: Harper & Row, 1980)

——(ed.), *The Eisenhower Diaries* (New York: W.W.Norton, 1981)

——(ed.), *Dear Bess: The Letters of Harry to Bess Truman, 1910-1959* (New York: W.W. Norton, 1983)

Baron Gladwyn (H.M.G.Jebb), *The Memoirs of Lord Gladwyn* (London: Weidenfeld & Nicolson, 1972)

Louis J. Halle, *The Cold War as History* (London: Chatto & Windus, 1967)

Sir William G. Hayter, *A Double Life* (London: Hamish Hamilton, 1974)

Nicholas Henderson, *The Birth of NATO* (London: Weidenfeld & Nicolson, 1982)

Frank L. Howley, *Berlin Command* (New York: G.P.Putnam's, 1950)

Edvard Kardelj, *Reminiscences: The Struggle for Recognition and Independence — the New Yugoslavia, 1944-1957* (London: Blonds & Briggs, Summerfield Press, 1982)

George F. Kennan, *Memoirs, 1925-1950* (London: Hutchinson, 1968)

——*Memoirs, 1950-1963* (London: Hutchinson, 1973)

Nikita Khrushchev, *Khrushchev Remembers* (London: Sphere Books Ltd., after André Deutsch, 1971)

Béla K. Király, "The Hungarian Revolution and Soviet Readiness to Wage War against Socialist States" in Király, Barbara Lotze and Nandor Dreisziger (eds.), *The First War between Socialist States: The Hungarian Revolution of 1956 and its Impact* (New York: Social Science Monographs, Brooklyn College Press, distributed by Columbia University Press, 1984)

Arthur C. Krock, *Memoirs: Intimate Recollections of Twelve American Presidents from Theodore Roosevelt to Richard Nixon* (London, Cassell, 1968)

Jenny Lee, *My Life with Nye* (London: Jonathan Cape, 1980)

Wolfgang Leonhard, *Child of the Revolution* (London: Collins, 1957)

Sir Fitzroy H. Maclean, *Eastern Approaches* (London: Jonathan Cape, 1949)

René Massigli, *Une Comédie des Erreurs, 1943-1956* (Paris: Plon, 1978)

Merle Miller, *Plain Speaking: An Oral Biography of Harry S. Truman* (London: Victor Gollancz, 1974)

Walter Millis (ed.), *The Forrestal Diaries* (London: Cassell, 1952)

Bibliography

Jean Mons, *Sur les Routes de l'Histoire: Cinquante Ans au Service de l'Etat* (Paris: Eds. Albatros, 1982)

Lord Moran, *Winston Churchill, the Struggle for Survival, 1940-1965* (London: Constable, 1966)

Sir Harold Nicolson, *Diplomacy*. (London: Oxford University Press, 3rd edn, 1963)

Nigel Nicolson (ed.), *Sir Harold Nicolson, Diaries and Letters, 1945-1962* (London: Collins, 1968)

Paul Nitze, "The Development of NSC 68", *International Security*, IV 4 (1979-1980), pp. 170-176

Anthony Nutting, *No End of a Lesson — The Story of Suez* (London: Constable, 1967)

K. M. Panikkar, *In Two Chinas — Memoirs of a Diplomat* (London: Allen & Unwin, 1955)

Lester Pearson, *Memoirs 1948-1957: The International Years*, vol. 2 (London: Victor Gollancz, 1974)

Kim Philby, *My Silent War* (New York: Ballantyne Books, 1968)

Eugenio Reale, *Avec Jacques Duclos au Banc des Accusés: A la Réunion du Kominform à Szklarska Poreba (22-27 septembre 1947)* (Paris: Plon, 1958)

——"The Founding of the Cominform" in Milorad M. Drachkovitch and Branko Lazitch (eds.), *The Comintern: Historical Highlights* (New York: F. A. Praeger for the Hoover Institute, 1966), pp. 253-268

Robert Schuman, *Pour L'Europe* (Paris: Nagel, 1963)

François Seydoux, *Memoires d'Outre-Rhin.* (Paris: Bernard Grasset, 1975)

Evelyn Shuckburgh, *Descent to Suez: Diaries, 1951-56* (London: Weidenfeld & Nicolson, 1986)

Walter Bedell Smith, *Moscow Mission 1946-1949* (London: Heinemann, 1950)

Charles G. Stefan, "The Emergence of the Soviet-Yugoslav Break: A Personal View from the Belgrade Embassy", *Diplomatic History*, VI (1982), pp. 387-404

Cyrus L. Sulzberger, *A Long Row of Candles — Memoirs and Diaries, 1934-1954* (London: Macdonald, 1969)

Béla Szász, *Volunteers for the Gallows - Anatomy of a Show-Trial* (London: Chatto & Windus, 1971)

Harry S. Truman, *Memoirs: Years of Trial and Hope*, vol. 2 (London: Hodder & Stoughton, 1956)

Arthur Vandenberg Jr. (ed.), *The Papers of Senator Vandenberg.* (Boston: Houghton Mifflin, 1952)

Francis Williams (ed.), *A Prime Minister Remembers — The War and Post-War Memoirs of Earl Attlee.* (London: Heinemann, 1961)

Philip William (ed.), *The Diary of Hugh Gaitskell, 1945-1956* (London: Jonathan Cape, 1983)

Wu Xiuquan, *Eight Years in the Ministry of Foreign Affairs (January 1950-October 1958) Memoirs of a Diplomat.* (Beijing: New World Press, 1985)

Bibliography

D. Newspapers and Contemporary Journals

The Birmingham Post
The Daily Graphic
The Daily Mail
The Daily Telegraph
The Economist
Esprit
The Express
Le Figaro
For a Lasting Peace,
   For a People's Democracy

L'Humanité
The Manchester Guardian
Le Monde
Newsweek
The New York Herald Tribune
The New York Times
The Spectator
Time and Life
The Times (London)
The Washington Post

Secondary Works

Louis Adamic, *The Eagle and the Roots* (New York: Doubleday, 1952)

Anthony Adamthwaite, "Britain and the World, 1945-49: the View from the Foreign Office", *International Affairs*, LXI 2 (Spring 1985), pp. 223-235

Hannes Adomeit, *Soviet Risk Taking and Crisis Behaviour* (London: George Allen & Unwin, 1982)

—— and Robert Boardman (eds.), *Foreign Policy Making in Communist Countries* (Westmead: Saxon House, 1979)

Agence Yougoslave d'Information, *La Coopération Culturelle entre la France et la Yougoslavie* (Paris: Service de Presse et Documentation, 1956)

G.M. Alexander, *The Prelude to the Truman Doctrine: British Policy in Greece, 1944-1947* (Oxford: Clarendon Press, 1982)

Graham T. Allison, *Essence of Decision — Explaining the Cuban Missile Crisis* (Boston: Little, Brown, 1971)

Percy A. Allum, *The Italian Communist Party since 1945: Grandeurs and Servitude of an European Strategy* (Reading: Occasional Publication of the University of Reading Graduate School of Contemporary European Studies, 1970)

Gamael Abraham Almond and G. Bingham Powell, *Comparative Politics: A Developmental Approach* (Boston: Little, Brown, 1966)

Stephen E. Ambrose, *Eisenhower — the President, 1952-1969* (London: Allen & Unwin, 1984)

Grant Amyot, *The Italian Communist Party — The Crisis of the Popular Front Strategy* (London: Croom Helm, 1981)

M. Andereth, *The French Communist Party — A Critical History, 1920-1984* (Manchester: Manchester University Press, 1984)

Christopher Andrew, *Secret Service — the Making of the British Intelligence Community* (London: Heinemann, 1985)

—— and David Dilks (eds.), *The Missing Dimension — Governments and Intelligence Communities in the 20th Century* (London: Macmillan, 1984)

Hamilton Fish Armstrong, *Tito and Goliath* (London: Victor Gollancz,

Bibliography

1951)

Drago Arsenijevic, *Un Voyage Oublié* (Paris: Eds. France Empire, 1976)

Sidney Aster, *Anthony Eden* (London: Weidenfeld & Nicolson, 1976)

Phyllis Auty, *Yugoslavia* (Norwich: Jarrold for Thames & Hudson, 1965)

Jean Balliou (ed.), *Les Affaires Etrangères et le Corps Diplomatique (Histoire de l'Administration Française)* (Paris: Eds. du Centre National de la Recherche Scientifique, 1984)

Elisabeth Barker, *Macedonia, Its Place in Balkan Power Politics* (London: Royal Institute of International Affairs, 1950)

——*British Policy in South-East Europe in the Second World War* (London: Macmillan, 1976)

——*Churchill and Eden at War* (London: Macmillan, 1978)

——*The British Between the Superpowers, 1945-1950* (London: Macmillan, 1983)

——"Yugoslav Policy Towards Greece, 1947-1949", in Lars Baerentzen, John Iatrides and Ole Smith (eds.), *Studies in the History of the Greek Civil War, 1945-1949* (Copenhagen, Museum Tusculanum Press, 1987), pp. 263-295

—— "The Yugoslavs and the Greek Civil War 1946-1949", ibid., pp.297-308

—— "Tito in 1954: Tightrope Walker or European Statesman" unpublished manuscript, 1985, by permission of the author

C.J. Bartlett, *The Long Retreat — a Short History of British Defence Policy, 1945-1970* (London: Macmillan/St. Martin's Press, 1972)

Milan Bartos, "Yugoslavia's struggle for equality", *Foreign Affairs*, XXVIII (April 1950), pp. 427-440.

John Baylis, "Britain, the Brussels Pact and the Continental Commitment", *International Affairs*, LX 4 (Autumn 1984)

James Bellini, *French Defence Policy* (London: Royal United Services Institute for Defence Studies, 1974)

Nora Beloff, *Tito's Flawed Legacy — Yugoslavia and the West, 1939-1984* (London: Victor Gollancz, 1985)

Barton J. Bernstein (ed.), *Politics of the Truman Administration* (New York: New York Viewpoints, 1974)

Nicholas Bethell, *The Great Betrayal — the Untold Story of Kim Philby's Biggest Coup* (London: Hodder & Stoughton, 1984)

Robert M. Blum, *Drawing the Line: the Origin of the American Containment Policy in East Asia* (New York: W.W. Norton, 1982)

——"Surprised by Tito: The Anatomy of an Intelligence Failure", *Diplomatic History XII* 1 (Winter 1988) pp. 39-57

Robert Boardman and A.J.R. Groom (eds.), *The Management of Britain's External Relations* (London: Macmillan, 1973)

C. Boborowski, *La Yougoslavie Socialiste* (Paris: Armand Colin for the Fondation Nationale des Sciences Politiques, 1956)

Frédéric Bon et al., *Le Communisme en France et en Italie*, 2 vols. (Paris: Armand Colin, 1969)

Oleg B. Borisow and B.T. Koloskow, *Soviet-Chinese Relations, 1945-1970* (Bloomington: Indiana University Press, 1975)

Franz Borkenau, *European Communism* (London: Faber & Faber, 1953)

Collette Bourdache, *Les Années Cinquante: la Vie Politique en France, l'Économie, les Relations Internationales, l'Union Française* (Paris: Fayard, 1980)

Claude Bourdet, *La Yougoslavie Ecartelée* (Paris: Conférences du Club Echos, no.81, 1949)

——*Le Schisme Yougoslave* (Paris: Eds. De Minuit, 1950)

Peter G. Boyle, "The British Foreign Office and American Foreign Policy, 1947-48", *American Studies*, XVI 3 (1982), pp. 373-389

Henry W. Brands Jr., "Redefining the Cold War: American Policy Towards Yugoslavia, 1948-1960", *Diplomatic History*, XI (Winter 1987), pp. 41-54

Jovan A. Brkitch et al. (eds.), *"Le Fédéralisme Yougoslave": la Lutte des Yougoslaves pour l'Europe et la Liberté, 1946-1955* (Paris: Eds. du Mouvement Fédérative Serbe, 1955)

Anthony Cave Brown (ed.), *Operation World War III: the Secret American Plan "DROPSHOT" for War with the Soviet Union, 1957.* (London: Arms and Armour, 1979)

Zbigniew Brzezinski, *The Soviet Bloc: Unity and Conflict* (Cambridge, Mass.: Harvard University Press, 1967, reprinted 1969)

Alan Bullock, *Ernest Bevin: Foreign Secretary, 1945-1951*, vol. 3 (Oxford, Oxford University Press, 1983, 1985 paperback)

Frederic S. Burin, "The Communist Doctrine of the Inevitability of War", *American Political Science Review*, LII 2 (1963)

Bernard Burrows and Geoffrey Edwards, *The Defence of Western Europe* (Thetford, Norfolk: Thetford Press for Butterworth Scientific, 1982)

Robert F. Byrnes (ed.), *Yugoslavia* (New York: Atlantic Books/Praeger, 1957)

John Campbell, *Tito's Separate Road — America and Yugoslavia in World Politics* (New York: Harper & Row, 1967)

——(ed.), *Successful Negotiation: Trieste 1954 — An Appraisal by the Five Participants* (Princeton N.J.: Princeton University Press, 1976)

David Carlton, *Anthony Eden — A Biography* (London: Allen Lane, 1981)

David Caute, *Communism and the French Intellectuals, 1914-1960* (London: André Deutsch, 1964)

Albert Chambon, *Mais que Font Donc ces Diplomates entre Deux Coctails* (Paris: Eds, A. Pedone, 1983)

Jacques Chapsal, *La Politique en France: de 1940 à 1948* (Paris: Presses Universitaires de France, 1984)

Harry Chase, "American-Yugoslav Relations, 1945-1956: A Study in the Motivations of U.S. Foreign Policy" (University of Syracuse, Social Science Ph. D. dissertation, 1957)

Chin O. Chung, *P'yongyang between Peking and Moscow: North Korea's Involvement in the Sino-Soviet Dispute, 1958-1975* (Alabama: University of Alabama Press, 1978)

Anton Ciliga, *La Yougoslavie sous la Menace Intérieure et Éxtérieure* (Paris, Iles d'Or, 1951)

Bibliography

Stephen Clissold, *Whirlwind — an Account of Marshal Tito's Rise to Power* (London: Cresset Press, 1949)

——*Djilas, the Progress of a Revolutionary* (Hounslow: Middx.: Maurice Temple Smith, 1983)

Kenneth Condit, *The History of the Joint Chiefs of Staff: 1947-1949*, vol. 2 (Joint Secretariat, Joint Chiefs of Staff, Washington, D.C.; Wilmington, Glazier, 1979)

John Connell, *The 'Office' — A Study of British Foreign Policy and its Makers, 1919-1951* (London: Allan Wingate, 1958)

Theodore A. Couloumbis, *Greek Political Reaction to American and NATO Influences* (New Haven: Yale University Press, 1966)

Paul Courtier, *La Quatrième République* (Paris: Presses Universitaires de France, 3rd edn. 1983)

Michael Cox, "The Rise and Fall of the 'Soviet Threat'", *Political Studies* XXXIII (1985), pp. 484-498

Bruce Cumings (ed.), *Child of Conflict: the Korean-American Relationship, 1943-1953* (Seattle: University of Washington Press, 1983)

Louis Dalmas, *Le Communisme Yougoslave depuis la Rupture avec Moscou* (Paris: Terre des Hommes — Documents, 1950)

Peter Danylow, *The Aussenpolitischen Beziehungen Albaniens zu Jugoslawien und zur UdSSR, 1944-1961* (Munich: Oldenbourg Verlag, 1982)

Philip Darby, *British Defence Policy East of Suez, 1947-1968* (Oxford: Oxford University Press for the Royal Institute of International Affairs, 1973)

Lynn Etheridge Davis, *The Cold War Begins: Soviet-American Conflict over Eastern Europe* (Princeton N.J.: Princeton University Press, 1974)

Karen Dawisha, *The Kremlin and the Prague Spring* (Berkeley: University of California Press, 1984)

Guy de Carmoy, *The Foreign Policy of France, 1944-1968* (Chicago: University of Chicago Press, 1970)

Diego de Castro, *La Questione di Trieste: l'Azione Politica e Diplomatica Italiana dal 1943 al 1954*, 2 vol. (Trieste: Lint, 1982)

Vladimir Dedijer et al., *History of Yugoslavia* (New York: McGraw-Hill, 1974, originally Belgrade 1972)

Paul-Marie de la Gorce, *La République et son Armée* (Paris: Fayard, 1963)

Ph. Aubert de Larue, "Le Neutralisme Yougoslave", *Politique Etrangère*, XXVI 4 (1961), pp. 327-342

Anne Deighton, "The Labour Government, the German Problem, and the Origins of the Cold War in Europe: a Study of the Council of Foreign Ministers, 1945-1947" (University of Reading, Ph.D. dissertation, 1987)

Lois Pattison de Menil, *Who Speaks for Europe? The Vision of Charles de Gaulle* (London: Weidenfeld & Nicolson, 1977)

A.W. DePorte, *Europe between the Superpowers — the Enduring Balance* (New Haven: Yale University Press, 1979)

Dominique Desanti, *Les Staliniens, 1944-1956, une Expérience Politique* (Paris: Anthème Fayard, 1975)

Isaac Deutscher, *Stalin, a Political Biography* (London: Oxford University Press, 2nd edn., 1967)

Bibliography

Marcel de Vos, *Histoire de la Yougoslavie* (Paris: Presses Universitaires de France, 2e edn 1965)

Piers Dixon and Corinna Hamilton, *Double Diploma: the Life of Sir Pierson Dixon — Don and Diplomat* (London: Hutchinson, 1968)

Veselin Djurdjevac, *La Yougoslavie: Socialisme et Non-alignment* (Paris: le Sycomore, 1983)

Michael Dockrill, "The Foreign Office, Anglo-American Relations and the Korean War, June 1950-June 1951", *International Affairs*, LXII 3 (1986), pp. 459-476

Bernard Donoughue and G.W. Jones, *Herbert Morrison: Portrait of a Politician* (London: Weidenfeld & Nicolson, 1973)

Georges Dupeux, *La France de 1945 à 1965* (Paris: Armand Colin, 1969)

Jean-Baptiste Duroselle and André Siegfried (eds.); *La Politique Étrangère et ses Fondements* (Paris: Armand Colin, 1954)

Jean-Baptiste Duroselle, *Le Conflit de Trieste, 1943-1954* (Brussels, Eds. de l'Institut de Sociologie de l'Université Libre de Bruxelles, 1966)

——*France and the United States, from the Beginnings to the Present* (Chicago: University of Chicago Press, 1976)

Maurice Duverger, *The French Political System* (Chicago: University of Chicago Press, 1958)

Fadil Ekmecic, *La Présence Yougoslave en France depuis 100 Ans* (Paris: Yougofranc, 1981)

Georgette Elgey, *Histoire de la IVe République*, 2 vols. (Paris: Fayard, 1965 and 1968)

Jean Ellenstein, *Le P.C.* (Paris: Bernard Grasset, 1976)

Herbert J. Ellison (ed.), *The Sino-Soviet Dispute — a Global Perspective* (Seattle: University of Washington Press, 1982)

Paul Ely, *L'Armée dans la Nation* (Paris: Fayard, 1961)

Matthew Evangelista, "Stalin's Postwar Army Reappraised", *International Security* (Winter 1982/83)

Herbert Feis, *From Trust to Terror: The Onset of the Cold War, 1945-1950* (London: Anthony Blond, 1970)

François Fejtö, *Chine-URSS: la Fin d'une hégémonie — les Origines du Grand Schisme Communiste, 1950-1957* (Paris, Plon, 1964)

——*Chine-URSS, de l'Alliance au Conflit, 1950-1957* (Paris: Eds. du Seuil, 1973)

Louis Fischer, *The Road to Yalta: Soviet Foreign Relations, 1941-1945* (New York: Harper & Row, 1972)

D.F. Fleming, *The Cold War and its Origins, 1917-1960*, 2 vols. (London: Allen & Unwin, 1961)

Martin H. Folly, "Britain and the Issue of Italian Membership of NATO, 1948-1949", *Review of International Studies*, XIII (1987), pp. 177-196

Dingle Foot, "Le Pacte Balkanique", *Revue de la Politique Mondiale*, 93 (Belgrade, 1954)

Michael Foot, *Aneurin Bevan: A Biography: 1945-1960*, vol. 2 (London: Davis-Poynter, 1973)

Rosemary Foot, *The Wrong War — American Policy and the Dimensions of the Korean Conflict, 1950-1953* (Ithaca: Cornell University Press,

Bibliography

1985)

Joseph Frankel, *The Making of Foreign Policy: An Analysis of Decision-Making* (London: Oxford University Press, 1963)

——*British Foreign Policy, 1945-1973* (London: Oxford University Press for the Royal Institute of International Affairs, 1975)

——*International Relations in a Changing World* (Oxford: Oxford University Press, 1979)

Lawrence Freedman, *Britain and Nuclear Weapons* (London: Macmillan for the Royal Institute of International Affairs, 1980)

——*The Evolution of Nuclear Strategy* (London: Macmillan, 1981)

John Lewis Gaddis, *The United States and the Origins of the Cold War, 1941-1947* (New York: Columbia University Press, 1972)

——"Was the Truman Doctrine a Real Turning Point?", *Foreign Affairs* LII (January 1974)

——"Containment, a Reassessment", *Foreign Affairs*, LV (1976-77), pp. 873-887

——"NSC 68 and the Problems of Ends and Means", *International Security*, IV 4 (1979-1980), pp. 164-170

——*Strategies of Containment — A Critical Appraisal of Postwar American National Security Policy* (New York: Oxford University Press, 1982)

Robert Garson, "The Role of Eastern Europe in America's Containment Policy, 1945-1948", *Journal of American Studies*, XIII (1979)

Kurt Gasteyger (ed.), *Die Feindlichen Brüder: Jugoslaviens Neuer Konflikt mit dem Ostblock, 1958* (Bern: Dr. Peter Sager, 1960)

Dietrich Geyer (ed.), *Sowjetunion, Aussenpolitik, 1917-1955* (Cologne: Böhlau Verlag, 1972)

Marc Gjidara, "La Politique extérieure de la Yougoslavie", *Notes et Etudes Documentaires*, no. 4354-4355 (Paris, la Documentation Française, 1977)

Joachim Glaubitz, *China und die Sowjetunion: Aufbau und Zerfall einer Allianz* (Hannover: Niedersächsische Landeszentrale für Politische Bildung, 1973)

François Goguel and Alfred Grosser, *La Politique en France* (Paris: Armand Colin, 8th edn. 1980)

André Goral, *Où Va la Chine? Un Travail de Sisyphe* (Paris: Eds. Renée Lacoste, 1956)

Léon Gouré, "Soviet Limited War Doctrine" (RAND Corporation, California, discourse delivered on 11th Military Operations Research Symposium, 1 May 1963)

William Edgar Griffith, *Cold War and Coexistence: Russia, China and the United States* (Englewood Cliffs, N.J.: 1971)

——*Peking, Moscow and Beyond: the Sino-Soviet-American Triangle* (Washington, D.C.: Centre for Strategic and International Studies, Georgetown University, Washington Papers 6, 1973)

A.A. Gromyko and B.N. Ponomarev (eds.), *Soviet Foreign Policy 1945-1980*, vol. 2 (Moscow: Progress, 1981)

Charles Grosbois, *La Chine en Nouvelle Democratie* (Rome: Instituto Italiano per il Medio ed Estremo Oriente, 1954)

Bibliography

Alfred Grosser, *La IVe République et sa Politique Éxtérieure* (Paris: Armand Colin, 1961)

——*Affaires Extérieures: la Politique de la France, 1944-1984* (Saint Amand-Motrand (Cher): Flammarion, 1984)

——*The Western Alliance — European-American Relations since 1945* (London: Macmillan, 1980)

John Michael Guhin, *John Foster Dulles: A Statesman and his Times* (New York: Columbia University Press, 1972)

Jacques Guillermaz, *Le Parti Communiste Chinois au Pouvoir, 1949-1972* (Paris: Payot, 1972)

Klaus Hänsch, *Frankreich zwischen Ost und West* (Berlin: De Gruyter, 1972)

Jon Halliday, "Anti-Communism and the Korean War", *The Socialist Register* (London: Merlin Press, 1984), pp. 130-163

Hugh B. Hammett, "America's Non-Policy in Eastern Europe and the Origins of the Cold War", *Survey*, XIX 4 (1973), p. 144 ff.

Paul Y. Hammond, *The Cold War Years: American Foreign Policy since 1945* (New York: Harcourt, Brace & World, 1969)

Thomas T. Hammond (ed.), *The Anatomy of Communist Takeovers* (New Haven: Yale University Press, 1975)

D.L. Hanley, A.P. Kerr and N.H. Waites, *Contemporary France: Politics and Society since 1945* (London: Henley, Routledge & K. Paul, rev. edn., 1984)

Kenneth Harris, *Attlee* (London: Weidenfeld & Nicolson, 1982)

Michael M. Harrison, *The Reluctant Ally: France and Atlantic Security* (Baltimore: Johns Hopkins University Press, 1981)

Robert Hathaway, "Truman, Tito and the Politics of Hunger" in William Levantrosser (ed.), *Harry S. Truman: The Man from Independence* (Westport, Ct.: Greenwood Press, 1986)

Irena Reuter-Hendrichs, *Jugoslawische Aussenpolitik 1948-1968* (Cologne: Carl Heymanns Verlag, 1976)

Guy Hentsch, *Staline Négotiateur: Une Diplomatie de Guerre* (Neuchâtel, Eds. de la Baconnière, 1967)

Jôrg K. Hoensch, *Sowjetische Osteuropapolitik, 1945-1975* (Kronberg/Ts.: Athenäum/Droste Taschenbücher, 1977)

George W. Hoffman and Fred Warner Neal, *Yugoslavia and the New Communism* (New York: 20th Century Fund, 1962)

Erik P. Hoffmann and Frederic J. Fleron (eds.), *The Conduct of Soviet Foreign Policy* (London: Butterworths, 1971)

Ole R. Holsti and Alexander L. George, "The Effects of Stress on the Performance of Foreign Policy Makers", *Political Science Annual.*, VI (1975), pp. 255-308

Townsend Hoopes, *The Devil and John Foster Dulles* (London: André Deutsch, 1973)

René Hostiou, *Robert Schuman et l'Europe* (Paris: Cujas, 1969)

Michael Howard, *The Mediterranean Strategy in the Second World War* (London: Weidenfeld & Nicolson, 1968)

——(ed.), *Restraints on War: Studies in the Limitation of Armed Conflict* (Oxford: Oxford University Press, 1979)

Robert Hunter, *Security in Europe* (London: Elek Books, 1969)

Bibliography

Robert Strausz-Hupé, "Yugoslav Counteroffensive in the Cold War", *The Yale Review*, XL (December 1950), pp. 273-284

——"The United States and Yugoslavia: A Reappraisal", *The Yale Review*, XLV (December 1955), pp. 161-177

Richard H. Immermann, "Eisenhower and Dulles: Who Made the Decisions?", *Political Psychology*, I (Autumn 1979), pp. 3-20

Ghita Ionescu, *The Breakup of the Soviet Empire in Eastern Europe* (Harmondsworth: Penguin, 1965)

Egbert Jahn (ed.), *Soviet Foreign Policy — its Social and Economic Conditions* (London: Allison & Busby, 1978)

Robert V. Rhodes James, *Anthony Eden* (London: Weidenfeld & Nicolson, 1986)

Novak Jankovic, "The Changing Role of the U.S. in Financing Yugoslav Economic Development since 1945" (paper presented at the Symposium "Policy Options of American Governments" at the John F. Kennedy Institute, Free University, Berlin, July 1987)

Roy Jenkins, *Truman* (London: Collins, 1986)

Robert Jervis, "The Impact of the Korean War on the Cold War", *Journal of Conflict Resolution*, XXIV 4 (December 1980), pp. 563-592

A. Ross Johnson, *The Transformation of Communist Ideology: the Yugoslav Case, 1945-1953* (Cambridge: Mass, the MIT Press, 1972)

——*The U.S. Stake in Yugoslavia, 1948-1968* (California: Southern California Arms Control and Foreign Policy Seminar, 1972)

Chalmers A. Johnson, *Peasant Nationalism and Communist Power: the Emergence of Revolutionary China, 1937-1945* (Stanford, Ca.: Stanford University Press, 1962)

Peter M. Jones, "British Defence Policy: the Breakdown of Inter-Party Consensus", *Review of International Studies*, XIII 2 (April 1987), pp. ·111-132

Peter Jones and Siân Kevill (eds.), *China and the Soviet Union, 1949-1984* (London: Keesing's International Studies, 1985)

R.B. Manderson-Jones, *The Special Relationship: Anglo-American Relations and Western European Unity, 1947-1956* (New York: Crane, Russak for the London School of Economics, 1972)

Robert S. Jordan, *The NATO International Staff/Secretariat 1952-1957* (London: Oxford University Press, 1957)

Aleksandar Jovanovic, *Le Système Socio-Politique Yougoslave* (Belgrade, Medjunarodna Politika no. 31, 1969)

Jacques Juillard, *La IVe République: 1947-1958* (Paris: Le Livre de Poche Ed. Revue, 1981)

Karel Kaplan, *A Victory for Democracy, Czechoslovakia 1945-1948* (Prague: Orbis, 1963)

——*Dans les Archives du Comité Central: 30 Ans de Secrets du Bloc Soviétique* (Paris: Eds. Albin Michel, 1978)

——*Procès Politiques à Prague* (England: Chaucer Press, Eds. Complexe, 1980)

——*Der Kurze Marsch, die Kommunistische Machtübernahme in der Tschechoslowakei, 1945-1948* (Munchen: R. Oldenbourg Verlag, 1981)

——*Political Persecutions in Czechoslovakia, 1948-1972* (Munich:

Research-Project "Crises in Soviet-type Systems", 1983)

——*Unterwanderung, Gleichschaltung und Vernichtung der Tschechoslowakischen Sozialdemokratie, 1944-1954* (Wuppertal: POL Verlag, 1984)

Lawrence S. Kaplan, *A Community of Interests: NATO and the Military Assistance Program, 1948-1951* (Washington D.C.: Office of the Secretary of Defense, Historical Office, 1980)

Stephen S. Kaplan, *Diplomacy of Power — Soviet Armed Forces as a Political Instrument* (Washington D.C.: Brookings Institution, 1981)

Michael Kaser, *COMECON, Integration Problems of the Planned Economies* (London: Oxford University Press, 2nd edn., 1967)

Curtis Keeble, "The Roots of Soviet Foreign Policy", *International Affairs*, LX 4 (Autumn 1984), pp. 561-578

——(ed.), *The Soviet State — the Domestic Roots of Soviet Foreign Policy* (London: Gower for the Royal Institute of International Affairs, 1985)

Richard Kindersley (ed.), *In Search of Eurocommunism* (London: Macmillan, 1981)

Robert Knight, "Die Kärtner Grenzfrage und der Kalte Krieg", *Carinthia*, I (1985), pp. 323-340

Siegfried Kogelfranz, *Das Erbe von Jalta — die Opfer und die Davongekommenen* (Reinbeck bei Hamburg: Spiegel Verlag, Rowohlt, 1985)

Dimitrios G. Kousoulas, *The Price of Freedom: Greece in World Affairs, 1939-1953* (Syracuse: Syracuse University Press, 1953)

——"The Truman Doctrine and the Stalin-Tito Rift: A Reappraisal", *South Atlantic Quarterly*, LXXII (Summer 1973)

Bennett Kovrig, *The Myth of Liberation: East-Central Europe in U.S. Diplomacy and Politics since 1941* (Baltimore: Johns Hopkins University Press, 1973)

Annie Kriegel, *Les Communistes Français* (Paris: Seuil, 1968)

Walter La Feber, *America, Russia and the Cold War, 1945-1967* (New York: John Wiley & Sons, 1967)

Mathilde Landercy, *Le Cardinal Stepinac: Martyr de ses Droits de l'Homme* (Paris: Apostolat des Editions, 1981)

Branko Lazitch, *Tito et la Révolution Yougoslave, 1937-1957* (Paris: Fasquelle Eds., 1957)

David D. Larson, *United States Foreign Policy towards Yugoslavia, 1943-1963* (Washington, D.C.: University Press of America, 1979, 1st edn 1965)

Derek Leebaert (ed.), *Soviet Military Thinking* (London: Allen & Unwin, 1981)

Lorraine M. Lees, "The American Decision to Assist Tito, 1948-1949", *Diplomatic History*, 2 (1978), pp. 407-422

——"American Foreign Policy Toward Yugoslavia, 1941-1949" (Pennsylvania State University, Ph.D. dissertation, 1976)

Melvyn P. Leffler et al., "American Conception of National Security and the Beginnings of the Cold War, 1945-1948", AHR Forum, 1983

René Lejeune, *Robert Schuman, une Ame pour l'Europe* (Paris: Eds. St.

Bibliography

Paul, 1986)

Jeannine Verdès-Leroux, *Au Service du Parti: Le Parti Communiste, les Intellectuels et la Culture (1944-1956)* (Paris: Eds. de Minuit, 1983)

Julian M. Lewis, "British Military Planning for Post-War Strategic Defence, 1942-1946" (Oxford University, D.Phil. dissertation, 1981)

Charles Edward Lindblom, *The Policy-Making Process* (Englewood Cliffs, N.J.: Prentice-Hall, 1968)

William Roger Louis, *The British Empire in the Middle East, 1945-1951: Arab Nationalism, the United States, and Postwar Imperialism* (Oxford: Clarendon Press, 1984, paperback 1985)

Peter Lowe, *The Origins of the Korean War* (London: Longman, 1986)

Geir Lundestadt, *The American Non-Policy towards Eastern Europe 1943-1947 — Universalism in an Area not of essential Interest to the United States* (Tromsö: Universitetsforlaget, 1978)

Peter Lyon, *Neutralism.* (Leicester: Leicester University Press, 1963)

William McCagg, *Stalin Embattled, 1943-1948* (Detroit: Wayne State University Press, 1978)

Neil McInnes, *The Communist Parties of Western Europe* (London: Oxford University Press for the Royal Institute of International Affairs, 1975)

Malcolm Mackintosh, *Juggernaut — A History of the Soviet Armed Forces* (London: Secker & Warburg, 1967)

David S. McLellan, *Dean Acheson: the State Department Years* (New York: Dodd, Mead, 1976)

Michael Mandelbaum, *The Nuclear Question: the United States and Nuclear Weapons, 1946-1976* (Cambridge: Cambridge University Press, 1979)

Lilly Marcou, *Le Kominform: le Communisme de Guerre Froide* (Paris: Presses de la Fondation Nationale des Sciences Politiques, 1977)

——*Le Mouvement Communiste International depuis 1945* (Paris: Presses Universitaires de France, 1980)

Eduard Mark, "The Question of Containment: A Reply to John Lewis Gaddis", *Foreign Affairs*, LVI (January 1978), pp. 430-440

Stephen C. Markovich, "American Foreign Policy and Yugoslav Foreign Policy", in Peter Potichnyj and Jane Shapiro (eds.), *From the Cold War to Detente* (New York: Praeger, 1976), pp. 78-96

——"The Influence of American Foreign Aid on Yugoslav Policies, 1948-1966" (University of Virginia, Ph.D. dissertation, 1968)

Voitech Mastny, *Russia's Road to the Cold War — Diplomacy, Warfare and the Politics of Communism, 1941-1945* (New York: Columbia University Press 1979)

——"Stalin and the Militarization of the Cold War", *International Security*, IX (Winter 1984/85), pp. 109-129

David Allan Mayers, *Cracking the Monolith: U.S. Policy against the Sino-Soviet Alliance, 1949-1955)* (Baton Rouge: Louisiana State University Press, 1986)

Klaus Mehnert, *Peking and Moscow* (New York: G.P. Putnam's, 1964)

Albert Meister, *Socialisme et Autogestion — l'Expérience yougoslave* (Paris:

Eds. du Seuil, 1964)

Ray Merrick, "The Russia Committee of the British Foreign Office and the Cold War, 1946-1947", *Journal of Contemporary History*, XX 3 (July 1985) pp. 453-468

Alexandre Metaxas, *Pékin contre Moscou* (Lausanne: Eds. Scriptar, 1959)

Pierre Miquel, *La Quatrième République: Hommes et Pouvoirs* (Paris: Bordas,1982)

Rudolf Mittendorfer, *Robert Schuman — Architekt des Neuen Europa* (Hildesheim: Georg Olm Verlag, 1983)

Jules Moch, *Yougoslavie: Terre d'Expériences* (Monaco-ville: Eds. du Rocher, 1953)

Valérie Anne Montassier, *Les Années d'après Guerre: 1944-1949: La Vie Politique en France, l'Économie, les Relations Internationales, l'Union Française* (Paris: Fayard, 1980)

Kenneth O. Morgan, *Labour in Power, 1945-1951* (Oxford: Clarendon Press, 1984)

Roger Morgan, "The Transatlantic Relationship", Kenneth J. Twitchett (ed.), *Europe and the World* (London: Lane, 1976)

Robert A. Mortimer, *The Third World Coalition in International Politics* (London: Westview Press, 2nd edn, 1984)

Leonard Mosley, *Dulles: A Biography of Eleanor, Allen & John Foster Dulles and their Family Network* (New York: Dial Press/James Wade, 1978)

Marcel-Edmond Naegelen, *Tito* (Paris: Flammarion, 1961)

Frank A. Ninkovich, *The Diplomacy of Ideas: US Foreign Policy and Cultural Relations, 1938-1950* (Cambridge: Cambridge University Press, 1981)

Joseph L. Nogee and Robert H. Donaldson, *Soviet Foreign Policy Since World War II* (Oxford: Pergamon Press, 1981)

F. S. Northedge, *Descent from Power: British Foreign Policy, 1945-1973* (London: Allen & Unwin, 1974)

Bogdan Novak, *Trieste, 1941-1954: The Ethnic, Political, and Ideological Struggle* (Chicago: University of Chicago Press, 1970)

Joseph S. Nye (ed.), *The Making of America's Soviet Policy* (New Haven, Ct.: Yale University Press, 1984)

L. Jay Oliva (ed.), *Russia and the West from Peter to Khrushchev* (Boston: D.C. Heath, 1965)

Ivo Omrćanin, *Enigma Tito* (Washington, D.C.: Samizdat, 1984)

Robert Endicott Osgood, *NATO, the Entangling Alliance* (Chicago: University of Chicago Press, 1962)

——*Limited War Revisited* (Boulder, Co.: Westview Press, Frederick A. Praeger, 1979)

Ritchie Ovendale, *The English-Speaking Alliance — Britain, the United States, the Dominions and the Cold War, 1945-1951* (Allen & Unwin, London, 1985)

——(ed.), *The Foreign Policy of the British Labour Governments, 1945-1951* (Bath: Pitman Press for Leicester University Press, 1984)

Stevan K. Pavlovitch, "The Grey Zone in NATO's Balkan Flank", *Survey* XXV 3 (Summer 1980), pp. 20-42

——*Unconventional Perceptions of Yugoslavia, 1940-1945* (New York:

Bibliography

East European Monographs no. CLXXXVIII, Columbia University Press, 1985)

Andrew J. Pierre, *Nuclear Politics: the British Experience with an Independent Strategic Force, 1939-1970* (London: Oxford University Press, 1972)

Joze Pirjevec, "Die Auseinandersetzung Tito-Stalin im Spiegel britischer diplomatischer Berichte", *Südostforschungen*, XL (1981), pp. 164-174

——*Tito, Stalin e l'Occidente* (Trieste: Editoriale Stampa Triestina, 1985)

Mosha Piyade, *About the Legend that the Yugoslav Uprising Owed its Existence to Soviet Assistance* (London, Yugoslav Information Service, 1950)

Raymond Poidevin, *Robert Schuman, Homme d'Etat* (Paris: Imprimerie Nationale, 1986)

Walter S. Poole, *The History of the Joint Chiefs of Staff, 1950-1952*, vol. 4 (Joint Secretariat, Joint Chiefs of Staff, Washington, D.C., December 1979; Wilmington, Glazier)

Milentije Popovitch, *Des Rapports Économiques entre États Socialistes* (Paris (?): le Livre Yougoslave, 1949)

Bruce D. Porter, *The USSR in Third World Conflicts — Soviet Arms and Diplomacy in Local Wars, 1945-1980* (Cambridge: Cambridge University Press, 1984)

John Prados, *The Soviet Estimate: U.S. Intelligence Analysis and Soviet Strategic Forces* (Princeton: New Jersey, Princeton University Press, 1982)

Peter P. Prifti, *Socialist Albania since 1944: Domestic and Foreign Policy Developments* (Cambridge, Mass.: the MIT Press, 1978)

George H. Quester, *Nuclear Diplomacy: the First 25 Years* (New York: Dunellen, 1970)

Catherine Quiminal, *La Politique Extérieure de la Chine* (Paris: Eds. François Maspero, Yenan Synthèses, 1975)

Gavriel D. Ra'anan, *International Policy Formation in the USSR — Factional 'Debate' during the Zhdanovshchina* (Hamden, Ct.: Archon Books, Shoe String Press, 1983)

David Reynolds, "A 'Special Relationship'? America, Britain and the International Order since the Second World War", *International Affairs*, LXII 1 (Winter 1985-86), pp. 1-20

Peter G. Richards, *Parliament and Foreign Affairs* (London: Allen & Unwin, 1967)

Jean-Pierre Rioux, *La France de la IVe République*, 2 vols. (Paris: Eds. du Seuil, 1980)

Olav Riste (ed.), *Western Security: the Formative Years — European and Atlantic Defence 1947-1953* (Oslo: Norwegian University Press, Universitetsforlaget, 1985)

Walter R. Roberts, *Tito, Mihailovic and the Allies, 1941-1945* (New Brunswick, N.J.: Rutgers University Press, 1973)

Philippe Robrieux, *Maurice Thorez — Vie Secrète et Vie Publique* (Paris: Fayard, 1975)

——*Histoire Intérieure du Parti Communiste Français 1945-1972*, vol 2

(Paris: Fayard, 1981)

Harry Rositzke, "America's Secret Operations: A Perspective", *Foreign Affairs*, LIII 2 (January 1975), pp. 334-351

Graham Ross (ed.), *The Foreign Office and the Kremlin* (Cambridge: Cambridge University Press, 1984)

Robert R. Rothstein, "Foreign Policy and Development: from Non-Alignment to International Class War", *International Affairs* LII 4 (October 1976), pp. 598-616

Victor Rothwell, *Britain and the Cold War, 1941-1947* (London: Jonathan Cape, 1982)

Alvin Z. Rubinstein, *Yugoslavia and the Nonaligned World* (Princeton: New Jersey, Princeton University Press, 1970)

——*Soviet Foreign Policy since World War II* (Cambridge, Mass.: Winthrop, 1981)

Dennison Rusinow, *The Yugoslav Experiment, 1948-1974* (London: C. Hurst for the Royal Institute of International Affairs, 1977)

Margit Sandner, *Französisch-Österreichische Beziehungen während der Besatzungszeit von 1947 bis 1955* (Vienna: Verband der Wissenschaftlichen Gesellschaften Österreichs, 1983)

Warner R. Schilling, Paul Y. Hammond and Glenn H. Snyder, *Strategy, Politics, and Defence Budgets* (New York: Columbia University Press, 1962)

A.W. Schlesinger, "Origins of the Cold War", *Foreign Affairs*, XLVI (1967), pp. 22-52

George Schöpflin, "Nationality in Yugoslav Politics", *Survey*, XXV 3 (Summer 1980), pp. 1-19

Stuart Schram (ed.), *Mao Tse-Tung Unrehearsed — Talks and Letters: 1956-1974* (Harmondsworth: Penguin Books, 1974)

Anthony Seldon, *Churchill's Indian Summer* (London: Hodder & Stoughton, 1981)

Avi Shlaim, Peter Jones and Keith Sainsbury, (eds.), *British Foreign Secretaries since 1945* (Newton Abbot: Devon, David & Charles, 1977)

Avi Shlaim, *The United States and the Berlin Blockade, 1948-1949: A Study in Crisis Decisionmaking* (Berkeley: University of California Press, 1983)

——"Britain, the Berlin Blockade and the Cold War", *International Affairs* (Winter 1983-84)

Marshall D. Shulman, *Stalin's Foreign Policy Reappraised* (Cambridge, Mass.: Harvard University Press, 1963)

Robert R. Simmons, *The Strained Alliance: Peking-Pyongyang-Moscow and the Politics of the Korean Civil War* (New York: Free Press/Macmillan, 1975)

Fred Singleton, *Twentieth Century Yugoslavia* (London: Macmillan, 1976)

Gaddis Smith, *Dean Acheson* (New York: Cooper Square, 1972)

Raymond Smith and John Zametica, "The Cold Warrior: Clement Attlee Reconsidered, 1945-7", *International Affairs*, LXI (1985), pp. 237-52

Richard C. Snyder, H.W. Bruck and Burton Sapin (eds.), *Foreign Policy*

Decision-Making (New York: Free Press of Glencoe, 1962)

William P. Snyder, *The Politics of British Defence Policy, 1945-1962* (Ohio: Ohio State University Press, Ernest Benn Ltd., 1964)

V.D.Sokolovskiy, *Soviet Military Strategy* (New York: Crane, Russak, 1975)

John Spanier, *American Foreign Policy since World War II* (New York: Holt, Rinehart & Winston, 9th edn., 1983)

Margaret Sprout and Harold Sprout, "Environmental Factors in the Study of International Politics", *Journal of Conflict Resolution*, I 4 (1957), pp. 309-328

W. Starlinger, *Derrière la Russie, la Chine* (Paris: Eds. Spes, 1957)

Zara Steiner, "Decision-making in American and British Foreign Policy: an Open and Shut Case", *Review of International Studies*, XIII 1 (1987) pp. 1-18

Lord Strang, *The Foreign Office* (London: Allen & Unwin, 1955)

——*Home and Abroad* (London: André Deutsch, 1956)

——*Britain and World Affairs — A Survey of the Fluctuation of British Power and Influence from Henry VIII to Elizabeth II* (London: Faber and André Deutsch, 1961)

——*The Diplomatic Career* (London: André Deutsch, 1962)

William Stueck, "The Soviet Union and the Origins of the Korean War", *World Politics* (July 1976)

——*The Road to Confrontation: American Policy toward China and Korea, 1947-1950* (Chapel Hill, N.C.: University of North Carolina Press, 1981)

——*Survey of International Affairs*, Pt. IV Yugoslavia (London: the Royal Institute of International Affairs, 1952)

James Tang, "Diplomatic Relations with a Revolutionary Power — Britain's Experience with China, 1949-1954" (Ms. Ph.D., University of London, 1987)

William Taubmann, *Stalin's American Policy* (New York: Norton, 1982)

Hugh Thomas, *Armed Truce — The Beginning of the Cold War, 1945-1946.* (London: Hamish Hamilton, 1986)

Herbert Tint, *French Foreign Policy since the Second World War* (London: Weidenfeld & Nicolson, 1972)

Zivko Topalovich, *Tito et Cominform: Yougoslavie de 1941-1949.* (Paris: Ed. du Groupe Socialiste Yougoslave, 1949(?))

Margaret Truman, *Harry S. Truman* (London: Hamish Hamilton, 1973)

Nancy B. Tucker, *Patterns in the Dust: Chinese-American Relations and the Recognition Controversy, 1949-1950* (New York: Columbia University Press, 1983)

Adam B. Ulam, *Tito and the Cominform* (Cambridge, Mass.: Harvard University Press, 1952)

——*The Rivals, America and Russia since World War II* (New York: the Viking Press, 1971)

——*Expansion and Co-Existence: Soviet Foreign Policy, 1917-1973* (New York: Praeger, 2nd edn, 1974)

Joan Barth Urban, *Moscow and the Italian Communist Party from Togliatti to Berlinguer* (London: I.B.Tauris, 1986)

Bibliography

David Vital, *The Making of British Foreign Policy* (London: Allen & Unwin, 1968)

Wayne S. Vucinich (ed.), *At the Brink of War and Peace: the Tito-Stalin Split in a Historic Perspective* (New York: Columbia University Press, 1982)

Irvin Wall, *French Communism in the Era of Stalin: the Quest for Unity and Integration, 1945-1962* (Westport, Ct.: Greenwood Press, 1983)

William Wallace, *The Foreign Policy Making Process in Britain* (London: Allen & Unwin for the Royal Institute of International Affairs, 1977 — first published 1976)

Geoffrey Warner, "The Korean War", *International Affairs* (1980)

———"Britain and Europe in 1948: the View from the Cabinet", in Josef Becker and Franz Knipping (eds.), *Power in Europe? Great Britain, France, Italy and Germany in a Postwar World, 1945-1950* (Berlin: De Gruyter, 1986)

Hugh Seton-Watson, *The East European Revolution* (London: Methuen, 3rd edn. 1956, reprinted 1961)

———"Contemporary Communism in Perspective" in J.D.B. Miller and T.H. Rigby (eds.), *The Disintegrating Monolith — Pluralist Trends in the Communist World* (Canberra: The Australian National University, 1965)

Donald Cameron Watt, *Succeeding John Bull: America in Britain's Place, 1900-1975* (Cambridge: Cambridge University Press, 1984)

Samuel F. Wells, "Sounding the Tocsin: NSC 68 and the Soviet Threat", *International Security*, IV 2 (Autumn 1979), pp. 116-158.

Alexander Werth, *France 1940-1955* (London: Robert Hale, 1956)

Nigel West, *A Matter of Trust* (London: Weidenfeld & Nicolson, 1982)

Cees Wiebes and Bert Zeeman, "The Pentagon Negotiations — March 1948: the Launching of the North Atlantic Treaty", *International Affairs* LIX 3 (1983), p. 353 ff.

Philip Williams, *Crisis Management* (London: Martin Robertson, 1976)

———*Crisis and Compromise — Politics in the Fourth Republic* (London: Longmans, 3rd edn. of *Politics in Post-War France*, 1964)

Philip Windsor, "Yugoslavia, 1951, and Czechoslovakia, 1968", in Barry M. Blechman and Stephen S. Kaplan, *Force Without War: United States Armed Forces as a Political Instrument* (Washington D.C.: Brookings Institution, 1978)

Peter Willetts, *The Non-Aligned Movement — the Origins of a Third World Alliance* (London: Frances Pinter, 1978)

Duncan Wilson, *Tito's Yugoslavia* (Cambridge: Cambridge University Press, 1979)

Thomas W. Wolfe, *Soviet Power and Europe, 1945-1970* (Baltimore: Johns Hopkins University Press, 1970)

Christopher M. Woodhouse, *The Struggle for Greece, 1941-1949* (London: Hart-Davis, MacGibbon, 1976)

Daniel Yergin, *The Shattered Peace — the Origins of the Cold War and the National Security State* (London: André Deutsch, 1978)

John Young, *Britain, France and the Unity of Europe* (Leicester, Leicester University Press, 1984)

Bibliography

——"Talking to Tito: the Eden Visit to Yugoslavia, September 1952", *Review of International Studies*, XII 1 (January 1986), pp. 31-41

——"Churchill, the Russians and the Western Alliance: the Three-Power Conference at Bermuda, December 1953", *English Historical Review* (October 1986), pp. 889-912

John Yurechko, "From Containment to Counteroffensive: Soviet Vulnerabilities and American Policy Planning, 1946-1953" (University of Berkeley, California, Ph.D. dissertation, 1980)

Stephen Xydis, *Greece and the Great Powers 1944-1947: Prelude to the 'Truman Doctrine'* (Thessaloniki: Institute for Balkan Studies, 1963)

Charles Zalar, *Yugoslav Communism — A Critical Study* (Washington D.C.: U.S. Government Printing Office, 1961)

Koni Zilliacus, *Tito of Yugoslavia* (London: Michael Joseph, 1952)

Index